FOR RICHER, FOR POORER

Two week

PERSPECTIVES ON GENDER

Series Editor:
Myra Marx Feree, University of Connecticut

Pleasure, Power, and Technology:
Some Tales of Gender, Engineering, and the Cooperative Workplace
Sally Hacker

Black Feminist Thought:
Knowledge, Consciousness, and the Politics of Empowerment
Patricia Hill Collins

Understanding Sexual Violence:
A Study of Convicted Rapists
Diana Scully

Maid in the U.S.A.
Mary Romero

Feminisms and the Women's Movement:
Dynamics of Change in Social Movement Ideology and Activism
Barbara Ryan

Black Women and White Women in the Professions:
Analysis of Job Segregation by Race and Gender, 1960–1980
Natalie J. Sokoloff

Gender Consciousness and Politics
Sue Tolleson Rinehart

Mothering:
Ideology, Experience, and Agency
Evelyn Nakano Glenn, Grace Change, and Linda Rennie Forcey (editors)

For Richer, For Poorer
Mothers Confront Divorce

Demie Kurz

ROUTLEDGE • NEW YORK and LONDON

Published in 1995 by
Routledge
29 West 35th Street
New York, NY 10001

Published in Great Britain by
Routledge
11 New Fetter Lane
London EC4P 4EE

Copyright © 1995 by Demie Kurz

Printed in the United States of America on acid-free paper.

Library of Congress Cataloging-in-Publication Data

Kurz, Demie.
    For richer, for poorer : mothers confront divorce / Demie Kurz.
      p. cm.   —   (Perspectives on gender)
    Includes bibliographical references and index.
    ISBN 0-415-91008-0 (alk. paper). — ISBN 0-415-91009-9 (pbk. : alk. paper)
      1. Divorced women—United States—Psychology.   2. Divorced women—United States—Social conditions.   3. Divorced mothers—United States—Psychology.   4. Divorced mothers—United States—Social conditions.   5. Separation (Psychology)
I. Title.   II. Series : Perspectives on gender (New York, N.Y.)
HQ834.K87   1995
306.89'082—dc20
                                                  95-8486
                                                    CIP

children after divorce

Elsbeth Neil. catt

CONTENTS

ACKNOWLEDGMENTS

I wish to thank the many people who made possible the research project, "The Status of Child Support in Philadelphia: Effects on Women and Children," which was the basis for this study of divorced women. This research was funded by a generous grant from the Pew Charitable Trusts to Women In Transition and was conducted by the Philadelphia Health Management Corporation. I also thank the Research Foundation of the University of Pennsylvania for funds to carry out parts of the data analysis.

The idea to do a research project on divorced women and their access to child support originated with Women In Transition, an organization widely recognized for the excellence of its programs, which provide counseling and training for many women, including divorced women. Former director, Lynne McMahon, hoped that research on divorced women and the child support process would help our understanding of how divorced women can obtain the resources to which they are entitled. Women in Transition along with Women's Law Project had developed a Child Support Project to inform, assist, and train divorced women trying to obtain child support. Lynne's successor, Roberta Hacker, the current director of Women in Transition, continued to support this research project on divorced women's access to resources.

I am very happy to have been associated with the Philadelphia Health Management Corporation (PHMC), where the research was carried out. Under the able leadership of its president, Richard Cohen, and Senior Vice-President, John

Loeb, PHMC has made significant contributions in many health-related areas through its unique combination of health research, policy development, and health-delivery programs. The leadership of PHMC provides an atmosphere that is not only highly professional, but stimulating and supportive. Many fine people work at PHMC, including Lynne Kotranski, director of the research and evaluation division, and Kris Olsen, former director of that division.

I was most privileged to have Kathleen Coughey as co-principal investigator on the grant which funded this research. Kathleen was a wonderful colleague, whose knowledge of divorce issues enriched the project at all stages. We spent many hours together designing the research, discussing the situations of the mothers we interviewed, and hoping for a time when things would be better for divorced women. Kathleen also did extensive data preparation.

I also wish to acknowledge Women's Law Project which, along with Women in Transition, developed the Child Support Project to inform, assist, and train divorced women trying to obtain child support. Women's Law Project, whose current director is Carol Tracy, continues to do excellent work counseling women on child support and other issues related to divorce. Dabne Miller expertly directs the hotline which assists divorced women and others in negotiating for child support and other resources to which they are entitled.

My colleagues in Women's Studies at the University of Pennsylvania, Carroll Smith-Rosenberg, Janice Madden, and Luz Marin, gave me valuable moral support. Sociology Department colleagues, Elijah Anderson, Jerry Jacobs, and Robin Leidner, read parts of this manuscript and gave me helpful feedback and encouragement, as did Barbara Woodhouse of the Penn Law School. Michelle Fine of CUNY Graduate Center and Vicki Smith of the University of California at Davis also read parts of the manuscript and offered welcome suggestions. I am grateful to Ann Freedman for her patience in explaining legal issues to me and for making excellent suggestions regarding parts of the manuscript. Dabne Miller provided valuable comments on the child support system, and an anonymous reviewer made some very good points about an earlier draft.

I want to thank Tanya Koropeckyj-Cox for doing an excellent job preparing the tables for this book and for offering invaluable suggestions about the data analysis and the findings. Barbara Goldoftas provided superb editing, and Myra Marx Ferree, the editor of the Perspectives on Gender series, made astute suggestions for improving the manuscript. Jayne Fargnoli, Sociology Editor at Routledge, was very supportive throughout the publication process, as were friends David Kairys and Mary Anne Layden. Xan Griswold provided cheerful and expert help in preparing the manuscript at a critical juncture, and Jennifer Fields and Christine Min helped with last minute book preparation. Of course none of these people are responsible for any errors in the findings or their interpretation.

Acknowledgments

My family has provided essential and loving support. My husband Bruce always believed in the project, was there to talk about the issues, and helped make sure I could finish the book. With great skill he cheerfully kept our family life going when I was buried in data. Our sons Ethan and Joshua, always lively, interesting, and fun, generously gave me sympathy and support. Thanks also to friends at Taylors Lane, to Julie Forsythe and all the folks at Small Meadows, and to other members of my family for just being there.

Finally, I wish to thank all the women whom we interviewed. Many said they agreed to the interview because they hoped that their speaking about their experiences would help other women in similar situations. I hope this book ensures that their words are heard.

Chapter 1

INTRODUCTION

While there has long been concern about the well-being of the family in America, in the 1990s, politicians, policy-makers, and academics express particular anxiety about the state of the family. They decry what they see as the family's "breakdown"—a term that is used to describe an interconnecting web of problems, including the high divorce rate, the growing number of single parent families, and the emotional pain of children who must live apart from a parent. These problems, it is commonly believed, bring unique harm to families, particularly to children who, frequently separated from their fathers, are said to pay the true price of family breakdown. The growth of single-parent families is also seen as detrimental to society in general. Compared with children from "intact" families, children from "broken homes" are believed to face particular problems in school, to have higher rates of delinquency, and to have more difficulty making family commitments as adults.[1]

In public forums and private homes, experts and citizens search for the cause of divorce and the "dissolution" of the family. The one offered most frequently is the breakdown in "family values." First associated with political tendencies on the Right, the loss of family values is now a common expression used to describe what is wrong with the family today. As it is usually used, the term "family values" refers to the values believed to bind together the traditional nuclear family of a breadwinning father and a full-time mother. A loss of family values, then, means a loss of the virtues associated with this type of family.

1

Consequently, the cause of the "breakdown" of the modern family and the rise of single-parent families is sometimes attributed to the fact that women and men are no longer bound by the commitments associated with traditional marriages: when they become dissatisfied with a marriage or family life, they simply walk away.

The cause of "family breakdown" and the loss of family values is also frequently attributed to factors of gender, particularly the behavior of women.[2] For example, some believe "family decline" has resulted from the entry into the labor force of large numbers of mothers, who are said to have little time to devote to their families and their children. Further, in the current climate of hostility to single-mother families, mothers are blamed for an array of social problems. They are blamed not only for the failures of their children, but increasingly for high divorce rates and crime rates, lowered educational standards, and an "epidemic" of teen pregnancy.[3]

As politicians and members of the popular media use the phrase "family values," it is also coded with racial meanings and class imagery. The "traditional family" usually refers to a white, middle-class family. Similarly, popular images of divorce are often associated with white families and rich families, as when the media raise the issue of divorce in stories about couples battling over multimillion-dollar divorce settlements. On the other hand, "the single-parent family" is frequently a code word for poor, often black families headed by women. Certainly the term "welfare mothers" too often calls up an image of black women. In this context, loss of family values refers to a belief that lower-income people, particularly African-American women, commonly have children out of wedlock, perhaps in order to get money from welfare.[4]

These class and race images are, of course, inaccurate. Divorce has traditionally not been primarily a middle- or upper-class phenomenon. While the divorce rate has risen at all class levels, divorce rates have always been higher for people with less education and lower income, and this is still the case. Contrary to the stereotype, divorced women have also always included a fair representation of black women, and in fact the divorce rate has always been higher for blacks than for whites. As for welfare, current estimates are that 51 percent of welfare recipients are white, and 42 percent are black. Further, roughly 35 percent of the women using AFDC, Aid to Families with Dependent Children, are divorced, separated, and widowed women.[5]

This book focuses on divorce, which is viewed in our society as one of the causes of family breakdown. The current divorce rate is high and causes alarm. According to recent estimates, if these rates continue, anywhere from 44 to 64 percent of today's marriages will end in separation or divorce. Over 60 percent of all single-parent households are composed of divorced or separated women. Two-thirds of divorces involve children, which means that four out of ten American children experience the divorce of their parents.[6]

While the divorce rate is high, many divorced men and women do remarry—two-thirds of divorced women and three-quarters of divorced men. For some groups, however, the remarriage rate is lower. Only 32 percent of black women and 55 percent of black men remarry within ten years after divorce. Some researchers claim that divorced women who are older remarry at lower rates then those who are younger. Further, the divorce rates for those who do remarry are similar to those of couples married for the first time. Four out of ten marriages in the United States involve a second marriage for the bride or the groom.[7]

In this book, I do not take the usual view of divorce as an expression of "family breakdown" and a loss of "family values." The views of divorce which I present in this book are based on interviews with a random sample of divorced women of different classes and races. While these women have experienced a lot of hardships, when viewed through their eyes, divorce looks different from the recent portrayals of "breakdown" and "decline."

The women in this sample focused on two issues as critical to their divorce experience. First, because they found their marriages to be very difficult and in some cases abusive, a majority of women in this sample are glad their marriages have ended. Those many women who experienced domestic violence and those whose husbands abused drugs and alcohol particularly felt that there was no choice but to end the marriage. For these women the real problem was not their divorce but the marriage. Many of these women hope to marry again, under better conditions. A minority of women in the sample do regret the loss of their marriage. Those women who were left by their husbands, especially for "other women," find their divorces particularly painful. Some of them wish their husbands had shown more commitment to the marriage because now they are struggling on their own to support their children. Thus, divorce may be an escape from a bad marriage or it may be a loss of a valued relationship, but for these women, it is not an expression of family values or their lack. Women do not divorce casually, or for trivial reasons.

The second major concern voiced by all the divorced women in this sample involves the conditions they faced at divorce. Divorce is a gender issue, with women and men facing very different circumstances after divorce. Women become not only the custodial parents of children, but their primary economic support. Legal, social, and economic policies in this country are constructed in such a way that the resources and standard of living of all divorced women declines, no matter what their background. Most women suffer hardships and become economically disadvantaged. The women in this sample are uniformly angry about their second-class treatment as divorced women and their diminished opportunities.

Unfortunately, as a society we often ignore the fact that many divorced women face poverty. An astonishing 39 percent of divorced women with children live in poverty. Twenty percent of divorced women receive some type of welfare income. Families with an employed single mother suffer a poverty rate 8.5 times that of families with two employed parents. Life for single mothers is very difficult, and there are insufficient social supports for them. We organize our family policies around the idea that a family has two parents, with the male as primary breadwinner and with mothers and children dependent on his wages.[8]

Further, our failure to address the hardship of women has a direct impact on the fate of children. Children usually live with their mothers after divorce, and thus their standard of living is intimately tied to that of their mothers. Unfortunately, as a result of the privatized nature of our social system, we have failed to address the hardship and poverty of both divorced women and other single mothers, and their children.

In addition to the disadvantages of gender there are other factors that create hardships during marriage and after divorce. Women with less education or women whose husbands do not have steady jobs face greater risks. Minority women can experience particularly severe difficulties after divorce. In general, they receive fewer assets from their marriages and have greater difficulty finding jobs to support themselves and their children at an adequate standard of living. Since there are higher rates of divorce in lower socio-economic groups, many divorced women have limited resources as they begin their lives as divorced women.

Men, of course, also suffer at the time of divorce. Their situation, however, is very different from that of their former wives. Their main loss is not economic; in fact they gain a higher standard of living at divorce. But most men do have greatly reduced contact with their children and this is painful for many fathers. A minority of men work strenuously to develop new roles as divorced fathers and continue to have significant relationships with their children, while the majority distance themselves from the family and lose meaningful connections with their children.[9]

Children also certainly suffer because of divorce. Many children would undoubtedly prefer that their parents not divorce. Some social scientists argue unequivocally that divorce harms children. So certain are they that divorce harms children that they believe that access to divorce should be curtailed to spare children from suffering and from long-term harm. However it is very important to stress that there is no agreement on the subject of whether divorce has a long-term negative effect on children. Some researchers believe that after a period of adjustment, children continue to lead lives that are as normal and productive as their counterparts in families where no divorce has occurred. Other researchers believe that children in marriages of poor quality where there is a lot of conflict fare worse than children of divorce. I will address the subject of the impact of divorce on children in chapter 7.[10]

The experiences of the women in this sample suggest that trying to improve general "family values" will not slow the divorce rate or improve family life. Fighting for family values typically means working for a return to families as usual. Some politicians would like to restrict opportunities for women to divorce and live outside of marriage. However, forcing women back to marriage as it is currently structured would not necessarily be good for women, and would not necessarily be good for children either. Before rushing to hasty judgments about the loss of family values, we must understand women's perspective on families and divorce. Without a better understanding of the impact of divorce on women we will not get to the root of the problems in marriages, but instead will create policies that are harmful to women and children. What we need to focus on are the real problems women face in and outside of marriage, such as domestic violence, hardships due to poverty, and a social system that promotes economic inequality between men and women.[11]

LISTENING TO WOMEN

This book on mothers and divorce is based on an interview study. The data presented here are based on interviews with a random sample of 129 divorced women with children. These women come from different racial groups and from a wide range of economic backgrounds, including the very wealthy and the very poor. The sample includes women with high-paying professional jobs and women who are high school dropouts and cannot find work. Most of these women hold jobs in traditional female categories, such as secretarial, sales, and pink-collar work.

To illustrate some of the problems divorced women face, in the following paragraphs I will give brief accounts from interviews with three of the women in this study. I will first present the story of Evelyn, whose circumstances show how difficult conditions can be for some divorced women. Evelyn is one of the 22 percent of women in the sample who live below the official poverty level. Like many other divorced women, Evelyn married young. Disproportionate numbers of divorced women married young, and disproportionate numbers of younger women divorce, in contrast to women in other age groups.[12] Along with 50 percent of the women in the sample, Evelyn experienced violence in her marriage at the hands of her husband. While like the majority of divorced women in the sample, Evelyn has adjusted to her divorce and is glad that her marriage is over, she faces many difficulties supporting herself and her children. Like the other poorest women, she is also unhappy about the obstacles she faces in escaping poverty.

Evelyn is a 36-year-old white woman with three children—ages 7, 13, and 15—from a fifteen-year marriage. She married her high school sweetheart and didn't finish high school. Evelyn started out happy in her marriage. According to her account, the difficulties started when the local company her ex-husband was working for downsized its workforce and he lost his job. He couldn't find work that he felt paid adequately and so he took a low paying job in a bar. Her ex-husband, she says, felt very badly that he was not supporting the family at an adequate level.

Evelyn believes it was at the bar that her ex-husband started drinking heavily. He then began using drugs. Evelyn says she would have "stuck by my ex-husband for anything else, but not drugs, because of what it was doing to the kids and me." When her ex-husband used drugs, he became violent. He didn't physically assault her much, she says, but he threw things at her, destroyed property, and several times threatened her with a gun, even shoving the gun down her throat. He would rip the telephone off the wall. She became afraid of her husband, as did the neighbors. Once she called the police, but when they found out that she was still married and wasn't injured, they said they couldn't do anything. When she called a local agency for abused women, they told her the same thing. Evelyn finally left her marriage.

> It was after a really bad incident, where he had chased me with a gun. I asked the police if they would come and give me protection while I cleared out the house. They said they would give me twenty minutes. I was staying somewhere else. I met them, grabbed garbage bags, and just emptied drawers into them. I went to my parents.

Her ex-husband called her parents' house in a nearby state and threatened to come see his children. Evelyn's father called the police, who said they would stake out the house and make sure her husband didn't come near.

Evelyn's ex-husband is now in prison for robberies he committed to support his drug habit. His new girlfriend says that he still loves Evelyn, but Evelyn says she can't think about that after all she has been through. Evelyn believes her ex-husband does care about the children. He calls every Wednesday night from prison to talk to the children, and he writes to them frequently. Evelyn can't take the children to the prison to see their father very often because she doesn't have a car and the prison is not accessible to public transportation. She says one of her daughters became particularly upset after the divorce: she became very angry and got into fights at home and at school. Evelyn took her to counseling, which helped her daughter a lot, and she seems happier now.

Evelyn is enrolled in the Aid to Families with Dependent Children (AFDC) program. She applied for AFDC funds during her separation, when her husband stopped sending his unemployment checks. She has never received child support. At the time of the interview, Evelyn was living on her AFDC payments and food stamps which totaled $9,000 a year (1988 dollars), putting her below the official poverty level. She gets money from an energy assistance program as well, and free cheese and rice from another program. The 22 percent of women in this sample who are on AFDC all live on similar amounts of money and live below the poverty level.

Evelyn would like to get off of welfare, but she can't because the jobs she has found don't offer her health care benefits. Welfare covers her medical expenses, which have sometimes been high because one of her children has had several accidents. AFDC also paid for her daughter's counseling. So Evelyn appreciates welfare very much, and she tries to keep a positive attitude, even while she must really struggle to survive.

> You can always manage. Like you can always have demonstrations in your house. I had one here last night—a Tupperware demonstration. So I get free Tupperware things. I've had jewelry demonstrations. That's how I got my kids' Christmas presents this year. They all got gold rings. They don't have to know how you got their presents—that you didn't pay for things.

Evelyn must also find a job where she can be at home when the children come back from school, which means that most full-time jobs are not available to her. When she has left her children alone, they have gotten into trouble fighting with each other and other children in the neighborhood. Evelyn won't work at night because that is when she helps her children with their homework. One of them brought home a failing grade last year. Evelyn says, "I said to him, 'This is it, no more.' I worked with him every night. The next quarter he came home with As." Next year Evelyn will have to take the children out of the Catholic school they are attending because she can no longer afford the tuition. This makes her sad because she attended Catholic school and would like to provide a similar education for her children.

Evelyn says the hardest thing about the divorce has been surviving financially. She manages to get by on her extremely low income with extensive help from her parents, although she says they don't have much money themselves. Evelyn's parents have tried to help her out with repairs, such as helping her replace the water heater so she did not have to spend the winter without hot water. Evelyn says her parents and her sister have given her tremendous emotional support as well; she can call on them night or day.

Evelyn's main concern is how she will get ahead in the future. She does own her home; this is her only financial asset, and she did everything she could to keep it after the divorce. The neighborhood she lives in, however, is gentrifying and she may have trouble paying the higher taxes. If she should sell the house, she would not get the money for it. The money from the sale would have to go to the welfare office as compensation for the welfare payments she has received. She resents the fact that the government makes it so difficult for women on welfare to improve their situation. She cannot marry her boyfriend, although they would like to wed, because married women cannot remain on AFDC and Evelyn fears she could not find an adequately paying job with health care benefits. He also earns a low salary and makes regular child support payments to his children from his previous marriage. Despite her hardships, though, Evelyn has managed to keep up her hopes, supported by her family and sustained by her love for her children. As she says:

> I guess the thing that helped most of all was my children. Sometimes we would be all sitting here at this table crying and I would think, "Oh my god, I have to pull things together for my kids." It's having kids that made all of this so hard. But also, it's really them that kept me going.

June is a black middle-class woman who was married for four years and has a two-year old son. June is much more financially secure than Evelyn. She has a masters degree in an educational field and a good job. However, like the majority of divorced women nationwide, and in this sample, June receives no child support from her ex-husband. This is very upsetting to her and she has spent many hours trying to enforce a child support order.[13]

June left her ex-husband because he began seeing another woman while she was pregnant. She remembers this as "the worst period of my life. I was on an unpaid maternity leave. I was a new mother. It was horrible." This was not the first time he had had an affair. June felt deeply hurt. She is very religious and has felt guilty about divorcing. But her pastor has reassured her that she did the right thing. June says she would never like to go through anything like a divorce again. Losing her marriage was "like a death. You mourn it." But she feels she is much stronger and also says, "I have a much better idea of what I want in men, what's acceptable in men."

The most troubling aspect of June's life now is that she cannot get child support from her ex-husband. He quit a steady job in one government office in order to apply for a higher paying one in another government agency. Unfortunately he didn't get that job and is now unemployed. Her ex-husband is receiving unemployment benefits, and friends tell June he has a job on the side that he is not reporting. June has spent hours at court trying to finalize a child support agreement based on her ex-husband's unemployment benefits. She has spent countless hours determining all her expenses and calculating all her expenditures. But she has still received no child support.

June feels especially angered by this because her ex-husband does not volunteer to do any of the chores associated with raising their son. Her ex-husband sees their son every week when June takes him to her ex-husband's parents' house. The grandparents tell June they are sorry their son has not paid any child support. They understand that she is angry and, she says, they would even understand if June stopped bringing their grandson over. But June's lawyer has told her that under no circumstances can she limit visitation just because her ex-husband is paying no child support. In the State of Pennsylvania this is illegal. Furthermore, June does not want to deprive the grandparents of visits with their grandson, whom they love very much, nor does she want to deprive her son of visits with his father and grandparents.

June is managing, although she and her son have had to cut back on their expenses for non-essential items. She got her lawyer for free as part of her benefits through the school system, and she also has health care through her job. She hasn't lost opportunities because of the divorce, but, as she says "I been terribly drained by it. I have had to completely regroup." She says she has been very frustrated about the time she has put into trying to get child support and is very upset she is not getting it. She doesn't know when this problem will be solved and feels like the divorce won't really be over until it is.

Finally, Anne is a white women who is an educational consultant and, like June, has a masters degree. She was married for 13 years and has an 11 year-old daughter. Anne reports that she and her husband had a lot of conflict during the divorce negotiations. There is still tension between her and her ex-husband. However, they have resolved the key issues of visitation and child support and they now share joint custody of their daughter.

Anne states that she and her husband made a mutual agreement to separate. During their marriage she and her husband quarreled constantly over their different values and particularly over issues of money, including how to spend family money, her husband's career decisions, and the accumulation of debts from his business. Anne supported the family when her husband's businesses failed. She says the fighting wasn't good for any of them, particularly her daughter. Anne was afraid of her husband's temper. She says he broke a lot of things during their fights, although he never hurt her physically.

> My husband could get very angry. He would break things; he didn't lay his hands on me. But if he broke things I would think, 'what next? What's the difference between a clock and me?'

The separation did not end the acrimony. Anne said:

> My ex-husband was into fighting for everything he could get. He constantly fights and argues. He's out for revenge. He even told me, "I'll miss fighting with you." That's just the way he is. My lawyer certainly saw a lot of it. We talked about how my ex-husband just had to "win the war." That was the whole point, winning the war.

Anne claims her ex-husband used his temper as a tactic, as she says, "to try and frighten me." She gave up trying to get child support or alimony during the separation to avoid the fighting. Anne says her ex-husband "didn't want to give the money he was paying for our daughter to me." So they reached an agreement that her husband would pay their daughter's private school tuition instead of paying child support. They also agreed to share custody of their daughter. This is the one thing they were able to agree on and never fought over. Anne says her ex-husband is a great father.

Anne says her ex-husband was able to pursue legal disputes over resources for an extended time because he obtained legal services through his business. Anne has been paying her lawyer over a period of several years. She has paid $7,000 and still owes more. While she also has debts resulting from the divorce, Anne says her financial situation is improving. Right after the divorce she was in a panic about her finances and the debts from her ex-husband's business failures. Her lawyer helped her sort out her financial problems. This reduced her fears and helped her get through the transition between her marriage and her divorce. Now she is on more solid financial footing.

This book examines the experiences of the divorced women of this sample and focuses on the questions that concern them—the hardships of their marriages, and the difficulties of surviving on a low income. In order to provide a framework for understanding the experiences of these divorced women, in chapter 2 I examine the views of social scientists who see divorce as "marital breakdown" and "decline" and then present my own, alternate perspective on divorce.

Chapter 3 examines how women describe the ending of their marriages. Many women experience serious conflict with their ex-husbands. They describe leaving their husbands because of physical violence, drug abuse, and general dissatisfaction with their subordinate position in the marriage. Some women are left by their husbands, often for other women. Many women in the sample have experienced physical abuse from their husbands. I examine women's accounts of violence they experienced during their marriage and the separation. I also report on the prevalence of domestic violence in the marriages of these women, women's perceptions of why it occurs, and the effect that violence can have on the divorce process.

In chapter 4 I consider the hardships women face at divorce. I examine how their standards of living decline, what their sources of income are, what sacrifices they must make, and where they turn for help. A small number of mothers receive generous child support and alimony awards and live relatively comfortably; most women, however, struggle to support themselves and their children at an adequate standard of living. The poorest mothers live on welfare in inadequate housing located in high-crime neighborhoods. A few of them have resorted to drugs and alcohol as a way of coping with their problems. African-American women have the greatest difficulty securing employment and adequate health care for themselves and their children.

Chapter 5 continues the discussion of how women survive on low incomes through an examination of women's negotiations for child support, which is critical to their ability to raise their standard of living. I describe new reforms that will greatly improve the child-support system, but show how, based on these women's experiences, these reforms will not ensure that women will get the amount of child support they need. There are some women, for example, who are reluctant to pressure fathers to pay child-support because they fear that the fathers will retaliate with physical force. This examination of the child-support system demonstrates how divorce perpetuates economic inequality for women.

Chapter 6 looks at how mothers and fathers negotiate over custody and visitation. These negotiations are key for determining what kind of role fathers will play in the lives of their children. Unfortunately, just as many fathers do not pay child support, many fathers are not involved in the lives of their children. Many mothers would like fathers to be more involved with their children. At the same time, other mothers report a lot of ongoing conflict between themselves and fathers over visitation. Those women who experienced violence during the marriage are particularly afraid that their ex-husbands could again become violent. This chapter demonstrates how our custody and visitation policies must simultaneously protect mothers while giving deserving fathers access to their children.

In chapter 7 I present women's assessments of how divorce has affected their lives and the lives of their children. Some mothers regret their divorces and believe that overall they are worse off because of their divorce. The majority, however, particularly those from marriages where there was violence and drug abuse, are happy to be divorced. These mothers also express anger at society's treatment of divorced women; most believe that the government should do more to help mothers and children face the financial and social hardships of divorce. When discussing the welfare of their children, women report a range of responses by their children to the divorce. Many say their children have adjusted to the divorce after a period of mourning the loss of the family as they knew it; others say that their children are better off not living in a conflict-ridden marriage; still others report that their children are experiencing ongoing problems. These women's reports of their children suggest that it is difficult to generalize about the effects of divorce on children.

In the conclusion to this book, I turn to questions of divorce policy. The policy questions about divorce are far-reaching and have significant consequences for women and children. The family is a hotly contested arena for debating critical questions about the role of women, the distribution of social and economic resources, and the welfare state. Unfortunately, the terms "family breakdown" and "family values" mask how much is at stake for women and the fact that women's interests can be very different than those of men. The term "family values" conceals political agendas. Too often "family values" are invoked to urge that women shouldn't have choices about family life. Some politicians are trying to muster people's anxieties about family life and women's roles in order to restrict opportunities for women to divorce or to live on their own without men. Currently, if women make such a choice, they are punished, and many voices are urging that such penalties be increased. Are we saying women should be kept in families regardless of what staying there means for them? Do we as a society today demand that women accept male infidelity and violence because the economic price of leaving is so high that the survival and security of women and children is endangered? I think we should see what women want. This book is an effort to look at just that.

Chapter 2

UNDERSTANDING DIVORCE
AND DIVORCED WOMEN

All social scientists bring to their research a set of assumptions that influence their understanding of the information they gather and the conclusions they draw. In examining divorce and its aftermath, our assumptions affect how we understand the entire divorce process and what prescriptions we make for reshaping family policy. For example, those who write of "family breakdown" believe that marriages are ending because men and women have forgone commitment to family life in order to pursue their own individual goals. To promote more happiness and well-being for family members, these analysts would like to strengthen commitments to the family as it is traditionally conceived. In contrast to these writers, I believe that divorce occurs because of the hardships that contemporary marriages cause for women, due to domestic violence, drug abuse, and alcohol abuse, as well as for reasons of personal dissatisfaction. I believe we should identify these problems in marriage and work to improve them. At the same time, we should enable women who leave their marriages to support themselves and their children at an adequate standard of living.

This chapter focuses on two key questions—why marriages end, and how divorce affects mothers and children. I first consider how those who write of "family decline" address the question of the ending of marriages and the hardship of divorce, and then offer my own perspective on these issues. I discuss at some length the policies and institutions that structure divorce in our society and shape the circumstances that constrain the opportunities of divorced women—the law, the labor market, and social welfare policy. These institutions are organized to make it particularly difficult for divorced women with children to gain the resources they need to maintain an adequate standard of living.

DIVORCE AS DECLINE

While there have always been social scientists who view divorce as a sign of decline, recently some have argued this position with particular urgency. Speaking out from new organizations they have formed to publicize their views, these writers call for a reversal of "family decline" and a return to the two-parent family. They locate themselves between "liberal" and "conservative" views, promoting what they view as a position which is in the best interests of all American families. These people include David Poponoe and Jean Bethke Elshtain, co-chairs of the Council on Families in America, David Blankenhorn and Barbara Defoe Whitehead, directors of the Council on Families in America, and sociologist Amitai Etzioni, founder of the Communitarian movement. In recent years they have written extensively and spoken out publicly on family issues. Poponoe, a prominent spokesperson for this type of thinking, summarizes many of the arguments of these researchers and policy makers in his widely cited book *Disturbing the Nest.*[1]

These writers believe that the family is declining because of people's changed values—specifically, that men and women have a weakened commitment to marriage. These writers attribute this decreased commitment to the rise of individualism, the belief that one's own needs can take precedence over the common good of the family. They frequently cite the work of Robert Bellah and his colleagues, who argue that the therapeutic ideal of self-actualization, rather than self-sacrifice or obligation, has become widespread throughout American life and has weakened commitments to the family.[2] Writers in this tradition discuss the position of women in the family, but usually only to consider how their behavior contributes to family decline. They point to women's increased interest in careers and expanded participation in the workplace as factors in the rise of "individualism" and the decreased commitment to the family in modern America. The portrait they paint of these career-oriented families is typically of a white family, usually one that is better off than average. They do not examine either the economic factors that pull women into the labor force or the double standard that assumes that it is women's responsibility to provide an alternative to market values.

In analyzing the effects of divorce on families, these writers point to how divorce injures all parties and how, in its wake, adults are left lonely and children are subjected to great emotional hardship. They are particularly concerned about what they believe are the uniformly negative consequences for children of growing up in a single-parent family. It is children, these writers believe, who pay the price of the loss of family values. They cite data which they believe shows that divorce has long-term negative consequences for children, including behavior problems, problems in school, and difficulties forming intimate relationships later in life. They claim that the best environment for raising mentally healthy children is the nuclear family, particularly large "intact" families with many routines and traditions. In their eyes, divorce disrupts the socialization of children to basic values and norms. The children who are the products of "broken homes" are then said to carry their problems to schools, workplaces, and future families, if not to jail. These writers have increasingly targeted single-mother families as the cause of a variety of social problems including school failure, poverty, and crime.[3]

Those who take the "family decline" perspective argue that, overall, the nuclear family has been seriously weakened: fewer people are marrying, and those who do tend to marry later in life, have fewer children, and divorce more frequently than was previously the case. While citing some benefits of divorce, including greater happiness on the part of many divorced people, these writers focus on its costs to children. Although they do not argue that divorce should be prevented, they seek to discourage divorce and reinvigorate the ideals of the nuclear family, and they urge the development of a new social movement whose purpose would be the promotion of families and family values.

Some Communitarians urge the government and business to support family leave and flexible working hours to strengthen family bonds. Etzioni also supports child allowances. However Poponoe argues vigorously against an expanded "welfare state," which he believes undermines "family values or familism—the belief in a strong sense of family identification and loyalty, mutual assistance among family members, and a concern for the perpetuation of the family unit." He does not take into account all those who have fallen through the family safety net in the past, or how certain family functions, like care for the elderly, are part of the welfare state he deplores.[4]

WOMEN, MARRIAGE, AND DIVORCE

Writers who focus on the family's decline raise some important questions. It is certainly the case that divorce can leave women, men, and children less nurtured, and that children can suffer emotionally and socially because of the behavior of their parents. It is also the case that the nuclear family can provide an excellent environment for raising children, and that raising a child as a single person can be difficult. Further, as these writers argue, marriage is not as permanent an institution as it once was. And finally, many would agree that "individualism," or the failure to invest in social institutions or projects for the common good, is a major problem in contemporary American society. Those writing from this perspective, however, misunderstand the basic problems of marriage and divorce. As they apply the concept of "individualism" to family life, they fail to consider who in the family is benefitted and harmed by marriage and by divorce. Their perspective minimizes the hardships of family life and the degree to which divorce can be a necessity in order for a woman to raise her children in a safe environment.

I analyze divorce from the point of view of a group of women from diverse backgrounds. Despite their diversity, these women have remarkably similar views about divorce and the divorce process. Seen from their point of view, the real issues and problems of family life look different than from the perspective of family "breakdown" or "decline." As noted in the previous chapter, many of the women in this sample feel they had to leave difficult marriages and that they are less harmed by their divorce than they were by their marriage. What has been hard for them, however, is surviving as single parents and, for most of them, being solely responsible for the financial and emotional well-being of their children.

Men and women frequently have different interests in marriage and at the time of divorce. Although it is valuable for some purposes to take the family as a unit of analysis, it is misleading to assume that the family exists predominantly above and beyond the interests of its members. While men, women, and children frequently act together as a unit in social and family activities, they also have different and potentially conflicting interests. I sometimes speak of the family as highly "gendered," meaning that the actions of members are influenced at every point by gender norms and opportunities. Women and men approach divorce from different social positions, with men usually having more access to power than women. As Myra Marx Ferree states: "Gender is, with race and class, a hierarchical structure of opportunity and oppression as well as an affective structure of identity and cohesion, and families are one of the many institutional settings in which these structures become lived experience." While nuclear family advocates portray the family as having a "natural," ahistorical character, the family, in fact, is not isolated but is deeply embedded in the opportunity structures of the wider society.[5]

Writers have long noted that there were two marriages, "his" and "hers," referring to the different pleasures, burdens, and duties husbands and wives experience in their roles. Further, it is generally agreed that "his" has traditionally been a more rewarding marriage than "hers." Similarly, a number of writers have argued that men and women continue to have different interests at divorce, based on the fact that at that time women become the full-time custodial parent of the children, and must support themselves and their children on a reduced standard of living.[6]

Causes of the Rising Divorce Rate

In order to provide a background for understanding the role of gender in marriage and divorce, I will first briefly examine the underlying causes for the rise in the divorce rate over the past decades. The question of the rising divorce rate is a complicated one, most of which is beyond the scope of this book. A brief examination of the recent history of the rise in the divorce rate, however, gives us a context for understanding the options women face as they consider marriage and divorce. There is one factor in the rising divorce rate that has been cited by all well-known scholars of the family—the entry of large numbers of married women into the workplace after World War II.[7] Prior to that time, many single women had worked in the paid labor force, as had married immigrant and minority women whose incomes were necessary to support their families. But most married women did not. It was expected that they would be supported by husbands, and laws made it difficult for them to enter the paid labor market.

After World War II, the service sector of the economy expanded greatly, increasing the demand for women workers. Women whose children were grown entered the workforce first, and then as wages rose, so did women with younger children. While in 1940 only one in seven married women was working outside the home, during the 1950s, many married women with school-aged children began to work. By 1960, 32 percent of the workforce was female, and by 1992, 47 percent.[8] Many of these women were motivated to enter the labor force by the fact that their husbands' wages were not rising and it was increasingly difficult to support a family on one income. The rise of the women's movement and its support for working women further legitimated this change, which was already underway when the women's movement began.

The growing number of married women working outside the home produced major changes in gender relations in the family. One particularly important change was that for those married women who were earning an income, it became easier to contemplate a divorce. Although the incomes of most women were and are relatively low, the fact that women have any ability to support themselves outside of marriage means that marriage isn't the necessity it was before. The increase in wages for women after World War II may also have enabled poorer women, who had always worked in the paid labor force, to consider divorce. At the same time these changes also undoubtedly enabled more men to leave their marriages, believing that their wives could support themselves.

Thus, one of the most important consequences of married women's entry into the labor force was that the continuation of a marriage came to depend more on the quality of a couple's relationship, or as some put it, on "emotional gratification."[9] Emotional fulfillment is a much less stable basis for a relationship than sheer necessity. With marriage based on this less secure foundation, more people began to divorce. Their increased numbers and visibility resulted in less stigma toward divorce, which in turn became another factor in the rise of the divorce rate. As a result of this greater acceptance of divorce, new laws in the 1960s and 1970s made legal divorces much easier to obtain.

Just because divorce has become a widely available option, however, does not mean that if marital partners are dissatisfied they are free to "walk away" from marriage. If anything, as the portrayals of women in Arlie Hochschild's book *The Second Shift* indicate, women may stay in unsatisfactory marriages even when they are not happy because they fear that life as a divorced woman will be so very hard. As Hochschild notes:

> Earlier in our century, the most important cautionary tale for women was of a woman who "fell" from chastity before marriage and came to a bad end because no man would have her. Among working mothers of small children, and especially the more traditional of them, the modern version of the "fallen woman" is the divorcee. Of course, not all women fear the prospect of divorce.... But the cases of Nancy Holt and Nina Tanagawa are also telling because their fear of divorce led them to stop asking for more help in the second shift. When life is made to seem so cold "out there," a woman may try to get warm inside an unequal marriage.[10]

Being married also remains very much a part of a women's identity. There is still a lot of social pressure on women to marry and stay married, to have a "normal" identity as a married woman. So one must qualify the view that everyone is now free to leave marriages and say that it is still far from easy for women with children to leave a marriage. In fact, looked at in this way, we could easily pose a different question: what is it that leads some women to divorce even when they know it is going to be difficult? This question should alert us to the fact that for some women marriage must be a significant hardship.

Other women, of course, don't leave marriages, but are left. Generally speaking, it is easier for men than women to leave marriages because they don't usually have the children to care for. Until recently they have not had to contribute any substantial funds for child support. This is not to say that men have no difficulty leaving marriages, but that since most men will not have to make sacrifices to take care of their children after divorce, they have a different set of considerations when thinking of leaving a marriage. Ehrenreich argues that the increased acceptance of divorce has left men free to leave behind the burdens of marriage and childrearing with relative impunity. They can buy food preparation and housekeeping services, which were once only available from wives, and due to less restrictive sexual norms, they can find new sexual partners relatively easily.[11]

Gender and Marriage

In order to provide a context for understanding what makes some women leave their marriages and why marriages end, we must now turn to the question of what marriages are like for women. In contemporary marriages, power imbalances still favor men and disfavor women. Traditionally in marriage husbands have controlled family resources and decision-making, and wives, who were considered the legal property of their husbands, had few rights. Until the 1970s, a husband had legal control over the family's assets and was the only family member with independent access to credit.[12] Recently, married women have gained many rights and advantages. Formal legal barriers to their entry into the labor force have been dropped, and with the entry of women into the paid labor force they have gained power in marriage. Feminist movements have spread an ideology of equality in marriage that many women have embraced, whether or not they identify with the label "feminist."

Despite these changes, inequality and power imbalances continue to shape contemporary marriages and put women at a disadvantage. Philip Blumstein and Pepper Schwartz point to the widespread acceptance of the male provider role—along with men's greater income—as the key factors in the maintenance of men's greater power in the family. Those women who do not work outside the home remain in what John Scanzoni calls "wife as complementary" roles, in which the needs and interests of a woman's children and husband are more important than her own. Other women remain in "junior partner" roles, exercising some bargaining power because they work outside the home, but consigned to a subordinate status because they earn far less than their husbands. In her study of working class families, Lillian Rubin found that working-class husbands had an ideology of male dominance, while middle-class couples subscribed to an ideology of equality. However, she found that middle-class marriages actually showed substantial inequality in that couples often organized their activities and made decisions according to the needs of the husband's work schedule. Other researchers report that even when wives in dual-career families have high-status positions, their careers are still considered secondary to those of their husbands.[13] It is still the wives who take time off if their children are sick or childcare problems develop. In a recent Gallup poll, 89 percent of respondents said that it was the wife who rearranged her schedule to take care of the child.

These power differentials in marriage create serious problems for women. First, women end up with the burden of the household work. A 1989 poll by Gallup surveyed 1,234 random people and found that while 57 percent now believe that the ideal marriage is one in which both the husband and the wife share the responsibilities of earning money and caring for the home, 70 percent reported that women did most of the housework in their families. Hochschild has studied the burdens that the double shift places on women and found that many wives who want to work outside the home also want their husbands to do a much greater share of household work. Many husbands, however, do not want to increase the time they spend doing domestic work, leaving their wives with a heavy workload in their "second shift," in addition to their paid labor. As noted above, Hochschild demonstrates how conflicts over housework lead some couples to consider divorce.[14]

Second, the belief that men should control family decision-making has led a frighteningly large number of men to be violent toward their wives. Nationally, estimates are that in a given year, 10 to 20 percent of women are beaten by a male intimate, and a quarter to a half of all women will experience violence at the hands of a male intimate in their lifetime. Most experts attribute the existence of "wife battering" to the husbands' desire to maintain control in the family.[15] As we will see in the next chapter, many women in the sample I have studied experienced domestic violence in their marriages and some left their marriages because of it.

Some social scientists have argued that in contrast to white marriages, black marriages are relatively egalitarian, in part because so many black married women have been in the labor force over the past decades, which has given them more power in marriage. But others argue that a significant degree of power inequality is also evident in black marriages, with black women being asked to play subordinate and stereotypically female roles. Gloria Joseph and Jill Lewis, and Michelle Wallace argue that some black men and women distrust each other, with men viewing women as domineering and women in turn believing that the men are chauvinistic.[16]

Black women have long been stereotyped as domineering because of the important economic role they have played in the family. Daniel Patrick Moynihan argued in 1965 that black families were constructed around a "matriarchy" and that black women dominated black men.[17] The inevitable conclusion was that black women were emasculating black men and weakening the black family. This view has been criticized as unfairly blaming black women for their strength under adversity. Unfortunately, this stereotype of black women as dominant and domineering persists today, and black single mothers are still blamed for socializing their children to inappropriate gender roles. There is no recognition of the fact that, as Joyce Ladner pointed out long ago, black women have been socialized to be self-reliant, economically independent, and hard working. Ladner claims that fathers and mothers have socialized black girls in this way so they could support themselves and their children even if their partners couldn't find jobs.[18]

At the same time, while many black women have been socialized to less traditional gender roles, research has shown that white and black women themselves have similar attitudes toward gender roles. According to a variety of researchers, both black and white males endorse traditional sex roles, including beliefs that the wife should put the needs of her children and husband before her own, and that she should not work while the children are of pre-school age because they might suffer. On the other hand, black and white females are more likely to endorse nontraditional attitudes toward the roles of mother, father, and wife. Other researchers report some variation on this pattern. H. Edward Ransford and Jon Miller found that black and white females were equally likely to hold a more feminist outlook. Karen Dugger argues that as white women have entered the labor force in larger numbers, the attitudes of black and white women towards gender roles have become more similar.[19]

How do women feel about their social position in relation to men? Terry Arendell concludes that a "gender gap" now exists in which women generally want more equality, while many men are resistant. While some women believe that traditional gender roles should continue, polling data indicate that increasing numbers of women are dissatisfied with their subordinate position. A 1989 *New York Times* poll found that a majority of women believed that American society had not granted women enough equality. In this same poll, the majority of men said that the women's movement had "made things harder for men at home." The American Male Opinion Index found that 60 percent of men opposed changes in sex roles and other feminist objectives in 1990, up from 48 percent in 1988. According to Morgan, "the family is an important location of a whole set of privileges that men enjoy and which they would be reluctant to relinquish; this may be especially the case for men workers with relatively few alternative sources of privilege in society." Thus, as wages decline, and as good jobs become more scarce due to the globalization of the world economy, men may increasingly resent the loss of family privileges.[20]

Race and Class Factors in Contemporary Marriages

The family exists not only in a gender context, but in a class and race context that creates great variability in family opportunities and resources. A person's socio-economic position has a strong influence on the likelihood that they will divorce. Despite the stereotype that divorce is a middle-class phenomenon, and despite increases in the divorce rate at all socio-economic levels, divorce rates have always been higher among lower-income people, and among those with less education. These patterns are related to higher rates of unemployment and job insecurity among workers from lower socio-economic backgrounds. While recession and the down-sizing of the labor force have affected workers at all levels, they have hit working-class and poverty-level people particularly hard, causing them to experience extensive layoffs and declining wages. However, despite the fact that the divorce rate is higher the lower one's education and income level and that the divorce rate is higher for blacks than for whites, the stereotype persists that divorce is a middle-class phenomenon.[21]

Many argue that it is difficult to sustain a marriage when a man cannot earn an adequate wage, a problem that occurs more frequently the lower a man's social class. In her study of white working-class marriages, Rubin, borrowing Joseph Howell's terms, found that the families she studied in which men had less job security and more unemployment had "hard-living" characteristics such as unstable family ties, violence, and alcoholism. By contrast the "settled-living" families she studied were cautious, conservative, and church-going. In her more recent study of working-class families, Rubin again found alcohol abuse a problem for some men, particularly, although not exclusively, the unemployed. Judith Stacey, in her study of working-class families also observed the tensions generated by unstable employment conditions. Many men who experienced reduced employment opportunities struggled with the loss of their masculine identity. Wives worked to supplement men's wages and keep families together. Among the families Stacey observed, divorce rates rose, and some of the younger men succumbed to the lure of the drug economy, which grew during the time of economic retrenchment. Recently, due to recession and down-sizing, employment conditions have become more insecure for middle-class workers. Katherine Newman has argued that middle-class families who experience a husband's loss of a job are also vulnerable to what she calls "the pathologies of downward mobility," including alcoholism, child abuse, divorce, and violence.[22]

Similarly, despite the stereotype of divorce as a white phenomenon, there have also always been higher divorce rates among black than white couples. Ten years after marriage, 47 percent of blacks have separated or divorced compared with 28 percent of non-Hispanic whites. Many attribute the higher rate of divorce among blacks to the fact that a higher percentage of blacks than whites must deal with difficult economic and employment situations. William Julius Wilson argues that these kinds of conditions create a serious problem for the marriages of African-Americans. He and others point to the high unemployment rate for black men as a key factor in divorce. The unemployment rate for black men aged twenty to twenty-four rose from 13 percent in 1960 to 25 percent in 1992. David Ellwood claims that after factoring in the percentage of men who have stopped looking for work, only half of civilian minority men in a given month are employed. These unemployment rates, combined with the high rates of mortality and incarceration among black men, have resulted in a steep decline in the number of what William Julius Wilson calls "marriageable men." These writers argue that many more black than white men cannot earn enough money to make a significant contribution to the support of a family.[23]

Literature on black marriages also portrays some families as having a "hard-living" lifestyle caused by poverty and erratic employment, a style which can be destructive of family life. Elijah Anderson, Eliot Liebow, and Robert Staples argue that some black men approach marriage with anxiety or shun it for fear they will not be able to support a family. They have difficulty playing the provider role because of their inability to find secure, well-paying employment. They claim that worsening economic conditions account for the high divorce rate and lower marriage rate for blacks. As Maxine Baca-Zinn, Rose Brewer, Patricia Hill Collins, and others have shown, deindustrialization has had a particularly negative impact on minority families, which have been forced to accommodate to declining employment opportunities for men as business leaders relocate jobs to the suburbs and to oversees markets with cheaper labor costs.[24]

In conclusion, after examining how structural factors of gender, class, and race shape marriage and family life, a different set of problems emerge than those that are typically said to cause "family decline." As will be described in the following chapters, many divorced women cite issues of inequality and control—particularly domestic violence—as major problems for their marriages. It is critical that we correctly identify the hardships women face in marriage, in order to shape social policies that can address the real problems which threaten families. The failure to understand the true threats to family well-being leads some to propose returning to family patterns that will exacerbate the problems of marriage, especially for women.

THE EFFECTS OF DIVORCE ON WOMEN AND CHILDREN

Unfortunately, when marriages end women face a new set of difficulties than the ones they experienced during marriage. Whatever the problems of their marriages, most women go on to experience economic hardship after divorce. Fortunately, over the past decade a number of researchers have recognized that mothers face serious economic problems after divorce and have argued for changes in social policy to improve their situation. However, while there have been some positive reforms that I will describe, our social policies continue to greatly disadvantage women after divorce, and these women continue to be vulnerable to severe poverty. In 1992, for example, 39 percent of all divorced mothers with children lived below the poverty level. Divorce is a major contributing factor to the "feminization of poverty." This term refers to the fact that women, particularly women with children, constitute an increasingly high percentage of the poor. Forty-seven percent of female-headed families with children are poor, compared to 8.3 percent of husband-wife families. However, it is important to stress that it is minority women who are particularly at risk for poverty. As will be described below, this feminization of poverty is fueled by the "racialization of poverty" that occurs in our society.[25]

Divorced mothers are left on their own to live on their wages and on whatever they can negotiate from their ex-husbands in the way of child support. Unfortunately, one-third of all divorced women working full-time cannot support themselves and their children above the poverty level. Their standard of living goes down by at least a third.[26] How divorced mothers can support themselves is a critical question not only for their own well-being, but for their children. Children of divorce live at the standard of living of their mothers. Thus, to the extent that a mother's way of life after divorce suffers, so does that of her children. To date, a great deal of attention has been focused on the emotional well-being of children after divorce, a topic which is very important, and which I will take up in chapter 7. Unfortunately, much less concern has been shown for the economic well-being of children after divorce, many of whom experience poverty.

Divorced fathers do not suffer in the same way as divorced mothers. Their incomes are higher than those of their former wives, and their expendable income goes up after divorce by 15 percent. While some pay child support, as will be explained in chapter 5, child support as it is currently calculated and awarded covers less than half the cost of raising a child; typically it is no more than 10 to 20 percent of a father's income, and never more than 30 percent. Thus fathers contribute much less to the support of their children than do mothers. Even poorer fathers have more usable income than many poor mothers. Men may have a new family to support, but this is often at the expense of their former wife and children.[27]

Thus the great majority of divorced single mothers are in a highly dependent, vulnerable position. Few social policies enable them to live at an adequate standard of living outside of marriage. Some must resort to welfare, which provides a standard of living that is typically below the poverty level. Further, to the extent that a mother's way of life after divorce suffers, so does that of her children. As Mary Ann Glendon states:

> We have made it easier and quicker for individuals to obtain a divorce than any other country in the West except Sweden. Yet our legal system and our public policies do less than those in any other country to help families cope with the consequences of divorce. In granting a divorce to parents, we are liberal; in assisting their children we are illiberal. Until recently, we did less than any other country to ensure that absent fathers support their children. The result is that

American children face the worst of both worlds: more so than children any-where else, they cannot rely on either their parents or their government to sup-port them.[28]

The following sections address the reasons why divorced women remain in such a disadvantaged position at divorce. First, the law doesn't provide adequate protections for women. Second, women must support themselves and their chil-dren by working in a labor market which seriously disadvantages women. And third, we define the situation of divorced mothers as their "private" problem and provide them with only meager social supports and resources.

The Law

Recently, reformers have publicized the hardships of divorced women. Some policy makers have become concerned about their situation and have proposed new legal approaches to dividing resources at divorce. However, these new reforms have serious limitations.

Divorce became legal with the passage of the Married Women's Property Acts in the 1840s, but the state tried to discourage divorce until well into the twenti-eth century. Lifelong marriage to the same partner in a traditional family com-posed of a male breadwinner and a female wife and mother was seen as the preferred and "natural" state. To keep families together and to "protect" women and the family, the state made divorce restrictive through a fault-based system that remained in effect until the 1960s. Under this system divorce could take place only if one party was able to prove the other guilty of adultery, cruelty, or other serious offenses. In the event that a divorce did occur, the wife was to be financially protected by her ex-husband. In theory, a husband remained finan-cially responsible for a former wife for the rest of her life, unless she remarried or was found "guilty" of adultery, cruelty, or desertion, in which case she could be denied alimony, and sometimes custody and property as well.

Some believe that the legal position of divorced women was better under the fault-based system. This was not the case, however. Since the state put no mech-anisms in place to enforce the fault-based system, it did not in fact protect women. Most women have never received alimony from their ex-husbands. Between 1887 and 1906, fewer than 9.3 percent of women received alimony; by 1922, 14.7 percent did; and in 1981, the figure was 14.9 percent.[29] Nor did most women obtain much property from a marriage because most couples have had little property to divide. Some poorer men and women, including many minorities, did not have the money to obtain divorces, and so they simply sepa-rated. In other cases, husbands deserted their wives. Thus, a major contradiction existed between the law's assumption that the wife was dependent and should be protected in her domestic role, and the fact that most women received no such protection.

By 1985 all states had passed "no fault" laws, based on the principle of "irretrievable breakdown" of the marriage, "incompatibility," or "irreconcilable differences," which permitted a divorce even if only one partner desired it. The no-fault system overturns the traditional view of women as dependent, stipulating that men are no longer responsible for the support of their former wives. The new model looks at marriage as a partnership between husbands and wives, much like a business partnership. At divorce, women are expected to support themselves through paid work, supplemented by child support and an equitable division of assets from the marriage. Thus alimony or lifelong financial support that in theory was available to a divorced wife, has been replaced by "spousal support" awards of short duration, typically to the former wife, until she can begin supporting herself through paid work. Similarly, women receive no special consideration in the division of property in the no-fault era. Property is to be divided equitably between divorcing spouses, much as one would divide property when dissolving a business.

While overturning the stereotypic view of women as dependents of their husbands was a positive development, the assumption that divorced women would be able to support themselves on their salaries and wages and on the assets from their marriages was seriously in error. First, as will be discussed in the next section, most women cannot earn enough in the paid labor market to support themselves and their children. Second, although women make an enormous investment in their marriage, after divorce they have little to show for it. Most women receive little property from their marriages. Some estimate that fewer than 50 percent of divorced women receive property of any value. In their study, Judith Seltzer and Irwin Garfinkel found that the median value of a family's assets at divorce was $7,800, with women receiving half that amount. The main asset of a couple is often the home, which in some cases is sold at the time of divorce so that each spouse can receive half its value. However, this usually leaves a woman and her children with smaller quarters and causes the children additional disruption.[30]

Recently, definitions of property have expanded somewhat to include more than tangible assets such as a house, a car, savings accounts, and investments; they can also include pensions, interests in a spouse's business, reputation, or career. These new regulations particularly benefit those women whose ex-husbands are better off. However, while many state laws provide guidelines for the "equitable" distribution of property, the law provides only broad-based discretionary standards mandating financial equity between the spouses, which leaves room for widely varying judicial interpretations of what constitutes equity in a particular divorce agreement. Weitzman and others claim that in a system with so much discretion, judges tend to be more supportive of men than women. Finally, one of the biggest problems for women is that, except in rare cases such as in the state of New York, laws concerning marital property do not include the most valuable asset of a marriage, earning potential, nor do they include items such as insurance and professional licenses.[31]

As well as having little property, only about one-sixth of divorced women receive spousal maintenance awards, most of which are of limited duration. Spousal maintenance awards are not large, and only half are paid in full. Weitzman and others believe that courts have been applying minimal and unrealistic standards of self-sufficiency and denying support to most divorced women. Based on her evidence, Weitzman claims that judges in California employ only a minimalist standard for rehabilitative alimony, which awards women the minimum amount needed for some job training. According to Weitzman, the California courts consider that "rehabilitation" has been achieved if the wife can survive without applying for public benefits.[32]

While divorced women have been unable to secure many assets from their marriage, in theory one resource remains available to all divorced women—child support. Most mothers are entitled to it, nearly all mothers need it, yet unfortunately few receive it. Approximately 85 to 90 percent of divorced mothers have physical custody of their children. Child support can help many of them stay out of poverty. Women who live near the official poverty level and receive child support can easily fall below the poverty line if the payments are eliminated. One study showed that about a third of the divorced and separated women who did not receive child support fell below the poverty line, compared to only 12 percent of the women who received such support.[33]

However, despite mothers' demonstrated need for child support, an adequate child-support system has not been achieved. The two elements necessary to ensure an adequate system are equitable child-support awards and effective enforcement of child-support payments. Traditionally, child-support awards have been very low and do not meet even half the costs of rearing the family's children.[34] Similarly, child support enforcement has been weak and only a minority of women have received full support. Fortunately, in the past decade the Federal government has enacted important child-support reforms by instituting stronger enforcement procedures and by requiring states to develop guidelines to establish greater fairness in the awarding of child support. Despite these reforms, however, as will be described in chapter 5, problems will remain for women attempting to collect their child-support awards.

In conclusion, under current law, divorced women remain in a vulnerable and dependent position. Laws regulating the distribution of assets at divorce do not address the fact that women are economically disadvantaged by their participation in a failed marriage. The amounts of money that women receive from marital assets and for child support do not reflect their contributions to their marriages or their needs for themselves and their children after divorce. In marriages couples typically invest in a man's career—he through time in his job, she through time in the home and family. The husband's career prospects are enhanced, while the wife's are impaired; his earning capacity may grow, hers diminishes. Thus marriage itself can be partly responsible for the dramatically different prospects that men and women face after divorce. Paula England argues that the reason divorce is economically disastrous for women is that the tasks in which they have invested so much time—childrearing and housekeeping—are not transferrable when a marriage dissolves, unlike the job skills in which men have invested so heavily. Further, the fact that career assets are not recognized as marital property means that the primary wage earner, generally the husband, is permitted to keep most of the assets accumulated during marriage. Thus, the husband does not suffer financially at divorce, while the wife, who has invested in her family and in her husband's career, is deprived of a return on her marital investment.[35]

Women's Participation in the Labor Force

Laws for allocating resources at divorce rest on the assumption that women are able to earn enough money for themselves in the workplace. The major source of income for divorced women is what they earn from paid work. Most women who did not work outside the home during their marriage do so after a divorce. Greg Duncan and Saul Hoffman found that the proportion of mothers who worked 1,000 or more hours per year increased from 51 to 73 percent after divorce. Divorced women constitute a higher percentage of the full-time workforce than any other group of women.[36] Unfortunately, despite legislation forbidding discrimination, labor force policies remain highly disadvantageous to women and the state takes only a minimal role in establishing rules and conditions that would enable women to be full participants in the workplace.

Women face discrimination in the workplace. First, in terms of wages, women currently earn 70 percent of what males earn. In 1991, the average woman college graduate, working full-time throughout the year, earned only 38 percent more than the average male high school graduate. Roberta Spalter-Roth and Heidi Hartmann found that in the mid-1980s, only half of working mothers earned what they call a "minimum sufficiency wage," or an hourly wage from a year-round, full-time job which is high enough to support a family of three at the poverty line. The differences in wages between women and men remain, even when men and women have the same level of education.[37]

The majority of women find it difficult to get jobs except in certain sex-typed fields. These are the jobs which their schooling prepares them for and which counselors, advisors, and employers channel them into. Disproportionate numbers of women end up in a relatively small percentage of female-typed job categories, which pay less than male jobs. In 1990, 70.6 percent of all women were employed in only six job categories: nurses and health technicians, elementary and secondary school teachers, sales clerks in retail trade, clerical workers, apparel and textile workers, and service workers. Black women are confined to even fewer occupations than white women and predominate in such jobs as chambermaid, welfare service aide, nurse's aide, and childcare worker. Further, black women can have more difficulty finding work than white women. While the earnings of black women are similar to those of white women, black women are 2.5 times as likely to be unemployed as white women.[38]

Additional problems prevent women from earning a decent living from paid work, in addition to low wages and the structure of the labor market. The workplace does not take into account that women are usually the primary caretakers of their children. Women need childcare, and neither the workplace nor the state provide it. For some women, this means they cannot work at all and must rely on welfare.

For other women, the need to care for their children and the lack of decent affordable childcare means that they work part time. While a higher percentage of divorced women work full time than other groups of women, about two-thirds of all women do not work at full-time, year-round jobs. Women who do not work full time usually do not receive health care benefits or disability insurance. It is also difficult to build seniority or other career advantages in a part-time job. In addition, part-time workers have less job security than full-time workers, and if they lose their jobs they have no unemployment insurance. Many women in these circumstances turn to welfare, formally known as AFDC, or Aid to Families with Dependent Children, "the poor woman's unemployment compensation."[39]

Sexual harassment also places women at a disadvantage in the workplace. Figures from a well-regarded study show that 42 percent of the women who work for the Federal government experience sexual harassment. Not only are women overwhelmingly the victims of sexual harassment, but they also bear most of its costs. As Diana Pearce says, "Every woman who has lost a promotion, quit to avoid further harassment, or mysteriously walked away from an opportunity has paid an economic as well as a psychic price for being a woman."[40]

This inequality in wages has serious consequences for women who are single parents. While 4 percent of families with a working male are in poverty, more than 25 percent of families headed by employed women have incomes below the poverty level. Of those who support their children principally through their own earnings, 60 percent earn a poverty-level income or below. Black single mothers are also poorer than white ones. Nearly one-third of black single mothers who worked for pay in 1987 lived below the poverty line, compared with 17 percent of white single mothers.[41] To date, the government has failed to pursue affirmative-action policies that would allow the entry of qualified women into higher-paying jobs outside of traditional female job categories.

Underlying government policies is the view that males should be the providers for their families, and women the nurturers and caretakers. Existing policies dictate, in effect, that family income should be distributed through men. These roles are woven deeply into the history and traditions of American society, beginning with the republican vision of the true citizen as a wage earner who could be self-sufficient and support himself and his family. Government legislation and social policies perpetuate this gendered division of labor by promoting the view that men must be supported in the public sphere to do "real" work, while women should take responsibility for unpaid work in the domestic sphere, work that enables men to be the "independent" wage earners.[42]

State Welfare Legislation and Social Policy

The only large-scale program that the state provides for single mothers is AFDC, which, until recently, has been considered an "entitlement program" for all those who meet the criteria of poverty as determined by AFDC regulations. AFDC is designed for mothers whose chief source of financial support, a male partner, is no longer present (whether through death or divorce) or never was present. Thirty-five percent of the women on AFDC are divorced or separated and about half the women on AFDC never married. Two-thirds of AFDC recipients are children.[43] Rather than being a comprehensive program for divorced mothers and other single parents or for families, however, this assistance is only available to women if they are very poor.

Historically the goal of AFDC has not been to help women escape poverty or to live independently, but to provide temporary assistance to widowed, divorced, and more recently, unmarried women until they can once again be supported by a man. Further, women on welfare have been viewed as a special type of woman, usually morally undeserving. This view can be seen in the contrasting payments received by AFDC recipients and those who receive income through other programs. The Supplemental Security Income (SSI) program, established in 1973, combined the previous Aid to the Blind, Aid to the Disabled, and Old Age Assistance programs into one federal means-tested program. The average monthly payment per person for an individual on SSI in April 1988 was $259, while for a woman on AFDC it was $126. Similarly, a foster parent receives four times the amount per child as a woman on AFDC, and in some states foster parents are paid seven or eight times what the child's own mother is paid to care for that child.[44]

While it has provided a critical safety net for many poor women and their children, through much of its history, AFDC has been restrictive. The Federal government has granted states the power to control who has access to welfare and how much income they should receive. Agencies have always used means tests to verify that women were in fact poor, and have excluded women if evidence showed that they were living with men who might support them. In many jurisdictions, AFDC regulations promoted intrusive "midnight raids" to determine if a man was present in the household.[45]

As part of AFDC's practice of supporting traditional gender roles, it has historically penalized women for working. Some women on welfare have worked at paid labor in order to survive, but traditionally, for every dollar a woman earned, a dollar was deducted from her AFDC payment. AFDC has always paid less than the lowest-paying job in order to discourage women from going on welfare, so the state would not be in competition with the market. In no state does the value of the AFDC benefit for four people equal 75 percent of the poverty line; in half of the states, it pays less than 50 percent. In addition, in return for AFDC payments the state is entitled to certain of the assets of AFDC recipients. In Pennsylvania, for example, any homeowner who has received AFDC has a lien put on her house. Before selling her home, the owner must pay back the amount of money she received in AFDC benefits or this sum will be taken out of the payment she receives for her home. States are also entitled to the child support received by an AFDC recipient. For every month that the children's father pays the required amount of child support to AFDC on time, the mother receives $50. The theory is that the woman should be "paying back" money to AFDC. Over the last few decades, AFDC benefits have frequently been cut back. Since AFDC benefits are not indexed to keep up with inflation, the value of AFDC benefits have, consequently, decreased every year. Thus AFDC has become less and less effective at keeping women and children out of poverty.[46]

Recently, AFDC policy has changed dramatically and now requires mothers to work in the paid labor force. The Family Security Act of 1988, authored by Senator Moynihan, mandated that women with children on welfare should work, and made participation in a jobs program mandatory. The government was to provide transitional day care, Medicaid coverage, education, and employment and job placement services. While helping poor women find jobs is a very important goal, mandatory jobs programs are usually limited because they do not provide enough of the training and childcare resources that women need in order to work. Thus the way this system was implemented almost guaranteed that AFDC would not raise women out of poverty and would not increase their income, work skills, and job opportunities. Instead, AFDC has worked to channel mothers into the low-wage labor market where they face earnings that are not much larger than their AFDC payments, no health care benefits, and additional expenses—for childcare, carfare, and suitable clothing. In addition, a full-time job takes them away from their children for many hours.[47]

No one is addressing the real problem—the need for jobs which pay a livable wage. A number of politicians, in the name of reforming welfare, are seeking to end it. Some would abolish assistance to single mothers altogether. Many favor putting welfare money in the form of block grants to states, a policy which would end the entitlement of eligible poor women to AFDC. Unfortunately most states favor restricting access to welfare. A few favor giving women on welfare more job training, but as just described, job training works only if states help women with health care and childcare costs both during the training and after they begin work. Unfortunately, few politicians talk about providing guaranteed health benefits or child care, reforming the low-wage labor market, or raising the minimum wage. Almost no one faces the reality of the scarcity of adequately paying jobs for low-wage workers or the punitiveness of making single mothers with small children work while taking care of children by themselves.[48]

The failure of the social welfare system in the United States to provide adequate levels of assistance to single-mother families is rooted in the belief that helping women live more easily as single parents destroys the family. These fears can be exploited in uncertain economic times when politicians want to reduce budgets by cutting social programs. Welfare mothers, who have no political constituency, are easy targets for politicians. They are portrayed as poor, usually minority women, who are morally unworthy. In fact, 51 percent of AFDC recipients are white and 42 percent are black.[49] Nonetheless, politicians continue to use racist stereotypes of black women to further discredit AFDC and blame it for "family breakdown."

False beliefs about the impact of welfare persist despite evidence that it is not welfare that has caused the increase of single-parent families. Wilson and Neckerman, and David Ellwood and Mary Jo Bane have concluded that welfare is not the underlying cause of the dramatic changes in family structure in the past few decades. White women tend to apply for welfare following the breakup of a marriage, and black women turn to AFDC because of the lack of opportunity to marry and the high poverty rate in the black community. Demographic evidence also undermines the theory that AFDC causes marital breakups and out-of-wedlock births. High rates of divorce and separation predated the welfare explosion and have continued to rise despite slowed growth of AFDC rolls and the declining value of AFDC benefits.[50]

WOMEN OF THE STUDY

Having set the context for the situation of divorced women, I will now describe the women who form the basis of this study. They reflect many of the characteristics of divorced mothers just described. These women come from a wide range of educational backgrounds. Some are professionals, others have only a high school education and are having great difficulty finding work. There are many black divorced women in the sample, as well as white. The diversity of this sample has many advantages. It enables us to examine the differences in women's experiences, while at the same time seeing these things that all divorced women have in common. Further, because this is a random sample it is possible to do statistical tests of significance.

Despite their diversity, many of these divorced mothers must live on relatively low incomes, and a certain percentage face serious poverty. The median family income of all women in the sample is $18,350 (1988 figures), which is 43 percent of the median income of a two-earner family ($42,709 in 1988). Twenty-five percent of the women in this sample live below the official government poverty level. This is actually lower than the poverty rate for divorced women with children nationally, which, as has been noted, was 39 percent in 1992. Forty-four percent of women in the sample receive no child support at all, 16 percent receive partial support, and 40 percent receive regular support. The average number of children for the sample is 2.25. The economic characteristics of the women in this sample will be explored in greater depth in chapter 4.

The Sample

The data for this study were gathered through interviews with a random sample of 129 mothers who obtained divorces through the Philadelphia Family Court in 1986, and who were interviewed in 1987 and 1988. The sample was restricted to women who had at least one child. Custody of the children was not a precondition for inclusion, but women had to have some financial responsibility for the child(ren). Women whose children were financially independent adults were not included. This means the sample does not include a large number of older divorced women. The average age of the women is 35, the median age, 34. Most women (61 percent) are between 30-39 years of age. The remainder are split evenly between under 30 and over 40. Most women live within the limits of Philadelphia County, which has the same borders as Philadelphia, a city of approximately 1,600,000. A small percentage of women in the sample live in the suburbs. The racial distribution of the sample approximates that of the city, with 61 percent white women, 35 percent black women, and 3 percent Hispanic women.[51]

Of the women contacted, 48 percent agreed to be interviewed, 11 percent declined, and 40 percent did not respond to the request to participate. This response rate compares favorably with response rates found in other studies of divorced women.[52] Divorced women can be a difficult population to find because many of them change their residence at least once, frequently several times. In the case of this study, for women who did not respond to the initial letter of invitation, we sent second and third follow-up letters, trying to trace them through different addresses where necessary, and calling women where we could obtain telephone numbers. The letter of invitation explaining the study was accompanied by a letter from the Administrative Judge of the Family

Law Division of the Common Pleas Court in Philadelphia, urging women to participate so that more could be learned of the situation of divorced women. The women were paid for their time—$25 an interview.

A review of the records of those who did not respond to the letter of invitation indicated that they included slightly more black than white women. Thus, a greater proportion of white women agreed to be interviewed for the study than black women. Asian women, although they were 1 percent of the city's population when the sample was drawn, were not represented in the sample. Further, some very poor women may also not be represented in the sample. The women who responded to the request to participate in the study only after receiving three letters of invitation were living a more marginal existence. Thus, the figures in this study may present a slightly better financial situation for divorced women in Philadelphia than exists in reality. Despite the diversity of the sample, no one interviewed identified herself as a lesbian. This could be because lesbian women did not feel comfortable sharing this information, or because they did not volunteer for the study. Some lesbians may have been fearful of volunteering for a study of divorce, given that a number of divorced lesbians have had difficulty gaining custody of their children.

The fact that this sample reflects the views of women who live in a large metropolitan area contributes to the representativeness of the sample. First, divorce rates are higher in urban areas in the United States. Second, this urban sample has a greater number of poor and minority women than one would find in some rural and many suburban settings. As indicated earlier, even the earliest divorce statistics collected in this country show a higher rate of divorce among lower-income and minority couples than their wealthier white counterparts.[53] Thus in terms of race and class groups, this sample provides a good representation of the different populations of divorced women.

The women in this sample share certain characteristics with all other divorced women. The women in a national survey of 209 mothers with physical custody of their children whose divorces were finalized in 1984 are almost identical to the Philadelphia sample in terms of age, education, and duration of marriage. There were some predictable differences between the two samples in terms of race, income, labor force participation, and number of children. The Philadelphia women are 62 percent white, as opposed to 86.6 percent white in the national sample; they have more children (2.2, as opposed to 1.8); they have higher average earnings ($15,588 as opposed to $10,504 a year); and they have a lower rate of participation in the labor force (73 percent as opposed to 84.2 percent) than women in the national sample. The greater number of minority women reflects the urban nature of this sample. The lower labor force participation of Philadelphia women could reflect the fact that more of the women in this sample are on welfare and are therefore not supposed to be employed and, as will be noted later, that some minority women report difficulty finding work. The Philadelphia women may have higher average earnings because of the higher salary scales of a Northeast urban area. Finally, it is very interesting to note that despite the fact that the sample was drawn from a large urban area, the official poverty rate of the women in this sample, 25 percent, is lower than the 39 percent rate of poverty for divorced women nationwide. High as the poverty rate is for the divorced women in this sample, it is lower than the poverty rate for divorced women nationwide.[53]

The women in this study were interviewed approximately two years after their divorces and had been separated an average of 3.1 years before their divorces. Thus the women in this sample had been living on their own, apart from their former husbands, for about five years. This is enough time for these women to have regrouped and reorganized their families. Constance Ahrons claims that divorcing families experience the greatest change and the most stress the first two years after the divorce.[55] These women had been together with their husbands for an average of 8.5 years (median 6 years). Fourteen percent of the women in this sample are remarried, 14 percent are engaged to be married, 5 percent are living with a partner, and 24 percent are dating. Forty-three percent of the women were not in any relationship at the time of the interview.

The interviews with divorced mothers lasted from one-and-a-half to three hours and included both fixed-choice and open-ended questions. Interviews were conducted by the author and another sociologist, Kathleen Coughey. Half the women were interviewed in their homes, and half in the offices of the research team, depending on the women's preference. As a result of the diverse nature of the sample, women were interviewed in a range of settings, in neighborhoods of relatively small city row houses, in neighborhoods considered dangerous, in the most expensive sections of the city, and in suburban developments with large ranch houses. Both interviewers were white. It would have been interesting to have both a white and a black interviewer. It is certainly possible that black women would have mentioned additional issues to a black interviewer, concerning for example their attitudes about the fact that judges and other court personnel are predominantly white. As will be reported, three black women volunteered information about how their race affected their experience of divorce.

Almost all the women wanted to share their experiences and spoke with a great deal of candor about their pain, their anger, and their hopes for the future. Before we spoke with them, many had only had the chance to share their experiences with a few friends and family. Most of the women voiced the hope that their participation in the study could "help other women in this situation."

Designating Social Classes

In order to understand the impact of divorce on women who come from a range of economic backgrounds, I divided these women into different social class groups. As will be discussed below, there are significant differences

Figure 2–1. Summary of Social Class Definitions.

Middle Class: Any woman who has any of the following characteristics:
— has a college degree, or
— has a house worth $150,000 or more, or
— works in a professional occupation.

Working Class: Any woman who has all of the following characteristics:
— has a stable job in a nonprofessional occupational category, such as "pink" collar, sales, technical, or clerical, and
— has an income higher than the Ruggles poverty level, but does not meet any of the above characteristics of the middle class, and
— does not receive Aid for Families of Dependent Children (AFDC), live in public housing, or meet any of the other criteria for the poverty level group.

Poverty Level: Any woman who has any of the following characteristics:
— has an income below the Ruggles poverty level, or
— is receiving AFDC/welfare, or
— is living in public housing, or
— does not have a high school diploma.

---

between the women in this sample based on their social class position, which underscores the importance of understanding how divorce has different consequences for women depending on what resources they bring to the divorce situation. In dividing women into social classes, I used education, occupation, income, and housing resources. My goal in using these different types of class indicators was to understand how women with a range of different resources experience divorce. Based on these indicators, women clustered into three class groups: middle-class and professional women, working-class women, and poverty-level women.

As indicated in Figure 2–1, if a woman had any one of the following characteristics, she was coded as middle-class: an education level which included a college degree; a house valued at least $150,000 in an affluent suburban location; or a professional job classification. I coded as working-class women who had none of the characteristics of middle-class women, but did have the following characteristics: a stable job in the following job categories: pink collar, sales, technical, clerical, and technician; a high school diploma; and a personal income higher than the Ruggles poverty level (see next paragraph for a definition of this poverty level). I placed in the third group, which I have called the "poverty-level" group, all those women who were living under the Ruggles poverty level and those who were on AFDC, or welfare, or who lived in public housing. These women had neither professional jobs nor high-priced homes. I called this group "Poverty-level" because there is little agreement as to how to describe lower-income people in a non-stigmatizing way.

For this study I have chosen to define poverty-level status using the definition devised by Ruggles rather than the standard, government-defined poverty level. Experts disagree on how and at what level to set the poverty threshold. As critics have pointed out, the government sets the poverty level at an unrealistically low level. In 1988, when many of the interviews for this study were done, the government set the official poverty rate for a family of three at approximately $9,500. Patricia Ruggles argues that the poverty level for a family of three in 1988 should actually be set at $15,000, that this is a "minimally adequate" living standard based on "current normative patterns of need and consumption." She claims that the current government poverty level is based on outdated norms and consumption patterns. Policy makers in some other countries also have higher poverty thresholds than those found in the United States. The European Economic Community, for example, sets its poverty level at half of the median family income of individual countries, which is much higher than the current U.S. government poverty rate.[56]

I chose to define social class using characteristics such as education, occupation, and housing, as well as income, because they have a significant influence on a person's opportunities and provide a more stable indication of a person's life chances than income alone, especially the income of divorced women. As many have noted, the income of women drops precipitously at divorce. After divorce, women frequently become temporarily unemployed or fail to receive child support payments for some period of time, with a resulting drop in income. Thus, more stable class indicators like education and occupation take into account resources that were available prior to and after divorce and which influence a woman's ability to cope with the economic changes which occur at divorce. Income alone is too sensitive to temporary fluctuations to be a reliable indicator of the situation of divorced women.[57]

In assigning women class groups, I used college degree, professional occupation, or owning a home worth at least $150,000 to determine membership in the middle-class because, although middle-class women can face many hardships, these resources do provide them with certain benefits. Working-class women also have some educational and occupational resources, although not as many as those of the middle-class women. All have high school diplomas and many have stable work histories and health care benefits, but their income levels can be low. In fact, if we looked only at income, in a few cases there would be overlap between the working-class and poverty-level groups. However working-class women, based on their education and on their access to stable jobs

Figure 2–2. A Portrait of Divorced Mothers.*

	Middle Class (n=25)	Working Class (n=58)	Poverty Level (n=46)
Average age (years)	39	35	33
Educational level	some college (29%) college degree (54%)	most have high school diploma (88%)	high school diploma (64%) or less (27%)
Average years of education	15.5	12.1	11.7
Average age at marriage (years)	25	22	20
Average number of children	1.7	1.9	2.8
Race	72% white 28% black	74% white 24% black 2% Hispanic	39% white 54% black 7% Hispanic

* All of the variables in this table show statistically significant differences by social class group. See appendix for details.

• The women ranged in age from 23 to 62, with 93 percent between 25 and 44 years old.

• All of the women were divorced in 1986. They had all been separated from their husbands for about five years on average at the time that they were interviewed.

• Women in all three groups were legally married for about eleven to thirteen years on average, ranging from one to twenty-eight years. Excluding separations, the women were married and living with their spouses for seven to nine years on average.

with benefits, have more resources than poverty-level women, many of whom are forced to rely on AFDC and public housing for basic necessities.

In assigning women to class groups, I did look at alternative ways of determining the poverty level by income. Using the classification scheme based on the 1988 government poverty thresholds, I classified the women in the study on

Figure 2-3. The Economic Status of Divorced Mothers.*

	Middle Class (n=25)	Working Class (n=58)	Poverty Level (n=46)
Employment Status	nearly all work full-time (71%) or part-time (13%)	nearly all work full-time (82%) or part-time (13%)	working for pay (30%) welfare (40%) unemployed (24%)
Average personal income[1]	$31,500 (professional) $14,900 (non-professional)	$16,700	$7,100
Average total family income[2]	$35,900 (professional) $37,900 (non-professional)	$23,700	$11,100
Receive no child support	22%	33%	69%

* All of the variables in this table show statistically significant differences by social class group. See appendix for details.

1. Personal income includes earnings from paid work, as well as disability and/or unemployment checks. Figures in all tables are from 1987–1988.

2. Total family income includes income from paid work, alimony, child-support payments, disability or unemployment checks, food stamps, and AFDC/welfare payments.

the basis of whether their incomes were below 100, 150, or 200 percent of the poverty threshold. Analyzing the data by different levels of poverty, however, did not change the findings. On all important variables the results were similar to the results I obtained by using the Ruggles poverty level. In conclusion, the three class designations I chose to analyze these data appear quite stable. Based on broader sociological principles, they are more useful and meaningful than using income alone.

Finally, it is important to note that, using the criteria for class which I have chosen means that there are sometimes income and other resource differences between women in the same class. In chapter 4, for example, I note income differences between those middle-class women who are professionals and those who are not. Similarly, among poverty-level women I differentiate between those who appear to be in poverty only temporarily and those who have fewer resources, who may remain poor for some time. However despite some differ-

Figure 2–4. Characteristics of Divorced Women by Race.

	Black (n=46)	White (n=79)
Average age (years)	35	35
Education level	7% have college degree 82% have a high school diploma 11% did not complete high school	13% have college degree 77% have a high school diploma 10% did not complete high school
Average education (years)	12.6	12.7
Average age at marriage (years)	21.7	22.1
Average number of children *	2.5	1.9

* Difference by race is statistically significant but is no longer significant after controlling for social class.

ences within classes, given the criteria for defining class that I used, the women in this sample tended to cluster into these three class groups. Figure 2–2 shows the important, statistically significant differences among women of different classes, including their age, number of children, education, and race. For a description of the research methods and results of the analyses, see the appendix. Figure 2–3 presents differences between women in terms of their economic characteristics, such as income, employment status, and receipt of child support. The higher a woman's class, the older she is likely to be, the fewer children she is likely to have, the higher her rate of employment, and the more likely she is to receive child support. Thus, these measures of class provide a good indication of how women with particular resources and backgrounds negotiate for resources as divorced mothers. Chapter 4 will present further details about class membership and its impact on the experiences of the divorced women in this sample.[58]

Large differences also separate black and white mothers in terms of their social class, poverty status, and reliance on AFDC. While black women comprise 35 percent of the women in the sample, they comprise 28 percent of the middle-class women, 24 percent of the working-class women, and 54 percent of the poverty-level women. Figures 2–4 and 2–5 summarize the characteristics of

Figure 2–5. The Economic Status of Divorced Women by Race.

	Black (n=46)	White (n=79)
Employment status *	43% employed full-time 13% employed part-time 11% looking for work 28% on welfare 5% unemployed or other	65% employed full-time 13% employed part-time ·3% looking for work 10% on welfare 9% unemployed or other
Average personal income[1]	$14,900	$15,900
Average total family income[2]*	$16,700	$26,000
On welfare *	28%	10%
Incomes below official poverty level *	41%	9%
Receive no child support *	64%	36%
Receive significant help from family	37%	34%

1. Personal income includes earnings from paid work, as well as disability and/or unemployment checks.

2. Total family income includes income from paid work, alimony, child-support payments, disability or unemployment checks, food stamps, and AFDC/welfare payments.

* Race differences for marked variables are statistically significant. See appendix for details.

these divorced women by race. Black and white women are similar in terms of age, age at marriage, and overall they have the same number of years of education. While black women have significantly more children than white women, this difference is not significant after controlling for social class.[59]

In terms of economic characteristics, it is important to note that black and white middle- and working-class women with jobs have similar incomes. However, as noted in Figure 2–5, a much higher percentage of black women (29 percent) are on AFDC than white women (10 percent). As a result, a full 42 percent of all black women in the sample live below the official poverty level, in contrast to 9 percent of the white women, while three out of the four Hispanic women live below the poverty level. Black women also have a significantly lower rate of employment and receive less child support compared to white women. These striking economic differences between white and black women persist despite the fact that black women have achieved the same educational level as white women, thus demonstrating how black women face discrimination and other serious disadvantages based on race.

I also examined age differences between women in this sample. While age has an impact on the experiences of the mothers in this sample, as will be discussed in chapter 7, the only point at which age was a statistically significant variable was in terms of a woman's social class. As noted above, poverty-level women were on average significantly younger than other women. Other than this difference, however, there were no other significant differences between women based on age in terms of the variables used in this study. The fact that older women in this sample did not significantly differ from younger ones could be due to the fact that to be included in this sample a woman had to have at least one child for whom she had some financial responsibility. Thus, the sample does not include many older women. Some researchers report that divorced women who are older face particular financial problems.[60]

CONCLUSION

In conclusion, our current conceptions of divorce do not adequately reflect the experiences of the diversity of divorced women. There is too much focus on divorce as a white middle-class phenomenon and as a product of "individualism," and too little understanding of how structural factors of gender, as well as class and race, impact on divorced women. This book, based on interviews with a random sample of divorced women of different classes and races, examines the reasons why women are leaving their marriages and how they view their marriages and divorces. These women's accounts show that many women wanted their divorces and are glad to be out of difficult, sometimes destructive marriages. At the same time, divorced mothers have difficulty supporting themselves and their children. Our social policies, which fail to address the situation of women and children who live outside of marriage, create hardship. Thirty-nine percent of divorced mothers nationwide live below the official poverty level. It is critical to understand the lives of these women and to understand the inequalities they face, so that we may create fairer policies which give divorced women the resources to which they are entitled.

Chapter 3

HOW MARRIAGES END

As noted in the previous chapter, some social scientists believe that a key factor shaping contemporary divorce is "individualism"—husbands and wives, influenced by corporate culture, personal growth movements, and the women's movement, now place a high priority on their own personal interests and needs, and so are more ready to divorce when they encounter difficulties in their marriages. Despite the widespread interest in the topic of divorce, however, we don't really understand why people end their marriages. While research shows that women typically initiate the divorce process, we don't know why this is so.[1]

In order to form accurate images and assessments of those who divorce, we need to know more about why couples are leaving their marriages. Are divorced women "selfish" and "misguided"? Are they "victims"? If women are leaving marriages simply to "see if they can do better," this phenomenon creates a different understanding of marriage than if they are leaving because of dissatisfaction with traditional sex roles, domestic violence, or their husbands' drug abuse or domestic violence.

Our views of divorced women in turn influence the policies we choose to respond to divorce. Depending on whether we believe that divorce is caused by the rise of individualism and the abandonment of commitments to the family, by men's unemployment and inability to support a family, or by women's wishes to escape a violent marriage, we will adopt one policy while rejecting another.

In this research I explored the reasons that women themselves give for their marriages ending. These women's views challenge contemporary perspectives on divorce which stress the role that individualism plays in a couple's discontent. Their stories illustrate how their decisions about marriage and divorce were rooted in family contexts that were significantly shaped by factors related to gender, race, and class. The domestic violence in these women's marriages, for example, was a major influence on their experiences of marriage and their decision to divorce. Economic hardship and poverty also placed heavy burdens on the marriages of some women. Their accounts demonstrate the disadvantages that divorced women can experience in marriage, and the ways that their marriages can be not only fraught with problems, but also destructive.

Women in this study were asked to describe the circumstances of their separation. Most women stated, "I left when/because ..." or "He left when/because...." These data do not tell us what "causes" divorce. An answer to that complex question would require an in-depth analysis of historical and demographic data, as well as more comprehensive data from women themselves. Nor did these women give extended accounts of the process of ending their marriages such as are found in some other studies. These data represent what a random sample of women chose to report in interviews an average of five years after their separation. Their descriptions of why their marriages ended relate to their understanding of their divorces at a particular moment in time; they would very likely differ at different points in the divorce process, with different interviewers, and at different historical periods. These women's accounts in many cases would also differ from those of their ex-husbands. As noted earlier, there are "his" and "her" versions of marriage and divorce based on the different social positions of men and women in the family.[2]

What is important about these accounts is that they provide women's perspectives on what shaped their marriage and divorce. These women's views of the ending of their marriage strongly influenced their entire experience of divorce. While being interviewed, the women referred repeatedly to these reasons for their divorces, indicating their enduring importance to their lives. They often reported that the circumstances of their separation had a strong impact on their experience of divorce as well, including their ability to negotiate for resources. For example, if a couple parts mutually and amicably, a woman may be more likely to obtain child support from her ex-husband than if they had serious conflicts. How a marriage ends also affects a woman's assessment of her divorce. A woman who is left by her husband against her wishes may see herself as having lost major opportunities because of divorce, while a woman whose ex-husband was abusive or violent may feel divorce gives her the opportunity to pursue a more fulfilling life. These women also reported problems in their marriages that have been widely noted as problems for families in the United States today, particularly domestic violence. And finally, their responses to questions about the circumstances of their separation are consistent with responses women have given other researchers who have asked similar questions about the ending of their marriages.[3]

Figure 3–1. Principal Reasons Women Gave for Their Divorce.

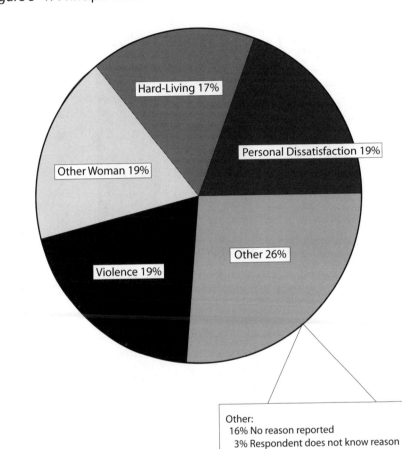

REASONS FOR DIVORCE

Based on their accounts of why their marriages ended, I have placed the women into four different groups. One group includes those women who reported having left their husbands because of personal dissatisfaction and those who termed their separation "mutual." A second group includes those women who said their marriages ended because their husbands were involved

Figure 3–2. Principal Reason for Divorce by Social Class.*

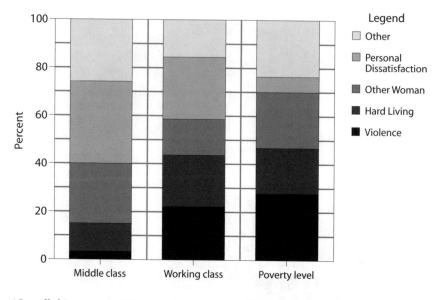

*Overall chi-square significant by class. See Appendix for details.

with other women. In some cases the men left their wives, in others wives said they left because of their husbands' involvement with other women. I placed in a third category those women who reported having left their marriages because of violence they experienced at the hands of their husbands. In a fourth category are those women who state that their marriages ended for what I call "hard-living" reasons, after Joseph Howell's description of certain types of blue-collar families in which the men's difficulties holding jobs led to alcoholism, extended absences from home, and related behaviors that threatened their marriages.[4] Figure 3–1 presents the percentage of women in each of these categories.

There were significant differences between reports of women in different classes (see Figure 3–2). The higher their class position, the more likely the women were to cite personal dissatisfaction as a reason for their divorce, while the lower their class position, the more they reported leaving because of violence. "Hard-living" divorces were more prevalent among working-class and poverty-level women and were significantly more likely to occur among white women. There were no other statistically signficant differences between women in terms of their race.[5]

Personal Dissatisfaction

I begin my discussion of the ending of these marriages with the category of what I have called "personal dissatisfaction," since this category is closest to the kinds of dissatisfaction that contemporary observers have said motivate Americans to divorce. The 19 percent of women who left their marriages for reasons of personal dissatisfaction stated that: they didn't love their husbands anymore; the communication in their marriages was not good; they fought too often with their husbands; their husbands had been too controlling; or they were tired of carrying the emotional load of the marriage. At the same time that they cited a variety of factors as critical to the ending of their marriages, however, women also identified certain patterns to the separation, particularly the importance of gender roles.

A few women spoke in gender-neutral terms about why they left their marriages. A 33-year-old white secretary, married twelve years, mentioned lack of communication in her marriage. A 31-year-old woman from a similar background said that she and her husband argued all the time.

> One of the problems with my ex-husband was that we didn't communicate well. I guess we were just different. He didn't talk much and he was very moody. I had to plan when I would say things to him. He did use drugs—but we all did, our generation. . . . But that wasn't the cause of our communication problem.
>
> I left him. And he was angry about that. He didn't want me to leave. . . . He just always wanted to have a good time. I felt that I gave the marriage my best shot. But all the arguing wasn't good for me and it wasn't good for the kids.

A 41-year-old working-class Hispanic woman, married seventeen years, said that she did not like or respect her husband. She claimed he had squandered their money on bad business ventures, and she didn't trust him anymore.

> I went to marriage counseling around the time of the separation. . . . It wasn't helpful. I knew the marriage was done. He had sold the house he bought with his mother right out from under her. . . . I thought, if he does that to her, what is he going to do to me?

Most of these women, however, gave what I call "gendered" accounts of how their marriages ended. By gendered I mean that women described leaving their marriages because of behaviors associated with the conventional male role. Typically, there is a division of family labor by gender, with women assuming emotional and caretaking functions and men expected to be the primary bread-winners. In addition, as discussed in chapter 2, despite norms favoring equality in marriage, men often still control decision-making in the family. Gender, of course, permeates all social interactions. As Joan Scott notes, gender is "a constitutive element of social relationships based on perceived differences between the sexes, and . . . a primary way of signifying relationships of power."[6]

First, women mentioned their ex-husbands' controlling behavior. One 34-year-old white middle-class woman, an administrator who had been married for eleven years, felt that because of her ex-husband's controlling behavior, she could not participate in decision-making during the marriage:

> I left him . . . he wasn't physically abusive, but he was emotionally abusive. . . . I didn't like how he made all the decisions. He always argued very logically with what I said. So it always seemed like what I said didn't make sense and what he said was right. I just didn't have respect for him anymore. I thought long and hard about leaving, for over a year. I tried to get him into counseling. He went but he didn't really participate. And when we got home it was just the same thing.

Several working-class women also spoke of their ex-husbands as being too controlling.

> I married him when I was young and dumb. I had a scholarship at [local university] I could have taken but I married him instead. He also wanted to control everything about my life. He wanted to control my friends, my time. [36-year-old black nurse, married for fifteen years with two children]

> One problem with my husband, he was like "women have their place." He would provide but the woman was to keep her mouth shut. (Now) I would look for somebody who would treat their partner as an equal. [39-year-old black part-time temporary worker, married for seventeen years with three children]

A few women spoke in both general terms and in more gendered terms about their marital relationships. One middle-class white woman whose ex-husband was an artist initially spoke of her ex-husband's "irresponsibility." She described how she felt guilty when she left "because my child was very young and she was very confused but at the same time I couldn't be with someone so irresponsible." They had tried counseling, but according to this woman, it was too late. "I had been up for that a year and a half before and he kept saying there was nothing wrong. Only when I got him out the door was he ready." However, later in the interview this woman gave a more gendered account of her marriage. She stated that what she liked about the divorce was "moving more in the direction I want." During her marriage, she said, "I'd been running in the direction he wanted."

Second, women stated that they did not get enough emotional support from their husbands. A 33-year-old white psychiatrist, who had been married nine years, spoke about the issue of emotional support in very gendered terms.

I had to do all the emotional work in the relationship and I wasn't getting anything back. I really tried to make it work for a couple of years. I kept thinking that it would change, that if I did the right thing he would become more emotionally active and responsive in the relationship. We went to therapy but things didn't seem to change. Finally I told him I wanted him to leave. He was very angry.

I knew I couldn't stay with someone who was so completely unsupportive. He was only looking out for what was good for him. I don't think all men are the same, but I believe it was very male behavior. I guess he was angry that he wasn't getting enough emotional attention. First, because we had recently had a baby. And then because I went back to school.

A 37-year-old white graduate student in education, who had been married six years, presented a similar picture:

It's a relief. I was carrying the emotional load of the relationship for so long. I was just always directing my energies toward making things better, toward trying to make him and the relationship happier. Now I'm starting to ask, "what do I want?" That's something I've never asked before.

A 34-year-old black poverty-level woman, a part-time classroom aide, spoke in a similar vein:

I want a supportive relationship. One where I can give support and get support. My husband thought a man was supposed to be a good provider and that was it. I want more than that. I want a real relationship.

Lillian Rubin has noted that many women are deeply dissatisfied with the lack of emotional support from their husbands.[7]

Third, a small number of women voiced discontent with their husbands' failure to be adequate enough providers. These women are discontented because their husbands are not working, or are not working hard enough. Those who are themselves working for pay are particularly unhappy. One white middle-class woman, a registered nurse, stated she left her husband because he remained unemployed throughout the marriage. She claimed that he accumulated debts and smoked a lot of marijuana, and that he didn't spend time with the children or help her take care of them. One woman, a 36-year-old white middle-class mother of two, who was married for twelve years, felt that her husband did not try hard enough to be successful in his work.

He is bitter. He feels he got kicked out. It was me that wanted the divorce. I didn't love him anymore. I didn't respect him anymore. He didn't have any ambition. I had to really push him to improve his business.

As Myra Marx Ferree notes, in accordance with prevailing gender norms, some women subscribe to the idea that men should be the primary providers and are uncomfortable when they believe their husbands do not live up to the primary breadwinner role.[8]

Those women who state that the decision to end their marriages was mutual also spoke of their husbands' controlling behavior. Anne, the educational consultant who was introduced in chapter 1, at first spoke of how her divorce was the result of a "mutual split."

> We just couldn't get along. My ex-husband is a nut. He has a terrible temper. He . . . constantly fights and argues. He even told me "I'll miss fighting with you."

However, she then continued with a story about her ex-husband's controlling behavior:

> My ex-husband didn't have an emotional vocabulary. Everything was fine or he was very very angry. He used his anger to control. It scared me. I would really try to prevent it. If I could tell it was coming, I would do things to prevent it.
> I was very frightened by the end. My friends were frightened too. He would throw and destroy things. My daughter was really upset too. She thought, if he can throw these things, what can happen to me?

A 38-year-old black senior computer program analyst stated that the decision to end her marriage was mutual; married for nine years, she had experienced a lot of violence before and during the marriage. She thought the separation would be peaceful, but found otherwise:

> When we first separated it was by mutual agreement, and I thought it would be amicable. But he would come over a lot and harass me in all kinds of ways. Like when he used to come to the house he would go to my bedroom and rummage through my drawers and throw all the clothes on my bed. He would say, "I want to find out about your love life." He's driven around my mother's house. They're afraid of him. They've never dealt with a person like him. . . . He almost caused me to lose my job. He really harassed people [at my workplace], including the guard.

One 40-year-old white working-class woman, who had been married for nine years, described her divorce as mutual, but spoke of feeling controlled by her husband.

> We knew it was over as soon as he moved out. I was terribly relieved when he moved out. I felt I had my freedom back. I'd been divorced before so I had no illusions about how easy it would be. But my ex-husband was really into power

and control. It got so I would just go along with everything and say, "yes, yes." I really haven't been all that assertive a person. So it was a relief.

In these cases, the report of a "mutual" decision to break up may conceal troubled circumstances that are far from mutual, and that reflect imbalanced power relations.

We need to know more about when women see their husbands as too controlling, since women raised this issue in all of the categories. Some women, like this 38-year-old black technician who did not give a reason why her marriage ended, described explicit controlling behavior.

When I was married, I stayed in. I was home with my son and he was always out. He said, "You should be home with the baby."

A 35-year-old white clerical worker who left her husband of sixteen years because of his use of drugs stated:

My ex-husband always got his way, even during our marriage. He'd ask me what I wanted to do about something. Then he'd do it his way. Then if I said anything he'd get angry. He'd say, "Well, I asked you what you wanted." I'd be totally stuck. I just couldn't win.

Other women, like this 49-year-old middle-class white woman who left her husband of ten years because he was seeing another woman, described a more indirect kind of control.

In my marriage I was afraid of saying what I really thought. He could always just leave. Even at 36, knowing everything I knew, I still walked on eggshells about that. . . . I am much better now than I was while we were married at telling him what I think. He's moody and also he can always win in an argument. When we were married I used to bite my lip and not say anything.

Several women commented that they were dissatisfied with the subordinate roles they adopted in their marriages and indicated that they would not assume these roles again.

I've learned from this experience [the divorce] not to give all of myself. Women have a tendency to love more than a man, to make him happy, to make things right for him. But then women get the blunt of the blow. Women get hurt. [36-year old black pharmacy technician, married thirteen years]

I'm not going to be somebody's servant. That's the way I was in my marriage, picking up all the time. My ex-husband was a slob. Love is not being a maid. Men don't know the meaning of love. My ex-husband treated me like his mother. [34-year-old unemployed working-class white woman, married eleven years]

My ex-husband was very impressive when we met. Anything that money could buy he got us— clothes, furniture. But he changed when we got married. Men do that. First they have to impress you. But when you marry them, they feel they own you. And when he says jump, you have to jump. [24-year-old poverty-level black woman, married five years]

These women's dissatisfaction with male control raises the question of a gender gap between men's and women's expectations of marital roles. As noted in the previous chapter, polling data show women want more equality in marriage, while men think there is enough. One group of researchers believes that the divorced population includes a higher percentage of men who have more traditional gender-role attitudes and women who have nontraditional views. They argue that particularly those women who are in the paid labor force are now in a position to leave a relationship in which they view their husbands' demands as unfair.[9]

Violence

Although the home is spoken of as site of love and caring, we know now that the prevalence of violence is alarmingly high in contemporary marriages. In a given year, anywhere from 10 to 20 percent of women are beaten by a male intimate, and a quarter to a half of all women will experience violence at the hands of a male intimate in their lifetime. Some are even beaten during pregnancy. At least four women in the United States are killed every day by male partners. The National Centers for Disease Control reports that in emergency rooms, more women are treated for injuries from battering than from (nonmarital) rapes, muggings, and traffic accidents combined. Children who witness domestic violence are believed to be at risk for emotional and developmental problems. The gravity of this issue has finally come to public attention, and national leaders in the fields of health care and criminal justice have urged groups to take action to stop domestic violence. However, despite more publicity about this problem, accounts of marriage and divorce fail to incorporate the facts of violence into their analyses. Violence continues to be viewed as a separate issue, in a different category from the study of marriage and divorce, or blended into a nondescript and misleading category called "family violence."[10]

In this sample, 70 percent of women of all classes and races experienced violence at the hands of their husbands at least once. Fifty percent of women experienced violence at least two to three times. Women were asked to check off on a list the acts of violence which they and their husbands committed during their mar-

Figure 3–3. Violence Experienced within Marriage or after Separation.*

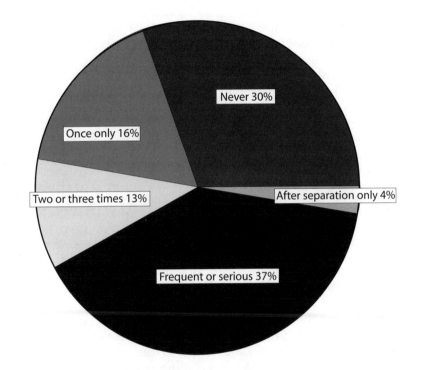

* 70% of respondents had experienced violence at least once during marriage or separation.

riage, and the frequency of their use of violence. The list included: throwing things at a spouse, pushing, slapping, kicking, hitting, beating up, threatening with a knife or gun, and using a knife or gun. As reported in Figure 3–3, of the 70 percent of women who reported violence, 16 percent reported that the violence occurred only once; 13 percent reported that it occurred two to three times during the marriage; 37 percent reported that the violence took place more than three times, or that there was one serious incident of violence; and 4 percent that there was violence during the separation only. An incident of violence was considered "serious" if a woman said she had been "beaten up" or she had sustained a physical injury.[11]

I will first discuss the experiences of the 19 percent of women in the sample who said they left their marriages because of violence; in the next section of this chapter

I will discuss the experiences of all the women in the sample who experienced violence. The accounts of these women resonate with fear and pain. One can easily imagine how the children who witnessed this violence were very fearful and deeply saddened. At the same time, a quiet courage runs through the accounts of these women as they assessed the costs and benefits of staying in their marriages.

While many women in the sample experienced violence, those who stated that they separated because of the violence had experienced much more serious physical violence than women who gave other reasons for separating. Many of these women stated that they left their husbands after a particularly serious fight. Some women, such as this 41-year-old white working-class mother of two, felt that their lives could have been in danger.

> It took a year for the separation to come through. I filed. We separated for the last time after he beat me up. It was Mother's Day. He beat me up in front of the kids and his parents. I was really scared then. I thought, "if he'll do this in front of them, what could he do next?" I had to get a protection order at the time and that cost $300.
>
> We had been going to a counselor. . . . The therapist called me one night and said to come right over. He said, "Your husband doesn't know right from wrong. He only thinks he is right. You'd better get away. He could kill you." I now believe that. At the time I thought he would still change.

This 31-year-old mother of one, a black woman living at poverty level, left an eleven-year marriage after a particularly serious incident of physical abuse. She addressed the question most frequently put to battered women, the question of why she didn't leave sooner, despite experiencing a lot of very serious violence throughout her marriage.

> We separated after a big fight where he was physically abusive. First I went to the Emergency Room. Then I went to the Police Roundhouse. The police came to the house and made him leave. . . . I got a restraining order. It lasted for a whole year.
>
> There was violence constantly for the 10 years. It would usually happen on the weekends. We would fight over small things like, if he would go out on Friday, I would say I want to go out on Saturday. But slowly over the years something was clicking inside. I said to myself, "Are you going to let someone else run your life?"

> Interviewer: So what made you realize that you wanted to get out of this relationship?

> I have thought about that a lot. Somebody told me people scheme on others but you scheme on yourself. First, I don't want to hurt or disappoint other people. So instead I get hurt. Also, there would be repercussions. Where would I go with three children? I didn't want to go back to my mother's. I get along with my mother but if I went home it would be like I had been a failure.

Another poverty-level woman also described why she didn't leave sooner.

> He degraded me constantly and he injured me. I've had a broken jaw. And see this scar on my face—it's not a dimple. We had violent fights three times a week. It started when the honeymoon was over. He said, "Now we're going to change all this shit." I had thought everything was fine.
>
> Interviewer: Did you think of leaving?
>
> That's what everyone asked, "Why don't you leave?" I said, where was I going to go? People who ask that question don't understand. [31-year-old black part-time classroom aide]

Like this woman, some other women also described injuries.

> There was no violence for the first five years, before the kids were born. Before they were born he was violent maybe only three times. But after the kids were born, it was often. He seemed to especially resent time I spent with the kids. I'd have to hurry them through their baths.
>   The night he broke my rib and my jaw I was giving the kids a bath. I guess he thought it was too long. He broke my rib because he was trying to throw me down the stairs. I was resisting and I guess he cracked my rib over the banister. . . . I would say there was a violent incident once a month. [42-year-old white secretary, mother of two, married sixteen years]

Some women left when the violence affected their children. One woman left when her husband sexually assaulted her son by a former marriage. She filed a criminal charge against her ex-husband, who is now serving time in prison for this crime. This poverty-level black woman left because of the effect of the violence on her children and on herself.

> All the violence was hard on my son. He saw me injured when he was two years old. He saw blood, he saw a lot. It's affected my son. He's mixed up.
>   I left because I was afraid of what this was doing for my son. I left because of what it was doing to me. I realized I could have shot my ex-husband. But I couldn't do that for my son's sake.
>   I finally realized the marriage wasn't working. I really wanted a marriage. I wanted that marriage to work. But I finally realized it just wasn't working. [28-year old black woman living at the poverty-level, mother of one, married six years]

As will be described below, some women also watched their husbands destroy property and found this frightening. This 33-year-old white middle-class mother of two, who owned and ran a business with her husband, described his violence:

> I was the one who left. My ex-husband had a terrible temper. He used violence a lot. He didn't hurt me physically very much but he destroyed property a lot.

He flew off the handle a lot. He was also an alcoholic. He had an explosive angry temper.

In conclusion, many of the divorced women in this sample were "battered women." We rarely think of divorce and battering together, instead viewing "battered women" and "divorced women" as two different categories. We must incorporate an understanding of violence into our portrayal of all aspects of family life, including divorce. There undoubtedly have always been women who left marriages because of domestic violence. Perhaps there are more at the present time because of increased publicity about wife battering. The problem is, because we do little to alleviate the hardships of divorce for women, we make them pay a heavy price for leaving marriages because of domestic violence.

Hard-Living

Seventeen percent of women gave "hard-living" as the reason for the ending of their marriage. As noted in the previous chapter, "hard-living" is the term Joseph Howell used some time ago to describe certain behaviors, such as heavy drinking and frequent absences from the family, which men, particularly working-class and poverty-level men, exhibit when they feel frustrated by unstable work conditions and high unemployment. Since Howell first described hard-living, alcohol abuse has continued to plague men with weak employment histories. Hard-living is usually associated with male behavior. Lillian Rubin argues that some men continue to use alcohol as a way of coping with unemployment and Katherine Newman stresses that alcohol abuse is associated with the downward mobility and job insecurity of male workers at all socio-economic levels.[12] It is important, however, to highlight the role of gender in hard-living; more often than not, it is women who are the victims of these behaviors.

Women in this sample who said they left because of hard-living behavior mentioned most often drug abuse, then alcohol abuse, followed by accounts of their husbands' absence from the home. Drug use has become a particularly serious problem during recent decades. It has devastated minority populations in urban neighborhoods, and—as is reported less frequently—it also has posed a threat to white blue-collar families. Judith Stacey relates the recent upsurge in drug use to the unstable employment conditions created by economic restructuring. Most of the women who left because of their ex-husbands' use of drugs or alcohol found their husbands' behavior very troubling and particularly disruptive of family life. The majority of women who reported leaving their marriages for reasons of hard-living are working-class and poverty-level women, although a few middle-class women reported that their ex-husbands abused alcohol, and one that her ex-husband used drugs. Said one woman living at the poverty level:[13]

He's still an alcoholic and he's still into drugs. That was the problem in our marriage. At first he'd be gone one night a month. I would stay up all night worrying and he would come in at 6:30 in the morning and take a shower and leave. I didn't realize what it was at first. Then it became more and more frequent and he was gone a whole lot. . . . It started getting to the kids. [34-year-old white bookkeeper, mother of two, married twelve years]

In some of these cases the husbands also used violence.

He kicked me out of the house, violently. It was our house. By then there was a lot of violence. Things hadn't been that way to start. Initially there was none. But around the time my son was born I noted he was acting funny. I didn't know what it was. I thought maybe he was jealous of the baby because I was paying the baby more attention. But then I came to realize it was drugs. [33-year-old white secretary, mother of one, married seven years]

Evelyn, one of the women introduced in chapter 1, said that drugs made her ex-husband behave in strange and frightening ways.

The reason for the divorce was drugs. I would have stuck with my ex-husband for anything else, including just plain robbery. But not drugs, because of what it was doing to the kids and me.

He's not a bad guy at all. But when people are on drugs they are fearless. It's scary. You could see all the neighbors stay out of his way. Nobody would cross him. I wouldn't cross him. No way. I think he liked that feeling. The neighbors called him a crazy man. When he was on drugs he would throw things around here. He wouldn't harm me physically very much but he destroyed property. He also liked guns. He would put a gun in my mouth, to my throat. When he started fights he would rip the phone off the wall.

The women were particularly concerned about the effect of drugs on their children.

I was married a long time. Things were fine for six years. We got along pretty well. Then he decided he wanted other women. He wanted a wife and a girlfriend. But I won't be number two. I told him good-bye and good luck. I also found out during the last eighteen months of our marriage that he was selling drugs. Then I knew I wanted out. That's no way to raise a child. [38-year-old black middle-class office manager, mother of one, married fifteen years]

And of course, men who use drugs or alcohol are more likely to have employment problems and thus not be able to support their families.

During the marriage we lived off my unemployment insurance. My ex-husband didn't keep jobs. He used alcohol a lot and was a drug addict. When I was eight months pregnant he still didn't have a job. I said, "That's it. We're having a baby in one month and you can't take any responsibility." [33-year-old white poverty-level homemaker with a year-old child]

Women also reported that their ex-husbands were rarely home. These women say their husbands never took any responsibility for the marriage. Some men "hung out" on the street with other men. Said two white working- class women:

We got married very early. I had gotten pregnant. Almost from the beginning of the marriage he was gone a whole lot. He would come home from work and take a shower and go out again. He was young. He just wasn't ready for the responsibility. He just wanted to be with his buddies all the time. . . . He would hang out down the street from our apartment. I never saw anyone because I had a baby so I would sometimes take the baby down there [down the street] at night. It wasn't the usual place you take a baby, but I had to get out.

For a long time I went on this way. I just accepted it. I had always wanted to be a homemaker. I like taking care of people. But after five years or so I decided I wanted more—that there was more to the world and that I was worth more. My ex-husband didn't used to think I was worth much. As I said, he never stayed around. I began to want to be with someone who would love me in the way I wanted to be loved. [27-year-old white waitress, married seven years]

I kicked him out finally. The problem was he was never here. He was always with his friends. He worked, but then he would go out. Or all his friends would be here. Sometimes I would wake up in the morning and his friends would be here. He was like a big kid. He just didn't want to be married. At first we had married friends. But then he made friends with a single guy and after that all his friends were single. [26-year-old white data processing clerk, married four years]

This poverty-level woman thought her husband was "fooling around" with other women. He was also sometimes violent towards her.

Most of the time my husband wasn't even at home. He would go out with groups of people and screw around. Sometimes he was violent when he came home. I think he was guilty. If I asked where he'd been, he'd get mad. If I didn't ask, he'd say I didn't care.

He was gone weekends at a time. I was at my mother's most of the marriage. One time I went back for six months but it didn't work. It was tense. I got an addiction. I used to drink and take Valium just to forget he was there. I wish he had just left. [26-year-old white mother of two, married six years]

Eleven percent of the women in the sample said their husbands were never around. Their comments may reflect gender differences in commitment to the family. Various studies of poverty-level and working-class marriages indicate that husbands and wives have separate leisure-time activities, and that some men in these families prefer to spend their leisure time fraternizing with male friends, not staying at home.[14]

Other Women

Nineteen percent of the women reported that their ex-husbands were involved with other women. These women described two different kinds of experiences. One group of women stated they were left by their ex-husbands for other women. These women suffered a lot of emotional pain. A 51-year-old white middle-class woman with two college-age children who had been married for twenty-seven years said:

> After he said he was leaving for another woman I was in very, very bad shape. I went into a depression. It continued into the separation. We were in counseling together and I was in alone at the same time. I personally suffered a lot and it can't be measured or weighed. It's taken a toll.

A 31-year-old black teacher with a two-year-old child explained how it was when her husband said he was leaving:

> It was a horrible experience. I was on an unpaid maternity leave. I was a new mother. I had been hoping things would work out in the marriage. We had been having problems, but I thought we could work them out. But he was running around with another woman. And he had been, even while I was pregnant. I felt a lot of hurt and a lot of frustration. . . . The separation was the worst period of my life.

One woman, a 44-year-old white teacher, said that after two children and twenty-one years of marriage, her husband left for a younger woman. She described the experience as "devastating." She developed panic attacks, insomnia, and alcoholism and has seen a therapist for several years to cope with her emotional problems. She is now on friendly terms with her ex-husband, who has broken up with the woman he fell in love with. She finds she still loves her ex-husband and recently went on a date with him. She thinks she would like to remarry her ex-husband but she believes he is in a mid-life crisis.

> I would like to be married to my ex-husband again, if he would only straighten himself out. . . . The therapist says maybe he's learned now and he wants to come back. But the other possibility is that he'll just keep going off and having affairs. He won't go to a therapist. He says it wouldn't do any good. He talks like he hasn't been a success, he hasn't done the work he wanted to do. I don't know what the problem is because he did fine in his job.

Men who leave their marriages for other women are also presumably experiencing some kind of "personal dissatisfaction" with those marriages. They are in a different situation from their former wives, however. They are freer than women to leave marriage and pursue new relationships because unlike women they rarely have to consider that they will have full-time care of their children. Three women did report having affairs after they had decided to separate. For one woman, the affair resulted in remarriage. However, while most of the women who left for reasons of personal dissatisfaction said they would like to remarry, they are not currently in a serious relationship, and unlike their husbands they did not leave their marriages for another relationship.

Women of all classes expressed the same feelings of rejection and emotional pain when they were left by husbands for other women.

> I took my husband's finding another woman as rejection. I felt I failed. The other thing was money. I got really down. I was a candidate for [a local mental institution]. [33-year-old working-class black woman, part-time retail clothing, married seven years, one child]

> There was a period of about nine months . . . I knew he was leaving . . . for the first six months I was okay but then I wasn't okay. By not okay, I mean not functioning. I was not a functioning parent, not a functioning daughter, nothing. It's an upheaval and then a tremendous adjustment. [41-year-old white working-class woman, legal secretary, married twelve years, three children]

> I'd like to stay married to him . . . I still love him. He's the man I married. He will never change. He lives with that lady and he goes to bars. He's a macho man. He still doesn't want me to talk to any man and he finds out if I go out with any man. The year he left I tried to kill myself. I was really depressed cause I never thought this would happen. [40-year-old poverty-level Hispanic woman, married nineteen years, three children]

All of these women experienced great emotional pain, and spoke of being "devastated" and very depressed.

> Emotionally it ripped me apart. I depended on him and when he left me I felt rejected and lonely. The kids played a major part in my life. I lived for them. I didn't want them to get hurt by the divorce. I wish I had gone to counseling earlier to face the reality sooner. [33-year-old white working-class woman, part-time accountant, married twelve years, three children]

A few women mentioned that their ex-husbands wanted to come back when their affairs didn't work out, but these women had lost trust in their husbands and were not willing to try and reconstruct the marriage.

Within the category of women who reported that their marriages ended because their husbands became involved with other women, some women reported that they left their husbands because their husbands were seeing or "fooling around" with other women. Particularly poverty-level and African-American women reported having left for this reason, in contrast to the majority of white women, whose husbands left them. These women whose husbands were "fooling around" were upset not only because of their husbands' involvement with other women, but also because these men were rarely at home and did not take any responsibility for the household. Thus "fooling around" is related to the hard-living category of never being around. The quotation below reflects these women's concerns about their husbands' lack of responsibility.

> My marriage began to change when I had my son. I stopped working then. Then I saw how things were. Without my income we couldn't pay for anything. I began to look at where the money my ex-husband was making was going. It was going into gambling.
>
> The bills were not getting paid. Finally the electricity was cut off. When the electricity was cut off, he moved in with his mother. That's when I knew something was really wrong. Also, he threatened me a lot. And once he cracked up my car and just left it there. These things seemed to change at my son's birth. Even at the birth, my ex-husband wasn't supportive. I was in there going through labor and he was out in the hall talking to everyone, grandstanding.
>
> Then I finally asked my ex-husband about his fooling around with other women. He was fooling around a lot. He finally admitted it and that's when I said I was going to get a divorce. This was important because I am a Jehovah's Witness, and in our religion that's the only grounds for divorce. Otherwise we believe that you should really work things out yourself. But because he admitted that I was able to get a divorce. Otherwise I would still be in the marriage. [34-year-old black childcare worker, married eight years, one child]

These women's accounts sound like Elijah Anderson's descriptions of relationships among poor, urban black youth. Anderson claims that if these young black men marry, they still do not plan to give up the freedom their peers have taught them to desire. Their goal is to conquer women, not to settle down and be breadwinners. Anderson argues that these young men want a reliable partner who will be like their mother and not question the time they spend with other "ladies" or with male friends. The women, who had hoped for a male breadwinner and a "typical" marriage, then leave when they see that their marriage will not conform to this ideal. According to Anderson, the origin of these conflicts lies in the fact that many young black men, due to high rates of discrimination and unemployment, have little hope of earning enough to support a family.[15]

On the whole, however, we don't know under what circumstances men and women choose to have affairs. Recent data show that 25 percent of men and 15 percent of women in marriages have affairs. Presumably they have affairs when they experience personal dissatisfaction with their partners and their marriages. In this sample, however, when women left for reasons of personal dissatisfaction, they did not leave for a man. Thus, according to these women, when they left they were becoming single parents, while their ex-husbands left to begin relationships with other woman.[16]

Other Reasons for Ending Marriage

I categorized 26 percent of women as having "other reasons" for ending their marriages. Six percent of these women gave no reason for ending the marriage. An additional 10 percent said they were left by their husbands but did not say why. Three percent were left by their husbands but didn't know why. Of the remaining 7 percent, 4 percent said they left their husbands because of their husband's sexual orientation. One woman left her husband because he came out as a transvestite, another because her husband had come out as a gay man. One woman left because of her husband's mental illness. Three percent of women said their husbands had left them for assorted reasons. One woman said her husband had left her because she decided to go back to school for a graduate degree.

According to their accounts of their divorces, the experiences of these women do not support the idea that women are putting their own interests ahead of other family members and leaving their families because of weak commitments to the institution of marriage. These women reported marriages embedded in different gender and class contexts. There was a lot of violence and a lot of hard-living in many of the marriages, and many women reported being left for other women. Even those women who reported leaving for reasons of personal dissatisfaction say that gender issues were part of these reasons and that they were very discontented with male controlling behaviors.

A major factor in these men's behavior, in addition to gender, was class. A higher level of hard-living and violence was evident among working-class and poverty-level men, particularly poverty-level men. Some of these men come from disadvantaged educational backgrounds and employment histories. Forty-one percent of the ex-husbands of poverty-level women did not have a high school diploma. These men, whose median income was $19,500, worked as security guards, cab drivers, truck drivers, or factory workers, or they held jobs in construction, roofing, or maintenance. Some poverty-level women reported that their ex-husbands were unemployed or in prison. Several women spoke sympathetically about the difficulties their ex-husbands had faced making a living. Here are the words of a 33-year-old white woman, now living below the poverty level, whose ex-husband used drugs:

> He had a job. Then he got into drugs. I think what made him change is that he felt he didn't make enough money. He came from a poor family. His father did the

same thing; he deserted the family. His mother had to raise five children. I know he felt he should be providing better for me. He always loved the mountains. I know he wanted a place in the mountains. But that was out of the question. And I know that he wanted to get a special wheelchair for his mother. She's an invalid. But he realized he couldn't do these things. He only had a ninth-grade education.

In addition, another factor, age, contributed to the patterns of divorce among some poverty-level women, who, as reported earlier, married earlier than other women. Age has long been a factor in the divorce rate. Women who marry young have always divorced at a higher rate than older women. A number of poverty-level women spoke of marrying young when they "didn't know what they were doing."

> I got pregnant. My father said, "You have to marry him. No daughter of mine is going to get pregnant and not be married." Of course I hadn't known anything about birth control. I had been very sheltered. . . . It turned out my husband wasn't responsible. He doesn't want a wife, he wants convenience. [30-year-old poverty-level black woman, married thirteen years, seven children]

> The marriage was a mistake. I was young, seventeen, and I had no guidance. My mother left home when I was eleven. I lived in different homes. [30-year-old poverty-level Hispanic woman, no high school education, married eleven years, four children]

> I got married [at a young age] because my mother and his mother made us. I already had my son and I was pregnant with my daughter. I told my mother I didn't want to. She now realizes it was a mistake. . . . [26-year-old white poverty-level woman, no high school education, married six years, two children]

> I made a mistake marrying him . . . I was living at home. I was planning to go on to school. I did have a child already but I told my mother, "I'm going to school but I don't want to take your money so I'm going to work for a year." But it was difficult to get along with my mom. And my husband said, "Come move in with me." But I realize now I didn't get married for the right reason. It wasn't really for love. But I believe in a strong family so I decided to try and make it work. [28-year-old black poverty-level woman, high school education, seeking employment, married seven years, three children]

These women sound like the working-class couples described by Rubin and others, who live at home until they marry and use marriage as way to leave their family of origin. They believe that marriage will provide them with the autonomy they desire. Instead, they are disappointed to find that early marriage and child-bearing quickly create new burdens.[17]

VIOLENCE IN MARRIAGE AND AT SEPARATION

As we have seen, 18 percent of women in this sample stated that they left their marriages because of violence. But, as noted, 70 percent stated that they experienced violence on at least one occasion, and there were no significant class or race differences between these women. In this section I will examine these women's experiences of violence. Women's experience of violence has implications for a variety of issues: it is an indicator of inequality and control in marriage; it affects women's negotiations during divorce; it influences how these divorced women view their marriages; and it influences how the public views divorce. Indeed, our continual separation of the issue of violence from divorce has made violence invisible as an important issue in divorce. What follows is a discussion of these women's reports of the frequency and severity of their ex-husbands' use of violence, of their own use of violence, and of when the violence occurred.

As noted earlier, women were asked to check off on a list the acts of violence which they and their husbands committed during their marriage, and the frequency of their use of violence. The list included: throwing things at a spouse, pushing, slapping, kicking, hitting, beating up, threatening with a knife or gun, and using a knife or gun. As reported in Figure 3–3, of the 70 percent of women who reported violence, 16 percent reported that the violence occurred only once; 13 percent reported that it occurred two to three times during the marriage; 37 percent reported that the violence took place more than three times, or that there was one serious incident of violence; and 4 percent that there was violence during the separation only. Some women experienced violence during the separation and the marriage. Unfortunately, women who reported violence during the marriage were not specifically asked to differentiate between violence they experienced during the marriage and during the separation. Eleven women who experienced violence during the marriage also described incidents of violence during the separation, in addition to the five women who described violence during the separation only. As will be described in chapter 5, additional women stated that their husbands threatened to use violence during the separation.

For this analysis of the role of violence in the lives of the women in this sample, I considered the experiences of the 54 percent of the women who experienced at least several incidents of violence during the marriage or the separation. While one act of violence certainly could have serious repercussions for a woman's outlook and behavior, the 16 percent of women who reported just one act of violence were not included in this analysis. Unlike the majority of the women who experienced violence, they themselves stated that the violence, usually a slap, was an isolated event that did not affect other aspects of their lives. The amount of violence experienced by women who reported several or more incidents of violence is similar to rates of violence reported elsewhere, which suggests that their reports of their ex-husbands' use of violence are reliable. Studies by Marjory Fields and by Barbara Parker and Dale Schumacher found that between 50 and 75 percent of divorcing wives reported being assaulted by their husbands at least once during their marriage. Mark Schulman found that two-thirds of divorced women in a Harris poll reported violence in their former relationships. These figures are higher than those reported earlier for married couples, which showed that 10 to 20 percent of women will be beaten by a male intimate in a given year, and a quarter to a half will be beaten by a male intimate at least once in their life.[18]

Increasing numbers of researchers have turned their attention to violence which takes place during separation. Recent nation-wide surveys in Canada indicate that women experience more violence during and after the ending of a relationship than in the relationship itself. Martha Mahoney has proposed the term "separation assault" to describe what she sees as men's use of violence to prevent their partners from leaving the relationship, and to continue to control them after they leave. Similarly, homicide data have shown women at greatest risk of being killed during the period of separation.[19]

As indicated in Figure 3–4, there are statistically signficant differences by class among the women who experienced violence at least two to three times during the marriage or separation. Sixty-five percent of the poverty-level women experienced violence during their marriages, in contrast to 52 percent of the middle-class women (40 percent during their marriage, 12 percent only during the separation), and 47 percent of the working-class women (43 percent during the marriage, 4 percent during the separation). As for race, 51 percent of the white women and 63 percent of the black women experienced violence more than once, but these are not statistically significant differences. Further, the experience of frequent or serious violence within marriage is significantly related to class. Poverty-level women reported a dramatically higher incidence of frequent or serious violence compared to other women. Black women also experienced more serious violence than white women, but these differences were not significant after controlling for class.

We do not know whether poverty-level women actually experience more violence, or whether they are more willing to report it. The literature does not help us answer this question. Some researchers claim there are no class differences in woman battering. On the other hand, in their first nation-wide survey, Murray Straus et al. found that the greater a person's education, income, and occupational level, the less likely he or she will be battered, and also that there was more husband-to-wife violence among blacks than whites, particularly among the lowest-income black husbands.[20]

If there are indeed any class and race differences in men's rates of violence toward women, they could be due, as Robert Staples suggests, to class and race differences in husbands' attempts to control wives. While some women in this sample reported that husbands used violence, others sought different means of controlling

Figure 3–4. Violence Experienced within Marriage or after Separation, by Social Class.*

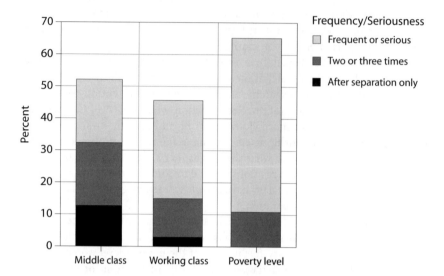

*Overall chi-square on incidence of violence is significant by class but not by race. For more details, see appendix.

___

their wives. Women of all classes reported controlling behavior by their husbands. Some of these women experienced no violence but reported being intimidated by their husbands' anger; frustrated by their husbands' attempts to control their time, their friends, or their work; or angry that their husbands, who insisted that their point of view was the correct one, would not listen to their views.[21]

While I only discuss physical abuse here, women did report other types of violence. All women were questioned about whether their ex-husbands ever forced them to have sex. Seventeen percent of the women said they had, a figure consistent with national estimates of marital rape.[22] We did not probe for further details, so I cannot describe their experiences of marital rape. Some women volunteered information about other types of violence they had experienced. While this information, which was volunteered, cannot be used to determine the frequency of these experiences, it demonstrates the broad range of violence to which women were subjected. One woman reported being beaten while pregnant, and in her words, "the baby died." Two women had charged their husbands with offenses for which these men were convicted and for which they are currently in prison: one woman's ex-husband was convicted of committing incest with their daughter, the other of committing sodomy with her son by a previous relationship. One woman reported that her ex-husband had raped her mother, as well as herself, while they were married.

There were several instances where women did not experience physical violence, but spoke of feeling abused. Four women mentioned that their husbands had committed significant damage to family property, and the same number reported serious mental abuse. Finally, as noted in the previous section, some women mentioned their husbands' controlling behavior. While controlling behavior and violent behavior may take different forms, their roots are the same. A variety of researchers agree on the primary cause of violence toward wives—husbands' attempt to control their wives.[23]

Finally, some women reported that they sought help in order to stop the violence. Unfortunately women were not asked about seeking help in a systematic way. Twenty-five percent of women who experienced violence, however, volunteered that they had either called a hotline for abused women, called the police, or secured a protection order from the police or from another criminal justice official to keep the abuser away from the home.

Causes of Violence

Women were not asked what caused the violence; a quarter of the women who experienced violence, however, raised this subject on their own. While these women's experiences cannot be generalized to all the women in the sample, they are noted here because they are consistent with women's accounts of violence in other studies.[24] Among the several reasons women gave for the violence, the most common reason was that violence occurred when they attempted to act independently:

> He was violent when I would go out and do things on my own. He didn't like that. For example, I went out and found myself a job. He didn't want that. He wanted me to always be home. My father gave me a car and I would take the kids places. He didn't like that. [28-year-old black poverty-level woman, high school education, seeking employment, married seven years, three children]

A working-class white woman reported that the violence started during the separation when she "started to change," that is, when she began to voice her own opinions.

> He wasn't violent during the marriage, but during the separation. When I started to change, that's when it started. During this time he was violent about once a month, including once in front of the kids. He usually took the phone off the wall when it happened. [27-year-old white working-class waitress, married seven years]

Another woman reported that her husband attempted to control arguments.

> He wasn't that violent a person. But if we're disagreeing he'll come and get me by
> the wrists or the shoulders. He knows karate. He broke my wrist. [36-year-old
> poverty-level black woman, married two years]

Another reported that her ex-husband was violent when things did not go his
way:

> He would look in the cabinet and the glasses wouldn't be standing straight, or
> the kids ate the last piece of cake, or I'd be five minutes late and he'd accuse me of
> being in a motel. The children wouldn't go on a merry-go-round, it makes them
> sick, and he ended up beating me up in the parking lot. He used to go for my
> throat. [44-year-old, white secretary, married eight years, three children]

These women also spoke of generally controlling behavior on the part of their
ex-husbands.

> I have friends now. Before I couldn't 'cause he would insult them and give me a
> hard time. He didn't want me to have anybody. I had to be totally dependent on
> him. [29-year-old poverty-level white woman, unemployed, married eight years,
> three children]

> I had no friends. I wasn't allowed to have friends. I stayed in. I couldn't say hi to
> anyone on the street. That's why I wasn't allowed to work. When I was thirty I
> started talking back. He said I watched too much Phil Donahue and talked to my
> friends too much. I couldn't go to the movies with my sister. [33-year-old poverty-
> level white woman, married fourteen years]

> He was very insecure. He wanted me at home.... He didn't mind if I worked
> when he was working, but if he got laid off, which he did sometimes, then he
> wouldn't let me work. One time he said that the worst thing that ever happened
> was that I went to school.... He also wanted to control everything about my life.
> He wanted to control my friends, my time. He wouldn't let my son see my
> brother, who is a successful businessman. [36-year-old black nurse, married fif-
> teen years, two children]

Several of the women mentioned that the violence occurred in connection with
their ex-husbands' use of drugs or alcohol.

> My ex-husband was an alcoholic. He was also violent a lot. The majority of the
> time he was violent because he was drinking, but not all the time. [41-year-old
> white working-class woman, cleans houses part-time, married seventeen years]

There was violence constantly, whenever he came back down from the drugs. When he was on drugs he was mostly as nice as he could be, but when he came down, I was constantly on edge. I had to watch everything I did. One time I had my son on my lap. He was one year old. My ex-husband threw something at me. It hit my son. He'll have a scar on his lip forever. [24-year-old poverty-level black woman, attending catering school, married five years]

In some cases women stated that their ex-husbands became violent after their children were born.

I just walked out finally. My ex-husband was very irresponsible. The first three years were good, but the last two were crazy. I could have gotten killed. I felt like I lived in a graveyard. There was a lot of violence. I almost had to get violent myself. I feel like around the time I got pregnant he went crazy. He got a real demon in him. [28-year-old poverty-level black woman, married six years, one child]

And in a few cases women mentioned sexual jealousy.

He'd get violent on holidays. I got dressed up and he would start up. I was in the army reserves. He didn't like that so he threw out all my uniforms. He didn't like me to be near the men. He thought I had to be with them sexually 'cause I was in their company. [26-year-old black poverty-level woman, married five years]

Several women reported that their husbands destroyed property. As noted earlier, one woman said:

My ex-husband had a terrible temper. He used violence a lot. He didn't hurt me physically very much but he destroyed property a lot. He flew off the handle a lot. [33-year-old white middle-class woman with three part-time jobs, married seven years with two children]

As described in chapter 1, Anne, an educational consultant, became fearful when her husband destroyed property:

My husband could get very angry. He would break things; he didn't lay his hands on me. But if he broke things I would think, "What next? What's the difference between a clock and me?" [47-year-old white middle-class woman, speech pathologist, married thirteen years, one child]

A few women mentioned mental abuse.

There was violence constantly for the first ten years. It would usually happen on weekends.... The mental abuse was worse. I think that was really starting to get to me. He played games on my head. He said, "You'll never get a job."

The main problem was that he didn't think I should work. Also he wanted me home all the time. A lot of times he wanted me with my hair in curlers when he came home. It's not the kind of person I am, but I did it. [31-year-old black poverty-level woman, married eleven years, three children]

Several women mentioned a kind of mental abuse associated with their ex-husbands' use of guns.

He wasn't violent with me very often, but he threatened me with guns. One time we were watching TV and I got up at the commercial to get a glass of water. Just before I got up I heard a bang and some plaster fell on me. I said, "what's that?" and he said, "I pulled the trigger by mistake." He had been playing with a gun. He did that a lot. He likes guns. He has a real thing about guns. [33-year-old white poverty-level woman, high school education, married fifteen years, three children]

Third, women mentioned that their husbands used violence when the women said they were going to leave the marriage. One woman had decided to leave her husband because he had never been home during the marriage. He spent his leisure time with his male friends. She said:

He wasn't violent during the marriage, but during the separation. When I started to change, that's when it started. During this time he was violent about once a month, including once in front of the kids. He usually took the phone off the wall when it happened. [27-year-old white waitress, married seven years, two children]

The following woman had been physically abused throughout her marriage. She tried to leave a number of times but went back because she couldn't find anyone to watch the children while she worked. During the marriage she had called the district attorney and gotten a warrant for her husband's arrest. She described the time her husband locked her in a room.

He beat me up and locked me in a room for three days. My brother had to break down the door to get me out. He did this 'cause I was threatening to leave. He always threatened that if I left he would come beat me up and beat anyone who was with me. [33-year-old white poverty-level woman, married fourteen years, two children]

One woman, whose husband was very violent throughout the marriage, spoke of sexual violence at the end of the relationship.

There was a lot of sexual violence in the last year. I was very angry. I was trying to get him to leave and he wouldn't. So I started denying myself to him and then he would force himself on me. [28-year-old black poverty-level woman, seeking employment, married seven years, three children]

As noted above, Martha Mahoney believes it is critical to recognize "separation assault," attacks which male partners make on women to prevent them from leaving the relationship, to retaliate against them for having tried to leave, or to force them to return. It is an attempt by men to continue to control the relationship. Mahoney emphasizes that separation can be a particularly difficult time for a woman. Terry Arendell found that after separation, 40 percent of the men in her sample used violence against their former wives or explicitly threatened violence.[25]

Women's Use of Violence

As in other surveys, approximately three-quarters of the women who experienced violence reported using some type of violence themselves.[26] Women were very forthcoming about their own use of violence, suggesting that their reports were reliable. As data presented below demonstrate, however, women saw themselves using violence for different reasons than their ex-husbands.

Data on the severity of the violence used by ex-husbands and wives were obtained by asking women whether they or their ex-husbands had used particular acts of violence during the marriage. Figure 3–5 indicates that, among other acts of violence, 37 percent of the women reported that their ex-husbands had beaten them up, and 11 percent that their ex-husbands used a knife or gun. The most frequent violent act, for both husbands and wives, was "pushing," with 65 percent of women reporting that their ex-husbands pushed them and 41 percent reporting that they had pushed their ex-husbands. Figure 3–5 shows that for all categories of violence, women committed fewer of these acts than men, particularly in the case of more serious acts of violence.

When women were questioned about what acts of violence they used, special care was taken to have each woman describe her use of violence and to establish whether the violence was "mutual." When women spoke about acts of violence, the interviewers would make statements such as, "You seem to be describing mutual violence, he was violent, you were violent." As indicated below, almost all women stated that they did not view the violence as mutual, but rather they used violence primarily in self-defense. Also, women were asked not only to indicate acts of violence they had committed, but also to describe when they used violence. These accounts provide a context for their use of violence that is not presented in most studies of violence, in which men and women simply check off acts of violence they have committed on a list. Almost all of the women who spoke of using violence spoke of protecting themselves, which is consistent with previous research findings.[27]

> My ex-husband did all those things on your list except use or fire a gun. I did the first two—threw something at him, and pushed him.

Figure 3–5 Types of Violence Used by Husbands and Wives during
Marriage or after Separation.*

	By ex-husband (%)	By respondent (%)
Pushing	65%	41%
Throwing	51	36
Slapping	51	31
Kicking	43	30
Hitting	45	26
Beating up	37	6
Threatening with a knife or gun	22	13
Using a knife or firing a gun	11	4
Other	27	4

* Based on the reports of the divorced female respondents.

Interviewer: So was your violence the same as his?

I used violence to protect myself when he came after me. [33-year-old white secretary, married seven years, one child]

He did all those things on your list . . . I did all those things too.

Interviewer: So why did you do those things? You were angry at him?

I'm not a violent person. It was because he was violent. I had to protect myself. [29-year-old black poverty-level woman, married eight years, four children]

Interviewer: So what about you?

I did threaten him with a razor.

Interviewer: So you used violence too.

I sometimes pushed or shoved him in retaliation. But he made the first moves. I defended myself. I sleep with a knife.

Interviewer: How often did he get rough physically?

About twice a week; when we had arguments. But I have the right to say what I want. [36-year-old poverty-level black woman, married two years, two children]

Some women, as well as using violence in self-defense, decided to fight back. In response to the interview question about when she had committed the acts of violence she had described committing, this woman said:

I never started the violence. You don't attack men. They're bigger. After a while I started fighting. I wasn't going to let him just do me in so I would fight too. I felt like, I ain't going to let him just hit me. [34-year-old black poverty-level woman, unemployed, married fifteen years, four children]

Another said:

He provoked me a lot. He did all the things on your list. I did the same things.

Interviewer: So you behaved the same way he did?

I did these things because he approached me. One time I woke up in the night and I had this terrible headache. Then I realized he had hit me on the head. Another time he was trying to push me around. I said, "I don't want to do that, I don't want to play around." He kept doing it. I went downstairs and got a kitchen knife. I came upstairs and he was lying on the bed. I just put the knife at his throat and said leave me alone. He looked really scared. Then I realized what I had done. I scared myself. I'm not really like that. So I went to stay with my mother for a few days to cool off. [38-year-old black middle-class woman, married nine years, one child]

And another said:

We were married five years. In the beginning he was violent once or twice a year. Then for a couple of months it was once a week. I got black and blue a lot. At first I never hit him. But then I figured I might as well get some shots in. . . . One night I thought I might kill him. I went after him with a pitchfork. He was scared that night. He locked himself in the bathroom or I might have killed him. Sometimes I wish I had. [26-year-old white poverty-level woman, married six years, two children]

A few other women also wanted to use extreme violence.

After about five years the violence started. It happened once every two months. I mostly got black eyes. I got a broken jaw once. That's the only time I went to the Emergency Department. Sometimes I felt like I could have killed him. [34-year-old black poverty-level woman, unemployed, married fifteen years, four children]

A variety of things keep women from initiating violence or using violence as a tactic of control. For some women it is that they were not socialized to use violence. For many, it is fear. Most of these women were afraid of their husbands, whom they believed to be much stronger than they were and very capable of seriously injuring them. Many women were afraid that if they used violence, their husbands would retaliate and harm them.

In conclusion, half of the women in this sample experienced the pain of violence in their marriages. These accounts show a lot of suffering. They also show women taking deliberate action to minimize the violence in their lives, to protect themselves and their children, and to get out of these destructive marriages. These women's accounts also provide evidence of extensive attempts at male control in marriage. Such accounts raise questions about traditional conceptions and images of marriage and divorce.

CONCLUSION

While these women's accounts do not enable us to determine the causes of contemporary divorce, they do allow us to make certain observations. First, according to their accounts, more women than men in this sample, as in other samples, are leaving their marriages. These women, however, do not fit the picture of the divorced person leaving a marriage because of personal incompatibility with her partner, or a failure to make marital commitments. They reported leaving their marriages because of discontent with male control and traditional gender roles, violence, and their husbands' use of drugs and alcohol. Many women described divorces that involve frequent and severe violence. These accounts support the notion that there is a gender gap between the attitudes of divorcing men and women, with women favoring more equality in their relationships.

Second, men, too, leave relationships, undoubtedly for a variety of reasons. But unlike women, many leave for other relationships. While the women leave and become single parents, many of the men, as reported by these women, leave to form new relationships. Some men do not technically leave their marriages, but one could argue that to be on drugs and never to be around is also to "leave" a marriage. Other men, disillusioned by their marriage or their inability to earn a living wage, become involved in activities outside the marriage and spend little time with their families. These data show that we must reshape our notion of divorce as a general failure of commitment to include the gender-specific reasons women leave their marriages.

These findings have implications for our theories of divorce. To those who feel the family is declining, with negative consequences for all family members, particularly children, we must ask, "declining for whom?" Theories and descriptions of divorce must be much more sensitive to gender. Many writers speak of the family as a unit, with husbands and wives more or less equally responsible for the fate of marriages, and ignore factors of gender, class, and race, which create serious difficulties for women in marriage. Women's perspectives must be taken seriously in these accounts. These data show that from the perspective of a number of women in this sample, there would be many costs to staying in marriage, particularly for those women in marriages with violence and other kinds of "hard-living" behavior, and those in which men exert a lot of control. Similarly, we can no longer afford to study divorce and violence separately. We must incorporate the facts of widespread violence into our descriptions and analyses of divorce.

The data presented here suggest that we should be asking more complex questions about divorce, rather than the simple question of why the family is declining. Such questions include: What are the costs of traditional marriage? Why are men abandoning marriage? Why are unequal gender roles so hard to eliminate? How can we end domestic violence in marriage? What are the costs of violence and other forms of hard-living?

Chapter 4

COPING WITH DIVORCE

By far the most difficult aspect of their divorce, said the mothers studied, was living on a reduced income and managing as a single parent. Divorce creates hardship for women with children because they can no longer maintain an adequate standard of living. Mothers of all social classes become economically vulnerable at divorce. Their income drops sharply, with the result that 39 percent of all divorced women with children live below the official poverty level.[1] Since children's standard of living is intimately tied to that of their mothers, children in divorced families also have high poverty rates.

This chapter will examine how mothers cope with a drastic drop in their standard of living after divorce and where they turn for help. A major problem for divorced mothers is that they are confined to jobs that pay low wages, wages frequently insufficient to raise a family. Further, due to family responsibilities and lack of daycare, not all women can work full-time, although divorced women have a higher rate of full-time employment than any other group of working women, 80.3 percent compared to 67.8 percent for married mothers.[2] Those who can't work or can't find work, are forced to rely on welfare. Child-support payments from fathers enable women to raise their income but, as will be described, child-support awards are generally low, and many mothers receive no child support at all from their ex-husbands.

While almost all women suffer economically at divorce, however, there are also large differences in income and standard of living among women. Middle-class women have the greatest decrease in income at divorce. In this and other samples, the higher a woman's family income before divorce, the greater the reduction in her post-divorce income. At the same time, other women may be vulnerable to reduced incomes in ways that middle-class women are spared, and some are forced to live below the poverty level. Many of these women cannot find jobs, and lack health care insurance and adequate housing.[3]

The fate of single mothers and their children is part of the larger issue of how we will allocate resources in our society. While we have helped other groups to maintain an adequate standard of living, we have taken few steps to improve the economic position of women and children. For example, between 1978 and 1987, federal expenditures for the elderly increased by 52 percent, and because of increased benefits through Medicare, housing, and social security policies, the poverty rate of the elderly dropped dramatically and is now lower than that of the population at large. This is an important achievement. During this same period, however, expenditures for children fell by 4 percent, and their poverty rate rose.[4]

THE ECONOMIC STATUS OF THESE DIVORCED MOTHERS

Figure 4–1 shows the personal and family incomes of these women which, with a few exceptions, were relatively low and insufficient for maintaining an adequate standard of living. Even the median income for remarried women was relatively low, lower than that of non-remarried professional women who received child support. At first glance this is surprising, given that remarriage is assumed to be the best way for a divorced woman to regain her standard of living. The situation of these remarried women becomes clearer, however, when their incomes are examined according to their social class. While the median income for the remarried women was $33,600, for the middle-class remarried women it was $52,500, well above the median income of a two-earner family ($42,709 in 1988, roughly the time of the interviews), and for the working-class remarried women it was $42,570, roughly at the median for a two-earner family. Thus, for these divorced women, remarriage did guarantee an adequate standard of living. Among poverty-level women however, remarriage did not guarantee an adequate standard of living. Their median income after marriage was $16,220. One of the married couples in the sample lived below the official poverty level.[5]

The data presented in Figure 4–1 enable us to compare the basic incomes for unmarried divorced women of different social class groups. First, there was an interesting split among middle-class women, with one group having substantially more income than the other. The small group of professional women, 7 percent of the sample, had the highest family incomes of women in this sample.

Figure 4–1. Median Levels of Personal and Total Family Income by Group.*

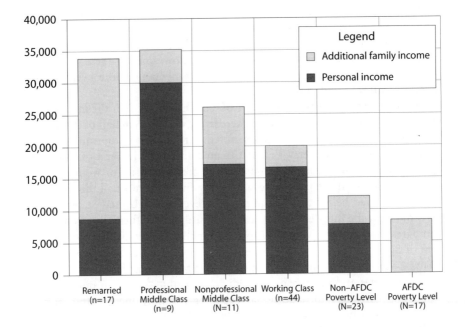

* The total height of each bar represents the median total family income for women in each group. Except for the remarried women, all of the other groups are made up of unmarried women. Personal income includes earnings from respondents' paid work, as well as disability and/or unemployment checks. Additional family income may include alimony, child-support payments, food stamps and/or AFDC/welfare payments, and income from new husbands. Group total does not add up to 129 because of incomplete income data.

They lived at 82 percent of the median income for a two-earner family in the United States in 1988. While the incomes of professional women were higher than those of any other group, however, they still were not living at the median level of income of two-earner families.

By contrast, the second group of middle-class women, nonprofessionals, had an income from their jobs that was very similar to the income of working-class women. The middle-class women, however, received more child support than the working-class women, which increased their family income to 61 percent of the income of a two-earner family. The working-class women had low family incomes. They live at less than half (47 percent) of the income of a two-earner family. This is only $5,000 above the Ruggles poverty level. As noted in chapter

2, the Ruggles poverty level, which is higher than the official government poverty level, is considered by some to more accurately reflect the condition of poverty. The final group of women, the 36 percent of women who lived below the Ruggles poverty level of $15,000, had the lowest incomes. Of these women, those on AFDC, whose primary source of income was from the state, were the poorest and had very little money aside from their AFDC payments and their allotment of food stamps. As will be reported below, some of these women did have part-time jobs, but Figure 4–1 reports only median income levels, so their income is not reflected in this table.

Overall, these figures paint a picture of hardship. Except for the middle-class women, all of the unmarried women were living on less than half of the median income of a two-earner family. As noted earlier, the European Economic Community defines poverty as half the median family income of individual countries. Thus by European standards, the great majority of women in this sample are living at the poverty level. Twenty-five percent of all the women in the sample lived below the official poverty level of the United States, and 36 percent below the Ruggles poverty level. The situation of these divorced women compares with that of divorced women nationally. As previously noted, 39 percent of divorced women with children live below the official poverty level, and 10 to 20 percent of divorced women receive welfare income.[6]

The incomes and poverty of these divorced women are even more striking when one considers the additional expenses a family incurs after divorce. Divorce creates two households. Thus the fixed costs of running a household, such as housing and transportation, must now cover two households even though there is no additional income. There are also frequently additional costs to divorce, such as relocation costs and legal fees. The burden of these additional costs falls disproportionately on women because they have the children. It is estimated to take 2.11 times as much income for one adult and two children to achieve the same standard of living as for one adult.[7] The burden of divorce also falls on children. In this sample, 32 percent of the children lived below the official poverty level, and 45 percent of the children lived below the Ruggles poverty level.

The economic situation of these women tells us a lot about the problems of divorced women with children. First, with the exception of professional women, these women's jobs failed to provide them with enough income to maintain an adequate standard of living. They found themselves in female job categories—such as secretary, sales, technical, or low-level service sector—which pay only slightly more than one-and-a-half times the official poverty level. The types of jobs held by the poverty-level women, such as nurse's aide, department store cashier, and low-skilled assembly-line worker, were even lower paying. Due to discrimination and their need for flexible hours, most women cannot break out of these job categories. These women's low wages reflect nationwide patterns. As noted in chapter 2, Roberta Spalter-Roth et al. found that in the mid-1980s, only half of working mothers earned what they call a "minimum sufficiency wage," or an hourly wage from a year-round, full-time job high enough to support a family of three at the poverty line.[8]

In addition to income from paid work, in theory women have available to them alimony, child support, and property. However, very few women in the sample received alimony—now known as maintenance or spousal support awards. Currently only about a sixth of all divorcing women receive maintenance awards, only about half the awards are paid in full, and most consist of relatively low amounts of money paid for limited duration. Courts have denied support to most divorced women because they have been concerned to enable fathers to "move on" and begin new lives and families, and consider that "rehabilitation" has been achieved if the wife can survive without applying for public benefits.[9]

Similarly, few women in this sample received property. The main type of property they received is the family home. Fifty-four percent of the middle-class women received a house as part of the divorce settlement, 28 percent of working-class women, and only 16 percent of poverty-level women. Having a home not only constitutes a very important additional resource for women, but home and neighborhood represent one kind of status that women of all classes try and hold on to. It is difficult to interpret these data, however, because many of those who received the family home also inherited large mortgages, which they were struggling to pay. Other women had to sell their homes because they were not able to keep up with the mortgage payments.

As noted in chapter 2, fewer than half of all couples nationwide receive any significant assets at divorce. One study done in Wisconsin showed that the value of couples' assets at divorce was $7,800, with mothers receiving a little over half of these assets. Also noted in chapter 2, definitions of property have expanded recently to include more than tangible assets such as a house, a car, savings accounts, and investments; they can also include pensions, interests in a spouse's business, reputation, or career. These new regulations particularly benefit those women whose ex-husbands are better-off. However, the definition of property still excludes the most valuable asset of a marriage—which, since most couples own little property, is the post-divorce income of the father. This failure to view men's income as marital property disadvantages women, whose own incomes are so much lower than those of their ex-husbands.[10]

Thus, besides their salaries from paid work, the only other means by which divorced women can raise their incomes is through child support. While women in higher classes receive more child support than other women, child support is very important to the incomes of all divorced women and in fact comprises a similar percentage of the income of women in all social class groups. For those women in this sample who received it, child support constituted 22 percent of their income, slightly higher than for women nationwide

Figure 4–2. A Profile of the Receipt of Child Support.[1]

	Overall	Middle class	Working class	Poverty level
Average amount of annual child support received per child *	$2,840	$4,400	$2,450	$1,520
Average total amount of child support received per year *	$5,070	$7,340	$4,350	$3,750
Percentage of total income made up of child-support payments	22%	24%	21%	22%
Percentage of women receiving no child support *	44%	22%	33%	69%

1. Averages were computed for all women who were currently receiving child support. Women who received no child support or who were on welfare were excluded.

* Differences by class on these variables were statistically significant. See appendix for more details.

(see Figure 4–2). At the same time it must be emphasizedthat the small size of most child-support awards is one reason that the women's total incomes are so low. Nationwide, child-support awards have been so low that they have not met even half the costs of childrearing. For many custodial parents, the cost of childcare currently exceeds their entire child-support award. The same was true for women in this sample. As indicated in Figure 4–2, the average child-support award was $2,840 per child per year. For many women in this sample, most of their child-support award is consumed by the costs of childcare. After paying for childcare, these women had little money left over from their child-support payments to pay for children's food, clothing, healthcare, educational, and recreational expenses.[11]

Unfortunately, one group does not benefit from child support payments—women on AFDC. Currently we have what Amy Hirsch refers to as a "two-track child-support system." One of the tracks is for poor women. Federal law dictates that women on AFDC can receive only $50 a month for child support; AFDC takes the rest of the father's payment as a kind of reimbursement for the welfare subsidies mothers and children have received. Thus, the group most in need of child support is denied that support by a federal program, which requires in effect that they pay back the government while they are still in poverty, thus making their attempts to escape poverty more difficult.[12]

A second major problem for women, in addition to the fact that child support awards are often too low, is that many women do not receive child support at all. In this sample, 44 percent received no child support, 16 percent received partial support, and only 40 percent received full support. These percentages are similar to those for the overall population of single-mother families. As indicated in Figure 4–3, the lower a woman's class, the less likely she is to receive child support. Second, significantly more white mothers than black mothers received full child support—60 percent compared with only 33 percent. Twenty percent of the white women and 17 percent of the black women received partial support, which means they received their child-support checks late; fathers might be anywhere from several weeks to several years behind in their payments, from several hundred to several thousand dollars "in arrears."[13] In the next chapter, I explore the reasons for nonpayment of child support, as well as women's attempts to enforce their child support orders.

The figures on the economic situation of these divorced women, in addition to showing their limited income from jobs and the relatively low levels of the child support they receive, also show how many of them can fall into poverty (see Figure 4–4). Of the 36 percent of women who fell within Ruggles poverty level, only 52 percent received government assistance, primarily AFDC and food stamps. Of the women on AFDC, 88 percent lived below the official government poverty level. Only 14 percent of these mothers reported that they were working, and they held part-time jobs as stockroom clerks, check processers, classroom aides, and nurse's assistants, bringing their incomes up to $11,000 to $13,000 a year. Because AFDC regulations discourage women's employment by deducting $1 from the AFDC award for every dollar earned, it is quite possible that other women were working but were afraid to report it. Roberta Spalter-Roth and Heidi Hartmann found that four out of ten AFDC recipients in their sample engaged in paid work for a substantial number of hours each year.[14] Despite their low incomes, few AFDC recipients receive child support and, as will be discussed in the next chapter, the child-support collection system for AFDC recipients has had a very low rate of success. AFDC recipients, however, do have one advantage over poverty-level women not on AFDC—guaranteed healthcare. As will be

Figure 4–3. Receipt of Child Support by Class.*

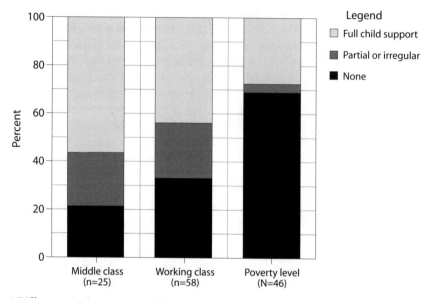

* Differences in the receipt of child support are highly significant by social class. See Appendix for more details.

reported below, many women stay on AFDC because the only jobs they are able to get provide no healthcare coverage.

As indicated in Figure 4–4, the incomes of the poverty-level women who did not receive AFDC were higher than those of the women who did. Fifty percent of the non–AFDC mothers were employed, although they did not make much money from their jobs, and 45 percent received full child support. Of the poverty-level women not on AFDC, however, a full 48 percent were not covered by health insurance. The children of these women were also at risk: 32 percent had no health insurance coverage. As just noted, AFDC provides basic health-care coverage for all women—and almost all the middle- and working-class women, and almost all of their children had healthcare coverage either through the mother's employment or through the father. Therefore, mothers not on AFDC were more vulnerable than any other women in the sample to lack of healthcare coverage. Seventy percent of the women not on AFDC, with no health insurance, were black, and 30 percent were white; and almost all the children who were not covered by insurance were black.

Figure 4–4. A Profile of Poverty Level Women.

	AFDC (n=24)	Non-AFDC (n=22)
Average age (years)*	31 years	34 years
Average number of children	2.8	2.7
Race	54% black 33% white 13% Hispanic	55% black 45% white
Average total family income[1]*	$8,180	$12,300
Percentage of group below official poverty level*	87.5%	36%
Employment status[a]	0% full time 14% part-time 86% unemployed[2]	36% full-time 14% part-time 48% unemployed
Receive no child support	83%	55%
Health insurance coverage*	100% on Medicaid or other insurance	50% uninsured

* Differences by AFDC receipt on these variables were statistically significant. See appendix for more details.

1. Total family income includes income from paid work, alimony, child-support payments, disability or unemployment checks, food stamps, and AFDC/welfare payments.

2. Includes women who report being unemployed because of AFDC requirements.

Finally, race is another important characteristic associated with poverty. Among the poverty-level women, the black women suffered higher levels of poverty than the white women. A higher percentage of black than white women were within the poverty-level group, and more black women than white women received welfare payments: 54 percent of the women on AFDC were black, 33 percent were white, and 13 percent were Hispanic. Among the poverty-level women not on AFDC, black women faced two particularly serious problems. The first was that only 42 percent of the black women not on AFDC were employed, compared with 67 percent of the white women. Further, a full 42 percent of the black women not on AFDC stated that they were seeking employment, while none of the white women who were not on AFDC were. These black women have more difficulty obtaining employment than white women despite the fact that they have the same level of education as white women.

The second major problem contributing to the higher rate of poverty among black women is that they receive less child support than white women. Seventy percent of the white poverty-level mothers not on AFDC received full child support in contrast to 17 percent of the black mothers. Child support was especially important for these women because poverty-level women who are not on AFDC, have on average 2.7 children (2.8 for whites, 2.6 for blacks). One particularly harmful consequence of these black women's poverty and lack of employment is that they and their children are more at risk than any other group for no healthcare coverage.

In conclusion, the family incomes of these divorced women were low in comparison to national norms for two-earner families. Further, they were low in comparison to the incomes of their ex-husbands, even when their husbands paid child support. The middle-class women reported a median income of $52,500 for their ex-husbands. This means that those middle-class fathers who paid child support still had a median income of more than twice the family income of the nonprofessional middle-class women and more than a quarter more than the family income of the professional women. Mothers must live at a much lower standard of living than fathers, even though they are paying almost all the expenses of the children, and even though, as noted above, it is estimated to take 2.11 times as much income for one adult and two children to achieve the same standard of living as for one adult. Similarly, while the working-class women's median income from jobs was $17,000, and their median family income was $20,800, their ex-husbands had a median income of $30,000. This means that even though working-class mothers who received child support were paying the great majority of the expenses for the children, they were living on three-quarters of what their ex-husbands made. Even poverty-level fathers had more income than poverty-level mothers.

ECONOMIC LOSSES

Middle-Class Mothers

How do middle-class mothers live on these reduced incomes? Only one woman in the entire sample reported no financial difficulties.

> I've been very comfortable. My ex-husband did very well. He owned several companies. I live off the interest from the settlement I got (one company), although lately I've been feeling I want to work. I feel as if I want to be contributing to the children, not just him.... Of course, my standard of living is much below that of my ex-husband. [49-year-old white middle-class mother of two, married ten years]

A few other middle-class women had a comfortable standard of living because of their professional jobs. A psychiatrist with a relatively good income felt she must watch her money, but she also believed that her ability to make a good income had made her life much easier than it otherwise would have been. One 37-year-old white woman who was married for six years also led a comfortable life. Her ex-husband, a physician with an income of $350,000, paid generous child support and also alimony, which she was using to put herself through graduate school in education. Although she can now afford a housekeeper, when the alimony ends in six years she will have to support herself and her daughter on own her salary as an educator with a Master's degree. In addition, while her standard of living was still comfortable, this woman had to find a new social identity.

> Then I'd say there were a lot of issues to do with my identity. What was my status? My status through my ex-husband wasn't there any more. Because of his income I was one of those small group of women who don't have to work at all. I still have a connection to those people through my daughter. But I had to decide whether I still wanted to be part of that group or not.... I had always felt a little bit different from them. But on the other hand, when we separated I wasn't sure I wanted to be separated from that group.

Most of the middle-class mothers, however, who had half the income of a two-earner family, were struggling to hold on to elements of their middle-class lifestyle. Half the median income of a two-earner family is only $6,000 above the Ruggles poverty level. Said one 41-year-old white woman, a therapist who had been separated for ten years, "The last five years have been financially difficult. My salary hasn't increased, I've had medical problems and my son is older and his needs are more expensive." A 34-year-old black woman with a Master's degree in psychology was determined, despite the adversity she faces, to finish her Ph.D. Although she received child support, she had endless financial struggles and many debts.

> My husband left the day I started graduate school. He didn't want me to go. So first of all, I had to get a part-time job in a library, which I hadn't planned to do. I had planned to go to school without working. I was totally unprepared when he left. I had tremendous financial responsibilites and few resources, and I had total care of my daughter, because when he left he chose to go to California for a while.
>
> I couldn't cut back on my expenses like tuition and the mortgage and the car. So I've had to borrow. I've worked it out, although it's been very difficult, but it's catching up to me. I've reached the end of my borrowing capacity.
>
> Sometimes it's really scary. I can balance things, like not pay the mortgage one month. But that's scary too because then I owe $800 the next month.

Trying to maintain their middle-class lifestyle, many middle-class women worried about mortgage payments, payments on their cars, and their children's educational expenses. The women were particularly reluctant to give up their homes. One 37-year-old white woman, who had three children and was married for seventeen years, still lived in her expensive suburban home, which she owned. A part-time employee of a telemarketing firm, she was living far below her former standard of living, which included a cleaning person, and she frequently could not pay her bills. She was accumulating debts, and the condition of her house was deteriorating. If her ex-husband missed any child support payments, which he sometimes did, she was in great difficulty. At times she was desperate for money. As she said: "The children were used to a good life style. I had a housekeeper. My Ex gives us no money. At one point we were without electricity for three days. He says my parents should pay." The only way she could continue to live where she did was because she received extensive financial help from her parents. According to this woman, her ex-husband lived nearby in a house worth $500,000.

A nurse with three children and an income of $30,000 also was fighting an uphill battle to keep her home. She received a total of $5,000 a year in child support (an average of $1,670 for each child) and had two liens on her house, one from the time when she went on AFDC because her ex-husband was sick and could not work, and another from the time she went on AFDC briefly after the separation. She cannot sell her house until she pays back the amount she received from AFDC. As noted earlier, in Pennsylvania any homeowner who has received AFDC has a lien put on her house. Before selling her home, the owner must pay back the amount of money she received in AFDC benefits, or this sum will be taken out of the payment she receives for her home.

For some middle-class women, divorce means losing the status of suburban housewife. This 36-year-old white woman had many friends who were also suburban housewives, and they saw each other frequently for lunch and other social activities. Now she worked as a secretary full-time for relatively low pay, and found this adjustment difficult.

> The hardest thing has been the financial situation. The divorce itself wasn't so hard on me. It's what I wanted. I have learned that I can live as an independent person. But I don't like working. I want to be at home. I have no time for friends and no time for myself. I am last on the list. I've really had to change my priorities. I know that a lot of other women have it really hard and maybe this doesn't sound like much to you.

A 33-year-old mother of two described how her dislike of her reduced standard of living and her dislike of being a single parent led her to remarry too soon.

> We owned a house. I had to get an apartment and a job and childcare. It was emotionally very hard. I know that I didn't have it as bad as a lot of people. I hated living in an apartment. I was stuck there. There was no yard. There was no babysitter in the apartment building that I would leave my kids with.
>
> What I did which wasn't so good was to get remarried too fast. I did it because of the kids. But it wasn't good for me. I didn't enjoy being single with the kids. So I didn't have a lot of choices.

These women lost the security that many middle-class families take for granted, and the sense of lifestyle choices and options. In their struggle to hold on to elements of their middle-class lifestyle, particularly housing, they have made compromises and settled for less than they expected. They sometimes expressed resentment that their husbands typically have not had to face this same struggle.

As for health care, seven middle-class women stated that they put off seeking health care unless they were very sick. The 39-year-old black mother of one who is a Ph.D. student in psychology had health care coverage which did not include medical or dental office visits. She said, "I don't go for my gynecological check-ups because I'm not sick. I don't get check-ups and I only go to the dentist when I have a cavity." According to a 41-year-old white woman with a particular health care problem, "I should see an endocrinologist four times a year but his bills are sky high, so I'm only seeing him once a year."

Middle-class mothers also reported great difficulty and stress securing and keeping adequate childcare. In addition to the cost of childcare, all of these women cited a real cost of time in arranging it.

Arranging child care has been a real adventure. Our society does not accommodate children. The work world does not accommodate children. You wait anxiously for that 3 o'clock phone call to hear that your children are home safe. I had a secretary who mothered my children over the phone when I wasn't there. I've been reduced to tears over the phone with the children. I think we are very behind the civilized world. [40-year-old white unemployed social worker, mother of three, married fourteen years]

It's been a lot of juggling [between summer camps and childcare programs]. I don't think he's been hurt by it though. I think his socialization's been good, but finding the camps, the sitters, the schools, and checking them out and integrating their requirements has been difficult. [41-year-old white family therapist, mother of two, married fifteen years]

Sometimes these mothers felt they were compromising the care of their children. At the present time, the woman just cited leaves her 12-year-old son home alone after school, which he does not like. The women also had a difficult time when their children were sick. Frequently they had to stay home from work and use their sick time or vacation time. While married women and men also have difficulties arranging childcare, for them the burdens of arranging this care can in theory be shared between a husband and wife; a divorced mother working full-time, however, has little flexibility in her schedule.

Working-class Mothers

Working-class women found living at less than half the median income of a two-earner family, only $5,000 above the Ruggles poverty level, to be difficult. These mothers spoke in terms of struggling to meet basic expenses, with little money left for such basics as clothes.

Since the divorce what's been hard is worrying about paying the bills—having enough money for food for my son. I don't even get to think about buying him new sneakers. [35-year-old white secretary, married sixteen years, one child]

The big adjustment at the separation was financial. I had to live on less. I couldn't buy the food I used to buy. I couldn't shop for clothes—I still don't. It was hard to pay the rent. [39-year-old black clerk-typist, mother of two, married twenty-one years]

I struggle every week to make ends meet. I don't have any money in my checking account left at the end of the week. [37-year-old white bookkeeper, mother of two, married twelve years]

Another woman, a 27-year-old waitress and mother of two, said:

I still never know if I'm going to make my bills. You can see I have marked on the calender when I need to get the bills in. This weekend I hope I can make the rent. If I can't then I'll get behind on that. Fortunately the landlady here is very understanding. She knows my situation. She says, just give me some so I can tell them it's coming.

This woman's comments also reflected the fact that she understood that she now shouldered full responsibility for her children's well-being. She concluded, "If something should happen to me though, I don't know what would happen with the kids."

Some of those who came from "hard-living" marriages had additional problems. One woman's ex-husband was addicted to drugs. At the separation she had no money to begin living on her own.

My ex-husband was doing a lot of drugs. Most of the time we didn't have a dime. I had to go back to work when my son was only three months old. Even the money I put away, he would blow on drugs. Finally, I got him out of the house one morning. I had the locks changed the next day and called him and said his bags were packed and on the front porch.

I didn't know how I was going to do it. I called the electric company and told them I would pay as soon as I could. The gas company was the worst. I told them, "look, you can't do anything to me. I'm paying you what I can, you can't do anything to me." [30-year-old white office worker, married two years, one child]

Some of those who experienced domestic violence had to leave their homes— sometimes abruptly—to escape the violence. One woman had to move out of her house to escape from her ex-husband even though she had a protection order against him. Her ex-husband refused to leave the house.

We moved out of the house and got an apartment. It was in a really bad neighborhood, though. . . . People would knock on the door at 4:00 in the morning. The last straw was when a man got killed in a house three doors down. . . . So then we moved back in the house. It was almost funny. My husband would come in the house and go straight to the bedroom. [36-year-old white police officer, mother of two, married 13 years]

Finally he moved out. But since their divorce agreement stipulated that they would sell the house and split the money, this woman and her 4-year-old son had to move again.

Then I bought the house we live in now. It's a real mess. Most of the houses in the neighborhood cost $50,000 but this cost $20,000 so you can imagine what it's like. When I first moved in we had to take down the walls to clean out all the dead bugs.

These mothers' reduced standard of living affected their children in a variety of ways. Some women saw their children less.

> My parents keep the children during the week and I have them on weekends.... They keep the kids in the summer and if they are sick.... I wish I could be home with them but that is the best. I don't get any support from the father, so it's hard to work two jobs and raise a family. [31-year-old black record clerk, married seven years, two children]

Other mothers stopped hiring babysitters as soon as they felt their children were old enough to be left alone. One woman with a twelve year-old son said:

> For the past four years my son has come home to the house himself. He has a key and lets himself in. I'm not happy with this, although he is only alone from 3:45–5:00. But a babysitter wanted $25 a week for one hour a day and I just couldn't afford it. [39-year-old black clerk-typist, married twenty-one years, two children]

Some had to compromise on the quality of daycare. One woman, speaking of the summer program where her child was enrolled, stated, "I know there's better but I just can't afford it. There's a lot of programs I'd like to get my son into." A 28-year-old white medical secretary with one child would have liked to have been able to afford a babysitter other than her parents. A 39-year-old office worker with three children said:

> I think having my parents do so much childcare is good and bad. I wish I could afford a babysitter, where they could do things. My parents are getting older. They are stuck in their ways. I think it's good and bad.

A few women who had enrolled their children in private schools, typically Christian academies, because they felt their neighborhood schools were not good, withdrew their children because they could not afford the tuition any longer.

A key factor in the difficulties these mothers faced in maintaining the standard of living they would like was the low wages their jobs paid. Many mothers wanted higher-paying jobs to make up for their reduced income, but encountered a variety of barriers to obtaining such jobs. Some women faced discrimination. One had had job training in traditionally male fields:

> If I could change something I would go back to school. I don't know what I would study. I don't like to type. I liked the masonry and carpentry but the unions hired the men and none of the women. [39-year-old black mother doing part-time secretarial work, married seventeen years, three children]

Others wished for higher-paying jobs, but they were not able to compete for them because of the difficulties of combining work and single parenting. Some stayed at their current jobs because they provided flexible working hours.

> I'd like another job although the waitressing job is really good. It's so close by and they understand my situation. It can accommodate my situation. [27-year-old white waitress, mother of two]

> My unit in the hospital is a good one. The supervisor is sympathetic to single parents and people allow you to be a bit flexible about your hours. That's one reason I've stayed on the job as long as I have even though the pay is not good. [39-year-old black clerk-typist, married twenty-one years, two children]

One woman, whose parents were supporting her temporarily, was concerned about finding a job with summers off so she would not have to pay for child-care.

> I'm looking for work in a school system so that I'll have the summers off. I don't want to have to pay all that money for childcare in the summer. That's why it's taking me a long time to find work. I want to find the right job so I don't have to keep changing jobs. [34-year-old white woman, seeking employment, married eleven years, two children]

A few women could not work because of emotional problems that were the legacy of "hard-living" divorces. One had been married to a violent drug user.

> I was trying to get the money together to buy him out so I could get the house. I was in a panic. I had to get money together because he threatened me.... I had a gun pointed at my head. He threatened to burn the house down; he said, "you'll get no peace...." I had a restraining order. He busted in my door at 3:00 am...I was too sick with my nerves to work. [35-year-old white customer service worker, married sixteen years, three children]

Fortunately her ex-husband stopped threatening her and this woman now had a full-time job.

Poverty-level Mothers

Poverty-level mothers struggle to pay for basic necessities. One white woman who had been married for twelve years was now a full-time bookeeper who earned $13,000, had two children, ages six and eight, and lived with her mother.

"I struggle every week to make ends meet," she said. "I don't have any money in my checking account left at the end of the week." Another woman said:

> My ex-husband never paid a thing. I raised my kids single-handedly. It was tough. Some days I didn't know what I was going to feed them. I only had a dollar sometimes. I'd think, "What can I get for a dollar?" [43-year-old black woman seeking employment, high school degree, married twenty-two years, three children]

One 29-year-old white woman with three children (ages 4, 6, and 7) remained unemployed in order to care for one child who was handicapped. She lived on child support and food stamps:

> I had to give up my comfortable living. I don't have the money to get the kids sneakers or anything. I have to deal with utilities trying to shut things off.

Women also spoke of great difficulties paying for basic house repairs, replacing broken hot water heaters, and, for those who owned homes, paying the mortgage. One woman had to take her family to the Salvation Army one night because the heat was turned off. Another said she was pleased that she had never had any utilities cut off. She attributed this to help from her parents and an energy assistance program. She felt "lucky" compared to "a woman a block away who lived in a dilapidated house all winter with no hot water."

Many women had difficulty securing adequate housing and a few had to use public housing. Sara McLanahan reports that divorced mothers move far more than those who are married. Two-fifths move in the first year after divorce, and thereafter about 20 percent move per year, a third more than married women. Many of these moves are not by choice.[15] In this sample, one 33-year-old white woman with two children was still moving to different houses. She now lived with her boyfriend's parents. "I have no stable life, nowhere to live. I have to depend on people. If I had not had to move, I would be OK." This woman left her ex-husband because of domestic violence. According to her, her ex-husband refused to move out of their three-bedroom house, where he lived by himself. At the separation, this woman and her 8- and 12-year-old children moved into her mother's house. However, her sister and brother-in-law were also living there with their two children. Things became tense, so she moved.

Another woman who had three children was now living with her sister. She had gone on AFDC at the time of the separation in order to pay the rent.

> We moved into public housing, into the projects up on the avenue. We lived there for five years. It was very hard. My place was robbed a couple of times. There were bugs everywhere. You couldn't get rid of them. The bugs ran over our food. My children were beaten up a lot. [31-year-old white poverty-level woman, no high school diploma, married nine years, three children]

One black woman, who had two children and recently remarried, was currently unemployed and was enrolled in a training program in a business institute. Like the other four women poverty-level who remarried she was still struggling financially.

> It took me a long time to find it but we ended up in public housing. It's pretty terrible. And now that I've remarried they just raised the rent—from $86 to $267. There's no security. I hear shots every night. There are about eight drug dealers in the lobby all the time. We can't even get the police to come here. I go down to meet my daughters when they come home from school.
>
> I read those stories about children getting killed on elevators and I really worry about my daughters. Also, the other day I went to the parking lot to get my car and I passed a dead body, a man with half his face blown off. Thank God my daughters didn't see that.

One mother, a 39-year-old black woman, spoke of her exhaustion from working two jobs for many years while she raised four children. She also spoke of her fear at having to leave the children home alone while she worked. She lived in a high-crime neighborhood.

> One very very hard thing is that I had to work two jobs. I would work one job and come home and spend time with the children and then go back to work. I worried very very much about leaving the children here while I was at work. You never know what will happen. Oh my God it's so hard. The girls especially. But none of my girls got pregnant.

For this woman, the church was crucial keeping her children out of trouble.

> One thing I did with the children was send them to church all the time. Even when they didn't want to go to choir or church camp I said, "You're going," and pushed them out the door. I pushed them out the door and onto the bus. I knew that would keep them out of trouble.

These mothers were particularly vulnerable when they lost any part of their support system, financial or social. One woman's ex-husband stopped paying child support. She worked at a full-time job at a department store and had to take a second job as a part-time cashier at a convenience store, to make up for the money she was not receiving in child support. She was thinking about rearranging childcare for her children, ages eleven and thirteen, to accommodate two jobs.

> While I do my full-time job, the children will come home from school and be by themselves. Even though it's not that long, I still don't like it. I'm starting to train

the children now how to do it. I do hate to leave the children in the day, but I have to. For my night job, I'll get a babysitter.

These women had the same work-related problems as women in the working class. One woman, who had just begun a business training program, spoke about her lack of confidence.

I went for a job interview recently. I did great until I came to the part where you have to type something on the computer. I did bad. They must have thought I was lying. I froze up. Also, they didn't have machines like that at [business school], not at all. One thing that happened during my marriage was that my confidence in my ability to work got a bit destroyed. He tore me down all the time. Fortunately my new husband has given some of that back to me.

And several women encountered discrimination.

I looked for a job during the separation and had a terrible time. For a while I earned $90 a month working in the kitchen at the kids' school. I was turned down for a job so many times because I was a single parent with two children. They kept saying, "Who's going to take care of your children?" I would say, "I'm reliable," because I needed the money, but I couldn't get a job. [34-year-old bookkeeper, married twelve years, two children]

In a few cases these women's husbands would not let them work during the marriage, so they had not developed many job skills.

I wanted to work but my ex-husband wouldn't let me. He said I might meet a man. He was very jealous. But then I did work for a while in a firm that a relative owned. He said that was OK because he knew the men there. [33-year-old white woman, home taking care of a one-year-old baby]

COPING WITH FINANCIAL HARDSHIP

Given their precarious financial situations, these women used various strategies for getting by on their reduced incomes. The most prevalent strategy was getting help from their parents. Many researchers have documented the use divorced women make of kin networks for important material assistance. Naomi Gerstl notes that divorced women, more than divorced men, make use of these networks to help them care for the children. In one study 17 percent of divorced women with young children were living with their parents. Some divorced women rely on grandparents for help.[16]

Help from Families

Many women in this sample received substantial financial help from their families, even after being separated from their ex-husbands for five years. There was a significant difference between women of different classes in terms of the assistance they received from their families. Forty-eight percent of the poverty-level women, 30 percent of the working-class women, and 20 percent of the middle-class women currently relied on their parents for substantial amounts of assistance and said they could not make it without their parents. Within the middle-class, however, there were real differences between how many professional women sought help from their parents in contrast with nonprofessional women. While very few professional women reported receiving help from parents, about a third of the nonprofessional women did. Thus nonprofessional middle-class women sought help from kin at the same rate as working-class women. Except for the white middle-class women, as many white women received help from their parents as black women. Many relied on their parents for babysitting. These women spoke of both the positive and negative benefits of this assistance.

> Because of my mother, childcare is not a problem. I'm lucky. I can just drop him off there and it's the same as if I were taking care of him. My father's there too when he comes home from work. My son has asthma attacks sometimes and they can get him at school. I put him in a school near there. I know I'm lucky; I'm the exception to the rule. [38-year-old black office manager, married fifteen years, one child]

Other women disliked being dependent on their parents again.

> I got a lot of help from my parents—financial and babysitting. But my relationship with them is harder. They're more protective of me. It's like being back at home. [28-year-old white employee in a telephone company, married six years, one child]

Working-class women received extensive help from their families. Seven women (six white, one black) currently lived with their parents, and four women, currently living on their own, lived with their parents at some time after the separation. An additional 19 percent of the working-class women had relied heavily on their parents in the past. This help was especially important for women who did not receive child support; a higher percentage of these women relied on parents than those who did receive child support. The following comments reveal the kinds of help these women received from their parents.

My dad started paying the mortgage after the separation. I paid my expenses. Without that I could never have kept the house; I would have had to sell it. [34-year-old white woman seeking employment, two children, married eleven years]

The children and I moved in with my mother. . . . I worked nights and she worked days so we were able to care for the children. We lived that way for two years, till I found the daycare and that freed me to find a good paying job. . . . We couldn't have done what we did without my mother. I had to regroup myself. [37-year-old white woman, clerical worker, two children]

At the separation I had to leave. There was no place to go except my mother's. Fortunately I could go there. It was very hard. I was emotionally and physically drained. I've always worked and I worked throughout the marriage. But I was only making $15,000 a year. And I was paying out $70 a week in childcare. It was very hard financially. I lived with my parents for two years. [31-year-old white secretary, married seven years, two children]

Many women still got babysitting and daycare help from their families. One woman got extensive assistance from her ex-husband's mother. She credited this help with enabling her to have the job she wanted.

If I didn't have my mother-in-law to babysit and an inexpensive place to live I wouldn't make it. I don't pay my mother-in-law but I make it up to her at Christmas. I give her a VCR, a TV. I give the biggest gifts to her. I feel bad cause there's other people to give to, but. . . . My son sleeps over there about three nights a week. It's better than any babysitter I could get. He's a bit spoiled but. . . . I wish I didn't have to work nights but since I do this is the best. If I didn't have my mother-in-law, I couldn't have picked the job I wanted. [29-year-old white woman who works in sales, married eight years, one child]

Since some writers have argued that working-class families are more oriented toward kin, this reliance on families is not so surprising. However, writers have typically emphasized how black families help each other in times of need.[17] In this sample, except in the middle class, white women were just as likely as black women to rely heavily on their families. While many aspects of these helping networks are positive, some women felt there were disadvantages to relying so much on their parents. As this woman explained, "going home" can feel like being a child again.

At the time of the separation I moved in with my parents. I don't know what I would do without my parents. Everything is so expensive that to make it on my own I would have to work all the time and then I wouldn't have any time with my son. Also, you have to have some time for yourself. I found that out.

> My mother has done everything. She raised my son during his young days. I
> feel as if she got to see my son during the best years. I feel like a sister to my son.
> My relationship with my mother isn't always easy. We disagree on a lot. My
> mother likes things her way and tries to make me do them her way sometimes.
>
> At the separation I went right back to work and my mother watched my son. I
> would like not to live with my mother. But it makes sense to live with her.... he'd
> be with her a lot of the time anyway—why bring him home for just three hours?
> [31-year-old white working-class woman, married nine years, one child]

Other studies report that women can experience conflicts as a result of relying on parents for help, and that relying on parents can make it more difficult
for divorced women to find a new, independent role for themselves after
divorce.[18]

Among poverty-level mothers, women not on AFDC got more help from their
parents than women on AFDC. Fifty-nine percent of women not on AFDC were
receiving significant help from their parents, and five women, all white, currently lived with their parents. Only 25 percent of women on AFDC received
such assistance. What was striking here was, again, the great majority of white
women, as well as black, who made extensive use of family networks. These
women's lives would be extremely difficult without assistance from their families. Help from parents also undoubtedly enables some women to stay off AFDC,
if this is their goal. Conversely, some women may go on AFDC because they do
not have kin who can help them, or because they do not want to become dependent on their families of origin.

Second Jobs

Women of all classes also take second jobs to meet their expenses. They feel
they need the income, but they find that second jobs have real costs in terms of
quality of life. Three middle-class women in the sample had second jobs. Said
a white 44-year-old mother of two and an elementary school teacher with a
Master's degree, "I worry about money and I don't know what will happen in
the future. So in addition to my job as a second grade teacher, I tutor eight to
nine hours per week." Another, a 38-year-old black middle-class office manager from nine-to-five, noted how taking a second job meant less time with
her child:

> I work a second job, so I can keep us in the lifestyle we're accustomed to. I work
> at [a clothing store] from 6:00–9:30 p.m., and Saturdays from 1:15–9:30 p.m.
> Because of my mother, childcare is not a problem.... But I wish I had more time
> with my son.

Even more working-class mothers took second jobs. Sometimes they had to quit their second job because their lives became too stressful.

> I get regular child support, but I couldn't make it. What I didn't figure into my living expenses was repairs on the house. I didn't make the "miscellaneous" category big enough. I had car repairs, roof repairs, and the upkeep of the house. I also wish I had gotten a cost of living increase in the child support.
>
> So I was faced with a choice: go back to work or take him back to court. I knew that taking him back to court would require first laying down $200 for a retainer fee. When you can't even put food on the table you can't do that. So I went back to work. I worked three nights a week and Saturday and Sunday—seventy-five hours a week.
>
> But my kids started getting in trouble. Not terrible things but I would get calls from people about how they were here and there. I was also exhausted. I went to my ex-husband and said, "Give me some money or take the kids more." He said he would take the kids more. It worked for a few weeks. But he does shift work so it just didn't work out. [39-year-old white working-class woman, company dispatcher, married seventeen years, two children]

The following woman worked overtime. Her ex-husband had disappeared and she received no child support.

> My life is extremely stressful. I work overtime a half-hour a day and four hours on Saturday. I feel like all the money goes to daycare. I never get a break, I have no time to myself. At first I just gave all my extra time to my son but I knew I needed some time for myself on Friday nights. Now I just go out no matter what, no matter what. I have to. But it's been difficult from day one. [39-year-old white working-class government worker, married seven years, one child]

Social Welfare Programs

Several mothers relied on social welfare programs, which they found very helpful. A few mentioned subsidized housing and housing subsidies as essential to their ability to reestablish themselves, such as this 28-year-old woman on AFDC.

> [After the separation] I lived with my mother for two months. Then fortunately Section 8 came through, low-income subsidized housing. I have a voucher and it means I only have to pay 30 percent of my rent. The best thing that happened to me is that the apartment came through. It meant that I could start again.

The program women identified as most critical for them was AFDC. Eight working-class women and three middle-class women used AFDC for some months after they were separated, in order to look for jobs or get training. Then they were able to find work. One woman discussed relying on AFDC, although she did not want to, and working two jobs after getting off AFDC in order to make ends meet. Her words show once again how hard it can be for divorced mothers to maintain an adequate standard of living.

> After I left it was very hard. It's very very hard to make it by yourself with a baby. I had to leave a house for a one-bedroom apartment. I went to an apartment which my aunt owned. She helped me out by giving me a cheap rate.
>
> But then I had to go on welfare. I hated it. I felt like charity. But I couldn't get any childcare to get to work. I was on it for about six years. Then when my son went into first grade I went back to school. I got certified in hairdressing and in bartending. Then I started working. I worked two jobs; I had to, for the money. I worked 10:00 to 4:00 as a bartender Monday to Friday, and then on weekends as a hairdresser. I just lived day-to-day. I worked to survive. [39-year-old white working-class woman, former hairdresser, remarried, home taking care of one-year-old child]

The poorest women are the mothers on AFDC. As stated earlier, they are younger than any other group, and have less education, fewer job skills, and more children. While women were not systematically asked why they went on AFDC, many women gave reasons for going on welfare. Several mentioned their inability to find daycare. One 25-year-old white mother of two living at the poverty level, who cleaned houses part-time, said, "Right after I got separated, I had a hard time getting babysitters. My sister-in-law babysat, but then she didn't want to do it anymore so I lost my job. Then we had to apply for welfare." Several women left their jobs and went on AFDC because they feared for the well-being of their children. One couldn't leave her children alone because when they returned from school they fought with each other and got into trouble. Another woman had been forced to move to a more dangerous neighborhood after her divorce. Her children began getting in trouble with the law after school, so she quit her job and went on AFDC.

Several women mentioned that they needed the healthcare benefits that AFDC provided. As Evelyn, one of the women introduced in chapter 1, said, "I'd much prefer to work, although I won't work a factory job. But the real reason I just can't go off welfare is because of the health benefits. We've done very well health-wise because of welfare." Some women were afraid they would not be able to find jobs that will pay them adequately if they got off AFDC. The following woman, whose two children were 8 and 9, did not have a high-school diploma and had not been able to find work with adequate pay.

> I'd like to get off welfare. I hate being on it. But at my last job, at the cookie store, I worked my way up to manager. They said I had to be there at 5:30 a.m. and stay

until 7:00 p.m. But all they would pay me is $200 a week. I wasn't going to work any more for that lousy pay. Now I hope to work for the guy whose factory is next door. [26-year-old white woman, married 6 years, 2 children]

Several mothers went on AFDC after they were unable to secure child support from their ex-husbands. A few women mentioned that they went on AFDC because of emotional disturbances related to their divorces, which prevented them from working. A white woman who used drugs with her husband during her marriage, and whose husband was violent toward her, lost her job because her boss said her personal manner frightened customers. She went to see a counselor. According to her, "My boss has said that he'll try to give me a job when I get all this straightened out through counseling."

Some women went on AFDC because they had little job training or experience due to having married and having children at a young age.

I was going to nursing school. But I got pregnant. I gave it up because I had to take care of the children. [31-year-old black woman, part-time classroom aide, married eight years, three children]

I should have waited to marry. We married after knowing each other for only 3 months. I wanted a perfect story-book marriage. I wanted my son to have a father.... I was close to being hired by ... [a major airline]. I could have made it. It's harder now with my son. [28-year-old white woman on AFDC with a high school education, married six years, one child]

Several women had no job skills because they were not allowed to work during their marriage.

I was not allowed to go out. I wasn't really allowed to talk on the phone.... I wasn't allowed to have a job. I wasn't allowed to have friends. [34-year-old black woman, no high school diploma, married fifteen years, four children]

This woman had been on drugs along with her ex-husband.

I was on welfare in ... [nearby city]. My ex-husband was a pusher. We had to come to Philadelphia because we were on the run. He had to get out of there so we came to Philadelphia. He put us up in a hotel. Then we went to live with my aunt. Then two months later he left us.

All of a sudden I had to take care of the kids on my own. I got on assistance. I had to pay the bills. I stayed with my aunt until she died. Then I enrolled in a program and got my GED. I sent my kids to my mom's for a year so I could go to school and get myself on my feet. [24-year-old black woman going to catering school, married five years, two children]

A 30-year-old Hispanic mother of four, married eleven years, received training from AFDC. She had no family to rely on, she was lacking basic education credentials and job qualifications, and she received no child support. A domestic-violence shelter and a sympathetic landlord also helped her. Her story shows how important AFDC can be as a safety net.

The marriage was a mistake. I was young, 17, and I had no guidance. My mother left home when I was 11. From the beginning he was seeing other women. I didn't know it but from the beginning he was also using drugs. Things were OK in the marriage until he started getting into drugs heavily. That's when the violence started. He was violent every week. Every time I said something he didn't like, I got hit.

I went on welfare fairly soon after our marriage. I saw that he wasn't going to keep a job. He never did. He always had excuses. But we had no money. When he got into drugs he stole money from me.

It was bad for the kids. The oldest one, he was six then, he felt he had to protect me. I had nowhere to go and no family. I did have two sisters, but they were afraid to take me in because they were afraid of him. They were afraid of the violence.

He left all the time but he would come back. One day he came back in the middle of the night and beat my legs with a lead pipe. It was terrible. The next day I went to a church because we didn't have any food. I went to get canned goods. The man there looked at me and said, "You're having a bad time, aren't you?" I guess he could see my red eyes and see that I had been crying. I said, "Yes I am." He gave me the number of the shelter. He gave me carfare to get there. He even called the shelter and told them I was coming. When I got there they were all ready for me.

It was very important for me to be in the shelter. That's where things turned around for me. They had daycare and school for the kids. I started going out and looking for places to live. That's when I found this place. But I lied to get it. Lord forgive me it's the only time I ever lied. I said I only had two kids. I got the apartment though. It was a one-bedroom apartment. We've been very happy here. It's safe.

Some of the neighbors, for spite or whatever, told the landlord I had four kids. He came and talked to me and said he'd heard I had four kids. I said I did and that I'd lied because I had to have a place to live. He said I could stay because I'd been responsible and everything. He said he would give me this apartment. He was fixing this part up then. I was the first to get it. It has three bedrooms.

Then slowly things started to get better. We got more peaceful. We got some peace of mind in the family. I also went back to school. There's my diploma. I'm working on my GED and I got my certificate for Nurse's Aide. I got it in June [she points to a big picture of the graduation ceremony on the wall]. I am very happy about that. I didn't get a job right away partly because my son broke his leg and it's taken a while to deal with that.

This woman's experience of domestic violence made it particularly urgent that she be able to live on her own, away from her ex-husband. In fact, many women in this sample who were on welfare experienced domestic violence in their marriages, and more of them stated that they left their marriages because of violence than any other group. Thirty-three percent of women on AFDC said they left their marriages because of violence, in contrast to 23% of poverty-level women who were not on AFDC, 16% of working-class women, and 4% of middle-class women. Similarly more AFDC women, 58%, reported experiencing serious violence at the hands of their husbands than women in any other group.

Some women's rights advocates who oppose the recent conservative "welfare reform" effort to eliminate as many women as possible from welfare programs, point out that such cuts leave women who are trying to escape the abuse of their partners in an extremely precarious position. Poor and minority women who have experienced violence are at particular risk for further hardship and abuse, as resources for them to begin independent lives are more scarce than for other women. Kimberle Crenshaw has urged that we give much more attention to the risks faced by poor and minority women who have been abused. These women need both material assistance and help dealing with the abuse.[19]

Being on AFDC, however, can be a liability for women, as well as an advantage. While some get training and schooling, others do not find ways to become more qualified for jobs during the time they are on AFDC. As noted earlier, for those women who own a home, AFDC prevents them from building equity in that home. The longer they are on AFDC, the more liens they have on the house. Further, as noted earlier, a woman can obtain only $50 per month of the child-support money her ex-husband owes. AFDC takes the rest of the award to reimburse the state for the woman's AFDC payments.

Certain facts about these women suggest that some will go on to find jobs and get off AFDC more easily than others. The fact that they are the youngest women in the sample, and have more younger children suggests that as they get older they may be able to work in the paid labor force, as long as they can find jobs. A quarter of the women on AFDC in this sample were currently in some type of training—catering school, word-processing school, computer school, community college—and these women hoped to be working soon.

Other data suggest, however, that certain AFDC mothers have a greater number of disadvantages and therefore may have difficulty finding jobs and escaping poverty. These women were poorer during their marriages and so had fewer resources with which to begin their post-separation lives. Forty-six percent of the women on AFDC had been living on AFDC or at a poverty-level income during their marriages, in contrast to 18 percent of the poverty-level women not on AFDC. The median income of the ex-husbands of poverty-level women not on AFDC was $24,000, while for AFDC women it was $14,100, with some of the AFDC women reporting that their ex-husbands were unemployed. This suggests that many fewer AFDC women than other women will receive assets from their ex-husbands which they could use to work their way out of poverty.

COPING WITH SOCIAL AND EMOTIONAL DIFFICULTIES

Managing under such difficult economic circumstances has made the lives of these divorced women very stressful. All mothers reported stress in dealing with their financial situation and in being single parents, both at the time of the separation and in the present. This woman, like several others, used the word "overwhelmed."

It's overwhelming at the separation. There are so many things that happen at once. I felt I was drowning emotionally. I wasn't sleeping. I was terrified of my financial situation. I didn't make all the right financial decisions either. [47-year-old white middle-class speech pathologist, married thirteen years, one child]

It was devastating to me when he left. I did immediately start getting alimony and child support but I was still extremely worried about money and I didn't know what would happen in the future. [44-year-old white middle-class teacher, married twenty-one years, two children]

I couldn't even pay the money to get the divorce. It was just tearing me up. I had to take out loans to pay off charges. I had a very bad case of nerves over all of this. [39-year-old white working-class woman, government employee, married seven years, one child]

Several women, like Evelyn, introduced in chapter 1, mentioned that their children helped them keep going under such difficult circumstances. The following woman, a 37-year-old white working-class department store clerk who had been married for thirteen years said:

The hardest thing has been coping with a reduced standard of living. I have managed. I did it myself. I knew when he left and I was sobbing right there by the door that I was all alone, that I had to do it all myself. If it hadn't been for my son I would be a dead duck.

As well as dealing with finances, many mothers also experience emotional difficulties as a result of the hardships of being a single parent, of recovering from the exposure to drug addiction and domestic violence, and, for those who were left, of feeling rejected by their ex-husbands. A 51-year-old college-educated mother of two who had been married for twenty-seven years, spoke of the difficulties of making decisions by herself.

The hardest thing is knowing the decisions have to be made on your own, also loneliness and trying to develop a new way of life. I had a lot of fears and a lot of anxieties. . . . Being alone was fearful. When you're married a lot of years, thinking of being single is a fearful thing. . . . You are more nervous. I smoke more.

A 33-year-old mother of two pre-school children, married for seven years, mentioned having to deal with the children's emotions:

We owned a house. I had to get an apartment and a job and childcare. It was emotionally very hard. . . . The hardest thing was dealing with the kids' emotions. Sometimes it was a screaming festival. . . . My older son is still full of anger.

Some women experienced physical symptoms of stress, such as this white working-class clerical worker with two children:

The divorce was very hard on my self-image—everything that I went through was. . . . I have headaches and stomach aches. I also have gallbladder problems.

Poverty-level mothers particularly spoke of how their distress took its toll on their health.

I have high blood pressure. It runs in my family, but it was also due to stress. [31-year-old white woman on AFDC, no high school diploma, married nine years, three children]

My health is fair. It's OK, but the stress really gets to me. I feel tired a lot, more tired than I used to. I feel more stressed out. . . . I get headaches and I've got stomach problems. And I've been having trouble with my gallbladder. [30-year-old black woman on AFDC married thirteen years, seven children]

I haven't had counseling but I feel as if I could really use it. I have nerve problems. [37-year-old black woman with two jobs, two children]

Several women mentioned tension headaches, and one woman attributed her high blood pressure and ulcers to stress.

Poverty-level women, more than others, mentioned that they drank and used drugs to ease their anxiety and cope with depression over having to support and care for their families by themselves.

I drink a lot to cope. Both of my good friends are in bad situations themselves and they have drinking problems too. Theirs is worse than mine. In this neighborhood lots of people have drinking problems. [33-year-old white woman on AFDC, no high school diploma, married fourteen years, two children]

I did really go down after the separation, even though I wanted to be away from all the negative stuff he put on me. I never took it out on the kids. I did turn to reefer though, and to cocaine. I never spent money on the stuff though. The first time I saw that I was going to spend money, something said, stop. So I got turned around. I got off it. But I was depressed. I had a huge number of back bills—gas, electric, telephone, water. [31-year-old black woman on AFDC, no high school diploma, married eleven years, three children]

One woman never mentioned a drinking problem, but the interviewer had to bang loudly and repeatedly on her door to wake her up for an interview at ten o'clock in the morning. She had been sleeping on the living room sofa, at one end of which lay an empty liquor bottle. She lived with a friend and was planning on applying to AFDC to get job training. This woman's husband had not allowed her to work during the marriage. She left the marriage because of violence. Her ex-husband is now in prison for sexually assaulting their oldest daughter. Another woman lived in a neighborhood in which many people used drugs and she had to decide whether to use them herself when she felt depressed. A black 28-year-old woman on AFDC with one child, who reported that her ex-husband had beaten her often, stated:

I was thinking of going on drugs, I was so depressed. But just as I was coming out of my depression a friend asked me to come to a Narcotics Anonymous meeting. I was down because I didn't have money. I had to move because they were turning my place into a condominium. Things were bad with my boyfriend. My girlfriend had been on cocaine. But she got off the pipe. She told me to come to the meeting. I was just starting to snort.

Strategies for Dealing with Stress and Emotional Pain

Some women used therapy to deal with their stress and anxiety, and all of them felt that the therapy was extremely helpful. Fifty-seven percent of the middle-class women went to see therapists, in contrast to 25 percent of the working-class mothers and 20 percent of the poverty-level mothers. Twice as many white women as black women in each class group saw therapists. It is not clear why so many more white women than black women used therapy. It may have been because black women did not have enough money to pay for therapists. However, women on AFDC get therapy at a reduced rate, and still only 15 percent of the black mothers on AFDC used therapy, compared with 50 percent of the white mothers on AFDC. This could be because these black women did not believe that counseling was valuable or because they would prefer to see black counselors, but could not find them.

All women who saw therapists stressed how therapy helped them gain confidence to manage their lives by themselves, to be single parents, and to create a new identity.

> I did get counseling for the divorce. It was very helpful. It helped me to accept myself. It helped me to stop blaming myself. It also made me realize I was more independent than I thought. It also helped me to handle the fact that I was a single parent. At first I thought I just wouldn't be able to handle all this. [28-year-old white middle-class woman, married six years, one child]

> I could not have survived without my therapist. She got me through it all. . . . I found I was a very strong person. In the beginning, doing small things was a big thing. I had never handled finances, lots of little things. [white secretary, married twenty-eight years, three children]

> Counseling was the thing that helped me the most. I released a lot of anger and frustration and it gave me a clear picture of what I wanted to do. [24-year-old white poverty-level woman, factory worker, high-school education, three children]

Some women went to great lengths to save money to see their therapist, such as this middle-class woman, who had a lot of debts.

> I go to a therapist and it's been very helpful. I've been very scared of all the responsibilities I've had. I've had to deal with a lot of depression and a lot of fear. I owe the therapist $900 but fortunately he wants me to keep coming. He knows I'll pay.

One woman, whose ex-husband had been violent and was addicted to drugs, said, "I did go for counseling. It was helpful because they listened. I really needed to talk." [33-year-old white working-class secretary, married seven years, one child] Another woman said:

> I go to counseling now, along with Narcotics Anonymous. Both are very helpful. My counselor is seeing me every day this week because last week my boyfriend left. . . . Narcotics Anonymous is very supportive. I can call people at any time. It's a very loving group. I celebrate my three-year anniversary this May. [33-year-old white poverty-level woman, married fifteen years, three children]

Another woman, who experienced a lot of violence and used tranquilizers, mentioned how her mother helped her to get over her depression.

> I did use tranquilizers. I was so tense. I was really down because of everything that happened. Really down. One thing that helped me out of it was my mother.

She just kept saying over and over, "How long are you going to feel sorry for yourself? You've got a child. That's your responsibility, your purpose in the world." That helped me get going again. [38-year-old black middle-class woman, married nine years, one child]

Several mothers mentioned using nerve medications. One of these women experienced a lot of domestic violence, while another's husband was an alcoholic and had disappeared.

The counseling I had was very helpful. I also got an anti-depressant, under a doctor's care. That helped stop the crying. I also got Zanec which helped lessen the tension. It meant I could sleep. [37-year-old white working-class receptionist, married seventeen years, two children]

I have had a lot of problems with my nerves because of this. I have colon problems, a nervous stomach, a lot of diarrhea. I've taken Valium and Tagament for my stomach. [39-year-old white working-class woman, married seven years, one child]

One woman, who was left by her husband for another woman, described how medication helped her panic attacks:

I took Vanex and Valium. I had panic attacks and those things really helped. I started drinking a lot and the psychologist said you're doing that to cover over your problems, so I stopped that. I've had headaches and sleeplessness because of the stress. [44-year-old white middle-class teacher, married twenty-one years, two children]

A few women either refused to take nerve medications or got off of them.

It was scary at the time of the separation, having two little kids, being in the house by myself. I was a nervous wreck. . . . The doctor checked me out and said that physically I was fine, but that I was very nervous and that that might affect my children. He gave me some Valium to take. I took one and I felt like spacy, like in the clouds, on cloud nine. I woke up the next morning and looked in the mirror and I said to myself, you can't let him do this to you. I decided I wasn't going to take garbage from anyone. I decided I would be a stronger person and fight. I went in the bathroom, took the Valium, and flushed them all down the drain. [34-year-old white working-class woman seeking employment, two children, married eleven years]

When I was first separated and had two babies and no place to live a doctor gave me Valium. I also took Atavan. I had terrible tension headaches. I got myself addicted to nerve pills. But then I got off them. I did it myself. [31-year-old black poverty-level woman, no high school diploma, unemployed, two children]

Several mothers worked out their own self-help techniques for reducing their stress.

> I took my husband's finding another woman as a rejection. I felt I failed. The other hard thing was money. I got really down. I was a candidate for (a state mental institution). But then I realized it wasn't me. I started reading a lot of self-help books. I listened to my friends who told me that I was a great person and that it wasn't me. Then I realized I'd tried everything. I'd given it my best. It wasn't me, it was him. I said, I can't let him still have this influence over me. So I started doing things for myself, like going to school. [33-year-old black working-class woman, data transcriber, high school education, married seven years, one child]

Finally, some of these women mentioned their church as a strong source of material and social support. One woman, however, said her church was not helpful because the pastor tried to get her to go to counseling to see if she could reconcile with her husband who had used drugs and was violent during the marriage.

Despite their hardships, these women continue to manage their lives and carry out their responsibilities. Some rely on their own personal strength, some on the support of their families, and still others on the support of their communities. Some survive simply by necessity, because they believe they have to be there for their children. Others find inventive ways of managing at a lower standard of living. But there is frequently a price for being in the role of single mother. These mothers experience increased pressure and anxiety due to the responsibility of earning the family's living at their job; doing the family's housework, food preparation, and laundry; shopping for food, clothes, and household maintenance items; doing the caretaking tasks for their children; and spending "quality time" with their children. As a result they experience fatigue, no time for themselves, and a decreased ability to advance in their jobs or careers.

There are of course some divorced women and other single mothers who do not "make it" and one or two of the women in this sample may confront serious difficulty. As we have seen in this section, several women reported that they came close to "going over the edge" into drug abuse, or alcoholism. One may not overcome her alcohol problem. Another feels she will have to give up her children to foster care because she frequently has no money and is at a point of nervous exhaustion. Perhaps some of the women who did not respond to the invitation to be interviewed and therefore were not included in the sample had not made it. One wonders what happened to their children who, along with their mothers, pay the price of our neglectful social policies.

Certainly men suffer emotional pain at divorce as well as women. They suffer from separation from their children. If they have been left by their wives they face feeling rejected. Some argue that men experience greater loneliness after divorce than women.[20] However, what is unique to divorced women is that most of them carry the major burden of supporting the children financially, providing nurturance for the children, and doing the myriad of usually invisible tasks associated with raising children.

CONCLUSION

All the mothers in this sample, no matter what their class or race, experienced a decreased standard of living as a result of their divorce. The majority of women in the sample were living on less than half of the median income of a two-earner family. To understand how women with certain skills and resources fare after divorce, I defined these women's class position by education and occupation. However, if I were to define class simply by total family income, some of these women's class positions would change. For example, many unmarried, nonprofessional middle-class women would fall to a position below remarried working-class women.

As the words of these women vividly illustrate, however, their losses vary according to class and race. While there was a decline in standard of living among all these mothers, it had different consequences depending on their class and race. Like middle-class women in other studies, these middle-class mothers had less income relative to their ex-husbands than did women of other classes, and suffered a painful decline in their standard of living. However, a variety of factors enter into a decline in one's standard of living—healthcare, housing, the quality of childcare, the ability to get a job, the ability to purchase counseling. Some of these indicators can be measured objectively and show poverty-level women at a distinct disadvantage; they are at greater risk for losing healthcare benefits, living in substandard housing and dangerous neighborhoods, and settling for lower quality daycare for their children. Minority women due to the "racialization of poverty" are the most vulnerable. Perhaps the most useful way to think of a divorced mother's economic decline is to say that she falls to the bottom of the opportunity structure of her class. The lower her class, the less opportunity she enjoys and the greater the danger she will fall through the safety net into poverty.

Race was a powerful force in these divorced mothers' lives. While black mothers were found in all social classes, they were overrepresented among the poorest mothers. Forty-two percent of the black women in this sample lived below the official poverty level, in contrast to 9 percent of white women. Three out of the four Hispanic women also lived below the poverty level. Among poverty-level women, black women fared worse in terms of family income, child support, employment, and health care. These striking economic differences between white and black women persisted despite the fact that black women had achieved the same educational level as white women.

These data show that our image of divorced women needs to expand beyond the myth of divorce as a white middle-class phenomenon. Perhaps we continue to subscribe to these images because we do not like to face the fact of poverty among white women and children, and will avoid associating it with something as common as divorce. We cannot accept that our policies cause poverty and hardship for the large number of "decent," "hardworking" divorced women and their children. Similarly, we do not recognize that many black women, just like white women, have chosen marriage, looking forward to a life-long commitment, and have had those hopes dashed by the harsher realities of marriage and divorce.

Given the hardships of these women and their children, we must provide them with more resources. The proposals put forth for improving divorced mothers' economic well-being usually call for stricter child-support guidelines and stricter enforcement of child-support orders. This is without a doubt of critical importance for mothers of all classes. Women in this study who received child support had a much greater chance of keeping essential elements of their lifestyles. The poverty rate for women in this sample who received full child support was 10 percent, compared with 38 percent for women who did not receive child support. However, child support reform is not a panacea. As will be discussed in the next chapter, some women will always have difficulty obtaining child support. Further, child support alone won't help those mothers with the lowest incomes. Of those mothers living below the official poverty level, 18 percent were receiving regular child support and 7 percent received partial support. The poorest mothers needed not only child support but also other ways to increase their standard of living. Fathers with low incomes typically have difficulty paying child support and also need assistance raising their standard of living.

We must also increase women's pay so they can support themselves through jobs. The biggest problem for divorced women is that they cannot get jobs which pay adequately. We must raise the minimum wage and provide fringe benefits for women who currently must work in low-wage, low-benefit, and unstable jobs. If divorced mothers are to escape sex-segregated jobs and gain higher-paying positions, they will also need affirmative-action policies and affordable and accessible day care, job training, and health care. These supports are also critical for helping women get off of welfare and enabling them to support themselves and their children through the paid labor force. We need a much greater range of policies to ensure the well-being of divorced women with children and other single-parent families. We cannot leave women to rely only on private resources, or to be at the mercy of the market and the few social resources available in our meager social welfare system.

Chapter 5

DIVIDING RESOURCES

As the previous chapter demonstrates, the decline in the standard of living that divorced mothers face takes a severe toll on their lives, pushing some of them toward permanent downward mobility or into poverty. Their children, whose well-being is tied to that of their mothers, suffer a similar fate. This downward mobility and impoverishment of women and children at divorce result from several key factors. First, our society distributes resources in a way that is highly gendered, with disproportionate resources going to men at the expense of women and children. After divorce, mothers have to support themselves and their children by working at wages that are considerably lower than those of their former husbands. Further, due to their childrearing responsibilities, some work part-time while others, like some of the women described in the previous chapter, remain at low-paying jobs where employers are willing to accommodate their need for flexible hours.

In addition to their low wages, a second key factor that disadvantages women is that they are not compensated for the myriad of tasks and countless hours of time they spend taking care of their children, either within or outside of marriage. Women are designated as caretakers of children in our society, and many identify strongly with this role. However, in financial terms, women are penalized for adopting this choice. As a consequence, just setting up a household on their own outside of marriage is difficult for most divorced women. This treatment of women originates from policies which assume that women will raise children in families where there are men who are primary breadwinners.

Our society also distributes resources in a manner that disadvantages certain class and race groups and relegates some men to poverty. With the shift to a more integrated world economy, U.S. companies have transferred large numbers of jobs overseas, leaving many minority and lower skilled workers vulnerable to lower paying jobs and increased levels of unemployment. Thus even during marriage, some women and their husbands remain poor, while after divorce, these women's situations can become desperate.

Sadly, our social policies do not address these gender inequities nor the inequalities based on class and race, leaving women and children to pay the price of divorce. Our current system for supporting divorced women and children is based on the redistribution of private family assets, supplemented by meager public resources, principally from AFDC. In theory, divorced women have available to them various resources from their ex-husbands and from their marriages—child support, a share of the marital property, and alimony, or spousal support or maintenance. As described earlier, however, most women don't receive property or alimony of any significant value. The primary resource available to them is child support, which is critical to divorced women for improving the standard of living of themselves and their children.

Researchers have established that regular child-support payments improve the standards of living of women and children and would lift a number of them out of poverty. The child-support system, however, has been a disaster for women and children. First, most women have found it difficult to enforce their child-support orders. Fewer than one-third of single mothers receive regular child support, and only half of those actually receive the full amount. In 1989, of the 72 percent of divorced women nationwide who had a child-support order, 51 percent received full support, 24 percent received partial support, and 25 percent received none. Since many of those 28 percent of divorced women who do not have a child-support order receive no child support, the actual number of divorced women receiving no child support is much higher than would at first appear. Second, child-support awards have been so low that they have not met even half the costs of childrearing. Further, women have found it extremely difficult to obtain increases in their child-support awards as their children grow older and their expenses increase.[1]

Fortunately, new reforms have addressed this debacle. The Federal government now views the enforcement of child support as a priority. Public support for child-support reform has grown as support for social welfare programs—particularly AFDC—has decreased. Policy makers hope that increasing the likelihood that women will receive child support will enable them to stay off welfare. These new reforms are promising and will make a significant contribution to the well-being of women and children. The stakes are very high. Should significant improvements be made in the child-support system, women stand to gain a greater share of resources after marriage. According to the Government Accounting Office, "Of the nearly $35 billion in child support payments owed nationwide under the Child Support Enforcement Program, more than $27 billion remained uncollected at the end of fiscal year 1992. During that year, more than 5.7 of the 8.5 million noncustodial parents owing child support made no payment on the amount owed."[2]

This chapter addresses the promise of child-support reform, but also the remaining problems women face getting their fair share of child support. While the improvements in the child-support system will result in many more women receiving child support and in their receiving higher awards, I argue that women will still not receive as much child support as they should, and that some women will continue to receive none at all. The experiences of the women in this sample provide important data about the conditions under which women negotiate for resources and the likelihood that new policies will overcome basic gender inequalities. I demonstrate how women still remain in a less powerful position than their ex-husbands, both in terms of how the law divides resources, and in terms of their ability to bargain with their ex-husbands for resources from their marriage. I conclude by arguing for a system which guarantees child support for all single mothers with children.

RECENT REFORMS IN THE CHILD-SUPPORT SYSTEM

In the following section I discuss the promise and limitations of two major measures that have been enacted to reform the child-support system. The first are reforms to improve the enforcement of child-support awards, particularly income or wage withholding, a system whereby child-support payments are automatically deducted from the wages of the noncustodial parent and sent to the custodial parent. The second are child-support guidelines, or formulas for determining child support, which have been developed in recent years to address the problem of inadequate child support awards.

Reforms in Child-support Enforcement

The child-support enforcement system has been described as having two parts, a private system and a public system.[3] The private system has been under the authority and jurisdiction of states. In this system, women go to court where their child-support award is determined at a conference or hearing with court officers. A judge signs the final order. This system depends on the initiative and resources of the custodial parent, who must hire a lawyer as well as pay for locating the noncustodial parent and for requisite legal and administrative costs.

The other system is a public one. Over the last twenty years, the Federal government has become involved in the collection of child support in two ways. First, it has granted substantial funding to states to provide child-support services, including certain limited federal locating and enforcement mechanisms. Second, it has required states to pass legislation, like income-withholding measures. Title IV–D of the Social Security Act, passed in 1975 by Congress, created a federal Office of Child Support Enforcement and required states to establish state child-support offices, typically referred to as IV–D offices. Title IV–D requires states to provide welfare recipients and anyone else who wishes to use this public system with free or low-cost enforcement services. Mothers who use this system are generally poor or near poor.

In addition, there is really a third system, one for women on AFDC. AFDC regulations stipulate that recipients receive only $50 of the child support paid by the father. As noted in Chapter 4, AFDC appropriates the rest of the award to offset the cost of welfare to the family. The state is also entitled to any support owed to the mother from the time before she went on welfare. Some argue that this shows how the goal of welfare is not to help the poor, but rather to save costs for the state. Further, as a condition of getting their benefits, AFDC mothers are required to cooperate in getting child support. They must identify the father of their children and they and their children must undergo blood tests. A mother must appear in court proceedings and testify against the father, unless she has "good cause" for failing to cooperate. Federal regulations do not recognize physical harm to the mother as a reason not to cooperate unless it impairs "her capacity to care for child adequately."[4]

None of these systems has generated adequate child-support funds for women and children. As just noted, 40 percent of custodial mothers and 28 percent of divorced mothers do not have child-support awards, and only half of those with an award get the full amount. This is the same rate of collection as twenty years ago. The collection rate for the IV–D system is even lower. Only 19 percent of those who use this system receive child support. Problems of the system have been attributed to insufficient staff and resources at the state and local level; an excess of officials, including judges, court clerks, process servers, and sheriffs, who are outside the control of the IV–D agency; diverse and inconsistent state laws that make processing interstate cases difficult; and lack of automation. In 1990, nationwide case workers in the IV–D system were responsible for on average 345 cases each. In some states, workers were responsible for over 1,000 cases.[5]

The most important and effective reform for child-support enforcement enacted to date is income withholding, a procedure by which an obligator's (typically the father's) payment is withheld from his paycheck by his employer, who then sends the money to the state child-support agency. The Family Support Act of 1988 required that by 1994 all states adopt laws that contain a provision for immediate wage withholding for the amount of child support awarded. An initial evaluation of ten counties that instituted routine income withholding showed that this procedure increased child-support payments by between 11 and 30 percent. Child support reformer Irwin Garfinkel estimates that income withholding will "increase the national amount of child support collections out of total child support obligations from 59% to between 65% and 77%."[6]

Further, many states have established other procedures for strengthening the enforcement of their child-support orders, including measures that would have been unimaginable until the recent change in attitude toward child support. Laws now mandate referring difficult child-support cases in the IV–D system to the Internal Revenue Service (IRS) for collection, imposing liens on real and personal property, and reporting arrears to credit agencies. Some states, such as California, are withholding state professional licenses when a parent is in arrears. Others, like Virginia, even refuse to issue driver's licenses, car registrations, or hunting and fishing licenses to those who are behind in their child-support payments and have made no arrangements to meet their obligations. A few states have gone so far as to seize lottery winnings of the delinquent fathers.[7]

Reformers have also made progress in ensuring that children receive health insurance as part of their child-support agreement. Many children are eligible for health insurance through their fathers. This coverage is useless, however, unless the fathers enroll the children in a plan, provide claim forms to the mothers, and give the mothers the insurance payments when the mother has already paid for a service. Mothers, however, frequently do not receive payment for their children's healthcare costs. Fortunately several states have enacted laws requiring employers to put children on their fathers' health insurance plans, to inform mothers about the plans, and to honor mothers' signatures on claim forms, which facilitates direct reimbursement. In 1993, Congress mandated that all states adopt such laws.[8]

While these reforms are important steps in increasing the number of women who receive child support and the levels of child support they receive, at the same time, according to Garfinkel's figures, between 23 and 35 percent of women will still not receive child support after income withholding is instituted. Many problems remain with new systems of income withholding. First, there has been no child-support enforcement system for women whose ex-husbands or former partners are self-employed. Fathers who are self-employed do not have employers who can withhold child support from their income. Second, there have been no effective mechanisms for enforcing interstate cases. In 30 percent of all child-support cases, parents reside in different states, and only $1 out of every $10 collected in child support is from an interstate case.[9]

The system also breaks down when men change jobs frequently or work in the underground economy. Third, the new reforms do not address the inequalities in the child-support system. Poor fathers are incarcerated more and pay at higher rates than other fathers. This inequity is rarely recognized and certainly not addressed.

Child Support Guidelines

A second important reform in the child-support system has been the development of child-support guidelines. The Family Support Act of 1988 mandated that states develop standardized formulas or guidelines to set more uniform and fair levels of child-support awards in order to make the awards conform more closely to the actual costs of raising a child; to eliminate inconsistencies between the awards of people in similar circumstances; and to decrease the time delays in processing the awards. Guidelines apply to all women except those on AFDC, who, as noted above, receive only $50 of the child support paid by the father.

However, while the establishment of guidelines, which most states have now adopted, is an important step in improving the child-support system, initial evaluations of the impact of child support guidelines are mixed. On the one hand, an early study of their impact in three states showed that the implementation of child-support guidelines resulted in awards that were 15 percent higher, a positive development. Yet this increase is far short of the 70 to 100 percent increase some had predicted. Further, according to this study, the main effect of the guidelines has not been to increase all child-support awards, but rather to raise the substandard award levels found in some jurisdictions to more average levels. The other main effect, according to the study, has been to increase the number of noncustodial mothers paying child support to custodial fathers. A recent study of the effect of guidelines in Massachusetts showed that while the guidelines call for child support orders to total 25 percent of the obligated parent's gross income, actual orders averaged only 14 percent of gross income. Some researchers believe that guidelines could increase the amount of child support collected by 50 percent. But this is still far short of the increases which had been hoped for.[10]

Why haven't the levels of child support risen? First, there are some loopholes in the law that contribute to lower awards. Guidelines have often been set in accordance with vague standards that permit the courts to decide what is "reasonable and just." Garfinkel argues that "because courts are permitted to depart from guidelines when the outcome is deemed to be unfair to any of the parties, it is possible that this loophole will be used to undermine the intent of the law."

Second, for women who have some type of joint custody agreement, courts may reduce the support award, reasoning that because the custodial parent—typically the mother—is getting more help from the father in raising the children, she should receive less child support. However, this kind of reasoning fails to take into account the lower earnings of the mother and her need to maintain an adequate standard of living, the high fixed costs of having children, and the costs of maintaining two homes.[11]

Further, there are problems in how the guidelines are determined. States have not established child-support formulas and guidelines that will distribute the costs of raising children between custodial and noncustodial parents in an equitable manner. The dominant approaches to allocating resources for child support have been an "income shares" approach, or a "percentage of income" approach. The goal of these approaches is to ensure that the noncustodial parent, typically the father, contributes the same proportion of his post-divorce income to his children as he did during the marriage.

These methods of calculating child support, however, are based on the costs of raising children in a two-income family. They do not take into account that divorced single mothers have many additional costs in establishing a new household. Second, these guidelines do not consider the nonmonetary costs of childrearing and do not compensate women for the time they invest in child-rearing or for their forgone earning opportunities. Women get no compensation for the task of mothering, which remains a kind of "invisible work," despite its difficult and time-consuming nature. These approaches to determining child support have also been criticized on the grounds that they exclude savings and investments from their formulas and do not include some important expenses, such as educational costs, for example. In many states, fathers' financial obligations end when the children turn eighteen and fathers have no obligation to contribute to their children's college education. Thus, a mother can be left with many expenses as her children finish high school.[12]

To be fairer, child support would have to be allocated through an "income equalization" approach, which would ensure that children continue to have the same standard of living as the nonresident parent. Because it is impossible to separate the standard of living of the child from that of the resident parent, income equalization attempts to establish some rough parity in the postdivorce standards of living of the father's and the mother's households. An income equalization formula adjusts for the "economies of scale" of the custodial parent; after a divorce it takes more money for a parent to live alone with a child than during a marriage. An income equalization approach would greatly increase the child-support obligation of most upper-middle- and upper-income nonresident fathers, and raise the standard of living of mothers and children.

Some have advocated this approach, but no state has adopted it and it is doubtful that any state will. State authorities undoubtedly hold attitudes similar to judicial authorities who have been more concerned with ennabling fathers to start new lives. They also share the widely held belief that the income that fathers earn belongs to them, and are reluctant to rule that a larger share should be transferred to former wives, even if the money is for the children. There is, however, evidence of some public support for increased child-support awards. One recent survey of Maryland residents concerning what they considered to be appropriate levels of child-support awards found that most respondents supported award levels that were considerably higher than the guidelines of their states, with only a minority giving answers which suggested that they thought the guidelines had been set too high. These researchers also found that, while female respondents favored higher awards than male respondents, it was not by much.[13]

Irwin Garfinkel advocates adoption of the percentage-of-income standard, a set percent rate for child support, as a realistic and achievable goal for determining child-support awards. For one child, a noncustodial parent would pay 17 percent of his or her income, an amount which increases to 25, 29, 31, and 34 percent for 2, 3, 4, or 5 children, respectively. Garfinkel believes that not only is this standard easy and efficient to use, but it also provides for automatic increases in awards as the noncustodial parent's income increases or decreases. Current laws do not address the issue of updating child-support awards, which has long been a serious problem. The Family Support Act of 1988 mandated that by 1993 states have a procedure to review and adjust child-support awards every three years to make them current. According to Garfinkel, however, "the review need not lead to updating. Moreover, updating every third year, rather than annually, is expected to reduce average award levels by about five percent." Garfinkel fears that courts will find the updating of awards so burdensome and costly that they will resort to a cheap method of review, one that avoids updating in the vast majority of cases. Garfinkel believes that in the past, lawmakers, in order to avoid overburdening the courts, have made it difficult to raise child support awards.[14]

Some reformers have called for the formation of a national child-support guideline commission to develop a set of fairer national child-support guidelines. One group recommends guidelines that would ensure that children would enjoy "a minimum decent living standard" of at least 1.5 times the federal poverty level. If this would result in impoverishing the noncustodial parent-payer, then the children should at least receive an award at the poverty level. This group recommends that awards from fathers in higher income categories should ensure that children will enjoy a living standard that is comparable to that of the higher income parent. This would be accomplished by ensuring that both households were in the same quintile of family income. Where either parent has additional children, guidelines should ensure that the children in the two households are treated in a comparable way.[15]

PROBLEMS IN NEGOTIATING FOR
AND ENFORCING CHILD SUPPORT ORDERS

In this section, based on the experiences of the women in this sample, I address the problems mothers will continue to face in negotiating for child support, even after the passage of recent and proposed child-support reforms. These include problems in securing awards that are adequate, and problems in enforcing child-support orders. The mothers in this sample received child support at a rate similar to national averages for divorced women.[16] Of those women with a child-support order, 56 percent received child support regularly, 23 percent received partial support, and 21 percent received none at all. Including both women who did and did not receive a child-support order, 40 percent received child support on a regular basis, 16 percent on a partial basis, and 44 percent not at all. Also, 29 percent of the women in this sample had income withholding arrangements, so it is possible to draw some tentative conclusions from these data about the possible successes and limitations of this new form of child-support collection enforcement.

Under current procedures, to obtain child support and other resources women must go through a process that involves negotiations with various parties, particularly their husbands, and frequently lawyers. Women must still depend on their ex-husbands to cooperate in this process by supplying the correct financial information and keeping appointments, and by being willing to make agreements. In some cases women are able to cooperate with their ex-husbands, but as we shall see, sometimes they experience serious conflicts with them over the payment of child support. Women also feel dependent on lawyers because they lack critical information about how formulas for child support work, what they can and cannot ask for, or how long they are eligible for awards.

In their negotiations for child support, the women in this sample reported four serious problems: difficulty securing legal help; inability to collect child support from ex-husbands who can evade the child-support system; fear of reprisals from their ex-husbands; and their ex-husbands' inability to pay child support. The data show that due to these problems, some women have difficulty negotiating their initial child-support awards, updating their awards at a later time, and enforcing their awards. These problems demonstrate the various ways men can use their power to further their interests, while women remain vulnerable. Despite the fact that, as Terry Arendell describes, men feel they have lost power at divorce and that their former rights and prerogatives have been stripped away, as I will demonstrate, they still have many advantages in the negotiations for resources.[17]

Before proceeding to the problems women experience, I will briefly note the experiences of a few of the minority of mothers who reported that fathers willingly pay child support on their own and who have had no problems with child-support enforcement. These reports show how some fathers, whatever their feelings about their former wives, are able to focus on their children's needs. A 37-year-old middle-class woman who was married for six years and had one child said:

> My ex-husband has a strong sense of family. He felt bad about the divorce and about our daughter. So providing good child support was his way of making his claim as a good parent.

A 51-year-old bookkeeper, married for twenty-seven years, finds herself in a similar situation. Her ex-husband is paying all expenses for two daughters in college, including tuition, clothes, allowances, and some travel. She said, "I'm lucky he likes to play father. If they have a problem, I say, 'go to your father.'" Another, a 44-year-old white teacher with two children, believes that her ex-husband is actually paying more child support than he is legally obligated to pay. She believes that he felt guilty about leaving her and their two children for another woman and agreed to the child-support settlement without examining it carefully or negotiating over its contents.

One working-class woman with three children who works in accounting simply wrote her own agreement about child support with her ex-husband. According to her, "I knew I could trust him about child support. We knew we could trust each other." Another couple easily reached a child-support agreement between themselves and even negotiated their own income withholding arrangement.

> There's never been a problem with my ex-husband paying child support. We both belong to the same Police and Fire Credit Union. We instructed them that when his paycheck comes the child support should just be credited to my account. [39-year-old working-class dispatcher, married seventeen years, with two children]

One poverty-level woman reported that her ex-husband has always paid, except when he lost his job. When he got a new job, he wrote the court at his own initiative and the court began withholding his income from his wages.

Lawyers and Legal Assistance

The majority of women in this sample obtained a child support order through Family Court. When women begin the process of obtaining child support, they have almost no information about how to negotiate the child support system. In some cases, a couple determines the amount of child support together with their lawyers before going to court. In other cases, the couple goes to court with or without a lawyer and the award is determined at a support conference or a pre-trial hearing. Court appearances can be confusing and time consuming. A hearing officer reviews the income and expense statements, income tax records, and pay stubs of each party and uses the guidelines to calculate an amount of child support. If either party objects, the divorcing couple goes before a master or permanent hearing officer. The hearing before the master is a full evidentiary hearing, at which either party can introduce evidence or call witnesses. If neither files exceptions, the master, either at the hearing or at a later date, will issue a recommended order for support and the judge will sign the order. If either files exceptions, there is a hearing before a judge.[18]

A minority of women in the sample, typically middle-class women, had their lawyers negotiate child support agreements with their ex-husbands' lawyers. If these women did not receive their child support payments, however, they also went to Family Court to try and enforce their child support orders. A few women considered divorced mediation. None, however, chose this option.

Almost all the women in this sample wanted to retain lawyers who would provide them with information and help guide them through the process of negotiating for resources, which they saw as a difficult one. All women began their negotiations for child support with little information about how to obtain resources, and most were overwhelmed at the prospect of collecting all this information and believed that lawyers could be very helpful to them. Many women felt very dependent on their lawyers. Research shows that divorced persons with lawyers secure more assets from the marriage and also have a greater chance of securing favorable custody arrangements.[19]

Lawyers can benefit women in many ways, such as by helping them to determine their own and their husbands' assets and to establish whether their husbands may be concealing any assets. Further, women whose ex-husbands have a lot of assets need information about what share they are entitled to receive and what they are worth. Also, lawyers sometimes are able to secure advantageous agreements for women by making tradeoffs between different kinds of property and child support. For women whose ex-husbands have few assets or may be chronically unemployed or change jobs frequently, lawyers can help them estimate their ex-husbands' worth.

While women need good legal help, however, the first problem they face is gaining access to lawyers. As demonstrated in Figure 5–1, while the majority of the women in this sample had lawyers, 17 percent had no legal assistance, and in the remaining cases women used their ex-husband's lawyer or shared a lawyer with their ex-husband. Further, there were statistically significant class and race differences in women's use of lawyers. While 81 percent of the middle-

Figure 5–1. Use of Legal Representation in the Divorce Process.*

Type of legal representation	Proportion of women
Private lawyer	63%
Legal aid	14%
None	17%
Other	6%

* Overall chi-squares by class and race are highly significant. Significance of race for the likelihoods of having a lawyer or using legal aid are no longer significant after controlling for social class. The likelihood of having no legal representation during divorce proceedings is significant for race and class, and race is still significant after the effects of class are controlled.

___

class and 83 percent of the working-class women had their own private lawyers, only 29 percent of the poverty-level women had private attorneys. Thirty-eight percent of the poverty-level women obtained their lawyers from Community Legal Services (CLS), a legal service for poor people in Philadelphia which arranges divorces at a low cost. Similar percentages of black and white women had lawyers, except among poverty-level women. A full 30 percent of the poverty-level women had no legal help at all from any source, including 17 percent of the white poverty-level women, and 36 percent of the black poverty-level women. The difficulties poor women face in obtaining legal assistance are even worse than they might appear to be. While 38 percent of poverty-level women obtained their lawyers from Community Legal Services, CLS does not handle negotiations for custody, child support, or property. Thus, while CLS is helpful to poor women in obtaining their divorces, they are left without any help in negotiating child support or property.

The 17 percent of women who had no legal assistance—many of them living at the poverty-level, many of them black—gave a variety of reasons for why they had no lawyer. Several women did not retain lawyers because they believed they had made adequate agreements with their ex-husbands, and they thought these would be sufficient. But some of these women, such as the following woman—a white working-class clerical worker with one child—are now sorry they did not retain their own lawyer.

I didn't have a lawyer because it was a pretty friendly divorce and I trusted that my ex-husband wouldn't go back on his word. But he did some. He said he would give me the car, and I never saw it. He traded it in and got a brand new car. He gives me $50 a week for child support, but I feel it should be more now. He says "no, we agreed to $50."

Several others mentioned that they wanted to avoid a fight with their ex-husbands.

I didn't have a lawyer 'cause it had all settled. I wish I had as far as custody goes, not anything else. That's a constant that hangs over my head. The main reason I didn't go to court was because I knew it could get nasty. I'm gonna be in contact with him the rest of my life so.... [31-year-old black woman living at the poverty level, married eleven years, three children]

I didn't have a lawyer. I never bothered. I didn't have any money. My ex-husband was being fair. And I didn't want to get into a fight. If my ex-husband gets nasty, he can be vindictive, like if somebody pushes him. And I didn't need any more money. [32-year-old white poverty-level woman, part-time convenience store worker, married fourteen years, two children]

Finally, several women said they had no need for a lawyer because there were no resources from the marriage, and several didn't get lawyers because they didn't know where their ex-husbands were.

Another group of women initially had lawyers, but said they couldn't afford to hire a lawyer to go back to court and raise their child-support awards. In theory, with new legislation mandating the periodic review and update of child-support awards, women should have an easier time securing increases in their awards. In practice, however, as Garfinkel has said, the loophole in the law allowing courts to depart from guidelines if they think it would be fairer to one of the parties may enable those husbands or wives who have legal assistance to take advantage of loopholes in the law. Not being able to raise an award can cause a great deal of hardship for a woman, such as the 39-year-old white working-class woman, cited earlier, who had to take a second job to meet her expenses.

Now I wish I had gotten more child support. I couldn't make it on that amount. What I didn't figure into my living expenses was repairs on the house. I didn't make the "miscellaneous" category big enough. I had car repairs, roof repairs, and the upkeep of the house. I also wish I had gotten a cost of living in the child support.

So I was faced with a choice: go back to work or take him back to court. I knew that taking him back to court would require first laying down $200 for a retainer fee. When you can't even put food on the table you can't do that. So I went back to work. I worked three nights a week and Saturday and Sunday, seventy-five hours a week.

This woman had to quite her second job, however, because she became exhausted and because her children, who were unsupervised while she worked, began to get into trouble. Her ex-husband refused to increase his child support payments.

The second problem women face is the quality of lawyers. Women in this sample reported a great variety of experiences with lawyers. Some middle-class women expressed satisfaction with the services of their lawyers. They looked carefully before they chose a lawyer, they paid their lawyers a lot of money, and in return they learned about their rights and received a lot of advice. Says a 35-year-old black computer analyst who was married nine years, "I had a good lawyer. He gave me a lot of information. I really shopped around for him. He specializes in divorces." Some women commented that their lawyers were particularly good at helping them manage with the emotional side of their negotiations. This advice is less tangible, but the women felt it was very helpful.

> I liked the advice my lawyer gave about how I should act. That was very important. He said, "Save your anger until later." He said, "Your husband is very guilty now and that will help you. If you fight, or drag it out, you won't get as much as you want. Keep the bitterness out. Use the fact that he wants the divorce and give it to him." This strategy worked. [34-year-old white teacher, mother of two]

However, a number of middle-class women did not have good experiences with their lawyers. One 36-year-old woman, a mother of two who had been married for twelve years, reported that her ex-husband's income had doubled since the initial child-support agreement was made, and she went back to court for more child support. Because she did not have the money to hire her own lawyer, she sought advice from her uncle, who got one of his law partners to handle her divorce for free.

> I would never do this again. It was all right for the divorce but when we went to the appeal to negotiate for child support the lawyer didn't come. He sent one of his assistants. The judge and my ex-husband's female lawyer, who is very good, made mincemeat of this assistant. The assistant didn't even look at my file until we were out in the hall getting ready to go in. I could have done a better job myself. I thought for sure it would be reversed at the appeal, but it wasn't. I've never said anything to the lawyer. I see him socially. I've felt like saying, "Why did you send that bimbo?" If I were doing it again I would pay my own lawyer.

Like many other women, these women complained about the cost of their lawyers. In metropolitan areas, divorce lawyers charge anywhere from $125 to $350 an hour. Some women complained that their lawyers didn't inform them of how much their divorces were costing until the fees had become very high, and they never received itemized bills from their lawyers. Some divorced women in other locations have complained of being exploited by lawyers, and a New York State judge has issued new rules requiring divorce lawyers to provide itemized billing and forbidding lawyers from taking women's homes when legal fees are not paid.[20]

Even more working- than middle-class women expressed discontent with their legal assistance. Many women stated that they sought the cheapest legal advice they could find. Some obtained the services of a lawyer as a favor to them, and complained that because of this they felt they could not ask things from this lawyer that they would have liked to have asked. Most working-class women believed that the fact that they had to settle for whatever lawyer they could get put them at a disadvantage in negotiating for child support, and prevented them from getting the information they needed. This woman, a 39-year-old white woman who was married for seventeen years, reported:

> I got a lawyer through a friend. The lawyer kind of did it as a favor. He's a more big-time lawyer who usually doesn't handle smaller things like this. He got me the divorce. But I wish I'd gotten more things now, like I would make sure and get child support in the event that my child went to college.

This woman had an experience shared by some other women—her lawyers did not show up in court.

> Everything worked out OK in Family Court except that my lawyer didn't show up. I felt very annoyed and nervous and upset. It was because he was doing me a favor and he had other things to do. However, we were in a little room and we were able to call my lawyer on the phone. He said everything in the agreement sounded OK.

These working-class women seemed to have less knowledge of their rights and less satisfaction about their agreements than the middle-class women. They felt they did not get basic information from their lawyers. Some women who did have lawyers for their divorce claimed they were never told about getting child support.

> I don't think I got good legal advice. He never informed me of my rights. I just filed the papers and got a basic divorce. I only found out later from talking to my friends some of the other things my lawyer could have done. [33-year-old black working-class woman in data processing, married for seven years, one child]

> The lawyer had a clerk do it. He just didn't keep me informed, he didn't know what was going on. When you pay a lawyer you expect him to know what's going on. For example, he didn't tell me how to go about getting child support. [28-year-old white medical secretary, married six years, one child]

So few poverty-level women have private lawyers that it is difficult to discern a pattern in their experiences; one or two women had good experiences, but the remainder did not. Like working-class women, they felt they did not receive much advice. Said a 37-year-old white department store clerk, "The lawyer didn't tell me what to do at all. He just said, 'I'll do whatever you tell me to do.' I still don't know if it was good advice or not." As noted above, for 38 percent of poverty-level women, Community Legal Services was their only legal service. CLS offers assistance for obtaining a divorce, but not for obtaining child support or child custody, so these women go without this type of assistance.

In conclusion, the majority of women, who have little money for lawyers, feel they do not get good legal advice. Of course having a good lawyer does not guarantee getting child support. As the following sections make clear, a number of men can successfully evade paying child support despite the efforts of lawyers. It is also the case that some divorce clients can have unrealistic expectations of what they can get from divorce settlements, and that well-meaning divorce lawyers and their clients may have honest differences over negotiations for child support and other resources.[21] However, it seems safe to conclude that the ability of many women to secure satisfactory child-support awards and to raise their awards as their expenses increase is flawed by their difficulty in paying for legal assistance. Some men also face difficulties paying for lawyers, particularly unemployed men. Since the incomes of many men are substantially higher than those of their ex-wives, however, on the whole men have less difficulty than women in securing legal help.

Some advocate efforts to encourage women to proceed without a lawyer, or *pro se.* They argue that women feel empowered by being able to control their own cases and not being beholden to a lawyer who makes many decisions for them and charges high fees. In many states, however, custodial parents are forbidden or discouraged from acting *pro se.* Even if a woman does handle her own case, she still has to pay legal fees and costs. And, of course, if the effort to secure child support fails, she must then hire a lawyer.[22]

Evasion

It has long been known that many women do not receive child support because their ex-husbands can successfully evade paying it. Recent child-support reforms have tried to address this problem. Income withholding should greatly reduce the ability of fathers to evade paying child support. The experiences of women in this sample indicate, however, that even with income withholding, some women will not get child support because their ex-husbands will still be able to successfully evade the system.

In this study, 29 percent of women had income withholding arrangements for obtaining child support. At the time these interviews were conducted, Pennsylvania courts were supposed to automatically attach the wages of the noncustodial parent if he had failed to pay thirty days' worth of child support. At the time, income withholding arrangements were called "wage attachments." Of the women with wage attachments, 27 percent received no child support, a figure consistent with Garfinkel's estimates that 23 to 35 percent of women nationally will still not receive child support even with income withholding. The experiences of these women give us an indication of the potential successes and problems with new income withholding procedures and show why, even with income withholding, there will be mothers who will not receive child support and will be left with inadequate resources to raise their children.

Evasion was the major problem reported by those women who had wage attachments and were not receiving child support. Said a 31-year-old mother of two who had been married seven years, "I got the wage attachment. When he found out he was going to court, he quit his job. He started dancing; he makes money under the table." Another said:

> My ex-husband doesn't pay child support at all. I've contacted the court. They say they've written him and that they're going to attach his wages. When my ex-husband found that out he called me and said he would make sure his employer said that he didn't know him. [34-year-old black woman, daycare worker, married eight years, separated one year after marriage, one child]

Nineteen percent of the women who have wage attachments were receiving only partial amounts of their child-support awards and also reported evasion as a problem. A 28-year-old white mother of one had to get her ex-husband's wages attached several times. She had to track him down through several states and several different jobs. She said:

> So I told the court he wasn't paying after two checks didn't come, and they said they attached his wages. But he quit his first job. So then I informed the court that he was working somewhere else. I called his sister-in-law and found out that he was working at. . . .
> The court caught up with him there and I got two months' worth of pay.
> Then he never told me he quit that job. I had to write the court again and tell them where he was working. I have been getting paid now since November. If he changes jobs again, I'll have to get his wages attached again. I don't like the system. It's the woman that has to do everything.

One woman stopped receiving child support when her ex-husband became unemployed. She is now trying to arrange to have his unemployment check attached.

Women without wage withholding agreements reported similar problems of evasion. Some reported that their ex-husbands lied about their financial circumstances, and although they were working full-time, they would tell the court that they were not working, or were working only part-time. A number of women report that their husbands were "working under the table."

> When we went to court the judge looked at his salary and said he should pay $30 a week for me and $20 for my son. My ex-husband looked at him and said, "You're kidding." And then the next day he quit his job. He said, "I'll never work above board again." [39-year-old white woman, married sixteen years, separated four years after marriage, two children]

> It's the same game. All the guys do it, it's a game. They work under the table. I told the judge. He told me to bring pictures of him working. It's ridiculous. [31-year-old white secretary, married seven years, two children]

This woman also said that her ex-husband's employer will "cover" for him.

> His employer lies and says he doesn't work there. The employer covers for him in a lot of ways—like he cracked up the company van. The reason his employer covers for him is that he has a lot on the employer. He knows a lot. It's one crook helping another. My ex-husband also has a couple of social security cards. And sometimes he doesn't even give his own name. He gives his uncle's name. [31-year-old white woman living at the poverty-level, married nine years, separated two years after marriage, three children]

Another woman, a 33-year-old mother of three living at the poverty level, said she didn't try to get child support because "there was no way to prove he had any income. He was stealing. I realized that the only thing that trying to get child support would do would be to aggravate me. He wouldn't show up. It would make no sense." One woman was going to try and do her own detective work to prove that her ex-husband was working under the table.

> Through welfare I gave information about my ex-husband to the case worker. I guess my ex-husband told them he wouldn't pay. And since he doesn't pay any taxes they can't get him that way.
>   I told the person at welfare where he worked. I gave them all that information. But they didn't do anything. Now I'm going and taking pictures myself. I'm slowly collecting information myself, with a friend. We're going to take pictures. I'm going to take him to court.
>   He told me, "You take me to court and I'll leave town." I said, "Fine." I wish he would. I want him to pay though. He sees the kids every Sunday. He won't pay a thing though. He doesn't give them any money. [26-year-old white woman living at the poverty level, no high school diploma, married six years, 2 children]

Some women reported that some fathers just disappeared. One 39-year-old white working-class woman with one child, married for seven years, could not find her ex-husband, who is an alcoholic.

My ex-husband makes sure he can't be found. The lawyer said if we knew his residence or his job we could go after it. But we don't. And I don't have the money to
hire a private detective. If I did I would go after him in a minute. I don't see how
he can live with his conscience.

Fathers' ability to evade the child-support system can also result in women
receiving lower child support than they are entitled to. Some women complained that the awards were inadequate because their ex-husbands, who were
working under the table, did not report their full income. According to one
woman:

> The lawyers decided that my ex-husband should pay $120 per week and that's
> what he pays. I showed the agreement to my lawyer and he said that was very
> good, more than most get—that's right isn't it?
> Of course the amount was based on my ex-husband's income tax returns. That
> didn't show all the money he was making under the table. . . . I sure didn't want it
> to go through the courts. I know what that's like. I've seen my neighbor go
> through that. You go to court all the time and you lose time from work and they
> never track them down. [40-year-old white working-class woman, married nine
> years, three children]

A white working-class woman with two children reported a similar problem.

> I don't know if it [the child support award] is fair. I don't want to really rob him.
> I guess if I thought he could afford more I wouldn't think it was fair. But I don't
> know how much he earns because his overtime, which he gets every other week-
> end, is off the books.

Another woman stated that her ex-husband, who owned a jewelry store and
sold jewelry, claimed in court that his business only did jewelry repair, not jewelry sales. This greatly reduced his reported income. The woman's lawyer chal-
lenged her ex-husband in court about why his store had cases filled with new
jewelry, but the judge did not take this into account in awarding child support.

One woman did have a way to find out her ex-husband's income because
they had run a business together. She knew that her ex-husband was not
reporting his actual income, but a lower one. However, she was fearful of
exerting her rights.

> The fight over property and child support could have gotten bad. I had Xeroxed
> all the business records to show how much money he made. We were making
> $60,000 as I told you, but my husband, for tax purposes, was saying that he made
> $17,000. I Xeroxed everything because I didn't want my ex-husband to claim that
> he was only making $17,000 and then have child support based on that.

I didn't want him to know at first that I had done that. I told the lawyer not to let them know I had done that unless it was necessary. I knew it would make my ex-husband angry. We did have to tell them and he was angry. . . . Through all of this time he made threats and he destroyed property. [33-year-old white middle-class woman, married seven years, two children]

Some women reported that their ex-husbands had gone to another state and were impossible to locate. The following woman reported that her ex-husband did not appear at a hearing at Family Court. She got word that he had moved to North Carolina. Even his attorney did not know where he was. Once a year she goes to Family Court to provide an update on the situation.

The court said that if he got a job they could pick him up through IRS. But he'll never pay taxes. When he had his maintenance business, he only filed once. He won't pay taxes both because he doesn't want to and also to avoid paying child support. I feel like I lost a lot of time going to court. [42-year-old black secretary, married sixteen years, separated three years before divorce, two children]

In some cases the court makes an effort to find these men, in other cases not.

Twenty-one percent of all the mothers in this sample received only partial amounts of their child-support awards. These women said that their ex-husbands were behind in their payments, or "in arrears" in average amounts ranging from several hundred to several thousand dollars. A working-class woman stated:

He doesn't pay regularly. I don't expect it. I look at it as a gift. . . . Sometimes he'll send $20 or $30 for a few weeks in a row and then he won't send anything for three months.

He won't pay if he doesn't want to. My husband works through the union—he's a roofer—so he can just go down to the union hall and work for a few days for someone else. He can work under another name if he wants. They can't attach his wages. [36-year-old white working-class woman, married thirteen years, two children]

Another woman, who said that her ex-husband was $400 behind in his child-support payments, stated, "The terrible thing is that he is seen as good because of that. My friends say, 'he's only $400 behind, that's good.'" She claims that her ex-husband works under the table for additional income. She believed that the only reason he negotiated a child-support agreement at all is because he was afraid that he could be investigated by the Internal Revenue Service.

Some fathers in Arendell's sample reported various strategies of evasion which corroborate the stories of these women. Several remained unemployed or underemployed in order to avoid paying child support. Some reported working in the underground economy to avoid payments. They shared a view that child support was "their" money. Refusing to pay it was resisting unjust authority.[23]

Fortunately, some states have developed measures to reduce fathers' ability to evade paying child support, such as requiring employers to report all new hires or rehires. Some states also include a new-hire report as part of the W–4 reporting system that employers already use for collecting tax-related information. Other states have developed child-support registries to collect abstracts of support orders and financial data about parents. Employers send support payments to the central registry with a list of the parents from whom the support was withheld, and the registry credits the property account and disburses payments.[24]

As noted, some women in this sample reported that they received no child support because they were unable to locate their ex-husbands, who have gone to another state. In interstate child-support cases nationwide, where the father lives out of state, women also receive little child support. Despite the fact that interstate cases comprise 30 percent of the total number of child support cases, only $1 out of every $10 collected in child support is from an interstate case. Locating a parent who lives in another state requires that two or more states have sophisticated computerized "locating" systems. The legal issues regarding which court or agency has jurisdiction to enter an order are complex, and the provisions of benefits such as medical expenses are problematic when the employer is in a different state from the mother. Typically in interstate cases, women get less of everything.[25]

Finally, women reported that enforcing their child-support orders was difficult because going to Family Court was frustrating and time consuming. Many complained they could not get through to the court by phone or find someone helpful to talk with. The following woman stated:

> Family Court is awful. You just can't get anywhere with them. You call on the phone and you hang there till they answer—often fifteen minutes or more. Nobody treats you nice. [33-year-old white woman, an emergency room technician, married two years, one child]

Others voiced similar complaints. This woman also did not like having to be with her husband again.

> I hate Family Court. You're treated horribly. The whole environment is bad. They send you to all different floors and people tell you that's not where you are supposed to be. Also, it gives my ex-husband a chance to follow me again. Every time we do this my ex-husband freaks out. . . . I hate going to court also because I have to take so much time off from work. [38-year-old black middle-class mother of one, married nine years, separated three years before divorce]

The introduction of income withholding will reduce the time women spend in court. Equally important are initiatives to computerize child-support systems. While until recently child-support systems had not been computerized, beginning in 1980 the federal government offered to pay 90 percent of the costs for states to develop modern computerized record systems for their child-support enforcement systems. Unfortunately it has taken states a long time to computerize. Until recently, administrative and judicial branches of government and state and local government agencies failed to cooperate with each other to institute new procedures. Federal legislation requires all states to have statewide computer systems by October 1995 and the U.S. Commission on Interstate Child Support hopes to build these different state systems into an integrated national system. Most states have computerized their systems. According to a General Accounting Office report, however, many of the state systems are seriously flawed and will not be functioning in 1995, nor will the computer systems of one state be able to interface with those of another.[26]

Wage withholding, computerization, and employer reporting systems will markedly improve the child-support system. Some men, however, will continue to go to great lengths to avoid paying child support. Arendell claims that many fathers view paying child support as having to give away "their" money. As noted, some fathers in her sample did not pay child support in order to exert their power. Angered by their loss of authority, and by the ability of the court to order them to pay child support, they refused as a symbolic act of resistance.[27]

In this study, some women said their ex-husbands believed that child support payments would be used by their ex-wives for their own benefit, rather than for the children. As a 28-year-old medical secretary with one child said, "Do you want to hear his excuse for not paying any child support? He says he doesn't want to pay for my luxuries!" Another woman said, "When they give money, they think they're supporting you. They think you're getting the money, the person they can't stand." The following woman made a related point about how men lose touch with the costs of raising children.

> Men's lives change. They date. They get into other things. They don't realize how expensive it is to raise children. They think, "I'm giving this $45. That should be enough." [31-year-old white secretary, married seven years with two children]

Feeling Fearful and Avoiding Conflict

Women also report that they are fearful of their ex-husbands during negotiations for child support and that this affects their ability to obtain adequate child support. The question of whether women fear violence and conflict during their negotiations for resources is a very important one for them and for debates about divorce and custody policy. As will be discussed here and in the next chapter, many commentators warn of the dangers for women of "custody blackmail," a term used to describe a father's threat to sue for custody even when he doesn't want it, to force a mother to bargain away her rights to spousal and child support. These commentators believe that custody blackmail has become more prevalent since courts began relying on the "best interests of the child standard"—which allows for courts to award custody to either parent, depending on which placement is deemed better for the child—rather than the "maternal presumption." In Lenore Weitzman's study, one-third of the women reported that their husbands threatened to sue for custody as a ploy to make them reduce their demands for financial resources. Other investigators, however, have not found evidence of custody blackmail.[28]

In describing their negotiations for child support, the women in this sample did not use the phrase "custody blackmail," and not many stated explicitly that they bargained away their right to child support in exchange for custody. The few who made a direct connection between fear of losing custody and receipt of child support make comments like:

At the hearing [for child support] I was afraid.... During the previous meeting I had had with my ex-husband he had been very threatening.... I was afraid he might snatch our child. I was there by myself with my child. My ex-husband brought his uncles. [34 year-old black poverty-level woman, married eight years, separated one year after marriage, one child]

I didn't know how custody would go. That was a threat he would use, he and his mom would take custody and he wouldn't pay support and I couldn't survive. [29 year-old white poverty-level woman, unemployed, married eight years, three children]

I gave up getting child support. I was so tired of waiting I would have done anything to get the divorce. It was just not worth going to court and arguing. And I was working. I was very afraid some of this time.... I was afraid he would come and take my son. [31-year-old woman, white working-class, unemployed, married nine years, separated one year after marriage, one child]

This woman, however, went on to describe explicitly trading custody for property.

The lawyer told me I could get a cash settlement but I was afraid I would never get it and this would really drag things out. What I was really concerned about was custody. I traded custody for anything else.

Several other women spoke of trading custody for property.

Figure 5–2. Women's Fear during the Divorce Process.*

Women who reported experiencing fear during:	Percentage (%)
— child-support negotiation	30%
— custody negotiation	38%
— property negotiation	35%

* None of the variables is significantly related to either race or social class. Each of these variables is significantly related to the experience of violence within marriage or after separation.

We sold the house and split the money. I ended up paying a $1000 bill we owed.

Interviewer: Why did you pay that?

He always threatened to take my son during this time.

Interviewer: Were you afraid?

Not in a physical way, just the fear of losing custody. [26-year-old white working-class woman, mail clerk, married five years, one child]

One woman, who said her ex-husband got most of the assets, including the furniture and the cars, stated:

I didn't care. Anything to get rid of him. I was willing to settle for nothing, as long as I got the kids. The main thing I cared about was custody. The rest I didn't care about. I knew I could replace anything. I told my ex-husband, "I'm not going to fight over furniture. The only thing I'll fight over is the kids." [42-year-old black secretary, married sixteen years, separated three years before the divorce, two children]

While most women did not speak explicitly of trading child support for custody, 30 percent of all women in the sample stated that they were fearful during their negotiations for child support, with few race or class differences among them (Figure 5–2). There is overlap between those who reported being fearful while negotiating for child support and those who reported being fearful during negotiations for custody and for property. Of those fearful during the latter, 74 percent were also fearful during negotiations for custody, 62 percent, during the negotiations for property.

Figure 5-3. Women's Fear during Child-support Negotiations as Related to Violence Experienced within Marriage.*

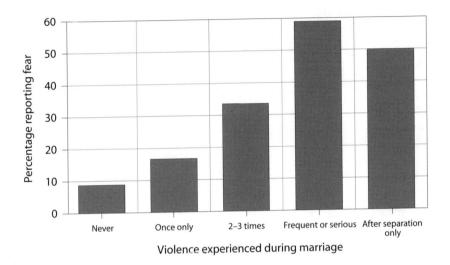

* Overall chi-square is highly significant. Fear is also highly related to whether a woman has ever experienced violence in marriage (41% reported fear) and to whether she experienced violence more than once (51% reported fear).

These women's fears are strongly related to their experience of violence during marriage. As indicated in Figure 5–3, there is a statistically significant relationship between women's fear during the negotiations for child support and their experience of violence during marriage and separation. Figure 5–3 demonstrates how women's fears during child-support negotiations are related to the frequency with which they experienced violence during marriage. The more serious or frequent the violence these women experienced, the more fearful they were during negotiations for child support.

Some women are also fearful because of their experience of violence during the separation. As described in chapter 3, increasing numbers of researchers are concerned about high levels of violence during separation, or "separation assault." Unfortunately, from the data gathered for this study, it is not possible to determine exactly how many women experienced violence, or threats of violence, during the separation, beyond the 4% of women who reported violence during the separation only. As noted in chapter 3, however, a total of seventeen women in this sample indicated that they had experienced violence during the separation. Six additional women reported an immediate threat of violence dur-

Figure 5-4. Current Receipt of Child-Support Payments and Its Relation to Women's Fear during Child Support and Custody Negotiations.*

	Full child support	Partial or irregular	No child support
Women who reported fear during child-support negotiations (n=29)	34%	21%	45%
Women who did not report fear during child-support negotiations (n=67)	60%	21%	19%

* Overall chi-square is statistically significant. Relation between fear and receiving no child support is most prominent.

---

ing the separation. The six women who reported an immediate threat of violence reported that their husbands forcibly entered their houses by breaking down the door and then destroyed property. One husband pointed a gun at his wife, and one threatened violence in the courtroom during negotiations for child support. The judge ordered him handcuffed and removed. The other women were pushed, including being pushed down the stairs, hit, and beaten. Three women had a police restraining order during the separation, two had the police at their home, and two called the police to report their husbands' threatening behavior. Similarly, in Arendell's sample, 40 percent of the men "described incidents in which they had threatened or resorted to acts of violence against the former wife since the end of their marriages." Arendell also reports that almost a quarter of the men in her study had followed their former wives during the months after the separation, in order to "gain information," or "spy," as some men termed it.[29]

There are strong indications that fear caused some of these women to reduce their demands for child support. There is a statistically significant relationship between feeling fearful during negotiations for child support and receipt of child support (Figure 5–4). Only 34 percent of the women who reported being fearful received regular child support, in contrast to 60 percent of those who did not report fear during negotiations for child support.

Some women who received no child support reported that their fear influenced their ability to negotiate for it. One 33-year-old white working-class woman said, "I was fearful he would become verbally or physically violent." A 24-year-old woman with two children on AFDC initially spoke of just wanting to "get away from her husband." But on further questioning, she said that she was fearful of him.

> I really wish now that I had gotten money for child support. I feel like I just threw it away. Then I was trying to get away from him. I just wanted to get away and to get divorced.
>
> Interviewer: What do you mean?
>
> I was afraid. I felt that if I had pushed him for things, he would have beat me up. I also figured he never would pay.

A 38-year-old black middle-class woman with one child reported that her ex-husband had been harassing her by following her to work, showing up unannounced at her home, and driving around her parents' home, and that one time he tried to take their son from daycare. She is ready to give up on trying to get child support.

> I have told my ex-husband that if he would stop harassing me I would stop taking him back for child support.
>
> Interviewer: You actually told him that? You would actually give up child support?
>
> Definitely. That amount of money is not worth the harassment at all. I find the money very useful. It helps pay the bills. But nothing is worth the harassment. I get terrible headaches. Terrible ones. I get very tense.

Another woman said:

> [During negotiations for child support . . .] he was going to kill me, take the house away from me, blow the house up, have me put into jail, you name it . . . I was fearful for all of us, my family, my friends. I didn't know what I was up against . . . He hit me and one time he hit my [four-year-old] son. [29-year-old white poverty-level woman, unemployed, married eight years, three children]

Further, while some women who were fearful gave up trying to get child support, others reported receiving a lower child-support award than they wanted. They were afraid that if they demanded more child support their ex-husbands would retaliate against them.

We came up with a figure for child support in Family Court. He made an offer, we did, he did, and we went down. I feel like I've been compromising all along. It sounded like a good figure 'cause it would pay the rent. I felt very rushed. I felt that I was not in control of my life being decided in court.

I was fearful the whole time. He was always threatening. By this time I had been to abuse court. He was under orders not to come near the house, the kids or me. The teachers were notified.... I was terrified he would take the kids. [44-year-old working-class woman, secretary, married twenty-eight years, separated three years before the divorce, three children]

Several women who were trying to obtain increases in their child-support awards at a later time, when their expenses for their children had increased, also mentioned their fear of violence. Two women were afraid for their children.

Someone at court told me I should take him back to court and get more. I said I was afraid to because I don't want him to hurt my daughter. He threatened to kidnap her and hide out in the woods upstate and I would never see her. After we came out of court he also said he was going to kill me. He ran at me and my lawyer stopped him.

The woman in court said, "Honey, you should take him back to court." I said I was afraid to 'cause I don't want him to hurt my daughter. [26-year-old, white working-class, part-time retail clerk, married three years, one child]

One woman was afraid for her life. She wanted to go to court for more child support, and because her income was so much lower than that of her husband, a policeman, she thought she could get more.

I could still take my ex-husband back to court, but I don't want to make any waves. I'm still afraid of him. I wouldn't put it past him to have me finished off. I definitely wouldn't put it past him. [41-year-old white working-class woman, married twenty-one years, two children]

This woman's fears had been confirmed by a counselor who had called her after a session with her husband and told her he felt she could be in danger and that her husband was capable of seriously harming her. Like this woman, other women's fears are grounded in their experiences of violence.

In addition to compromising on child support due to fear, some women reported that they compromised on child support in order to avoid conflicts with their ex-husbands. They were afraid that if they requested more child support their ex-husbands would be angry and that conflict over child support would threaten future family harmony. As one 37-year-old white middle-class woman said:

Part of the reason I just accepted the offer [the total financial award including child support] was because it seemed reasonable. But part of it was that I felt a sense of powerlessness. I didn't have a lot of resources. I was afraid to challenge what my ex-husband was proposing. I didn't want a long, drawn-out battle. It would be painful for everybody in our families and the end result would be the same or worse.

Another thing is that I will be communicating with my ex-husband about my daughter for the rest of my life. Once you have children your ex-husband is in there the rest of your life. We have a decent working relationship now. It's not worth it to jeopardize that. If you're angry about things, that spills over onto the child and working things out with the child. It has to. I've seen that. If you have a lot of anger it will spill over to the money and everything.

Like this woman, a number of women stressed that their actions were constrained by their concerns over future negotiations with their ex-husbands over many issues in their children's lives, not just child support. The following woman, a white 27-year-old waitress with two children, was dissatisfied with the amount of child support she received and talked about all the extra expenses which her husband did not realize she had to pay. She would not go back to court to get more money, however, because she did not want to disrupt the family.

I have a lot of expenses that my ex-husband doesn't realize I have. Every time I go in the store the kids want something. And there's always birthday parties and all kinds of things. Also I have a lot of expenses for medical bills. The kids' ears have been bad. I make sure and tell my ex-husband that I've paid this and that medical bill. He says, "Oh, that's what my money goes for." That's why I tell him—so he realizes that the money is really needed for the kids.

But I would not ask my ex-husband for more money. Right now we're getting along. We can talk about things about the children without fighting. But if I went for more money it would just cause trouble.

Another woman, a 41-year-old working-class Hispanic woman with one child who worked in a clothing store said:

I also didn't want to create bad vibes between him and me and between my daughter and him. I didn't want to create tension. I knew I wouldn't get anything. He would say he didn't have the money.

Finally, several women mentioned that their ex-husbands do not want to be pressured to pay child support, or that their ex-husband "does not want to be told what to do," and this sometimes made them fearful.

The lawyer wanted me to ask for child support. But I thought it would cause problems if I pushed, and my ex-husband said he would pay child support. My ex-husband doesn't like to be told to do something by the law. He said he wanted to give money for his son because he wanted to do it. . . . Also, my ex-husband is the kind of guy where if you keep bugging him, he's less likely to do something, he'll put it off even more. [35-year-old, white working-class clerical worker, married sixteen years, one child]

Some women also stated that they did not want to be too "pushy" at the time of the divorce. These women blamed the fact that they did not push harder for child support on their ignorance of negotiating skills. Unlike men, women have typically not been socialized to bargain for their own interests.

It was an amicable divorce. Now I realize I could have pushed a little harder—twenty-twenty hindsight. It wasn't the lawyer. I feel I could have done more myself. I feel women are intimidated and I could have investigated. We women haven't dealt with the legal things, with finances, and with lawyers and we don't know how far to push. [51-year-old white middle-class bookkeeper with a college education, married twenty-seven years, two children]

One woman reported that her lawyer counseled her to demand more from her ex-husband but that she was trying to be "nice," which she later regretted.

I definitely would do things differently if I were doing them over. I wouldn't be so agreeable. I wanted the pain to stop, to get on with life. That was my goal. Also, I was trying to be nice. I was raised to be nice, to be polite, to sit in the corner. [37-year-old white poverty-level woman, a store clerk, married thirteen years, one child]

A second woman disregarded her lawyer's advice in order to be "honest," a decision which she too later regretted.

The first lawyer tried to negotiate a settlement with me. . . . I guess I was not too cooperative. I don't know where you want to put this in your report, but I would suggest that women not be so honest. His advice was to bulk things up 'cause the other side will chew it down. I wanted to say, "This is what we really need." By not playing as the lawyer wanted and being honest, I don't feel it went that well for me. Child support was based on me while I was working full-time and had a 20-hour part-time job. [41 years-old, white working-class legal secretary, married twelve years, three children]

These women's comments reflect Weitzman's view that in negotiating for child support women sometimes empathize with others, and in their concern for feelings and relationships are willing to compromise their own interests.[30] This pattern was not widespread among the women in this sample, but some of these women showed evidence of women's socialization to "think of others." For the most part, however, these women are realistically assessing the costs and benefits of seeking and enforcing child support orders. As we have just seen, some conclude that the costs of pursuing child support are too high. Others find creative ways of getting as much support as they can.

What can be done to help those women who are too fearful to gain their fair share of child support? Wage withholding may be particularly beneficial to women who are fearful by reducing the occasions for conflict between women and their ex-husbands. As one woman said:

> I didn't like it [before I had wage attachment] because I hated asking him for money. I felt like a child. And we would always get in a fight. . . .
>
> Now his wages are attached. . . . I like it so much better. We don't have fights now. If the check is late, I don't get mad at him. And my ex-husband doesn't have any tool to use against me. Also he doesn't really miss the $90. He's used to his paycheck without it. [26-year-old white working-class data processing clerk, married four years, one child]

Unfortunately, however, some women may be at risk of violence when courts begin to withhold their wages. Some Legal Aid lawyers report that when courts have introduced wage withholding, there are fathers who have become angry and held their wives responsible for initiating a child support action. To respond to this problem, we must dramatically increase protection for, and services to, women whose ex-husbands are violent.[31]

In conclusion, these women described a variety of obstacles to obtaining child support, from their lack of experience in bargaining, to their fear of conflict with the men they depended on for valuable resources, to outright fear for their physical safety. These women were fearful of their husbands' anger. Their experiences suggest that we need to expand our thinking about "custody blackmail" to include not just what women specifically trade for custody, but also the climate of fear within which some women negotiate. It is these fears, which are related to their experiences of violence, which can lead them to drop or reduce their demands for child support.

Ex-husband's Inability to Pay

Finally, some of these women who received no child support reported that their ex-husbands could not afford it. Primarily poverty-level women reported this problem, particularly those on AFDC and minority women, who described their ex-husbands as not employed or not having any money. These men are more vulnerable than others to unemployment and discrimination. As noted earlier, they also typically must pay more child support than other men. Courts set proportionally higher levels of child-support awards for poorer men than for others and some of these men may have children to support through other relationships. In addition, proportionately more poor fathers are sent to prison for failure to pay child support. It is also the case, however, that in this sample, those husbands of AFDC women who were earning an income were making an average of $14,100 (this is similar to national figures, where the average income of AFDC fathers is $13,000 to $21,000). This is still considerably higher than the median income of $7,872, which their former wives receive from AFDC.[32]

According to income figures reported by women in this sample, most of the fathers could pay child support and still live at a higher standard of living than their former wives. As noted, mothers in this sample reported that middle-class fathers had a median income of $52,500 from their employment, while the median income of middle-class mothers from their employment was $21,750; working-class fathers had a median income of $28,000, mothers, $17,000; and poverty-level fathers, $15,500, and mothers, $6,500. Jay Teachman and Kathleen Paasch estimate that fathers nationwide could afford to pay three to four times what they are currently paying in child support and two to three times their current child-support awards.[33]

What child-support policies should we adopt when fathers' incomes are very low? Whose responsibility is it then to ensure that children are able to have an adequate standard of living? Different approaches to calculating the child-support obligation of low-income fathers have been suggested. One is that noncustodial fathers whose children are receiving AFDC should provide 25 percent of their income to support two children or, for those at the lowest end of the scale, $2,000 a year. Garfinkel argues that the percentage of income approach would also help address the problem of fathers with low incomes. If the father is poor or unemployed, under the percentage of income approach he will have a low child-support obligation.[34]

Another way to increase the ability of noncustodial fathers whose children are receiving AFDC to contribute to their children's support is to improve their job prospects. In the 1980s some localities, such as Prince George's County, Maryland, began to offer education and training opportunities to low-income fathers who were unable to meet their child support obligations. The idea of assisting low-income fathers so they in turn can support their children was adopted by Congress in the Family Support Act of 1988. This law authorized several demonstration projects to test approaches to training and employment for fathers of children on AFDC. The problem with this approach is that funds for such training programs are usually limited and unpredictable. Others have suggested different approaches in which, for example, teen parents "pay" their child support by going to school, attending parent classes, and babysitting, rather than with cash.[35]

Other Factors

Two additional factors may contribute to women's failure to receive the child support they are due. The first is that a fairly high percentage of women have no child-support agreement. Thirty percent of women in this sample, and 28 percent of divorced women nationally, have no legal child support agreement at all and receive no child support.[36] It is very unfortunate that such a high percentage of women do not become connected to the child support system. The 17 percent of working-class women and 40 percent of poverty-level women in this sample who had no child-support agreement reported facing the same problems in obtaining child-support agreements as the women just described—namely, evasion, fear, and lack of money. Poverty-level women, in particular, mentioned that their ex-husbands were not working and they did not believe there was any chance of their receiving child support. In some cases, the ex-husbands were drug users. A few other women stated that their ex-husbands were not paying child support because they were in prison. One woman had no agreement because her ex-husband was in prison for the sexual abuse of their daughter. Another woman reported that her ex-husband had just been released from prison and she hoped to begin receiving child support soon. These women also mentioned not being able to afford a lawyer.

One group of advocates for child-support reform believe that some women do not have awards because they are unaware of the child-support system, how it works, and what benefits might be available. They urge that those who work in the child-support system improve its outreach and accessibility by researching why some clients don't use their services. They also advocate that child support agencies develop public awareness campaigns, design simpler, clearer forms which would be available in different languages, increase working hours, and create 800 numbers.[37]

One further factor in the payment of child support that is mentioned in the literature is the charge that fathers fail to pay because mothers obstruct visitation. As will be demonstrated in chapter 6, however, most of these mothers reported that they did not prevent visitation. Many feared legal repercussions if they should do so. Pennsylvania law promotes a strict separation of visitation and child support, which states that a woman must allow visitation whether or not she is receiving child support.[38] So while many men might fail to pay child support, they still would have the right to visit their children, and almost all of these mothers feel compelled to allow visitation.

In conclusion, these women's experiences show that new reforms, particularly wage withholding, will greatly facilitate the payment of child support to divorced women with children; fewer men will be able to evade paying child support and women will be less constrained by fear. These data show, however, that the problem of evasion is far-reaching and cannot be completely overcome by wage withholding. Some fathers will be able to evade the system by disappearing or working under the table. Other mothers will get no child support because they are too afraid to demand it or because their ex-husbands are not working. Finally, women will continue to have less power in their negotiations with their ex-husbands as long as they do not have access to adequate legal services.

A PROPOSAL FOR CHANGE

We must make dramatic changes. First, the whole child-support system must be consolidated, and enforcement mechanisms seriously strengthened. Policy-makers dispute whether this should be done through federalizing the system within the IRS or the Social Security Administration, or strengthening the current state-based system. A strength of the state-based system is that it would build on existing practices and would engender little political controversy. States, however, will demand additional federal financial assistance to accomplish the changes, and federal funds remain scarce. If Congress merely recommends that states change, without mandating such change or providing sufficient resources, many states will continue to have inadequate systems.

Some reformers advocate federalization, which also enjoys some bipartisan congressional support.[39] Under federalization, an interstate registry of child-support orders would be established within the IRS. Child support would be deducted from the obligated parent's paycheck, and the employers would send the payments to the IRS, which would record and distribute the money. The IRS could also introduce a prepayment system for the self-employed, similar to estimated taxes. These reforms would also greatly facilitate collection in interstate cases.

Such efforts to improve the existing system must continue. Data from these women, however, show how lack of legal services, evasion, fear, and lack of income will continue to prevent some women from getting child-support. These limitations suggest that it is very important that income withholding and child-support guidelines not be seen as the solution to the problem of divorced women's economic insecurity. Income withholding is still a private transfer of funds and as such is contingent on the noncustodial parent having a sufficient income and on a certain amount of good will on the part of ex-husbands not to seek to evade the system. Thus, other measures must be taken to increase the independence and security of divorced women with children.

The problems the women in this sample identified demonstrate that we must adopt a child-support assurance system such as exists in some European countries and has been proposed in the United States. Such a system guarantees that if a woman does not receive all of the child support she is owed, the government will make up the difference to her while trying to collect the support from the father. Garfinkel has been a main proponent of such a system. He proposes a child-support assurance system that would not be income tested but would be available to all women without any stigma attached. He argues that an assurance program would reduce poverty and promote security and independence for all single parents, particularly women on welfare, who could become less dependent on AFDC. Garfinkel further argues that a child support assurance system can be cost effective because it can use the administrative structure that has been developed for income withholding.[40]

While the United States traditionally has enacted private solutions to social welfare problems, over the years the government has taken responsibility for some of these issues. As noted earlier, we have enacted social policies to greatly reduce the level of poverty among the elderly. We no longer view it as just the family's obligation to support them, and they have come to rely on the state for social security—Medicare and Medicaid and other social services—and on private pension plans. As Harry Krause points out, the social security system "nationalizes" that part of a person's income that could have been used to support their own parents, to fund the retirement of all.[41] Similarly, we must recognize the support of children as a public debt or investment, not a charity. Children eventually grow up and pay social security taxes on their income, which bring a critical element of security to the older generation. Given the current high divorce rate and the increasing numbers of single-parent families, unless we change our social welfare policy, more and more childrearing will be done in circumstances of poverty. As increasing numbers of children grow up poorer, there will be less retirement income for all.

Chapter 6

MOTHERS NEGOTIATE FOR CUSTODY AND VISITATION

Just as many fathers play a limited financial role in their families after divorce, many of them also withdraw and become socially and emotionally detached from their families. While a small group of fathers become co-parents with their ex-wives and/or have joint physical custody of their children, after divorce many fathers see very little of their children. According to recent figures from the National Survey of Families and Households, roughly 30 percent of divorced fathers did not see their children at all in the previous year, 60 percent saw their children several times or less during the year, and only 25 percent saw their children weekly. The more time passes after a divorce, the more fathers do not see their children.[1]

The public has become increasingly concerned about the failure of many fathers to maintain relationships with their children. Absent fathers often serve as a symbol of the breakup of the family. In response, legislators have devised policies to keep fathers involved with their children. Although, as will be discussed in chapter 7, there is no clear relationship between the frequency of fathers' visits and the well-being of children, it is widely assumed that it is better for the emotional development of children to have an ongoing relationship with both parents after a divorce.[2] Policy-makers also hope that more visitation by fathers will increase the rate of child support payments, since fathers who visit their children are more likely to pay child support than those who do not.

There is controversy, however, over whether fathers should have unconditional access to their children. As will be discussed in the next section, while some scholars and policy makers want to increase the access of fathers to their children, others fear that there are fathers who will use visitation as a way to exert control over mothers. They are concerned to protect mothers from harassment. They advocate custody arrangements which will not generate conflict between fathers and mothers.

Despite the importance of this issue, there is little data about how women feel about visitation, or about how fathers may or may not use visitation as a tool of harassment. In order to shed light on these critical debates, in this chapter I examine the experiences the women in this sample had in negotiating for custody and visitation with their ex-husbands. These women described a range of experiences, from cooperative to acrimonious. I argue that our policies concerning custody and visitation must take into account these different realities that mothers face in negotiating for visitation.

BACKGROUND ON DISPUTES OVER CUSTODY AND VISITATION

Social scientists, legal scholars, policy makers, and activist groups have conflicting views of the rights and obligations of mothers and fathers after divorce. The current standard of awarding custody—the "best interests of the child" standard—leaves open a wide range of interpretation as to what is in fact in the best interest of the child. Those who represent fathers' interests, including fathers' rights groups, have lobbied for more access for fathers to children and to decision-making about children's lives through custody and visitation statutes, particularly through gender-neutral joint custody statutes which legislate either shared physical custody of children or shared legal custody, or both. Shared legal custody is a new legal category developed to give the noncustodial parent, typically the father, the right to participate in decisions about the important issues of his child's life such as education and religious training, even if he does not have physical custody of the child. There is now a widespread presumption that joint legal custody should be awarded at the time of divorce. Over two-thirds of the states currently have some type of joint custody legislation to encourage fathers to participate in parenting after divorce, and some states have joint custody preferences.[3]

Despite this new legislation, fathers' rights groups remain convinced that the legal system is unfairly biased toward mothers and that many fathers are denied adequate access to their children. There are chapters of fathers' rights groups in every state that lobby for policies that will increase fathers' rights in custody and visitation, and many advocate mandatory joint custody. Interestingly, while these groups are angry about what they see as fathers' inadequate access to their children, since the establishment of joint custody statutes, fathers have not increased their participation in childrearing after divorce to any significant degree. Nor have these statutes fulfilled their other claims—that they would increase the number of fathers who pay child support and reduce conflict between mothers and fathers.[4]

Groups representing women's interests have an opposing set of concerns about mothers' and fathers' roles after divorce. There are some who also favor joint custody, to encourage fathers to stay involved in the lives of their children after divorce. These writers claim that joint custody statutes make a powerful symbolic statement that fathers should share parenting after divorce and that they help further the idea of gender-neutral sex roles that will encourage shared parenting. Some feminists, however, in direct opposition to the views of fathers' rights groups, are against any automatic increase in fathers' influence over custody and visitation. They claim that parents can have serious conflicts during and after divorce, and that by automatically granting fathers access to mothers and children, different types of joint custody statutes allow some fathers to harass mothers. Further, they argue that mothers have typically done the child-rearing and therefore should not suddenly, because of a divorce, lose what they have invested so much in.[5]

As noted in the previous chapter, some advocates for women have identified a particular form of harassment they call "custody blackmail," in which fathers can threaten to sue for custody even when they don't want it, in order to bargain for lower spousal and child-support awards. While the great majority of custody cases are not contested, when they are, fathers are more often awarded custody than mothers. Martha Fineman claims that "experts" and professionals have become key players in contested custody cases because the "best interest" standard is vague and indeterminate. She argues that these professionals have adopted a rigid gender-neutral ideology that prevents them from understanding how fathers can use custody as a tool of harassment.[6]

Some scholars are also concerned about whether judges take male violence against women seriously in awarding custody. While many states have recently enacted legislation mandating that judges take domestic violence into account in awarding custody, evidence suggests there is only sporadic enforcement of these laws and that judges have widely differing views of whether domestic violence is a serious problem at all. Some judges dismiss evidence of domestic violence in custody decisions even if there is a statutory requirement that they take it into account. Some commentators argue that when domestic violence is ignored, not only are women at risk, but the damage done to children by this violence is also ignored.[7]

Finally, Karen Czapanskiy argues that while joint custody statutes give fathers new rights and powers, they require no new duties or responsibilities. These statutes do not require fathers to participate in the activities that are the basis for joint decision-making. Thus, according to Czapanskiy, men can realize the promise of joint custody, while women do not.[8] For the women in this sample, their next most important concern, after their financial situation, was how to manage as single parents. While, as will be indicated below, these mothers definitely wanted primary physical custody of their children, they also stated that the burdens of single motherhood were overwhelming and they would like more help from fathers.

These different policy positions assume different realities about the post-divorce family. Proponents of joint custody statutes focus on the ability of families to cooperate and the power of the law to influence behavior, while critics of these statutes point to the potential for conflict between husbands and wives after divorce and believe that historically and up to the present, fathers have exercised inappropriate power over mothers and children. In order to develop fair social policies, we need more information about the nature of the post-divorce family to understand what issues and problems face mothers, fathers, and children.

This chapter presents mothers' accounts of their custody and visitation arrangements. I focus on custody and visitation patterns, including women's accounts of how they negotiated for custody and visitation with their ex-husbands, and how much visitation took place between the children and the non-custodial parent, typically the father, after divorce. While these data present only mothers' reports, other researchers have concluded that fathers' and mothers' reports of custody and visitation patterns are consistent.[9] I also examine factors associated with different levels of visitation by fathers, in order to understand why more fathers don't stay involved with their children.

Second, this chapter reports on mothers' accounts of conflicts between themselves and fathers over custody and visitation. Mothers described conflicts that occurred at the time of the custody award and conflicts that were still ongoing in their negotiations with fathers over visitation. We need to understand the extent and nature of conflicts between parents over custody and visitation. Conflicts endanger custody and visitation arrangements and introduce the possibility of harassment. Further, experts uniformly agree that parental conflicts are harmful to children.[10]

CUSTODY

This section presents the women's accounts of how they negotiated for custody of their children with their ex-husbands, including their reports of custody patterns and their accounts of issues and conflicts that arose during the negotiations for custody. Nearly all of the women (95 percent) in this sample had sole physical custody of their children; fathers had either partial or total physical custody of their children in the remaining 5 percent (6 cases). A full 34 percent of women in this sample did not have a legal agreement for custody.[11]

Why So Many Women Have Custody

The reason the women most often gave for why they were the ones to gain physical custody of their children was that both they and their husbands believed that it was "natural" that mothers, not fathers, be the primary caretakers of children. This belief was widespread among these mothers and reflects the traditional division of labor in North American families and the intense emotional bonds mothers typically feel for their children as a result of their primary caretaking work.

> The custody agreement is fine. It's fair. My ex-husband realized that a child should be with its mother. I mean that's just the way it is. It was assumed between us and we both agreed. [33-year-old white secretary, married for twelve years, with one child]

> I have custody because aren't the mothers supposed to get them? That's what I assumed. He never said he wanted them. [30-year-old white working-class office worker, married for fifteen years, with one child]

Even a couple with joint legal custody assumed it would be the mother who would have primary physical custody of the children.

> I knew the children would be with me, but I had it worded "joint custody" to be fair to the father. I told him I worded it that way. We discussed it. We're still on friendly terms. I said I assumed the children would be with me. I asked him if he had anything else in mind. He said he thought it was better that way. [37-year-old, white middle-class woman, two children]

Some women, such as this 34-year-old secretary, mentioned that they and their husbands felt that it was mothers who knew how to take care of children.

> It was assumed by my husband and me that I would get the child. He agreed with me that it's better for the mother to have the child. It's the mother who is there to do the homework, who's there in the middle of the night when the child gets sick, who's there for all the important things.

They added that their ex-husbands did not know how to take care of the children.

My ex-husband doesn't know what to do with the kids. He can't discipline them.... He just yells. He is learning a little. I was the one who had the time to raise the kids. [32-year-old poverty level, white convenience store worker, no high school education, married for eight years with three children]

Finally, many women stated that their ex-husbands had no interest in custody whatsoever. They said things like, "My husband didn't want to be bothered"; "He doesn't want children. There was no discussion"; or "I have custody because I guess he doesn't care. I can't even get him to take them out once in a while." One woman reported that she wished she could have shared custody, but her ex-husband didn't want the responsibility.

The reason I got custody was because although my husband wanted a relationship with his daughter, he really didn't want the responsibility. I would have shared custody. I was really hoping for joint custody, but he didn't want it. I talked to the therapist about it and then my husband and I worked it out. I don't feel this arrangement is fair for me. I like primary custody but it means primary responsibility. But it's best for my daughter and that's what counts. [34-year-old black middle-class woman, married for eight years with one child]

Several women talked about how their ex-husbands' physical abuse and drug and alcohol use made sharing custody a moot issue.

[I have custody because] I feel I'm a more fit parent than he was. He was a drug abuser and an abusive husband. Through the shelter I got a protection order. To do that you have to detail the abuse. This was brought to the judge's attention [and affected his decision about custody]. [24-year-old white factory worker, with three children]

There is no agreement. I just took my kids and left. He didn't care whether they ate or slept. All he was interested in was his beer and his women. I don't think he could handle the responsibility. He was always drunk. So, the best thing was to take my kids. [43-year-old black poverty-level woman, unemployed, married for twenty-two years, with three children]

While all women wanted physical custody of their children, a number of women mentioned that the custody arrangements did not seem fair because the fathers did not take responsibility for any of the parenting work.

I don't feel the custody arrangements now are fair. It's all one-sided. I have to rearrange my schedule completely for my childcare and he doesn't at all. I certainly want my daughter to stay with me. But I would like him to participate more. I want my daughter to have a man in her life. She's crazy about her Dad. [33-year-old black data transcriber, married for seven years with one child]

He lives a block away and the children don't feel they can go there except on Sundays. His parents don't care. They don't care that he's not paying child support either. . . . I don't feel it is fair I have them 99 percent of the time. He's not into their life. [33-year-old white woman living at the poverty-level, married for fourteen years with two children]

In the six cases in which fathers did have some joint physical custody arrangement, in two cases mothers and fathers had a cooperative arrangement for joint custody, in two cases mothers were ambivalent about joint custody, and in two cases fathers obtained custody against the mothers' wishes. The two middle-class women who had joint physical custody at the time of the interview felt it was working, despite the differences in lifestyle between the two households.

We have joint custody. It worked out that way because I felt the father has a right to be involved. . . . I like the arrangement because it gives my daughter time with her father and the burden is not all on me. One thing I don't like is that I don't always agree with my ex-husband's methods of childrearing. [34-year-old black middle-class manager, married for eleven years, with one child]

My ex-husband wanted to share custody. I didn't fight it at all. My ex-husband is a great father. There was no reason to fight for custody. Also, I felt that if I fought for custody that my daughter would eventually find that out and that it would make her angry. . . . I certainly could have gotten custody. . . . I would like to have my daughter more but that's the way it is. . . . We have different life styles though and that can be hard. [47-year-old white middle-class professional woman, married for thirteen years, with one child]

In two cases the father had custody of some of the children: in one case the father had custody of most of the children while in the other the father had custody half-time. In each case this was much more custody and visitation than stipulated in the legal agreements. The mothers in these two cases spoke as if they had to "give in" to their ex-husbands' wishes on custody. Both women reported that they were the ones who left their ex-husbands, who got angry at them for leaving. In two other cases fathers obtained custody against the mothers' wishes, one by suing for custody and one through a kidnapping. These will be described in the next section on conflicts over custody.

Women without Custody Agreements

Thirty-four percent of the women in this sample have no legal agreement for custody of their children. This means that a father is legally permitted to come and take the children to live with him, as they are still his children also. As indi-

Figure 6-1. Divorced Women with Physical Custody of Their Children but without Legal Custody.

	Percentage of Women without Legal Custody*
Overall	34
By Class	
Middle class	12
Working class	24
Poverty level	60
By Race	
White	19
Black	57

* Chi-squares by race and class are both highly significant. Difference by race is still highly significant after controlling for social class.

---

cated in Figure 6–1, there are statistically significant differences by class and race among these women. Disproportionate numbers of poverty-level women and black women do not have legal agreements for custody.

Women tended not to have legal custody for several key reasons. Most of them said that it did not seem necessary to get a legal agreement, because their ex-husbands didn't want custody of the children. They said things like, "We never discussed custody after he left. He came on Sundays to see the children. If I needed anything for them I could call him. There was no hostility." "There's no agreement about custody. It's based on nature. My ex-husband has no permanent residence and he goes from one woman to another." "My ex-husband doesn't want the responsibility." Some women implied that they were trying to save money and if they could arrange custody themselves, that was better. In a minority of cases, however, women had recently become fearful about not having legal custody of their children and were now trying to get it. As one woman said:

> I have custody, but it's not legal. I'm going to go get it made legal. I know they can take your kids. . . . I was afraid my ex-husband would try to take my son. One time he didn't return him. He was just going to keep him. I went down there and banged on the door and got him back. [28-year-old black woman living at the poverty-level, married six years, one child]

Figure 6–2. Divorced Women's Reports of Fear during Custody
　　　　　Negotiations and Their Experience of Violence
　　　　　within Marriage.*

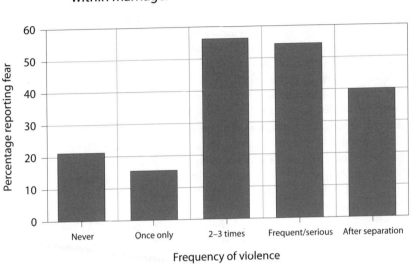

* Overall chi-square is highly significant (p=.004).

Another reason that fewer poverty-level women had legal custody agreements may certainly be that, as described in the previous chapter, compared
with women of other classes, fewer poverty-level women had lawyers. Further,
over half of the poverty-level women who had lawyers got them through Legal
Aid, which provides legal counsel for divorces but not for custody agreements.
Thus some poverty-level women may not have been informed about the desirability of securing custody agreements, and some may not have been able to
afford the legal fees to do so. In fact, a few of the poverty-level women in this
sample said they thought that getting a divorce meant that they automatically
gained legal custody of their children.

Fears and Conflicts over Custody Agreements

In this section I describe how some women had conflicts working out custody
agreements with their ex-husbands. Many women reported conflicts over custody. What I focus on in this section is the fear these women experienced as a

result of their conflicts, particularly fear that their husbands would become violent or would take or kidnap their children. All women in the sample were asked, "Were you ever fearful for yourself or your children during the negotiations for custody?" and 38 percent replied, "yes." There were almost no differences by race or class in their responses. These women's fears were related to their experiences of violence in their marriage. As indicated in Figure 6–2, there was a statistically significant relationship between these women's fears and their experience of violence in the marriage and during the separation. These women's fears during their negotiations for custody had serious consequences. As indicated in the last chapter, there was a statistically significant relationship between fear of losing custody and receipt of child support, indicating that because some women feared that they could lose custody during negotiations for child support, they reduced their demands for resources. Other researchers have also reported serious parental conflict over custody.[12]

Women expressed two types of fear during custody negotiations. Half of them spoke of having had one-time conflicts with their ex-husbands, which made them fear additional events of violence. Those who described one incident that made them fearful stated that fathers "threatened" to take the children. Women described these cases as one-time events, although it is certainly possible that their fear may persist and affect their behavior, as some of the quotations suggest. Some women described men as making threats when they were angry.

> I knew I wanted to file for custody when my ex-husband and I were having a fight and he threatened to take her. I knew he wouldn't but he knew how to scare me. [28-year-old white middle-class woman, married for six years with one child]

Some made threats to take the children and keep custody of them, sometimes to take them from school.

> He used to tell them that he would come and get them. At one point I had to go to the school and pick them up because he threatened to get them and lock me up. [37-year-old white working-class secretary, married for fourteen years with two children]

In two cases fathers made attempts to take the children but they did not follow through. One of these women, who left her marriage because of violence, stated:

> I got custody because he was abusive and because he skipped town. He didn't want the kids anyway. I would have really fought for my kids. He knew that was

the one thing I would really fight for. He threatened to take them. He tried to pick them up at school once. But I had told them not to let anyone take them. [42-year-old black working-class secretary, two children]

Sometimes the men made threats when they wanted specific things.

I got custody because my ex-husband doesn't want the responsibility. At one point my ex-husband threatened me by saying, "if you don't give me such-and-such I'll take the children." I had my lawyer call him and tell him if he didn't stop it he'd have him sent to jail. I wasn't truly afraid because I knew he just didn't want the responsibility. [41-year-old white working-class woman, married for twenty-one years, with two children]

The second group of women—the other half of those who stated that they were fearful during negotiations for custody—described either several incidents of conflict or one very serious incident, such as a kidnapping or a serious act of violence. Many of these women reported that the fathers had been violent during the marriage or were engaged in "hard-living" behavior—they used drugs, they were never around, they never worked. These women spoke of both verbal and physical conflict in the past over the determination of custody.

He used to tell me I was cracking up. It was a verbal war. He kept threatening to get custody. I had the police at the house quite a few times. Last October, the boys saw him hit my oldest daughter. I punched him. [37-year-old white middle-class woman, with three children]

He wanted custody. It was a long heated matter. He'd say I was an unfit mother. . . . I said I was going to get my own lawyer, then he would back down. He threatened to take my son off me. Sometimes I thought he would take him and not bring him back. [26-year-old white working-class mail clerk, one child]

One woman also spoke of physical conflict with her ex-husband when he tried to take the children.

I got custody. He had no choice. There was no way he could take care of them, because he was not working and he was doing drugs. . . . . . My ex agreed. But afterwards he tried to take them. He came to my house and tried to carry them out. We beat him up, my girlfriend and I. . . . I was afraid of physical harm. There were a lot of incidents. A couple when he tried to take them or harm me. [28-year-old white middle-class woman with two children]

Some women pointed to hard-living as an important factor in these conflicts.

I was afraid of him because he was taking drugs, really bad and he was abusive of me. That's why I left; my daughter was 11 months old and I was afraid he would hurt her. He didn't see the kids for a year. It wasn't because I was trying to be nasty but I was afraid. I wanted him to get help. [25-year-old white woman with no high school education, two children]

I got custody 'cause he's a drunk and a drug addict. When we were married, one of the things he did was not show up from Friday to Monday. That came out in court. He was going to kill me. He said that after we came out of court. He ran at me and my lawyer stopped him and my lawyer is smaller than me. He also threatened to kidnap her and hide out in the woods upstate and I'd never see her. [26-year-old white retail clerk, married for three years, with one child]

At the time of negotiating for custody, two women had protection orders—court orders mandating that their ex-husbands stay away from them and their homes because of the ex-husbands' physical abuse. A 49-year-old white mother of three had a protection order for a year. According to her, "He was not allowed on the premises or in the house. A police car went around here twice a day." A white working-class woman with two children reported that her ex-husband had been very violent: he threatened to kill the whole family.

I was very frightened during this time. One day he called from work and said, "Since we can't work this out I think it would be better if I killed you and the kids and myself." I got the kids out of the house for the night.

One quarter of the women who were fearful were afraid their ex-husbands could still take the children. Several did not have legal custody, which made them even more fearful.

In two cases, women lost legal custody of some of their children against their wishes. In one case, when the father petitioned for custody, the judge awarded one child to each parent. According to this woman, the judge asked the children where they wanted to live. The oldest son said he wanted to live in the house he had been living in, and the judge awarded custody to the father, who was living in this house at the time, although the mother was awarded the house shortly after the custody agreement was made. The mother thought the father sought custody in retaliation for her leaving. She described the experience as heartbreaking for her. She visited her son as much as possible while he lived with his father. She thought it was her ex-husband's mother who did most of the caretaking of the boy. In a second case, a woman told of a situation which had been devastating for her. According to this woman, she and her ex-husband had been estranged for some months. She did not have legal custody of her children and had decided to file for it when her ex-husband returned and told her he was sure they could become reconciled. She believed him. He took the children to his parents' home in another legal jurisdiction and never brought them back. This woman had no money to hire a lawyer to fight her ex-husband and his family for custody. She tried to secure help through Legal Aid but was told they could not handle such a case. Initially she began taking illegal drugs to handle her despair. After getting herself off drugs she now manages with the help of a psychiatrist who prescribes anti-depressant drugs for her.

Two other women reported that their ex-husbands kidnapped the children. In one case the father, who had been a drug user, took his son for two weeks without telling the mother and then returned the child himself. This woman, a black middle-class woman with one child, said:

> I got custody in September. I went to get it after he took my son in August. He took him for two weeks. I had no idea where he was. Boy, that sure ruins your work performance. He took him out of state.
>
> I didn't have trouble getting custody. It was decided with the judge there and the two attorneys. My ex-husband said he was the better parent. He was trying to get full custody. I produced a copy of the search warrants on him and bail bond. My lawyer gave a good speech. I also told my ex-husband that I would name names to prove that I was the better parent. That made him back down. But I was afraid that he would take my son and never bring him back.

In another case the father took the child out of state. The mother, a white woman living at the poverty level, had left the father after their baby was born because he had never held down a job and was gone a lot. After her divorce this woman began seriously dating a man whom she subsequently married. Her ex-husband came to visit this woman one day when her boyfriend was there and became very upset. The ex-husband grabbed the child and sped away in his car. The missing child was identified five weeks later by someone several hundred miles away in another state who saw a TV announcement about the kidnapping. This woman now has legal custody.

Research indicates that these women's fears have a strong basis in reality. In her study of seventy-five divorced fathers, Terry Arendell found that more than three-quarters of the fathers threatened a custody challenge after the divorce, with nearly a third issuing a formal threat through an attorney. According to Arendell, fathers undertook these custody challenges to harass their former wives, in particular to "balance out the power of their former wives by prohibiting maternal custody, which was the prime example of men's losses and women's disproportionate authority in divorce." A national study estimates that over 350,000 noncustodial fathers or father figures have taken a child in violation of a custody agreement or failed to return a child at the end of a legal visit

Figure 6–3. Frequency of Fathers' Visitation.*

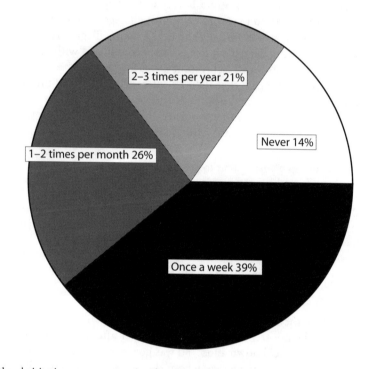

* Fathers' visitation rates are not significant by either race or class.

and kept the child for at least one night. As noted in the previous chapter, some fathers back up their threats with actual violence during the separation, what Martha Mahoney calls "separation assault."[13]

In conclusion, these women had two entirely different sets of experiences negotiating for custody with their ex-husbands. The majority had traditional parenting arrangements, with mothers doing much of the childcare. These women did not experience much conflict. These parenting arrangements are deeply gendered. The mothers said that both they and the fathers believed that maternal custody of the children is the "natural" arrangement, although many of these women would like more help from fathers in parenting their children. In almost a third of cases, however, fathers and mothers had conflicts over custody. In half of these cases the conflicts were serious: in some cases they were

Figure 6-4. Divorced Mothers' Experience of Fathers' Visitation.

	Visiting fathers (n=99)	Total sample* (n=106)
Involved Fathering	29%	25%
Detached Fathering	42%	35%
Conflict in Visitation	29%	25%
No Visitation	——	16%

* Excludes those mothers who had joint physical custody or whose ex-husbands were in prison or had died.

still going on. These conflicts made the women fearful and led some of them to reduce their demands for resources.

VISITATION

In this section I discuss women's reports of father's visitation patterns. These data shed light on the circumstances of mother and father roles after divorce and have implications for our policies concerning visitation. How much sharing of parenting can we expect after divorce? Could we change patterns of visitation? What kinds of conflicts over visitation do mothers and fathers report? What role should the law play in regulating parenting after divorce?

As indicated in Figure 6–3, in this sample 65 percent of mothers reported visitation on a weekly or monthly basis, while 35 percent of mothers reported that visitation took place approximately twice a year or not at all. Although these rates were reported by mothers only, and fathers might give different accounts, other researchers have found that fathers and mothers report similar rates of visitation.[14]

Women who reported that some visitation took place described three different types of experiences: involved, detached, and conflicted (see Figure 6–4). Twenty-nine percent of them reported that the visitation went well, 42 percent wanted more visitation, and 29 percent wanted less. These reports of visitation are similar to those reported by Robert Mnookin and Eleanor Maccoby for their sample of 1,124 families.[15] I will describe these patterns both for women who reported visitation weekly or monthly and for those who reported visitation two to three times a year. I will then conclude this chapter with the reports of women who stated that no visitation takes place.

Positive Relationships between Fathers and Children

As indicated in Figure 6–4, 29 percent of all women who reported some visitation (25 percent of the women in the sample) believed that the visitation went well. Those women who were happy with visitation stated that the father and children like each other and get along, and that they, the mothers, were happy to have these relationships go well.

> My ex-husband and my daughter have a good relationship. They're close. They see each other a couple of times a week. She'll sometimes call and ask her father to take her and her friends to a dance or a game. He likes to do that for her, even if it's not so convenient, to be part of her life. He takes her to his mother's, shopping, to the movies, to his house. If she gets sick he comes over to see her. I'm really lucky that way. We all get along. I am still close to my in-laws. My mother, my mother-in-law, and I are all going to New York together on Saturday. [33-year-old white secretary, married for twelve years, with one child]

> We made the visitation agreement ourselves. He sees them every weekend. He takes them to McDonald's, to the zoo, the park, baseball games. They love each other a lot; he calls them and they call him. He buys them clothing and toys. It's good like this. [23-year-old Hispanic woman living at the poverty level, married for eight years, with two children]

In several cases mothers credited their ex-husband's new wife with improving his relationship with his children.

> He takes his daughter (8 years old) to his place. His wife is very good to her. His wife has improved the relationship between him and my daughter. They have a pretty good relationship now. She feels he cares. [38-year-old white middle class professional woman, with one child]

Several women reported that fathers' relationships with their children were now "better" than they had been before.

> He pays more attention to the children now. I guess before his attention was always fixed on me. I think he should have spent more time with the kids. But he

would come home and go right upstairs and watch TV in our bedroom both before and after dinner. [31-year-old black woman living at the poverty level, three children]

In the following case, the mother thought her ex-husband had become a much better father and credits him for learning how to do this.

My ex-husband has a strong sense of family. He felt bad about the divorce and about our daughter. He knew he hadn't spent much time with her. So good visitation and child support were his ways of making his claim as a good parent.

My ex-husband has really had to learn to parent. In the beginning he had to plan everything the whole weekend. It was parenting on the go. Sometimes he would organize all the children on the block to do arts and crafts. [37-year-old white middle-class woman, with one child]

One woman talked about how father and daughter worked things out. She said her daughter, who is now 15 years old, took the initiative to improve their relationship after seeing a counselor. As a result, she said:

He's doing more things for her now. I knew he would come through. She's an exceptional child. She has a relationship with him now. They had none for a while. She used to want a day with him so badly. Now they go to lunch. They can talk. She's older now. She worked on him. She is his only child. [41-year-old working-class Hispanic woman, one child]

In one case a mother reported that visitation was working well even though the father was a former drug addict.

He has a pretty good relationship with the kids now and he sees them once a week. In the beginning I was afraid of him because he was taking drugs really bad and he was abusive of me. That's why I left. And my daughter was eleven months old and I was afraid he would hurt her. He didn't see the kids for a year. It wasn't because I was trying to be nasty but I was afraid. I wanted him to get help. [25-year-old white poverty-level woman, no high school education, married for three years, with two children]

Some of these women voiced minor complaints. They sometimes found it difficult to accommodate the different childrearing standards in their ex-husbands' households with their own; their children sometimes cried when they went to their father's; and a few thought the fathers could spend still more time with their children. These women, however, were generally pleased. Their descriptions of positive father-child relationships sound like those given by the 9 percent of divorced fathers in Arendell's sample who participate actively in the lives of their children and cooperate with their former wives in arranging visitation.

More Visitation

A second group, 42 percent of those who reported that visitation took place, wanted more visitation and talked about how distanced the fathers were from their children. (This includes 28 percent of those who reported weekly visitation, 41 percent of those who reported monthly visitation, and 67 percent of those who reported visitation two to three times a year.) Those who reported visitation weekly or monthly felt that their ex-husbands were not visiting the children as much as they had agreed to, and they were discontent because they had to take responsibility for making the visitation work. They felt particularly annoyed about this because they were already carrying the overwhelming load of parental responsibilities.

> I had to talk my ex-husband into keeping up with visitation. He does now. I talked him into other things, like taking his son to a baseball game. I told him that my son needs to be around a man, since mostly he's around me, my two daughters, and my mother. I wish he'd take the kids individually and get to know them individually. I think for my son's sake (4 years old) my ex-husband should see him more. . . . He doesn't come to soccer games or anything. He puts in his six hours on Sunday and that's it. [29-year-old white medical secretary, married for sixteen years, with one child]

> He can see her anytime. He sees her about once a month. She goes to see him. He never comes to see her. I wish he'd see her more often and give me a break. [32-year-old black poverty-level, married for fifteen years, with two children]

> He wouldn't even fight to see his son. I had to write it in there [the custody agreement] that he was allowed to see him. . . . He visits his son at his mother's house and takes him to the arcade. He never takes him to his home. He doesn't know anything about his son. It's a very detached relationship, like weak. [29-year-old white working-class woman, works in sales, one child]

> I would like him to have joint physical custody too. They are his daughters and I think they should be sometimes with him. Like weekends. Not just pick them up for two or three hours and drop them off. [34-year-old black woman living at the poverty-level, married for thirteen years, with three children]

> He and his girlfriend and their child live nearby so once in a while the kids call him and say, "Can we come over?" He says yes, but they come back pretty soon. I guess they get over there and he says, "Well, it's not your day. . . ." He cares about the kids but he doesn't realize that he just sees them one day a week. The kids want to be with him, not the TV. He does remember their birthdays. [35-year-old white secretary living at poverty level, three children]

These women were also discontented because they believed that the fathers did not use their time with their children to do meaningful activities.

He can see the children any time. It's in the legal agreement, as long as he gives forty-eight hours notice. He does shift work though so it's hard for him to come and visit. In the first year he would come by about once every three weeks. But he would just stop by. There was no quality time, as they say. . . . Maybe he cares about the children but he puts his own self first. In the last three years he didn't take the kids on vacation except one time. He has four weeks vacation a year.

Interviewer: Why do you think that is?

He was spending time with his girlfriend. And his priority was him. [39-year-old white working-class woman, married for seventeen years, with two children]

Mostly they go to his mother's house. They watch videos. He loves them but he doesn't know what to do with them. His son especially really loves his daddy. My youngest daughter didn't know him before. She was just a baby. My oldest daughter loves him. [32-year-old white poverty-level woman, married eight years, with three children]

I feel he could spend more quality time with her. I said, "You don't realize how you're hurting her." He's remarried and has two step-daughters and my daughter got jealous. I don't see it getting better. [33-year-old black secretary, married for eight years, with one child]

I feel like he should see them more and he should do more things with them. He sees them one day a week. All he ever does is take them to McDonald's and another fast-food place. . . . He does really care about the girls a lot, but he just doesn't know how to show it. [44-year-old white teacher, married for twenty-one years, with two children]

Frank Furstenberg believes that the kind of father detachment these and other mothers refer to results from a process of "drift." He points out that while initially fathers may keep up a regular schedule of visitation, playing the ambiguous role of part-time parent becomes increasingly difficult because the authority of the role involves knowing what one's children are doing on a daily basis, a difficult task for fathers who aren't living with their children. Some then become marginal to their children's lives and begin a process of "drift." Remarriage and a new set of children may complete the process of disconnection. Another factor that contributes to fathers' exit from the family is that many fathers have never had as strong an emotional tie to the children as mothers, who often provide the emotional link between fathers and children. Thus at divorce, fathers, losing that link, can lose connection with their children.

Arendell also argues that some fathers distance themselves from their children in order to avoid the pain they feel at being separated from them.[16]

Other researchers have cited a variety of factors contributing to low father visitation, including nonpayment of child support and a father's remarriage. In this sample, nonpayment of child support was also associated with less visitation, but there was no clear effect of remarriage on visitation. Other factors that have been cited as associated with lower rates of visitation include fathers' lack of time and money, lack of space to entertain children, commuting time to the child's residence, and conflicts with children's schedules. Arendell reports that some fathers curtail visits to their children as a way of getting back at the mother. Unable to control the visitation process, these men "take charge" by refusing to cooperate or compromise with their children's custodial parent. [17]

The mothers in this sample felt very dissatisfied about the consequences of this detachment. First, they believed that their ex-husbands did not appreciate all the work of childrearing which they did, such as helping children with homework. The women, like some researchers, described helping with homework as a kind of "invisible work." [18]

> He sees them every Sunday. That was the agreement. They think he's great. On Sundays when they come home it's Daddy, Daddy, Daddy. It hurts sometimes. I'm the one that's here all the other days of the week. I'm the one that deals with their fighting. And the homework. They said once, "Daddy said we should get good report cards." I think that time I said it out loud, "I don't want to hear it. He has no right to say that. What's he doing to help you with your report card?" [35-year-old poverty-level white secretary, high school education, married for fourteen years, with three children]

Researchers find that divorced fathers do very little of the work of parenting. Jay Teachman reports that "fewer than one father out of 27 regularly assists his children with homework or attends school events. Over three-quarters of divorced fathers have never participated in the schooling of their children. Slightly more fathers (one out of 12) take their children on vacation, while a majority of fathers (three out of five) have purchased gifts." Frank Furstenberg and Andrew Cherlin report similar figures.[19]

Some women spoke of feeling "stuck" with these routine activities, such as this 34-year-old black middle-class woman, with one child.

> The legal agreement is that he can see her several days a week, every other weekend, two vacation weeks a year, and alternate holidays. The days in the week have shrunk to two hours down from five; he never takes her in the summer; and every other month he takes her only one weekend, to suit his convenience.

> He does care, but he takes very little responsibility for her, and no initiative. For example, I send clean clothes with her and they always send back dirty clothes. If she is sick, he won't take her. He won't take her to her music lesson. It's pervasive.

Several women disliked the fact that their children would return home with dirty laundry. While this does not seem like a significant issue, these divorced mothers saw it as symbolic of the difficulties of getting ex-husbands to share childrearing responsibilities. Some women mentioned difficulties over scheduling visitation, for example if a father did not come when expected. Fathers certainly experience difficulties scheduling visitation as well, and if the visitation does not take place, they do not get to see their children. The problem for mothers if fathers don't come when expected is that they get no break from single parenthood.

This extra "work" women feel they are left doing can include "emotion work." The following mother had to work at taking care of her daughter's feelings when she did not want to leave to go to her father's. She did this out of concern for her daughter and also because she felt she must make the relationship between her ex-husband and her daughter work to meet her own needs. She believed that if her ex-husband did not see his daughter he would lose the incentive to continue making financial contributions to the household.

> The one problem I've had is that my five-year-old daughter complains about going to my ex-husband's. She sheds a lot of tears. I've tried to tell her that if she doesn't see him then she won't be able to have a relationship with him. I've really worked at having my children have a good relationship with their father.

Women also mentioned feeling "stuck" with being the disciplinarian, which they felt was the most negative aspect of the mother's role. Said a 26-year-old mother of one, "His Dad's Candyland and I'm the disciplinarian." And a 25-year-old mother of two said, "He's not a disciplinarian. They can do anything they want. I'm the mean one." In one case, a mother reported that the father explicitly rejected the disciplinarian role because, given his limited time with his son, he wanted his encounters to be positive.

> He doesn't want to discipline them. He was complaining about my son's foul language. I said, "You tell him about it" and he said, "Not me, I'm not going to be the bad guy when I only see them five hours a week." [33-year-old white poverty-level woman, married for fifteen years with three children]

Similarly, a few women mentioned that they had become associated with doing boring household chores.

She hates being home on the weekend with me. I have to do the dirty stuff. She associates me with routines. On weekends when she's with him they go out to eat and do things. The weekends I have her I also do errands. I take her shopping with me. She doesn't like to go shopping, she hates it. I do those errands when I have her because I want to have the other weekends for me. [28-year-old middle-class white woman, married for six years, with one child]

Other researchers confirm this type of division of labor. Furstenberg and Cherlin note that even those fathers who are involved with their children behave more like relatives than parents, taking them shopping for toys and clothes, out to dinner, and to the movies, rather than doing routine parent-child activities. [20]

Finally, visitation raises issues for women that require additional emotional work. Some women in this sample still had negative feelings about their ex-husbands as a result of the divorce and wished they did not have to see them anymore, although most accepted this as an inevitable part of a divorce. A few women mentioned having to deal with their own hurt feelings that their children liked their ex-husbands so much.

My older son cares about him a lot. He's his Daddy, he's like a god. The older one really looks forward to seeing his father. The younger one sometimes doesn't want to go. He's attached to my apron strings. At first I took it personally how attached my older son was to his father. I sit there through all his tears with his homework and then Daddy is great. Sometimes when my son is angry at me he'll say, "I'm going to live with my father." [27-year-old white waitress, with two children]

Undoubtedly fathers, who spend so much less time with their children, have to deal with negative feelings about how attached their children are to their ex-wives.

Those women (21 percent) who reported that visitation took place only two to three times a year described even more distance between father and children. Among this group, two-thirds reported that their ex-husbands have no interest in visiting the children. One woman reported that her ex-husband initially saw the children frequently, but has seen them less since his remarriage; another that her ex-husband had never been around during the marriage and had not taken any responsibility for the family. She did not pressure him to see their child more because according to her, he would make promises to come and visit and then would not, and this upset their child. One woman, who reported that her ex-husband had also been very violent during the marriage, stated that her ex-husband never had a relationship with the children while they were married.

He got visitation any time. He does have to call, but he can visit any time. He made sure to get that and yet after all that he never sees them. In one year he has taken the kids out three times, to the movies or to miniature golf. He's called a few times. He didn't show up for my daughter's graduation or her dance recital. She invited him to both. He never really had a relationship with them. [37-year-old white receptionist, married for seventeen years, with one child]

Almost half the women in this category, however, gave "hard-living" reasons for infrequent visitation.

He's still an alcoholic and he's still into drugs. That was the problem in our marriage. The kids only hear from him two or three times a year. His sister calls and reminds him it's one of the kids' birthdays, although one of their birthdays is very hard to forget. He lives very close by too. I don't want him to be forced to come. He needs to come because he wants to. The kids don't really care anymore. He was never really home anyway. [34-year-old white bookkeeper, married for twelve years, with two children]

Most of these women reported that their ex-husbands used drugs. In principle these women wish their ex-husbands saw the children more, but at this point they don't want more visitation until their ex-husbands get off of drugs. Two poverty-level women spoke of their ex-husbands being "in and out of town" and said they did not know how to locate them. Another said her husband spent a lot of time in bars, and one said her ex-husband had always been "irresponsible" during the marriage and was violent. According to her, the father also abused the children. Half of the women who stated that visitations took place two to three times a year reported that their ex-husbands used violence more than three times during the marriage.

Less Visitation

Many researchers believe that conflict with the mother is a major factor in a father's failure to see his children. It is not clear from this research, however, what aspects of custody and visitation mothers and fathers disagree over. Twenty-nine percent of the women in this sample who reported active visitation (11 percent of the women in the sample) wanted less frequent or no father visitation because of conflicts with their ex-husbands. There was a lot of overlap between those who wanted less visitation and those who had serious difficulties negotiating for custody. A large proportion of those who experienced conflicts over visitation—85 percent—were fearful during the negotiations for custody. Wallerstein and Kelly and Ahrons report that almost a third of the families in their studies remained in conflict and hostile toward each other three to five years after the separation.[21]

Why do these women want less or no visitation? What is the nature of their conflicts? First, these women complained that their ex-husbands' visits were as much for the purpose of checking up on them as they were to see the children, and that their ex-husbands attempted to get more visitation in order to harass them.

> He visits the kids once a week, maybe a couple of times. I don't really know, he sees them at school. There is always a string attached, though. He plays with the kids outside the house sometimes, but then he uses that as an excuse to come and harass me. [29-year-old black woman living at the poverty level, married for eight years, with two children]

In the following three cases, women reported their ex-husbands continued to take them to court for more visitation as a way of harassing them.

> He keeps taking me to court for more visitation but then he doesn't use it. We have been to court five times over visitation. I really dislike the way my ex-husband is using visitation as a weapon. This is very disruptive of my life. Because of the harassment I have said that he can't pick up my son at my house. He picks him up at my mother's house or at the mall. But then Saturday mornings I have to get up—I can't sleep late— and take my son to a mall. And then he often doesn't show up. [37-year-old white middle-class woman, married for nine years, with one child]

This woman's ex-husband was a drug user.

> My ex-husband kept dragging me back into court for modified visitation. We saw all kinds of judges. I don't think that it should have gone on so long. I was on the defensive a lot. He charged me with child abuse. At the school they had to examine my son to see if he had been abused. I think my lawyer should have stopped this sooner. Every time I saved a little money I would have to spend it on this.
>
> My ex-husband sees his son every day. He cares about him. But I sometimes feel he has a hidden motive. That part of his caring is to keep track of me. [38-year-old black middle-class office manager, married for fifteen years, with one child]

A 30-year-old clerical worker and mother of two reported that her ex-husband's parents continued to take her to court for increased visitation. This woman said that her ex-husbands' parents would like to have custody of the children. She also said these grandparents reported to Child Protective Services that she and her new husband were abusing the children. According to her, agents from Child Protective Services visited them and found no evidence of abuse. [22]

Undoubtedly fathers' anger fuels such harassment. Arendell believes that after divorce fathers are very angry at their loss of power, which they blame on the legal system and on their ex-wives. They focus on this anger, and on their feelings of wanting to retaliate, rather than trying to maintain and strengthen relationships with their children. [23]

Second, some mothers wanted less visitation because they said their children were experiencing conflicts over the visitation. They gave a variety of reasons for this. In the following case, the children saw their father every other weekend.

> I wish the visitation were less. My kids just don't want to go, but kids have no say. They hate to go. They don't like their father. Actually, they hate him. They have no relationship with him. My son was only two months old when he left. My son doesn't have any idea what a daddy is. He asked me to get remarried so he could have a real daddy. [34-year-old white working-class woman, seeking employment, two children]

In another case the mother would have liked the father to take the children more so she could have more time for herself, but she believed that visitation should be decreased for the sake of the children, who had conflicts with the children of her ex-husband's girlfriend.

> Initially he was going to have the kids every other weekend. But that didn't work out because my kids and his girlfriend's kids fought. It was too painful for my kids. The other kids would call my ex-husband their father and my kids would say, "No, he's our father." So then we agreed on every Tuesday. He gets them around 5:00 and brings them back around 9:30 or 10:30.
>
> For myself, I wish the kids were with him more because then I would get more free time. But for the kids I don't think it should be any more time because the kids have to live in two different worlds, and it's messing them up. [33-year-old white woman, living at the poverty level, married for fifteen years, with three children]

Two women stated that their ex-husbands had been violent toward the children. One said her children did not want to go see their father because he had been "too rough on them physically." Said a 37-year-old secretary and mother of two:

> He doesn't see them because they don't want to see him. They told the judge. He was not good for them emotionally and physically. He was very rough on my son.

Third, some women mentioned their problems with their ex-husbands' drug or alcohol abuse, which made them worry about their children's safety whenever they visited their fathers.

> I wish my son didn't have to go there at all. I raise children with real guidelines and my ex-husband doesn't. There's a lot of cursing and drinking too. My ex-husband is an alcoholic. [34-year-old black child care worker, married for eight years, with one child]

> I'm upset about visitation because he gets high on drugs or drunk when he has her. My ex-husband was in a rehab program. They said he had a problem with violence and then they put him in a psychiatric hospital for three months.
>   The lawyer said if he shows up high I should say he has to take a drug test but he shows up fine. He comes back high. When we negotiated for visitation I wanted it supervised. They said I had to give him a chance. His lawyer said he would never take her in a bar. But his lawyer had just met him. I said, "How do you know, you just met him." He said he would put it in the agreement but it's not there. [26-year-old white retail clerk, married for three years, with one child]

> He does drugs and is a drinker. He drives like a maniac. If he were a different kind of person I would want him to see more of her. But I would never let her in the car with him alone. He is not very rational. [33-year-old white emergency room technician, married for two years, with one child]

The remaining mothers who wanted less visitation reported assorted fears. One woman was constantly arguing with her ex-husband about visitation because the father wanted more visitation than was stipulated in the agreement.

> In the divorce agreement it states that my ex may see his son every weekend and two weeks in the summer. He sees him that much and more. He always wants him on his days off and takes him for long weekends and more vacations.
>   I'm glad he takes an interest but I don't like the battles. My ex wants to have him more. He feels whenever he wants him he should have him because I'm the one who left. He feels I should have left, but left my son at his parents, where we lived and where he still lives. [28-year-old white hairdresser, one child]

Several women were still afraid that their ex-husbands would take the children. As reported in the previous section, two men actually took the children. Many women had heard stories of children being taken, which made them even more fearful. As the following woman said:

> I know he would never take the kids. His job is too important to him. But I still worry about it. I've told them at the school that they can't give the kids to him.

And I've told him and his wife that if they ever took the kids out of state or anywhere I would kill them. I mean it. You see these kids' pictures on TV. I know
how bad these women feel. It's terrifying.... My kids are everything to me.
They're my life. [34-year-old white working class woman seeking employment,
married for eleven years, with two children]

Over a quarter of the women who reported visitation two to three times a
year also stated that they had experienced a lot of conflict with their ex-husbands over the children. The women in this group had complaints similar to
the women who reported conflict but whose ex-husbands visited their children
more frequently. Several of these women stated that the fathers were visiting
primarily for reasons of harassment.

He comes when he wants to. I don't like this arrangement because I don't trust
him. He's still bitter about me divorcing him. It would be OK to drop by. I feel
he's up to something. I tell him but it seems like it goes in one ear and out the
other.... He has a Jekyll and Hyde personality. [29-year-old black woman, check
processor, married for seven years, with four children]

Another woman said, "I don't understand men. They use the kids just to see
the lady. They use the kids." The following woman had left her husband because
of physical abuse.

For a while my [8 year old] daughter really wanted to be with her dad. Finally we
agreed she could. She stayed for six months. She wanted to come back sooner
because of all the things she was seeing and being exposed to. I said, "No, you wait
until school's over, I can't be yanking you from one place to the next so often."
So I came to my ex-husband's to get her. He wasn't going to let her go. He
started threatening violence. She was in the middle and started screaming. I just
took her. [28-year-old black woman seeking employment, married for seven
years, with three children]

Fathers would undoubtedly have a different account of visitation patterns and
might complain that mothers were preventing visitation. I will address this
question below.

No Visitation

Seventeen women in this group stated that their ex-husbands never see the children. These women's views of visitation reflect a combination of sadness and
regret that their children do not see their fathers and at the same time a belief
that given the circumstances of the fathers' lives, no visitation was best. In two-

thirds of the cases in this category, women stated that their ex-husbands did not see their children because of their hard-living behavior. Many of these women reported that their ex-husbands were drug users.

> He can see the kids on weekends but he never does.... I feel a father should see his kids but the way he is I get the kids dressed and we wait and he doesn't show up. That hurts the kids and the way he is on drugs now, I'm afraid he'll hurt them or take them and I'll never see them again. [31-year-old working-class woman, a record clerk, married for seven years, with two children]

> My ex-husband has visitation rights. He can see his son Sundays, I think it is from 10:00 to 4:00. I was concerned about visitation, because of the drugs, but that's what the court decided. But he never sees his son. He's too messed up. It would interfere with his life to have a relationship with his son. He doesn't care. [33-year-old white secretary, with one child]

One woman, married sixteen years, deeply regrets that her son had to see his father disintegrate on drugs.

> I'm sorry now that I let my ex-husband see my son. I was trying to help him, and my son knew exactly how to get in touch with me if he had to. It wasn't good for my son. He saw his father disintegrating on drugs, losing his hair. It was terrible. My son hates drugs now. He also hates his father and never wants to see him again.
> We haven't seen my ex-husband in four years. The last time we saw him was right before he robbed all our things. He said he was coming to see us, but then when we arrived everything was gone. I had just gotten a new place and had bought a lot of new things for me and my son. My son had a new bike.
> Occasionally my ex-husband drives by, to see his son. My son will tell me he has seen him drive down the alley. My son pretends not to see him. [39-year-old white hairdresser, married for sixteen years, with one child from previous marriage]

Several women had experienced extensive violence during their marriages and like this woman, who had been beaten many times by her ex-husband, they arranged to have visitation take place at the courthouse. However, the fathers then stopped visiting the children.

> I have custody of the two younger children. He took me to court for visitation rights. I didn't want him to have them. That's because he was coming around harassing me. I told the judge that. I think my ex-husband wanted visitation so he could keep harassing me.... My ex-husband thought he could just come any time. He came here one time and banged on the door. I told him I would call the police. I did. By the time they got here he was gone. He never came back.

The judge said that he could have visitation but it would have to be on Sundays in the court nursery. For months and months we went down every Sunday. But he never came. I got tired of going down to court. So I went back to court to have his visitation stopped. The judge agreed with me and stripped him of his visitation rights. [30-year-old Hispanic woman living at the poverty level, married for eleven years, with four children]

Another woman who had experienced violence also arranged to have visitation at the court. Her ex-husband also did not pursue visitation.

At first my ex could see the children anytime. After he became violent and wanted to bring that woman around I had it so he would see them at court. When we went to court for custody is when it was set up. He was supposed to see them every Sunday. I took them down there and he never showed, not once. He never sees them now. They saw him a couple of weeks ago for about an hour. They used to call him but that is dwindling. He never calls them. [30 year-old black woman living at the poverty level, married for nine years, with three children]

A 31-year-old poverty-level mother of three told her husband she would call the sheriff if he came to the house. He had threatened to take the children, and the children reported that he sometimes drove slowly by the house looking at them and asking them to come drive with him in his van. This woman also spoke with regret. "It would be OK if he saw the kids if he really cared. I don't think he really wants the kids. He just wants to get back at me. I don't know why because I still don't even know why he left."

Several women said the fathers' failure to see their children was due to the fact that the children had a poor relationship with their father, who had physically abused them.

He never sees them. My son and him hate each other. He used to abuse my son. Mostly mental things. It wasn't all the time, but he would call him a faggot and a wimp and a baby. Once my son was playing with a matchbox and my husband put his foot on my son's hand and just ground on it and said, "Faggot, you're not going to cry are you?" And of course my son was trying not to cry. If my son had friends over, my husband would make him cry in front of them.

My son is a completely different kid now. He has friends and they come over to the house where before he couldn't have friends over. [36-year-old white police officer, two children]

Finally, a 24-year-old woman, married two years, said her ex-husband never saw their two children because he was involved with his children from a new relationship.

Some of the same factors may work to prevent visitation among these fathers, as work to decrease visitation by other fathers. Father visitation is hampered by anger at the mother and conflicts with her; many fathers resent their loss of power and being forced into a legal framework of "visitation."

WOMEN'S PREVENTION OF VISITATION

Do any mothers prevent visitation or report any behavior of their own which their ex-husbands might find harassing? This is the main complaint of fathers' rights groups, which insist that mothers routinely deny or obstruct their visitation with their children. As William Goode has noted, former spouses may act out their conflicts with each other in disputes over their children. [24]

A few women who reported weekly or monthly visitation prevented their ex-husbands from seeing their children on a temporary basis. One woman briefly prevented visitation as a way of disciplining her children.

> For a couple of months when I was disciplining the kids, if nothing else worked, like speaking sternly or yelling or paddling them, I would tell them they couldn't go to their father's a particular week. It was the only thing that really worked. My ex-husband said to me, "You're destroying me. I can't stand it when I can't see them on Tuesdays." I talked with a counselor and we agreed that I should stop, that it wasn't fair for the kids. I only did it for about two months.
>
> At first after the divorce I told my ex-husband, "You can't see the kids." But then I realized, what if he dropped dead and the kids said to me, "You wouldn't let us see our father." That would be very bad. [33-year-old white woman living at the poverty level, married for fifteen years, with three children]

One woman suspended visitation as a way of making her husband pick up and return the children on time.

> He takes them every Sunday. One time he didn't bring them home on time. Just one time. He didn't see them for a month. I said, you don't bring them on time, you have us all worrying, you don't pick the kids up when you say you will, then you don't see them. [26-year-old white woman living at the poverty level, married for six years, with two children]

Two women in the sample reported taking actions to discourage visitation by the father. In one case, a mother hung up on her ex-husband when he called to say he wanted to see the children. He had been promising to visit during the previous year and had not. This woman claimed she would get the children dressed up and they would wait and he would not come. She thought this was because he had started to use drugs in the last year. Now she felt that she did not want the children to go with their father. She was afraid he could hurt them or take them away. In another case, a mother reported that the father, who had been an alcoholic, had taken little interest in visiting his children during the first three years after the separation. After she found out that her ex-husband had dropped her from his insurance policy without telling her, she told the two children not to call their father, although she claimed the father was free to call them and did not. Her actions backfired. The father told the children that he, too, was prevented from calling them, and his 17-year-old son left to live with his father, after a lot of painful conflicts with his mother and stepfather.

Three of the women who reported infrequent or no visitation limited visitation themselves, one with the agreement of a judge. This woman felt like her husband's erratic visitation was being used against her.

> The legal visitation agreement was that he could see the children every other weekend but he only came once a year to see them. I went back to court to have visitation changed because my ex-husband was using that against me. He would come out of the blue and maybe I wouldn't be there or I couldn't rearrange my schedule. So then he'd say why should he pay if he couldn't see them.
>
> I told the judge that I didn't want our lives disrupted like that. That I wouldn't have that used against me and that also it was devastating to the kids to have him say that he was coming and then he wouldn't come. [31-year-old white secretary, married for seven years, with two children]

The two other women limited visitation because of their ex-husbands' use of alcohol. As one woman said:

> I talk with him now but I can't be around him too long and I would not trust him with the kids. He calls every once in a while and tries. He's an alcoholic and the last couple of times he tried he was drunk so I refused. [24-year-old white factory worker, three children]

Another woman limited visitation to once every three months. Her ex-husband was an alcoholic and she left because he abused her physically. After the divorce her ex-husband broke into the house once and fell asleep in her bed, drunk. The children liked their father and she felt he liked them, but felt he used visitation to try and see her.

A third of the women (seven) in the no-visitation category tried to prevent visitation. In three of these cases judges either prevented visitation or limited it to specified times with court supervision. Three of the women reported that their husbands were drug addicts or alcoholics. In the other cases, the women prevented visitation because of their ex-husbands' use of violence. Two women mentioned that their ex-husbands had threatened them with violence. A 31-year-old unemployed mother of two said, "After my ex-husband said that he would hurt me if I filed for child support, as far as I'm concerned he lost all rights to his child." In another case a woman described her ex-husband's behavior as "harassing," and in another, a woman said her ex-husband was threatening to take the children.

Despite the fact that some mothers could make it difficult for fathers to see their children, most women stated that they did not limit visitation. First, Pennsylvania law requires mothers to comply with father visitation, even if the father is not paying child support.[25] Most women had been informed of this by their lawyers.

> My lawyer told me that I'd better not limit visitation in any way. My lawyer says we have to keep child support and visitation separate. I hate being in the middle. I feel I shouldn't deprive my in-laws from seeing their grandchild because of their son. They even understand how I feel and don't blame me for feeling mad and wouldn't blame me if I stopped the visitation. The Court isn't helping. I think they shouldn't separate support and visitation. [31-year-old black middle-class woman, reading specialist, one child]

> I really hate that I have to uphold my end of the bargain and allow my ex-husband visitation and that he doesn't uphold his end. My new husband and I considered denying him visitation. But we decided that we better allow it so that when we go to court they can't tell us that we had denied him visitation. [34-year-old black woman, runs a day care center in her home, married eight years, one child]

Sometimes mothers did not prevent visitation because they felt that their children would someday blame them if they had not been able to see their fathers. This woman, who left her husband because of physical abuse, stated:

> I feel good about my decision to allow my daughter to see her father and him to see her when they need to see each other. That clears my conscience, if it comes up, "Mommy, why didn't you let me see my father?" [33-year-old, black secretary, married eight years, one child]

Even the woman whose ex-husband kidnapped their son did not prevent visitation because she never wanted her son to blame her for not letting him see his father.

> During the marriage we lived off my unemployment insurance. My ex-husband didn't keep jobs. He used alcohol a lot and was a drug addict. After the kidnapping I didn't want my ex-husband around for a while. Now he sees him on holi-

days. I'm never going to hinder my son's getting in touch with his father. I would never do that. I never want my son saying when he's older, "You wouldn't let me see my father."

On the other hand, I'm honest with my son. One time recently I couldn't find him in a store. When I did I screamed at him about where he had been. Later I explained that I still had fears about losing him left over from when his father had taken him.

Also, whereas I would never prevent or even discourage my son from seeing his father, I'm not going to work to make it happen or make my son stay in touch with him. [33-year-old poverty-level white woman, two children]

In addition to having the potential to manipulate visitation to suit their interests, women also have the potential to turn their children's affections against their fathers. Women were not asked about how they spoke to their children about their father, but several volunteered that they did not speak against their ex-husbands. Just as these women did not limit visitation, for the most part they feared that if they used their power to alienate their children from their fathers by speaking badly of their ex-husbands, it would be counterproductive.

I never speak badly of my ex-husband to the children. If I did I'd hear about it. What I say gets back to him, especially through my son. He'd be back at me, he would. It would definitely make things worse. [31-year-old black woman living at the poverty level, married eleven years, three children]

A 36-year-old dental assistant with three children explained that her 13-year-old daughter just went to live with her father. She said, "I figure, let her see the other side. One thing I never did was speak against him. Let them see."

While most women in this sample appeared to be trying to be fair in how they represented their ex-husbands to their children, it seems inevitable that both parents may communicate to their children some of their negative feelings about their former spouse. In this sample, two women described behavior of their own that fit in this category. One woman, whose son had regular visitation with his father, whom the mother claimed he loved very much, stated:

Sometimes when I get mad at him [the son] I say [in a threatening tone of voice] "So you want to go live with your father? Go see what that's like." Then he goes, "No, no." [37-year-old white department store clerk, one child]

Another woman indicated that she told her daughter, who is now an adult, that it made her sad when the daughter saw her father.

According to some mothers, their ex-husbands spoke badly of them in an attempt to make the children take "their side." One woman reported that her ex-husband told the children it was her fault that he had to leave, which made the children angry at her. This woman left her husband because he was taking no responsibility for supporting the family and was frequently gone. She said:

> It was hard when he left because the kids said, "Where's Daddy, why did Daddy have to leave?" And he told them that I was making him leave, so they kept at me, "why did you make Daddy leave, why did you make Daddy leave?" That was hard. He can come anytime he wants. I don't tell them bad things about their father. I don't want to do that. But I try to get across that if you are going to live somewhere you have to pay and be responsible. [30 year-old black poverty-level woman, married thirteen years, seven children]

Similarly, as in the case of women who reported frequent visitation, several women consciously decided not to speak badly of their ex-husbands to the children.

> I don't tell my son any bad things about my ex-husband. I want my son to see both sides. Kids always think the parent who isn't there is worth a million dollars. I know because my grandmother raised me. [28-year-old black woman living at the poverty level, married six years, one child]

> I wish he would see the kids more. There is no reason for him not to see them. Even though he's not paying I would like him to see them. I'm very careful about not badmouthing to the kids about their father. [34-year-old white bookkeeper, living at the poverty level, two children]

A 36-year-old practical nurse, a black woman with two children, reported that she would never say anything bad about her ex-husband because that would anger her son, who would tell his father. According to her, "My son thinks his father's word is the last authority. His father told him he was the boss in this family."

CONCLUSION

In this chapter I have described two predominant types of post-divorce families, each highly gendered. With the exception of the 19 percent of mothers who reported satisfactory visitation agreements with caring and involved fathers, most mothers reported that fathers were either under-involved or over-involved in the lives of their children. Those mothers who wanted fathers less involved reported conflicts with their ex-husbands over both custody and visitation. A third of the mothers were fearful during negotiations for custody due to conflicts with their ex-husbands. Some were still afraid that their ex-husbands might take the children. A few experienced threats of killing and kidnapping and several reported kidnappings by fathers.

Similarly, 27 percent of women in the sample who reported that visitation took place reported conflict with their ex-husbands and wanted less visitation, a figure consistent with Maccoby and Mnookin's finding that 25 percent of divorces were "highly conflicted" at an average of three-and-a-half years after the separation.[26] Many of the 14 percent of women who reported that no visitation took place believed that under the circumstances it was best that the father not visit their children. Some feared the effects of their ex-husbands' hard-living, such as their ex-husbands' use of drugs or violence. Some, particularly those who experienced domestic violence during their marriage, felt that their ex-husbands were using visitation to harass them. Still others were afraid of losing their children. Women who had experienced domestic violence were particularly fearful. This fear may create a climate where women are afraid to bargain for resources.

These data indicate that in analyzing post-divorce family relations we have not taken factors of hard-living and violence enough into account. Fathers not only drift away; those involved with alcohol, drugs, and street life engage in behaviors that are incompatible with family life. Even after they disappear, they may reappear and disrupt family life. Further, as Arendell describes, a number of fathers, angry because they have lost control over their wives and children, believe the divorce process has deprived them of their rights and use visitation as a way to harass their wives and "get even" for these perceived injustices.

Custody and visitation laws and policies must address the scope and severity of conflict and violence in families after divorce. The use of domestic violence should call into question the fitness of a parent. The law must be ready to limit or deny access to those who use visitation for harassment or engage in other threatening or dangerous behavior. Courts should consider evidence of abuse in awarding custody, in drawing up visitation agreements, in deciding whether to deny visitation or require supervised visitation, and in modifying custody and visitation awards. Further, courts should never deny battered women custody of their children because of their "failure" to protect them from the abuser, as has happened in some cases. We cannot punish women for abuse suffered at the hands of their partners.[27]

While protecting the rights of mothers and children, it is also possible to expand the access of fathers to their children. Arendell, for example, while advocating the primary caretaker standard, also advocates expanding the "standard visitation agreement," which is typically every other weekend with an overnight stay, and one evening a week, with additional time for certain holidays and during the summer months. Arendell believes this is too restrictive for fathers who are very close to their children.[28]

Observers have argued, however, that increased rights for fathers should go hand in hand with increased responsibilities. As Czapanskiy and others have pointed out, joint custody has given fathers new powers, but no new duties. While the father is given the right to participate in decisions on all issues in his child's life, he is not required to participate in activities. Nothing happens to the father who fails to provide care during a time period when the visitation agreement stipulates that he is supposed to be caring for the child; he is not even required to reimburse the mother for the expenses she incurred during the time when he was supposed to be taking care of the child. This is in contrast to the mother, who is required to allow the father to see the child, or face judicially imposed consequences. Thus men can realize the benefits of joint custody, while women do not. Further, fathers can use joint custody to reduce their child support obligations while not in fact increasing their participation in the lives of their children.[29]

Czapanskiy urges that we reconsider fathers' responsibilities under joint custody. She argues that since we have adopted the principle that both parents are required to support their children, we should extend that principle to include providing nonfinancial care to children. She argues further that state legislatures now assume that it is in the child's best interest to have continuing contact with both parents, a view that challenges the notion of the "volunteer" father and undermines the traditional claim that a father may ignore his child so long as he provides support. She proposes that a parent who fails to comply with a residential plan should face a staged series of penalties, beginning with make-up time for the visitation he missed.

Further, in those jurisdictions with parenting plans, Czapanskiy favors stipulating in those plans all aspects of parenting, including not just who will provide physical care but who will be responsible for attending teacher conferences, taking the child to the doctor and dentist, supervising homework, arranging for visits with friends, selecting extracurricular activities, and shopping for clothes and school supplies. She notes, "By listing and allocating the various tasks of parenthood, both parents and the court will come to an understanding and perhaps an appreciation of the detailed work of childraising, a complexity that is absent from the present scheme."[30]

Chapter 7

WOMEN AND CHILDREN
AT DIVORCE

This chapter addresses the question of how the women interviewed view their experience of divorce and its impact on their lives and the lives of their children. It is very important to hear women's own views about the impact of divorce on their lives. Various social commentators freely offer advice about how our society should respond to divorce. As discussed in chapter 1, some wish to strengthen the traditional family, others aim to cut benefits for single mothers to make it difficult for women to live outside of marriage, while still others wish to provide more benefits and social supports to single parents. All of these proposals have serious implications for the lives of divorced women. Restrictions on the ability to divorce would severely curtail women's ability to choose their way of life. Yet we have woefully little information on what divorced women themselves think about these issues.

Similarly, we need more information about how divorce affects children. As I will discuss in this chapter, some researchers and policy-makers claim that children are paying too high a price for the divorce of their parents and that the negative impact of divorce on children is cause for restricting divorce. Others, however, point out that children's reaction to divorce is variable and not uniformly negative. They claim that while some children may be harmed by the divorce itself, many are harmed by remaining in marriages which are torn by conflict.

WOMEN'S REACTION TO DIVORCE

In order to develop accurate theories of divorce and to shape social policy, we need to know how women themselves understand and interpret their experiences of divorce. Do their accounts show that women are less committed to marriage? Or, on the other hand, do women want more restrictions on divorce so they cannot so easily be left by their husbands? Do women want changes in the institution of marriage? Have their experiences caused them to reject marriage, or do they wish to remarry?

Research devoted to the question of how divorce affects peoples' lives, which is usually based on measures of psychological well-being, has yielded contradictory results. On the one hand, many researchers have focused on how divorcing spouses experience high levels of physical and mental health problems after divorce and how women particularly experience significantly more depression than men after divorce. Other researchers, however, have argued that divorce can be a positive experience, that the mastery of major life crises can have long-term positive, growth-producing effects for divorced men and women, and that women and men are on the whole positive about their divorces. A few researchers believe that women in particular, despite their symptoms of depression and stress, gain an increased sense of competency and control through successfully negotiating the difficult tasks of divorce.[1]

In order to move beyond these contradictory findings, we need to know what women think about their divorces. Some who have done lengthy interviews with divorced women found that many were positive about the increased independence they gained at divorce. Catherine Riessman suggests that women ultimately feel better than men about divorce because they find their marriages restrictive. She notes that many women in her sample were less upset about the ending of marriages than men. Riessman argues that these women have less to lose and more to gain from divorce than men because divorce enables them to escape psychological domination by their husbands and feelings of being subordinate, devalued, and discredited. These findings are consistent with recent polling data cited in chapter 2, which suggest that there is a substantial gender gap between women's and men's perceptions about how much equality there should be in marriage. In 1989, while a majority of women in a *New York Times* poll believed American society had not changed enough to grant women equality, only a minority of men agreed. In one survey, a majority of men said, however, that the women's movement had "made things harder for men at home." We must devote much more attention to the question of whether women feel that marriage as it is currently structured is restrictive for them.[2]

These women's accounts expand our understanding of divorce and help explain the contradictory assessments of divorce as both positive and negative.

As these women's words show, their reactions to divorce are intimately tied to their circumstances after divorce—particularly their unexpected poverty and the loss of companionship—and also to their views of their marriage. Further, the reactions of many of these women show a strong consciousness of their subordinate position in marriage and in the larger society.

The women interviewed were asked the question, "How do you feel about being divorced? Based on their answers, I coded women's responses into three categories: women who spoke positively about being divorced, women who felt ambivalent, and women who spoke negatively. The coding for these categories were determined by women's own assessments. Women who gave both positive and negative statements about how the divorce had affected their lives were categorized as "positive" if they made more positive than negative statements, "ambivalent" if they made an equal number of positive and negative statements about their divorces, and "negative" if they made more negative statements.

Despite their hardships, an average of five years after their separation, 63 percent of these women expressed positive feelings about being divorced, 12 percent expressed ambivalent feelings, and 25 percent expressed negative feelings (see Figure 7–1). In contrast to some other studies, there were no significant class or race differences in these women's attitudes toward their divorce. Thus, it was not their socio-economic position, but other factors that influenced these women's outlook on their divorces. What story did these women tell about their divorces? How is it that while almost all women felt overwhelmed by their lowered standard of living and the stress of managing as a single parent, so many spoke in a positive way about being divorced? What factors did they cite?

Women Who Spoke Positively About Being Divorced

The 63 percent of all women who felt positively about being divorced cited two reasons for their feelings. One group was positive about the chance to be more independent, the other about getting away from the difficulties of their marriages. The first group of women emphasized the positive opportunities for growth associated with divorce, including the ability to escape from confining roles. This group included more women who left their marriages for reasons of personal dissatisfaction and therefore more middle-class women. These women's comments reflect their belief that they could be independent for the first time in their lives and begin to create their own identity. The strength of their feelings reflects their view that in their marriages they had accommodated to their ex-husbands' wishes and subordinated their own identity to their marital and motherhood roles, which they now see as too confining.

Figure 7–1. Women's Overall Feelings about Being Divorced.*

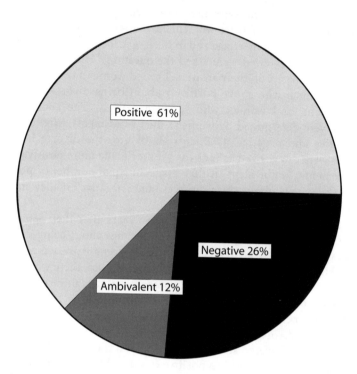

* Women's feelings about being divorced are not significantly related to either race or class. Also, the extent of positive feelings was consistent (around 60%) for all women regardless of their reasons for divorce.

I learned through all this that I am stronger than I thought I was, and I'm worth more than I thought I was. I learned I really don't need anybody. I can depend on myself. . . . I have no regrets. [27-year-old white waitress, married seven years, two children]

I wouldn't want to go through this again. It's like a death. You mourn it. I am much stronger. I have a much better idea of what I want in men, of what's acceptable in men. I'm more aggressive about myself just because I've had to do things myself. It's changed me. I'm stronger. The experience shook some reality into me. Life has ups and downs. You learn how to get up, and that you can. [31-year-old black teacher, with one child]

At the time of the separation I was lonely. But I was also free to concentrate on myself. I started to emerge as a person. I had more time. My life is better off now, definitely. Occasionally I wonder if I should have divorced, but not really. Before I always thought I needed to be married. But now I've learned that it's only me who can take care of me. Now I've put myself and my growth first. [49-year-old middle-class woman, married for ten years, with two children]

Sometimes women used language that reflected their experiences in therapy.

I've grown a lot. My consciousness has really been raised and my willingness to analyze things has really increased. I don't need as many external things to feel good about myself. [37-year-old white middle-class woman, married for six years, with one child]

Some women were happy to be free of controlling marriages. Said a 26-year-old white working-class mother of one who was married five years, "Being divorced let me out of a cell. The marriage kept me from growing up in many ways. I feel better." Another woman said:

Getting divorced is the best thing I ever did. I started going out. When I was married, I stayed in. I was home with my son and he was always out. He said, "You should be home with the baby." [38-year-old black middle-class woman, married for nine years, with two children]

Since my divorce I have stopped stifling myself. I wasn't a fighting person. I could never win arguments with him, never. So I just let it be. I shut up. [40-year-old white woman starting her own business, married for nine years, with three children]

A second group of women were happy to be out of difficult marriages, particularly hard-living marriages. More of these were working-class and poverty-level women. Many of them chose to leave their marriages, and for them the benefits of divorce also outweighed the costs. This 30-year-old woman, who supported her four children on welfare, left her husband of eleven years because of violence.

The best thing I did was getting away from that marriage. . . . You get tired when someone comes hitting you. You get fed up. He'd hit a couple of times a week. If you said anything back to him, he'd punch. I had to go to the doctor or emergency room about twelve times. Nothing was broken; it was lumps and bruises. It's painful to think of all that violence. [30-year-old poverty-level Hispanic woman, married for eleven years, with four children]

These two women, who left their marriages because of violence and drugs, voice similarly positive views.

> The day after I had him evicted, I went outside and said, "World, you're wonderful." It was the hardest thing I ever did. Through therapy I found that I am a very strong person. . . . All in all I've gained from the divorce. The only thing I lost was a Saturday night date. . . . I do worry how the children will handle it in the future, though. I couldn't get the two oldest to therapy. [44-year-old white secretary, married for twenty-eight years, with three children]

> My life is better than during my marriage because I'm free from a depressing environment and the fighting, and I have more independence. [28-year-old poverty-level black unemployed woman, married for seven years, with three children]

A 39-year-old mother of two, married seventeen years, was happy to be free of her ex-husband's alcohol abuse. She said, "I'm definitely happier now. I'm happy with myself. I got my self-respect back and opportunities opened up. I don't have to worry about the drinking anymore. My ex-husband drank a lot."

Some women were also happy to be leaving other kinds of abuses. A 40-year-old poverty-level woman with one child reported that her ex-husband gambled a lot, so during their twenty-one-year marriage they often couldn't pay the rent and had to move from place to place. Also, her ex-husband's violence caused her arm and leg to be broken. She said, "The most helpful thing I did was leaving. I lost fifty pounds after I left. And I'm calmer, I'm not nervous like I used to be." A 36-year-old black nurse, who described herself as experiencing a lot of mental abuse during her sixteen-year marriage, said that her ex-husband kept guns in the house and sometimes talked about using them. According to her, after her divorce, "I got my freedom, I feel much, much better except for finances. I felt like I was a prisoner." Another woman felt that she made the right decision:

> Maybe I could have stuck with the marriage but my ex-husband spent his time on the street. It isn't worth it to say you have a man. At a certain age you come to your senses. You ask what you want to get out of life, what's important. [36-year-old black dental assistant, married for thirteen years, with three children]

Women Who Spoke Negatively About Being Divorced

Twenty-five percent of the women expressed negative feelings about being divorced. Most of these women did not focus on the loss of their husbands or the life they had when they were married, but rather on the loss of opportunities and the difficulties of their lives. These losses shaped their assessments of their lives as divorced women.

First, some women said that as a result of their divorce they had lost a substantial investment. For example, some women believed their investment in their marriage prevented them from making a good investment in a job or career. This woman stated the problem clearly and dramatically.

> My dreams got shattered.... I have definitely lost opportunities. I could have furthered my career if I hadn't gotten married. I've reached the top of my field. I'm an optician. I want to be an optometrist. I wanted to go to medical school. I feel like it's not worth the time or the money now. And all the time I would have to spend away from my son. I've lost the opportunity to fulfill personal dreams—having more children, owning a house. [29-year-old white woman, married for five years, with one child]

A 37-year-old mother of two, who was married for fourteen years, said, "The hardest thing for me is the idea of wasted time." She wished she and her husband had ended the marriage sooner. A 31-year-old woman who was married nine years stated: "I've become much more wary and cynical about things. If I hadn't married, I would just have one child. I'd be out there working and furthermore my child wouldn't have psychological problems. The kids are the only two good things I got out of that marriage. It's a disgrace." This woman, like some others, then went on to explicitly compare her situation to that of men and concluded that women are given a bad deal.

> Men can get up and leave. I don't want to say women get stuck with the children. Women get left with the responsibility for the children. Then it's the children who suffer. Myself, I can handle it. But they can't.

A 39-year-old working-class mother of three, married nineteen years, felt that because she had become a single mother she was disadvantaged in beginning a new relationship. According to her, "It's hard to have kids and raise them today. I feel that's why the relationship I just had didn't work out. Nobody wants to be bothered with kids. Your life is over!"

Women also spoke of the stress of being single parents. According to one woman, what was so hard for her was not having been left by her ex-husband, but being a single parent. She said:

> It's so hard. The hardest is the kids, not that he left me. I paid $40 a week for childcare and had nothing left. You don't relax when you have the kids. You don't know what they will do. [32-year-old black poverty-level, unemployed woman, married fifteen years, two children]

Said a 30-year-old welfare mother with seven children, married thirteen years:

The hardest thing to cope with has been the money, and that the kids want a dad. The stress is really getting to me. I feel tired a lot, more tired than I used to. And I'm not as physically strong as I used to be. I get bills all the time. I've been getting headaches and I've got stomach problems. And I've been having trouble with my gall bladder. I may have to think about foster care. I have to keep the children's physical and mental health in mind.

One woman particularly stressed that it was not the divorce per se that bothered her, but rather seeing her ex-husband give financial support to another woman.

The divorce was not so devastating. My husband wasn't working. Between you and me, it was a relief. I have bitterness, though. I'm quite bitter. It's hard for me to see him give so much to another woman. I haven't asked for that much in child support. It floors me at times and depresses me. It's hard to get over. And I never even went on a honeymoon. [46-year-old black school bus monitor, married for thirty-one years]

Some women mention their dislike of being alone.

Sometimes you're so alone. I've been so alone. I do have my children. I don't know what I would have done to myself without them. I also have the Bible, and I have the church. [39-year-old poverty-level black woman on workman's compensation, married for twenty-two years, with four children]

It's scary, making decisions on your own. You're more nervous. You smoke more. There's loneliness and trying to develop a way of life, and a lot of fears and anxieties. I experienced a lot of personal suffering and it can't be measured or weighed. It's taken it's toll. [51-year-old white bookkeeper, married for twenty-seven years, with two children]

Finally, a few women did express feelings of sadness about losing their husbands. These women, who were left for other women, said they continued to love their husbands and wished they were still married to them. A 44-year-old woman who was married twenty-one years had dated and felt there were not many eligible men to be found. She said she would like to be married to her ex-husband again "if he would straighten himself out." But she was worried he would not change and she was angry because it was easier for her ex-husband as a man to find women to date or marry than it was for her to find a partner.

The therapist says maybe he's learned now and he wants to come back. But the other possibility is that he'll just keep going off and having affairs. He won't go to a therapist. He says it wouldn't do any good. I guess I feel angry that he doesn't have to go through what I do because he's a man. He has an easier time dating. [white teacher with two children]

These women's comments reflect the difficulty of being rejected by a partner. For women who go on to find a new partner, the rejection comes to matter less; it may be more difficult for those who do not find a partner.

Twelve percent of the women expressed ambivalent feelings about being divorced. These women gave similar reasons for being ambivalent as women who were negative about their divorces. First, they stressed that because of the divorce they lost a major economic investment. Said a 37-year-old mother of three, married seventeen years, who now works at a telemarketing firm: "I know I did the right thing in leaving but I have lost a lot of opportunities. My children had a good quality life with lots of money and it went to nothing." Another woman spoke with a lot of bitterness about lost economic opportunities.

> I've been held back by the divorce. If I were still married I would have a lot more money. I wouldn't have the childcare expenses. I would work too. I would have worked at night and my husband could have taken care of the children. [34-year-old white working class woman, seeking employment, married for eleven years, with two children]

She also said, however, "Divorce makes women stronger. You have to fight for what you want and say what you want. I'm glad I learned all that. I'm better off."

Second, women who were ambivalent mentioned the difficulties of living on a reduced income. This 36-year-old secretary and mother of two, married twelve years, said the problem for her was "the financial situation. The divorce itself wasn't so hard on me. It's what I wanted. I have learned that I can live as an independent person." A 37-year-old mother of one who worked as a clerk and cashier, spoke of how her life has been plagued by economic insecurity since she divorced after thirteen years of marriage. She currently lives with her mother, an arrangement which she dislikes intensely, but which enables her to survive on her low salary. While she is angry about her difficult economic circumstances, she also says: "I am a different person though. In some ways he did me a favot. I speak up at work, I speak up to my mother."

These views reflect the fact that our society still offers few alternatives to marriage as the place for women to find economic, social, and psychological well-being, and as the setting for raising children. Thus when a marriage ends, women lose not just a partner, but an investment. Those who can replace the old investment with a new one express less dissatisfaction. Some men may also feel like they have lost an investment after divorce, but they don't typically lose their standard of living and they can more easily make a new investment—

there are more women available to them as partners, and they do not have full-time childcare responsibilities.

Certain facts about these women reinforce the idea that for divorced women, the end of a marriage can represent losing an investment. An important factor in these women's statements of their well-being was whether they currently had a relationship with a man. At an average of five years after separating from their ex-husbands, 43 percent of the women were not involved in any intimate relationship with a man, while 14 percent were remarried, 14 percent were engaged, 5 percent were living with someone, and 24 percent were dating someone. Of the women who were not in a new relationship, only 48 percent reported being positive about their divorce in contrast to 74 percent of those who were remarried, 71 percent of those who were engaged, 86 percent of those who were living with someone, and 67 percent of those who were dating. While this difference is not statistically significant, there may be a tendency for women who have no new relationship to feel more like they have lost an investment.

Second, women's attitudes towards their divorces is related to their age. The percentage of women who felt positive about being divorced decreased with age: 72 percent of 25–29 year-olds were positive about being divorced, 67 percent of 30–34 year-olds, 58 percent of 35–39 year-old's and 44 percent of 40–44 year-olds (these differences are not significant). One could conclude from these figures that older women have less opportunity to find a new relationship and make a new "investment."

However, given the economic hardship that most divorces bring, it is striking how positive many women feel about being divorced. First, many women describe looking forward to forging new, more independent roles at divorce. Their views suggest that, at least in hindsight, many women view their marriage as having been restrictive. They speak as if the structure of their marriage was incompatible with their being a whole person. Second, some women, particularly those who left difficult marriages, are happy to have escaped from hard-living conditions. Their accounts demonstate that the literature which claims that being divorced is a uniformly negative experience underestimates how "rough" marriages can be. These women's accounts call into question the conclusion that women leave marriages primarily because of "individualism" or lack of commitment, or that divorce is uniformly a sign of decline.

At the same time, we must balance our understanding of the positive aspects of divorce with the reality of how difficult it is for many women to replace the resources that are distributed through the institution of marriage. Some women feel that the demands of being a single parent are overwhelming, that they are very alone, and that they lose a major life investment at divorce. Thus accounts of divorce that stress only its positive aspects are also misleading.

Figure 7-2. Divorced Women's Attitudes toward Remarriage.*

	Percentage of Sample (n=129)
Have remarried	14
Wish to Remarry	56
Unsure	18
Do not wish to remarry	10

* Attitudes toward remarriage are not significantly related to either race or class.

REMARRIAGE AND DATING

What are these women's attitudes towards remarriage? Given that the majority of women were relatively positive about being divorced, and given that a number of women experience "hard-living" marriages, are women rejecting marriage? Or are they happy to be free to search for new partners? Are they interested in making new commitments? As indicated in Figure 7–2, 14 percent of these women have remarried. Of those 86% who have not remarried, 66 percent said that they wanted to remarry, 22 percent said they did not, and 12 percent were unsure. There were no significant class or race differences between these women.

Those women who wanted to remarry believed that marriage provided a better way of life than any alternatives they could see. These women still believed in the institution of marriage. A middle-class black woman who was married for nine years described the feelings of many when she said, "I would like to remarry. I would like a chance for happiness. I'm not against marriage. It's just that this one didn't work out and I'd like another opportunity to have a good one." [38-year-old, computer program analyst, one child] Many women wanted the companionship they believed marriage could bring. This is not surprising, given that in our society we structure companionship through marriage. These women especially wanted a companion for the time when their children were gone.

> I would like to remarry. I think the species belongs in pairs—for nurturance and caring. Some day the kids will be gone. [40-year-old white working-class woman, married for nine years, with three children]

I would like to remarry to have someone who loves me—someone who's supportive and a companion. After a while the kids grow up, and when they grow up they don't seem to want to stick around. [33-year-old white poverty-level woman, married for fifteen years, with three children]

Some women did not like being alone and did not like being single.

Yes I want to remarry because I hate being alone, feeling alone. Sometimes it's nice to give away all the good things we have for ourselves and share that with another person. I think the family is a very good institution. [33-year-old black secretary, married for eight years, with one child]

And finally some believed it would be better for their children if they were married. A 37-year-old mother of two said, "I believe in marriage and the sharing of your life and I like the idea of the male and female roles in the house for the children." Similarly, another woman said:

I would like to remarry because I like the family life and because I feel as though the children are more stable when they have both parents. [34-year-old poverty-level black woman, married for thirteen years, with three children]

These women's words reflect the fact that while divorce and relationships outside of marriage are currently much more acceptable than in the past, many women believe that getting married is the surest way to obtain nurturance and caring.

By contrast, those women who did not want to remarry—22 percent of the sample—questioned whether the institution of marriage was good for them. These women spoke overwhelmingly of the joys of being in control of their own lives. The theme of independence, which was so strong in the accounts of women who were positive about their divorces, reappeared in their views of remarriage. Some of these women saw freedom and independence as incompatible with marriage. A 39-year-old poverty-level mother of four said, "I'm dating someone but I'd rather just be alone. I'd rather have the freedom." A working-class mother of two, married 21 years, commented, "The reason I would not like to remarry is because I might lose access to my husband's pension. Also I'm afraid I might lose my independence." Some women mentioned not only the desire to maintain their independence, but their desire not to be controlled by husbands.

I've lived with a man for ten years and had four children. But I don't want marriage. The problem would be possession. Marriage would give him more control. If I were his wife, "Mrs.," I would have to go along with what he says. This way I have much more say about myself. Legal paternity has been established . . . so if anything should happen to me, things are taken care of. [41-year-old black poverty-level woman, married for nineteen years, with two children]

I wouldn't want to give up my freedom, my identity, what I've fought so hard for. I won't give those up.... I would want to get married if I didn't have to give up those things. [37-year-old white receptionist, married for seventeen years, with two children]

I wouldn't like to remarry because I like my independence. I like to come and go and make my own decisions. Men expect things to be done for them. Men I date expect me to take care of them. Their attitude is "What can you do for me?" If that's their attitude, if I have to put out for them, I don't need it. [33-year-old black data transcriber, married for seven years, with one child]

A 49-year-old middle-class mother of two who was married ten years did not want to remarry at the moment because she wanted to make her own decisions and be in charge of her own life. She talked about how, unlike herself, her ex-husband's new wife refused to "wait on" her ex-husband. She wished she had done that and would make sure in future relationships that she did not subordinate herself to her partner's life. Finally, several mentioned that they could not remarry now because of their need to protect their children from new partners who might not understand their needs and their situation.

The 12 percent of women in the sample who were ambivalent about remarriage saw some of the same benefits of remarriage as those women cited above, but they also had doubts similar to those women who did not want to remarry. For example, these women were very concerned about keeping their independence and worried about whether they could do that in a new marriage.

I'm not going to be somebody's servant. That's the way I was in my marriage, picking up all the time. My ex-husband was a slob. Love is not being a maid. Men don't know the meaning of love. My ex-husband treated me like his mother. [34-year-old white working-class woman, seeking employment, married for eleven years]

They also worried about finding equal relationships with men.

I'm not sure whether I would like to remarry. One problem with my husband, he was, like, women have their place. He would provide but the woman was to keep her mouth shut. I would look for somebody who would treat their partner as an equal. [39-year-old black working-class woman, married for seventeen years]

Second, some women were concerned about dating in an era when the risk of contracting AIDS and sexually transmitted diseases has increased. This woman would like to remarry in order to reduce her exposure to diseases.

> Maybe I would like to remarry. It's dirty out there, AIDS, herpes.... It's nice to stay with one person. It's hard. You can't even trust your mate. [29-year-old poverty-level black woman, married for seven years, with four children]

On the other hand, for the following woman, her fear of AIDS made her hesitate to consider marriage.

> There's a lot of guys out there using drugs, plus AIDS is going around. It would have to be somebody really special who had a lot of money, a good job and loved my son like he was theirs. You don't know what they've done in the past. Most of the men I meet are high. [29-year-old white woman, high school education, married five years, one child]

In conclusion, roughly a third of the women had some serious reservations about the institution of marriage. Their reservations focused on whether they could achieve equality in marriage. Two-thirds of these women, however, still strongly believed in the legitimacy and desirability of marriage.

Problems of Dating

While a minority of women said they had no difficulty meeting men to date, the majority of the 43 percent of the women in this sample who were unattached, and many who were dating and would like to remarry, were pessimistic about finding men to marry. They stated that there were few men "out there" for them to date, and the men they did meet did not want to become involved with women with children. These women will generally have a more difficult time remarrying than their ex-husbands, who have a larger pool of women to choose from because it is more acceptable for them to pick partners who are younger and lower in status than they are. There are additional difficulties for women who wish to find new partners, foremost among them that they are full-time single mothers. The women in this sample were involved in fewer new relationships than their ex-husbands. While 33 percent of the women were remarried (14 percent), engaged (14 percent), or living with a man (5 percent), according to their reports, 53 percent of the ex-husbands were either remarried (24 percent) or living with a woman (29 percent) (women were not asked if their ex-husbands were engaged).[3]

These women's comments reflect the demographic facts—women have fewer choices of male partners than they would like. The women said things like: "There's not too much out there in terms of men." "As far as dating, what's left out there isn't so good." "There's nothing out there but other people's discards and scuzz." The following woman believed that unattached men are "messed up."

> I definitely want to get remarried. I like being married. But I don't think I'll find a man. I've looked. It's like what everyone said, there aren't men out there, but it's been harder to face than I realized. The divorced men are like my husband, messed up, they haven't dealt with their problems. I don't like the aloneness and I don't see any prospect of this ending. [44-year-old white teacher, married for twenty-one years]

For some of these women hard-living created conditions that limited the number of eligible men.

> I've become a loner because of AIDS. That really scares me. Also, a lot of the men in my neighborhood are into drugs so I don't bother anymore. [30-year-old poverty-level black woman, married for thirteen years with seven children]

Some women wanted to meet men who were emotionally supportive and were finding this difficult.

> I give out a lot of love, but you need some back. My husband couldn't do that. The guy I'm seeing right now can't either. He gives me a lot of material things. But that's not what I want. I wouldn't marry him for that reason. I'm not looking for a knight on a white horse. But I need emotional support—someone who loves me for what I am. [31-year-old white working-class woman, in accounting, married for five years, with two children]

Instead, they felt a lot of men are looking only for sex or, as some women said, "one night stands." Said a 35-year-old white secretary living at the poverty level, "The men out there all just want a one-night stand. And I'm not into that. Also they want to know, do you have money. And if you have kids, they're really turned off." One woman was more blunt about her view of men and sex.

> Men don't get to know the mind, just straight to the body. Get to know me, I think you'll like me. . . . I think women should run the world, you know, really . . . 'cause men are weak. Put some sex in front of their face and they're gone. [26-year-old poverty-level black woman, married for five years, with two children]

In reaction to this perceived attitude of men, several women said they were looking for older men. A 31-year-old with one child said, "There are just not that many men out there. Men think you're easy. Some of them are nice, but many are immature. I look for an older man. The younger ones are out for one thing." Some women feared new relationships because they had been physically abused: "When you get abused you don't want to think of getting close to anybody who'll treat you the same way but you hear a voice inside saying maybe not all men are the same." Another woman who experienced violence spoke in the same vein.

I'm not ready for a new relationship at all. I fear that I'm too set in my ways. I fear that the bitterness and animosity that I have because of what I went through would come out. Also it would be hard to give so much of myself again. [31-year-old black woman, poverty-level, three children]

One 34-year-old black woman noted a particular problem meeting black men in her profession. She said, "I would like to remarry for a sense of belonging. But I don't know where you look for men. I don't see any black men in my work life. The ones I might marry are married."

Finally, some women spoke of not wanting to date men who would try to control them. They said that they disliked being controlled in their marriages and that they wanted more equality in any new relationship. Said a 33-year-old working-class woman, who was married for seven years and had one child:

Men expect things to be done for them. Men I date expect me to take care of them. Their attitude is, what can you do for me. If that's their attitude—if I have to put out for them—I don't need it.

A poverty-level woman who was married for six years said:

Men will mess you up. The worst thing is if they come and live with you. They will hen and pen off you. Then they leave you in worse shape. There's always a catch. My current boyfriend will leave too. There's always a catch. He's slick. But he's paid his way. Once they give you money, then it gets bad even with a good man. They own you then.

In addition to experiencing difficulties finding the right kind of men, women stated that having children made dating much more difficult. Some said that men did not want to date women with children.

I've been alone for five years and I haven't met any compatible men yet. As soon as they hear you have three kids, they say forget it. [37-year-old middle-class white woman]

Some men can't accept women with children. They say, "They're not mine. The father's not doing for them, why should I?" [37-year-old black cashier, married ten years, two children]

Other women said they were afraid their children would become emotionally attached to new boyfriends and would get hurt if the relationship ended. Said a 28-year-old middle-class white woman, "A child can get close to somebody you're dating. That's happened now. I'm about to break up with the guy I've been dating and my daughter is close to him." Still others said that being with children all the time made it very difficult to find a time and place to be with men, a problem which their ex-husbands did not have.

> Dating was hard earlier. I couldn't do it because of the kids. There was no place in the house we could be alone. But my ex-husband could go out with whomever he wanted to. [41-year-old white working-class office worker, married for twenty-two years, with three children]

Some women did not feel comfortable bringing home men they were dating. Said a white working-class mother of two, "You can't teach them [the children] about morals and then do that." [31-year-old secretary, high school education, married for seven years] Finally, like the following woman, several women mentioned that they would have to take into account their children's safety.

> I'm very protective of my daughter. I would never bring anyone in the house if I thought he would ever lay a hand on her. I would definitely hurt someone if they bothered her. [36-year-old black hospital technician, married for thirteen years, with one child]

THE SITUATION OF DIVORCED WOMEN

Overall the women in this sample expressed both positive and negative feelings about different aspects of their situations as divorced women. The majority of the women were positive about being divorced; but a minority were negative. The majority wanted to remarry; while a minority had rejected marriage. Many were happy because they had remarried, had partners, or were dating; while 43 percent of the women had no intimate attachments, and many of them thought it was unlikely that they would find compatible partners. These women, however, were uniformly negative about one issue, their feelings about how divorce affected their lifestyle and standard of living. They expressed bitter feelings about their economic status. They believed that divorced women were treated badly in our society, and they felt like second-class citizens.

These women frequently compared their situation to that of men and believed their own situation to be much worse. They saw themselves as left "holding the bag."

> It's rough for divorced women. I really feel sorry for a lot of women, especially ones with more kids than I have. I only have two. Men walk out with no guilt. You could kill them, you really could. They leave debts behind. [34-year-old white working-class woman, married eleven years]

By contrast, they believed men could move on to new experiences.

> The situation of divorced women is terrible. They suffer. Men can pick up and go on like they are single. We keep on struggling with the kids. They party and have fun. [42-year-old black psychiatric technician, married for nineteen years, three children]

> The situation of divorced women is rotten. Legally women do not get their due. The children aren't protected. Also, there is no stigma for divorced men. They can make a new life. Women have to take what men will give. [44-year-old teacher, married twenty-one years, two children]

This woman deplored the inequality that women face.

> Women are still short-changed. It's still a man's world. It irks me that it's "natural" for women to assume all the responsibility for children. Why do I always have to be the one to take them to school and to the doctor? It should be 50–50.
> Actually though, it's really no different than when I was married. We were both working.... He worked pretty close to our home. He got finished with work at around 4:30 and then went to see friends or fooled around. I meanwhile had to kill myself to get from work to pick my daughter up at the childcare center. It was a terrible hassle. Then I would do all the cooking of dinner.
> But you know, I can't believe it. I never questioned that. I don't think I ever said anything to him. But it's just not fair. [31-year-old white working-class woman in accounting, with two children]

These women believed that men made rules and laws that promoted their own interests and disadvantaged women.

> Women's situation is pitiful. I think there's too much divorce and it's a man's world. They make the laws and they all profit by them. [41-year-old white legal secretary, married for twelve years, with three children]

> The situation of divorced women is deplorable, but it won't ever get any better. The judges have to pay attention and listen. They have to lower the cost of divorce. Maybe a woman should hear all divorce cases, or a man and a woman. [49-year-old white middle-class woman, married for twenty-six years]

Some women cited a long list of things which they believed should be changed to help divorced women.

> The loss of the alimony laws has been a real problem. The new laws haven't helped women at all and things have gotten worse for divorced women. I think enforcement of child support is helping. That's a real problem.... We need day

care and maternity leaves. Women shouldn't be spending half of their salaries on child care. [37-year-old white graduate student]

The situation of divorced women is unfair. They get no moral support. They have the children and they have to start a whole new life by themselves. A lot of women don't have extended families, and they have to find work. There should be groups to help women with the kids, so women can get away once in a while. Someone should help women make sure of their legal entitlement, so they don't just settle. They have to think about their future. [28-year-old poverty-level unemployed woman]

Other women focused on a particular issue, perhaps the issue that affected them the most, such as childcare.

The situation of divorced women sucks. Women's wages are so low that that overrides everything. If I could change something I would really work on childcare. I know there's childcare now in some big companies. But what about the small ones? [40-year-old working-class woman, married for nine years, with three children]

One middle-class white woman said she felt that at work she was "tested to see what comes first, my work or my child." Others mentioned jobs. Women were acutely aware of their low pay.

I think financially it's very difficult cause most women didn't have the education and secretarial jobs only pay about $13,000 and you can't support a family on that. [26-year-old white mailroom worker, married for five years, with one child]

Some women mentioned their need of food stamps.

We need more money. Divorced women with children should be able to get food stamps. Food is the largest expense. If I could get food stamps, it would be a big help and I could meet my other obligations. [46-year-old black school bus monitor, married for thirty-one years, with nine children]

Many women stressed that they need more information about services available to them.

The situation of divorced women is terrible. I don't think enough is done for them. If things are out there to help them, I don't think divorced women are aware of them. I think divorced women need information about how to get food stamps, medical care, assistance for paying utilities. I'm not talking about welfare. But why should we be penalized? Some politican should take this up, really.

He would get a lot of votes from divorced women. [37-year-old white reception-ist, with a high school education, married for seventeen years, with two children]

I think there should be classes to help divorced women to understand what they're going through and what they can get. It would really help them to talk to others in the same boat. [24-year-old poverty-level black woman, married for five years, with two children]

Several middle-class women mentioned the need for financial planning.

Women need expert advice in financial planning. I didn't know certain things, like about the cost of living for child support and the debt cushion. The problem is that women are thinking about "getting a divorce." They don't realize all the other things, that it means thinking about custody, financial planning, that they have to think and plan for a career. There were a lot of things I didn't think of until six months later—wills, beneficiaries, mortgage insurance. [34-year-old black middle-class woman, married for eight years, with one child]

Another middle-class woman pointed out that many women have no experi-ence managing finances.

Many women don't do financial things while they are married. Then after a divorce they feel like they've been raped legally. They don't know all the decisions that were made. They've lost out materially. Their self-esteem is already low. Women have to have partnerships in their marriages. They can't turn all those responsibilities over. [49-year-old middle-class woman, married for ten years, with two children]

Two women mentioned an ongoing need to be protected from abuse.

I feel myself, personally, I didn't really have that many problems, but talking to other women, they don't get any support. They're afraid of being beat up. There's a hell of a lot of women with a hell of a lot of problems. If a woman wants to go to school, it should be made easier. [43-year-old white waitress, married for twenty-one years, with two children]

Because of abuse some women still have the problem of harrassment. There should be some way to keep the men away, keep them out. [26-year-old poverty-level black woman, married for five years, with two children]

Women's comments on their economic situation form an interesting con-trast with their positive feelings about their current state of mind, which for many is now better than it was during their marriage. It is significant that so many women are positive about their divorces despite their negative feelings about their economic status, their inability to support their families in an ade-quate lifestyle, and their sense that they were treated unjustly. Their comments reveal, once again, how many resources for women in our society are tied to the institution of marriage.

CHILDREN

The question of how divorce affects children is critical to our understanding of the impact of divorce on families. Some believe that divorce creates many problems for children and has a generally negative impact on their well-being. They point to research showing that children from divorced families suffer higher high school dropout rates, higher teenage marriages, and greater rates of single parenthood, which can result in low self-esteem, emotional disorders, anti-social behavior, and depression. These problems can be exacerbated by changes in their residence and school and the loss of their familiar lifestyle. Some believe that children are paying too high a price for the mistakes and flaws of their parents. A few believe that this is an important enough reason to try and curb the divorce rate and keep families together.[4]

However, despite the fact that many researchers have studied the effect of divorce on the intellectual, social, and emotional functioning of children, many unanswered questions remain. This is because it is difficult to determine whether problems identified in children of divorce result from the divorce itself, from problems in the marriage, or from other circumstances that predated the marriage. Many studies of the impact of divorce on children assess children's adjustment at only one point in time. In these studies, researchers fail to compare the children of divorce with children in intact marriages. Such comparisons might show that problems observed in children were due to the stress and tension of the marriage, not the hardships associated with divorce. Others point out that studies fail to take into account the impact of the decline in the standard of living of the mother and children. And finally, the fact that many studies of the children of divorce are based on clinical samples calls into question their findings. Clinical samples, unlike random and representative samples, draw on selected populations from counseling or treatment programs. These samples often overrepresent the number of people with problems.[5]

Frank Furstenberg and Andrew Cherlin stress that to avoid overestimating the problems of children of divorce, these children should be compared with children from intact families. For example, they cite data from the National Survey of Children that found that 34 percent of parents who were separated or divorced reported that their children had behavior or discipline problems at school, in contrast to 20 percent of parents from intact families. Furstenberg and Cherlin point out that while, on the one hand, these figures would seem to indicate that children of divorce have more problems than other children, on the other hand, 66 percent of all children from families of divorce did not have serious behavior problems in school. Paul D'Amato concludes that when comparing children of divorce and children of two-parent families, the average differences between children are small rather than large.[6]

Some researchers now believe that children in two-parent families where there is a lot of conflict are actually no better off—and often are worse off—than children in divorced single-parent families. These researchers find that many of the problems which children of divorce exhibit, such as behavior problems and low scores on academic tests, were in fact present while their parents were still together. They also believe that children's level of adjustment is related to the level of conflict between their parents following the divorce. After examining the evidence on children's well-being after divorce, Furstenberg and Cherlin conclude that the best predictor of children's adjustment is a good relationship with the mother, and a low level of conflict between the mother and the father.[7]

Women in this sample were asked whether they thought their divorce had any impact on their children. It is important to compare mothers' accounts of their children's behavior and reactions, and their interpretations of that behavior, with data that is based on other measures of well-being. Do mothers identify the same factors as critical to the well-being of their children as do researchers? Are most mothers positive or negative about their children's emotional development? Of course mothers have their own biases that may affect their outlook on their children. As Susan Krantz points out, mothers who are depressed and unhappy about their divorces may see only the negative impact of divorce on their children, while those who are happy about their divorce may minimize its negative impact.[8] Nevertheless, it is very important to have the observations of mothers, who typically are the closest observers of their children's behavior.

Women were not asked fixed-choice questions about each child, but were asked to describe in their own words whether they thought the divorce had any impact on their children. A content analysis of their statements showed that a small percentage of women (8 percent) reported that the divorce was overall a positive thing for their children, and 54 percent reported the divorce had no effect on their children in the present, although some cited problems in the past. In contrast, 38 percent stated that they were concerned about some aspect of at least one child's behavior. Many of this latter group felt that the divorce had been very hard on at least one of their children.

There were no significant differences based on social class, length of time since the separation, or father's visitation in the mothers' reports of their children's well-being. More white women reported that their children had problems (42 percent) than black women (28 percent). Those with elementary and high-school children reported significantly more problems than those with younger children. One could speculate that this was because older children were more verbal about their discontent, or perhaps younger children were less attached to their fathers, whom they had known for less time before the divorce occurred. We really cannot draw conclusions about the effects of divorce on children of different ages, however, as it is difficult to separate the effects of age at divorce, length of time since divorce, and current age.[9]

Mothers Report Positive Reactions

The 8 percent of mothers who reported that the divorce had a positive effect on their children saw the divorce as lifting some kind of burden from their children. Most of these women and some of their children experienced physical abuse at the hands of fathers.

> She [8 years old] was thrilled that we separated, to be away from the abuse. She never wants us in the same space again. [33-year-old black secretary, married for eight years, with an 8-year-old child]

> The children are happy. With all that violence they were mixed up. The oldest was worried and didn't do very well in school. But all that is better now. They are good kids. [30-year-old poverty-level Hispanic woman, married for eleven years, with four children, ages 7, 8, 11, and 13]

A 31-year-old working-class mother of two [white waitress, married for ten years] talked about how her children were much "better" and more "relaxed," especially the older one who had seen her father's drug addiction and who had seen her father being violent to her mother.

One woman described how much better her son was now because he had been severely emotionally abused by his father, who had also abused her physically. According to this mother, her ex-husband would call her son "a wimp," "a faggot," and "a baby" and would sometimes make him cry in front of his friends. She stated that both her son (14 years old) and daughter (8 years old) hated their father and never saw him. She concluded:

> The divorce has made the children better people. . . . My son is a completely different kid. He has friends now and they come over to the house. Before he couldn't have friends over because my husband would embarrass him in front of his friends, or embarrass his friends. He has a lot of girls calling for him too. [36-year-old white police officer, high school education, married for thirteen years, with one 8-year-old and one 14-year-old]

Some of these women, however, did worry that at some point in the future the divorce could cause emotional difficulties for their child or children. One woman who experienced a lot of violence in her relationship stated:

I think the divorce had more effect on the children when we were together. When he left, a great burden was lifted. While he was here, my daughter just lived in her room. My daughter has really been helped by the counseling. But my son refused to go. I think he's going to have to deal with this at some time. Maybe it'll come up when he's 30. [37-year-old white receptionist, married for seventeen years, with two children, ages 14 and 17]

Mothers Report No Problems

Forty-six percent of the mothers reported that their children experienced no particular problems. These women gave several reasons for this. The greatest percentage of women in this group said there are no problems because the marriage ended when the child or children were so young that they did not remember life before the divorce. They said things like, "He was just little, he didn't know his Dad at all"; "He left right after my son was born, my son doesn't remember him being here"; or, "She doesn't know any other way of life."

These mothers also attributed their children's lack of difficulty to the fact that their husbands were never actively involved with the children during the marriage. In some cases this was because the fathers worked a night shift and were gone evenings; in other cases, the fathers were not emotionally involved with their children. Women said things like, "He was never there. The kids didn't know him that well"; or, "He worked nights, he wasn't around when the children were here"; or, as this woman said:

They never had a father who was there like normal fathers anyway. He wasn't an easy, typical father. So it wasn't really so different after the divorce. [41-year-old white supervisor, married for twenty-two years, with three children, ages 15, 21, and 22]

Still other mothers said that because their children were seeing their father regularly, things were not that different for the children. Said a 30-year-old working-class mother of two, "In the beginning, when we first separated, I think they felt partly responsible, but now it's cooled down. They have time with their father. It's a lot like it was." [white woman with a high school education, married for seven years] Another woman's son was in high school when she left her ex-husband because of violence.

At first my son didn't like the divorce. He wanted us to stay together. I think it affected him in school. His marks came down. After a while he got out of it because he was close to his father and he maintained that relationship. [42-year-old white poverty-level nurse's aide, married for eight years, with a 19-year-old son]

Another woman said her 15-year-old son was helped by the fact that she and her ex-husband got along. She claims: "He's been great, really good. He was affected for a little bit but knowing we're friendly helped a lot." [30-year-old working-class white office worker, married for fifteen years, with one child] One woman attributed her daughter's successful adjustment to a godfather.

> My daughter wasn't affected by the divorce. She has a fantastic godfather, my girlfriend's husband. He's the only male figure in her life but he's been very important, including disciplining her. [36-year-old black working-class woman, married for thirteen years, with a 12-year-old child]

Several women mentioned that they had to deal with their children's questions about their family situation.

> They don't remember living with their father so it hasn't hurt them that way. But my daughter [five-and-a-half] is starting to ask questions like "Why don't you live with Daddy?" She really wants to know that now, why she isn't like the other kids. [31-year-old working class woman, married for five years, with a 3-year-old and a 5-year-old]

Researchers report contradictory findings on the question of whether a child's well-being is related to contact with the noncustodial parent, typically the father; some believe frequent contact with the father is a factor in children's well-being, while others do not. Robert Emery concludes that there is "no clear evidence linking children's adjustment to a continuing relationship with the outside parent"; nonetheless, he believes that visitation with the noncustodial parent has considerable symbolic value for a child, which continues into adulthood. Furstenberg and Cherlin also report that a good relationship with a stepparent has a beneficial effect on children's well-being.[10]

Some women reported that their children experienced certain problems after the divorce, but were now fine. A 34-year-old woman who was married eight years said, "Initially my daughter was angry but now she feels she has the best of both worlds. She has two families, two intact sets of relationships, each with a different style." [graduate student, with one child] Another woman said:

> In the beginning the children kept saying they wanted him back. It was really hard. But now, they're just normal, adjusted kids. It doesn't bother them anymore. They go to school with so many kids who are in the same situation. [35-year-old white secretary, married for fourteen years with three children]

Some mothers reported conflicts with their children that began in the teenaged years and resulted in the children spending time at their father's home.

After they returned to the mother's home some months later, these mother-child relationships improved. According to one mother, when she and her daughter had conflicts, her daughter would say, "Well I'll just go to Dad's." This woman finally sent her daughter to her father's house, which was nearby. She stayed for several months and then happily came back. This mother said she and her daughter get along much better now. Another mother reported that she and her daughter had been very close, but started having conflicts when her daughter was 14. Her daughter frequently became upset and began challenging the mother. Things escalated to the point where the daughter threw something at the mother. This woman then sent her daughter to her father's. When she came back their relationship also was much better.

Finally, some of these women said their children were fine, but that they believed the divorce had had some effect on them, although they were not sure what that is. As one woman, who was separated from her husband when her daughter was an infant, said, "I think it will affect her. It has to." Or, as another said:

> They have generally reacted very well. They've had their moments of confusion, but as they get older, I feel they've handled it very well. I'm sure the divorce must have had an effect on them, although I can't say what particular effect. [47-year-old white medical secretary, married for twenty-two years with one child from her current marriage and five from her previous marriage]

A few mothers reported that their children were distancing themselves emotionally from their fathers. The implication was that the children were doing this because they were not seeing their father.

> I don't think my son really thinks of him as a father. At my son's school they had them go buy Christmas presents as a way of learning about money. My son bought a present for me, my mother, and my father. And he called my father Dad. [38-year-old black middle-class woman, married for nine years, with a 6-year-old son]

> One day my daughter [6 years old] said to me, "Mommy, Daddy's dead." I said "Where did you get that idea?" She said, "He just is." I guess that's the way she deals with her anger toward him. [36-year-old black pharmacy technician, married for thirteen years, with a 12-year-old daughter]

Mothers Report Concerns About Children's Well-Being

Thirty-eight percent of the women (42 percent of the white women and 28 percent of the black women) reported concerns about the behavior of at least one of their children, with no class differences between them. Women reported that children experienced some negative effects from the divorce itself, but even more from the conflicts and problems that occurred during the marriage. Women reported three major concerns. The first was how the hard-living that their children witnessed during the marriage could affect them in the future. While some of the women cited above said the divorce had been a positive thing for their children because it enabled them to escape from violence and drugs, in other cases women said that their children suffered from the effects of the domestic violence and drug use that took place during the marriage.

These women, who described their children as very angry and very hurt, worried about the long-term effects of hard-living and violence on their children. First, they mentioned the effects on their children of witnessing domestic violence.

> My daughter [14-year-old] doesn't like her father. You heard her. She says she doesn't want to get married if it means getting beaten the way I was. Sometimes she scares me she's so tough. I feel like my son [17-year-old] will have to deal with all this sometime. He has a happy-go-lucky attitude like everything will be OK. But he was affected. His father beat him. [41-year-old white working-class woman, married for twenty-one years, with two children]

> He's mixed up about his father. He wants us to live together. He remembers everything that happened. He saw me get cut badly when he was two. [28-year-old poverty-level black woman, married for six years, with a 5-year-old son]

Another mother said that her children, ages 11 and 13, refused to see their father because they were afraid of him. She said her ex-husband was "very rough on the children, physically and emotionally," particularly the son. The father took his daughter to court because she would not see him. The judge told the daughter she had to visit her father, but she refused. According to this woman, "My son hates his father for what he's done, but deep down inside he wants a relationship. With my daughter, when he took her to court, she really hated him and wants nothing to do with him."

Some researchers believe that children who are exposed to domestic violence experience more behavior problems, emotional difficulties, and reduced social competence than children who are not exposed to violence. While witnessing domestic violence has a strong negative impact on some children, however, it does not on others. A good relationship with the primary parent can act as a buffer against the negative effects of witnessing domestic violence.[11]

Another mother said that her ex-husband always "came and went" during the marriage and abused alcohol.

My son [five-and-a-half years old] has suffered. He's very anxious and clingy. There were times in the past when if I left my mother's to go to the grocery store he would scream. I guess he thought I might leave him too. He saw his father leave when he was 2. [39-year-old white working-class government worker, married for seven years, with one child]

One woman reported that her 14-year-old son was very angry at his father, who was a drug addict, and that because his father stole family property to support his drug habit, her son never wanted to see him again.

All of this has been very very hard on my son [14 years old]. . . . I felt damned if I did and damned if I didn't about my son's seeing his father. I'm sorry that I listened to my mother and sister and my son had to see his father disintegrate. But also if I had forbidden my son from seeing his father then he would have been angry at me. [39-year-old white hairdresser, married for sixteen years, with 2 children, ages 1 and 14]

According to another woman, whose ex-husband was an alcoholic and used a lot of violence:

The divorce really had an effect on my older son. He's full of anger. He's insecure. He saw so much wild, crazy stuff at home. . . . He's in counseling. He'll be in counseling for a long time. There's no problem with his school work but he has behavior problems in school. His Dad let him down a few times, like not being there when he said he would. That was really hard on him. Also, he got beat up by his dad.

The younger one is just confused. He was only 2 years old when we split up. I was so preoccupied with everything that I actually didn't feed him enough. He didn't complain, so I didn't think about it. [33-year-old white middle-class woman, married for seven years, with two children, ages 5 and 7]

The following mother described her son as growing angrier, as he has been unable to get his father's attention. According to this woman, her ex-husband drank a lot and eventually ended up on drugs.

My son [15 years old] wanted his father to pay attention to him all through the marriage. But all through the marriage it was me who did that. I was the one who took him to all his sports events; it was me there with the other fathers. My husband went to bars. He was more interested in being with his drinking buddies.

His father takes him once in a while. It's not the greatest places—the mall, the flea market, watching the VCR at his place. He always talked about how he would take his son hunting and fishing. This is hunting season, isn't it?

After the divorce my son used to call his father. But he's stopped doing that.

My son's starting to cool off to his father. Recently I asked him if he was going to call his father and he said, "I've had a divorce from him." Now my ex-husband is trying more to get in touch with his son. He realizes that his son is drawing away from him.

My son never had any trouble in school. He was a model student. But since the separation he's started acting out. He talked all the time in school for a while. Now I've just learned that he is starting to play hookey. I think he's just trying to get attention. But the person whose attention he wants—his father—he's not getting.

My son seems to be pulling away from my mother too. He was always close to her. I wish he would talk to a counselor. I try to get him to talk to me but it does-n't work. I know this is affecting him a lot. I just don't know what to do [sound-ing sad and scared]. I tell him never, ever to start drinking. [white office clerk, married for sixteen years, with one child]

In addition to the effects of domestic violence, drugs, and alcohol, women also mentioned fathers' visitation as a factor in their children's well-being. While research does not demonstrate a definitive link between children's well-being and the frequency of the fathers' visitation, some mothers believed their children were angry because they did not get to see their father enough. Said a poverty-level mother of three, "My oldest misses her father a lot. She has behav-ior problems in school and I think that's the reason. She doesn't feel quite whole. My son misses his dad." [32-year-old white store clerk, married for eight years with three children, ages 5, 7, and 8] Another mother reported that her son was "angry, violent, and rebellious" because he was not seeing his father enough. During the marriage, he was close to his father, but now, according to this woman, the father was always with his new girlfriend and did not spend time with his son, who had become very bitter. One time when the son was angry, he ripped the basement door off its hinges and then ripped the stairway banister off the wall [married for nineteen years, with one child]. One woman reported that her daughter, who was 13, had become more angry recently. She believed this was because her daughter had not been able to see her father much. He was in prison and was recently transferred to a prison further away. This mother had no car. She hoped her ex-husband's sister would be able to take the children to see their father. Another mother said her children were angry because their father spent time with children in another relationship.

It has been very difficult for the children. They're nervous and angry and they're hurt and they hate sharing their father with his wife and three kids. [33-year-old white woman, married for thirteen years, with two children, ages ten and 13]

Several women reported that erratic patterns of visitation were very hard on the children.

He sees them less than once a year. I don't like it because it hurts the children but there is nothing I can do about it. The children try to stay in touch with him but he's usually not available. If he is he makes false promises. They don't really have a relationship with their father. They say they don't have a father. [33-year-old poverty-level black woman who works in a bar, married for sixteen years, with two children, ages 14 and 16]

He could see them anytime but he only comes once every five or six months. I don't pressure him into seeing them. He can be obnoxious. He kept the oldest one upset. He promised to see her, she waits all day, and he doesn't show up. So I don't pressure him because he makes promises he doesn't keep. [52-year-old black secretary, married for eighteen years, with two children, ages 11 and 18]

In the following two cases, boys left their mothers' homes to live with their fathers and were not seeing their mothers. They were angry at their mothers, whose relationships with the fathers were also strained. In the first case, the mother said her son was very angry. She and her ex-husband, who was an alcoholic during the marriage, had a relationship that still had a lot of conflict.

We've been having terrible problems with my son. It's the hardest thing in my life. It's heartbreaking. My son has gotten kicked out of a lot of schools. Thank goodness I got him into the high school here. He's a senior but he's there by the skin of his teeth. All the counselors we've seen about his getting thrown out say he's a very angry young man. He's got his father's violent temper and my stubbornness.

My son has also been very unpleasant to my new husband. Finally one night two months ago my son hit him—my son's bigger than he is. And I said, "That's it, you're leaving." My son actually ran out of the house. He's been living with his father ever since. It's really heartbreaking [fighting tears]. I'm not sure I will ever see my son again. As I said, he's stubborn like me. [41-year-old white house cleaner, married for seventeen years, with two children, ages 17 and 20]

In another case, a mother reported that her son had been suicidal at one point and at the time of the interview had run away to his father's. His father used drugs during the marriage and still did.

Some women, whose ex-husbands left them for other women, reported that their children had particular problems. A mother of teen-aged girls thought their relationships with men would be affected by seeing their father leave.

The girls' legacy from this is that they'll have trouble trusting men. The older one, who felt betrayed, goes from boyfriend to boyfriend. The younger one was always scared of her father because he was away so much. [44-year-old white teacher, married for twenty-one years, with two children, ages 17 and 18]

Another woman worried about her son being burdened with her own sadness.

> My son [6 years old] has been through a lot. One time after my husband left I just had to cry and cry. My son came over to me and said, "Mommy why are you crying?" I said, "Because Daddy hurt my feelings." My son said, "Don't cry anymore Mommy, I'll take care of you." A child shouldn't have to go through that. Of course twenty minutes later he was in the next room throwing things. [37-year-old white working-class woman, married for thirteen years, with one child]

The following mother, whose ex-husband left her for another woman, was angry and bitter at her ex-husband. She spoke of her son being protective of her. Perhaps he sensed her sadness and loss, or perhaps he was worried that she would leave him. Or perhaps because of her own anger she could only see the negative effects of the divorce.

> My younger son [5 years old] doesn't want to be away from me very much. He's very protective of me, very protective. Even at the beach he wants to know if I'm OK when I've gone in the water. [34-year-old white working-class woman, seeking employment, married for eleven years, with two children, ages 5 and 9]

Finally, women expressed a variety of other concerns, particularly about their children's sense of security. Several women believed their children needed a male role model. One woman stated that her son was not sure of his manhood and craved male support. This woman worried even though the separation was fairly amicable and her daughter had developed a good relationship with her father.

> My daughter [6 years old] still longs for the family to be together. The divorce has affected her.... In the beginning my daughter had terrible separation anxiety from me. And when she went to my ex-husband's for the weekend, at first she cried and cried. It was terrible. It's fine now.... A good thing is that my daughter's relationship with her father has really developed.... I think a negative thing though is that children like this lose their childhood very soon. You should hear her talk. They have to handle things so early. And she still would really like us to get together. [37-year-old white middle-class woman, married for six years, with one child]

This woman was dealing with feelings of guilt about leaving her marriage because of the pain it has caused her children.

> I think sometimes that we adults are very irresponsible about our children and the pain we can cause them through divorce. I needed the divorce for myself but

it really hurt my children. I'll never forget the look and actions of my son when we were separated. He tried everything he could to get us together.... He had a lot of anger. The divorce made him more insecure. It interrupts childrens' lives.... The thing I feel worst about the whole divorce is how it affected the children. [49-year-old middle-class woman, married for ten years, with two children, ages five and eight]

While we cannot draw any definitive conclusions from these data because they are not longitudinal, nor do they compare children of divorce and children still in marriages, the accounts of these mothers indicate that, as is the case for the women themselves, children also experience very different "divorces." This makes it difficult to generalize about the effects of divorce on children. The majority of mothers believe their children do not suffer long-term adverse consequences due to the divorce. These mothers' views are similar to those of the middle-class mothers in Terry Arendell's sample who reported that their children experienced few long-term problems as a result of the divorce. Further, mothers in Arendell's sample stated that negative social stereotypes of children with single mothers made them feel discouraged and isolated from other mothers, who they believed subscribed to these stereotypes.[12]

As for the mothers who reported that their children have been adversely affected by the divorce, the majority were worried less about problems resulting from the divorce itself and more about the long-term effects of the father's violence and hard-living behavior during the marriage and after the separation. At the same time, some mothers did report problems for children resulting from the divorce itself, such as dealing with their father's leaving and their mother's anger and sadness. From these data there is no way of determining whether any of these will be long-term problems for the children or not.

CONCLUSION

Because so many economic and social resources in our society are distributed through marriage, women have a tremendous amount to lose at divorce. Almost all of these women, regardless of class or race, were very angry about their loss of resources, which they felt was caused by women's inferior social position. At the same time, the majority of the women felt positive about being divorced and were glad to be out of their marriages. This seeming contradiction is due to the fact that many women were happy to be away from hard-living, controlling, and confining marriages and to be able to be more independent— to begin their own lives and find their own identity. Their experiences left the women in this sample of two minds about remarriage. The majority still believe in the institution and would like a new marriage; they felt they had just happened to marry the wrong person and they expected to find a man with whom they could have a more sharing, equal relationship. A minority of women, however, rejected marriage because they believed it stifled their own personhood and growth.

These data further support the point that at the present time we are experiencing a disjuncture between men's and women's expectations for marriage. In her study of two-career couples, Arlie Hochschild describes most men as having a "transitional" gender ideology, favoring some but not full equality with their wives.[13] As we have seen in this study, many women want much more equality with marital partners. Some of the women in this study will undoubtedly go on to find more equality in new relationships, while others will not. There was also a high level of consciousness among these women regarding their subordinate social position. Many women were angry about what they perceived as injustices to women as a class, particularly divorced women. If women's movement leaders were to harness this anger, these divorced women's energy could be a force for making some of the changes they so desperately want.

As for the children, a signficant portion of the women felt that their children had not experienced long-term problems because of the divorce. For those women who were concerned about the effect of the divorce on their children, many were concerned about problems that originated during the marriage and preceded the divorce, such as hard-living. These data suggest that while we should continue to research the effects of divorce on children, at the same time we should avoid spreading alarmist views about the impact of divorce on children. We should more carefully focus on the specific harms to children that occur both within two-parent families and within single-parent families. Within two-parent families, children can suffer from violence, from the effects of drug and alcohol abuse, and from the lack of a close relationship with their father. Thus, to promote children's well-being we should improve conditions of marriage more generally. We should also make a major social commitment to promoting an active, meaningful conception of fatherhood in our culture.

Chapter 8

CONCLUSION

In this book I have examined the major factors that shape the circumstances and constrain the opportunities of divorced mothers. The experiences of the women in this study challenge the dominant frameworks used to describe the divorce experience. Those in the "decline" tradition, who believe divorce is an indicator of "family breakdown," argue that high divorce rates reflect men's and women's decreased ability to make commitments. They believe that children particularly are the victims of this excess of individualism. Some commentators have proposed reversing this trend with campaigns that promote family values, in the hope that these values will hold marriages together. The experiences of the women in this study, however, challenge the popular view that it is a loss of traditional family values that has led to a high divorce rate and to a breakdown of the family. The dominant approaches to divorce fail to take into account important realities of how women experience divorce. Further, they mask inequalities and divert attention away from the real issues—the unemployment, poverty, and male dominance which create hardship in marriage, and the unfair distribution of resources to divorced women and children. While excessive individualism may well be a problem in other arenas of American society, it does not characterize the behavior of these divorced women. For these mothers, divorce is part of a a larger system whose real problems are violence against women, the lack of social supports for single parents and children, the lack of concern for women's equity in the labor market, and the resulting economic hardship and poverty of divorced mothers and other single parents.

After divorce, all women and children experience a drastic reduction in their standard of living. Many mothers develop creative strategies to get by on their low incomes. Since our social system fails to support women outside of marriage, however, we end up making women and children pay a high price for divorce. The poverty rate for divorced women with children in the United States, 39 percent, is shocking. The women in this sample experienced the loss of their homes, the need to take a second job while doing all the child-rearing themselves, lower-quality child care, and the inability to buy basic necessities and obtain adequate health care for themselves and their children. Divorced mothers with less education and few job skills could not get jobs which provided medical insurance for themselves or their children or enabled them to live on their income. Many had to rely on AFDC, which forces women to live below the poverty level.

The reality of poverty among divorced women continues to be ignored. The prevailing image of divorce as a white middle-class phenomenon is not only inaccurate but serves to perpetuate the denial of hardship which can occur during marriage and divorce. Unemployment and job insecurity take a serious toll on marriages and are major contributors to divorce. Job insecurity is a growing problem at all socio-economic levels, yet it particularly affects lower-income and minority people. Thus, while all women face economic hardship at divorce, and divorce is a major contributor to the feminization of poverty, this is particularly true for lower-income and minority women. Gender inequalities in marriage and at divorce are further compounded by class inequalities and the racialization of poverty.

Finally, children suffer along with their mothers as a result of our policies. Some researchers estimate that two out of five children will see their parents divorce before their late teens. Twenty-five percent of all children live with only one parent. The poverty rate of single-mother families is 50 percent. Yet we continue to view the hardships these mothers and children face as their own, "private" problem.[1]

WOMEN'S VIEWS OF MARRIAGE AND DIVORCE

A variety of factors indicate that the women in this sample did not view divorce as a sign of family decline. First, the majority chose to leave their marriages. These mothers left their marriages for a number of reasons. However they particularly identified gender issues as reasons for leaving. Some left because of their dissatisfaction with traditional gender roles; they found their husbands too controlling or unsupportive emotionally. In a second category of cases, women left their marriage because of their husbands' violence. While many women in the sample experienced violence, those who left because of it experienced particularly serious violence. In a third category of cases, women left because of their husbands' "hard-living" behavior including drinking, drugs, and "running around," or spending time on the streets with other men—hard-living is often associated with men who experience unemployment and unsteady and unreliable working conditions. However it is important to highlight the role of gender in hard-living; more often that not, it is women who are the victims of these behaviors.

The fact that many women left their marriages because of hard-living and violence is significant. In recent years writers have focused on how middle-class values of companionate marriage have spread through all social classes. While this indeed may be true, these writers have not paid sufficient attention to the persistence of hard-living, which devastated the marriages of many of the women in this sample, or to the widespread existence of violence in marriages. Many women, even at great personal cost, are also leaving their marriages specifically because of violence. Indeed in the wake of increased publicity about domestic violence, many people now urge women to leave relationships when their husbands or boyfriends abuse them, and the public often looks down on women who do not leave abusive relationships. Unfortunately, we then make these women pay a high price for leaving, since we fail to provide adequate supports for them.

These women's accounts indicate that those who view divorce as a sign of "decline" do not ask who is experiencing the decline. They fail to understand how negative and destructive marriage can be. How could we argue that divorce is predominantly a negative event if we were really thinking about the high rates of domestic violence in marriage? While the problem of domestic violence is now more widely acknowledged, we have failed to understand its meaning and significance for marriage and divorce. It is as if acknowledging the existence of this problem constitutes a sufficient response. We engage in a collective social denial of this widespread and deeply troubling aspect of male treatment of women, of the toll it takes on marriages, and of the continuing role it can play after a separation.

Another factor that does not fit a picture of decline is the fact that the great majority of these women, no matter what their race or class, are glad that they left their marriages and, like women in other studies, glad to be divorced. While research shows that many divorced men also state they are happy to be out of failed marriages, it is striking that mothers are so positive about being divorced, given the high economic price they pay for leaving marriages. Some of the women were glad to be free of the situation of hard-living and violence, and some were happy to be free of the more subordinate roles they played during their marriages. At the same time, the majority of these women remained strongly committed to marriage and would like to remarry. Marriage is the avenue through which women in our society secure companionship, security, money, and—depending on the father—help with childcare. The women in this sample made a social, emotional, and financial investment in marriage, which they lost with divorce.

Some of the women, however, did have negative feelings about being divorced, such as the women who were left by their ex-husbands for other women. Women described either "being left for another woman," or leaving because their husbands were "running around." The women who were left experienced the end of the marriage as a painful rejection. Further, a minority of women viewed their overall experience of divorce as negative. These women believed they lost a major investment. They also felt "left behind" with the children, while their ex-husbands were free to move on to new relationships. Those who wished to remarry and had not were angry that they had less access to the economic and social resources that our society distributes through marriage. Some of these women were not hopeful about finding new partners.

At the same time, a third of all women in the sample questioned whether the institution of marriage was good for them. They felt that marriage would not let them be equals with their husbands, and that they could not realize the amount of independence they wanted in marriage. They spoke of equality and independence as incompatible with marriage. A number were afraid of being controlled in another marriage as they had been in their first one. Thus, the problem that these women expressed was not that marriage was declining as an institution, but that they wanted a different kind of marriage, a more equal kind of marriage. These women do not fit the picture of modern "couples" leaving marriages to pursue their own individualistic goals at the expense of their spouses and children.

Finally, while many women were happy that they divorced, all women in the sample expressed yet another problem with being divorced. They expressed uniformly negative feelings about their status as divorced women and were angry at the way they were treated as second-class citizens. They felt they were not treated fairly and that men in general, and their ex-husbands in particular, gained economic advantages at their expense. They also felt that being single mothers was very difficult. While a minority of men were active participants in the lives of their children, and a number of fathers did see their children at least once a month, many mothers felt burdened with more than their fair share of childrearing responsibilities and wanted their ex-husbands to be more involved with the children.

In conclusion, these women's accounts of their divorce experiences raise serious questions about the costs and benefits of marriage and about who gains and who loses during marriage and at divorce. How could marriage be improved? Should we worry less about marriage and work to improve the alternatives? This chapter will conclude with these questions. What is clear is that we should not pressure women who have left marriages to return to "marriage as usual." If we really wish to improve the quality of marriage and lower the divorce rate, we must do far more than make pronouncements about family values. We must work for more egalitarian relations in the family—for more sharing of household work, for ending male violence, and for changing the norms that dictate that men should control their female partners. To improve women's status as wives also requires raising the status of girls and women overall by giving them respectable jobs, paying them salaries of comparable worth, and ending sexual harassment and violence.

In schools and families we must also work to reshape men's roles to include meaningful fathering and meaningful participation in the domestic sphere. A small number of men do participate as equals in families before and after divorce. It is time for the majority of men to follow. To accomplish this will require a massive commitment by parents, by institutions such as schools, and by business and other work organizations which currently fail to accommodate the needs of family life.[2]

Finally, to improve marriage and reduce the divorce rate would also require decreasing class and race disadvantages that create unemployment and other economic hardships which are so destructive of marital relationships. Unfortunately, the outlook for improving class and race divisions is not promising at this time. Class divisions in the United States are deepening, intensified by the increased integration of the world economy, the loss of U.S. jobs to other countries, and economic and social policies which fail to curb inequality. Thus, for the foreseeable future, the conditions of marriage will not change dramatically and the divorce rate will not decrease. Given this reality, what specific changes do we need to improve the lives of divorced women and other single mothers with children? First, we must work to improve relationships between family members after divorce. As we have seen in this book, there are many problems which prevent good relationships between fathers and children after divorce. Second, we must improve the economic position of divorced women and their children and reduce the toll that economic hardship takes on their lives. More social welfare policies will be required to help mothers and children survive the destructive effects of economic hardship. I will address these two issues in the following sections.

SOCIAL POLICY AND FAMILY LIFE AFTER DIVORCE

To improve family relationships after divorce, we must examine the conditions of custody and visitation. The area of custody and visitation policy is a complicated one that must be given careful attention. As the data from this study have shown, there are two separate policy issues that affect fathers' participation in the lives of their children after divorce—the question of how to protect mothers and children from abusive fathers and the question of how to encourage contacts between deserving fathers and their children after divorce. The difficulty is achieving both goals, since they each have different and somewhat opposite requirements.

Custody and visitation laws and policies must address the scope and severity of conflict and violence in families after divorce, particularly now that the recommended arrangement for custody is joint legal custody. The high level of violence toward women in marriages and the ongoing serious conflict between a significant minority of couples after marriage makes it imperative that there be no automatic guarantee of mandatory joint residential custody. The law must be ready to limit or deny access to those who use visitation for harassment or engage in other threatening or dangerous behavior. Courts should consider evidence of abuse at every point in negotiations for custody and visitation. In addition, courts should never deny battered women custody of their children because of their "failure" to protect them from the abuser. Further, as various people have recommended, judges should be trained about domestic violence and its legal, sociological, and psychological implications. Simply passing laws does not guarantee that judges will apply or enforce them. State legislatures that vote on custody and visitation rights must also be educated about domestic violence. Some state legislators continue to promote mandatory joint custody, ignoring how much harm this could inflict on women and children. Similarly, if a woman has experienced violence from her partner, we must reconsider policies such as those imposed on AFDC and other single mothers, which require them to identify and maintain contact with fathers. Given the amount of separation violence and harassment which women encounter, such policies may be harmful and even dangerous.[3]

Court-sponsored programs which monitor families in conflict and provide supervision of the exchange of children in safe, neutral places are currently being evaluated. Pending the outcome of their evaluation, courts should continue to provide support services for families with serious conflicts over custody and visitation. Such services include assessment and mediation of visitation disputes, the development of more specific, enforceable court orders, and monitoring visitation by letter or telephone. "Case managers" should be assigned to families which are having a lot of conflict. Such programs are needed for the safety and well-being of mothers, but also for children. Conflict between parents is harmful to children. Mediation teams should be trained in gender dynamics and composed of a man and a woman so that the power inequities in marriage are not duplicated in the mediation process. These mediators should also be trained to detect and respond to physical and sexual child abuse and child neglect as well as to violence against women.[4]

The problem of "childsnatching," or the kidnapping of children, must also be addressed. In addition to the extreme mental anguish for those who experience it, the fear that their children could be taken can lead women to reduce their demands for resources. David Finkelhor and his colleagues propose a variety of measures to reduce the kidnapping of children, including the creation of emergency hotlines, more efficient and tougher legal measures for responding to these cases, strong enforcement policies, and wide publication of the penalties for these crimes.[5]

Finally, the debate over appropriate standards of custody should continue. Some researchers advocate replacing joint custody statutes with the primary caretaker presumption, which awards custody to the parent who has done the caretaking during the marriage. They believe this standard would decrease the number of custody disputes, including "custody blackmail," and reduce the number of court hearings for spurious charges. This would end the problem, described by Terry Arendell, of custody becoming a symbol of "victory or defeat." Some prefer the primary caretaker standard because of the attachment and continuity it provides in the lives of children, whose primary emotional bond is typically with the mother, who usually knows more about the children. According to Arendell, "the rights to be secured would be explicitly and firstly children's: the right to the stability and security of the primary parent-child relationship." Others point out that this is the fairest standard, since mothers invest so heavily of themselves in childrearing, which can then disadvantage them in the job market. Barbara Woodhouse, writing from a child-centered perspective that focuses on children's needs, argues for "earned parenthood" based on the active involvement of fathers and stresses the need for crafting legal standards that reward active caretaking by fathers. At the very least, the idea of there being a limitless ability to challenge custody should be changed. There should also be affordable mediation services available to those with joint custody to work out their disputes.[6]

The access of deserving fathers to their children must also be protected. Arendell advocates expanding the "standard visitation agreement," which is typically every other weekend with an overnight stay, and one evening a week, with additional time for certain holidays and during the summer months. She recommends the development and implementation of more flexible access guidelines for the noncustodial parent. She also proposes the development of a schedule specifying when the noncustodial parent will telephone the children, so the noncustodial parent is assured not only regular access to his children but also telephone conversations with his children that don't have to be mediated through the custodial parent.[7]

However, as Karen Czapanskiy and others have pointed out, fathers who wish access to their children should also take responsibility for their children. Joint custody has given fathers new rights, but not new responsibilities. While the father is given the right to participate in decisions on all issues in his child's life, he is not required to participate in all facets of the child's activities. Nothing happens to the father who fails to provide care during a time period when the visitation agreement stipulates that he is supposed to be caring for the child. This is in contrast to the mother, who is required to allow the father to see the child or face judicially imposed consequences. Thus men can gain advantages from joint custody, while women do not. A parent who fails to comply with visitation agreements should be required to make up the time he missed. The law should also encourage the development of parenting plans that stipulate which parent will be responsible for different caretaking activities.[8]

Finally, while the law certainly has some power to bring about change, we must also look to other arenas for promoting fathers' involvement in childrearing. The law is a crude tool for changing deep-seated social patterns. For those who wish to increase fathers' participation with their children after divorce, these data show that certain major social-structural factors work to distance fathers from their children, including traditional gender roles, expectations, and hard-living, as well as violence toward children and wives. Therefore, social initiatives for change are as important as legal ones. If we are really serious about creating a new ethic of shared family responsibility, we should embark on a massive campaign to raise boys to be nurturing and to be involved in childrearing. We should also pressure workplaces and other institutions to create family-friendly policies. And of course, we must work to stop violence toward women and children and to decrease poverty, which can be disruptive to family life.

PROMOTING THE ECONOMIC WELL-BEING OF DIVORCED WOMEN WITH CHILDREN AND OTHER SINGLE MOTHERS

This book has shown that there are multiple hardships for divorced women with children. Our society is willing to tolerate outrageously high poverty rates for this group, with 39 percent of all divorced women with children living in poverty and many others living not far above the poverty level. Our society has chosen to ignore the economic hardship and vulnerability of divorced women with children and other single mothers. Attention that should be focused on the terrible rates of poverty experienced by women and children gets expended instead on rhetoric about family values. The hardships divorced women and children encounter are further masked by our false image of divorce as a problem of middle-class, primarily white women, whom we erroneously assume can go out and earn lots of money. We should focus our efforts on helping women get resources from ex-husbands and from the state, so that they and their children can live at an adequate standard of living.

Because children live at the standard of living of their mothers, current divorce policies promote a systematic disinvestment in the next generation. While in 1960 and 1970 the poverty rate for children was only one-third the adult rate, in 1986 the proportion of children living in poverty was almost double that of adults. We penalize women and children with an unjust distribution of resources, and we blame single parents for their own poverty. At the same time, we create many social policies that enable the middle class to maintain a more comfortable standard of living, and some to accumulate a lot of wealth, although these benefits are frequently hidden in the tax code and social security benefits. We must begin to enact reforms in the law, in women's job prospects, and in social welfare policy. As noted earlier, the United States "stands at an extreme point" in comparison with Western European countries in its failure to provide either public or private support for women who experience divorce and for single parents generally.[9]

The Allocation of Private Resources at Divorce

Current divorce law is based on the assumption that men and women stand on equal footing at divorce. This effectively assigns custodial mothers primary responsibility for both caring for and supporting their children. Our current system of high rates of maternal custody and low levels of child support means that women bear a disproportionate share of the burden of childrearing without access to a commensurate share of the family's resources.

We must reform our laws to ensure that women receive a fairer share of assets from their marriages. Women's domestic work, their forgone earning opportunities, and other investments that they have made in their marriages entitle them to more of the marital assets. We must not continue to penalize women for their childrearing work. We must adopt new formulas for dividing property that share equally the financial rewards of the marriage and that look toward equalizing living standards between households after a divorce.

Martha Fineman, Jana Singer, and Stephen Sugarman have proposed the creation of new models of post-divorce income sharing that, in Singer's words, "recognize that marriage is an economic partnership in which spouses make joint investment decisions with the aim of sharing equally the financial rewards of those decisions." They favor reforms that would seek to achieve comparable standards of living between households after divorce, either for a period proportionate to the length of the marriage or until the children reach the age of majority, whichever is longer. June Carbone and Margaret Brinig argue for post-divorce income sharing that focuses on the situation of the children. They propose formulas for equalizing the income of ex-spouses' households during the children's minority.[10]

Under these models, income would be considered as marital property in the division of assets, and income sharing would be required to equalize living standards between former spouses after divorce. Singer proposes that each spouse receive an equal share of the couple's combined income for a set number of years after their divorce. She argues that the duration of this post-divorce arrangement would depend on the length of the marriage.[11]

While new income-sharing proposals would promote the overall well-being of the custodial family, child support remains critical to all mothers so that they can pay for the immediate expenses of their children. Fortunately, some attention has focused on the need for the reform of child-support legislation. The establishment of child-support guidelines and the development of child-support enforcement procedures, particularly income withholding, are very important reforms. A national child-support guideline which mandates higher levels of awards than current guidelines should be developed. Studies show that most fathers could pay higher child support without seriously compromising their standard of living. At minimum, a percentage of income standard should be established for awarding child support. As proposed by Irwin Garfinkel, all child-support awards would be determined by taking a percentage of the income of the non-custodial parent, usually the father, prorated for the number of children. This would also address the problem of raising child-support orders when children's needs increase. Care must be taken, however, that low income fathers not be assigned higher awards than they can pay. Further, as noted above, our child-support policies should not force cooperation from divorced or single mothers who have reason to fear harassment or violence from their ex-husbands.

Other reforms are also essential. If we care about children we must create enforcement mechanisms for child support that work. States must be able to find fathers. Child-support offices must be able to access computer files in their own state and in other states to find fathers. They should also be able to access Federal records such as tax returns to establish appropriate awards. Enforcement of child-support orders should be put in the hands of the Internal Revenue Service, which would use all its regular enforcement mechanisms to collect child support. The IRS should also have a national registry of child-support orders, should administer wage withholding, and should develop a payment system for the self-employed, similar to the quarterly payment system some use for their taxes.

Child-support reform, however, is not a panacea for improving the standard of living of divorced women with children. Some men cannot pay child support, and some men can still successfully evade the child support system. For these reasons we need a child-support assurance system, such as exists in other countries, that ensures that all custodial parents receive child support. Such a system guarantees that if a custodial parent does not receive all of the child support she is owed, the government will make up the difference to her while trying to collect the support from the father. A child-support assurance system would reduce poverty and promote increased security and independence for all single parents.

Financial Resources: Work and the State

Our society must face the fact that single parents endure financial hardship and high rates of poverty. Federal and state governments must take strong measures to raise the standard of living of single-mother heads of households. We can no longer define the plight of single mothers as their "private" problem and cut them off from social welfare benefits. Instead we must take a variety of measures to keep women and their children out of poverty and enable them to live at an adequate standard of living.

First, dramatic steps must be taken to improve the position of women in the labor market. We must end the disgrace of women's low pay, which fails to keep large numbers of women above the poverty level, and keeps many women far below the median income of a two-earner family. We must reform the low-wage sector by increasing the minimum wage and adopting policies of equal pay for work of comparable worth. We must also provide additional income support such as unemployment insurance and temporary disability insurance, which provide coverage for the types of earning losses common to single mothers who must sometimes take time off from work in order to meet their extensive family responsibilites. According to Roberta Spalter-Roth and Heidi Hartmann, such strategies could mean that a larger number of women would qualify for Earned Income Credit benefits and for unemployment insurance. Other necessary reforms include strong affirmative action policies ensuring that minority women have access to the labor market, and job training for women with little experience in the labor market. Effective enforcement of sexual harassment policies is also necessary to enable women to be productive and improve their economic opportunities in the workplace.[12]

Second, we must provide better wages and benefits for those mothers who work part-time in order to care for their children. At the present time, two-thirds of mothers in the labor force do not work at full-time year-round jobs, largely in order to combine work with family responsibilites. Single mothers should never be forced to work full-time, nor should they be penalized for working part-time and caring for their families. We should also institute flexible workplace policies which allow all parents who take care of children to combine work and family life.

Third, in order to enable women to work, to find and take better jobs, we must provide childcare. Our failure to provide childcare is a major obstacle keeping women from work and contributing to their poverty. Some women go on welfare because they cannot get childcare. Barbara Bergmann argues, on the basis of data from the United States and comparative data from other countries which have comprehensive daycare policies, that a large government role in the provision of childcare and after-school care would go a long way toward eliminating child poverty.[13]

Fourth, women need health care benefits. Currently many women in the low-wage labor market receive no health care benefits. As a result some women resort to welfare as the only way to obtain health care benefits. Going to work would jeopardize their access to health care. This is an intolerable state of affairs. It is bad enough that adults have to go without adequate health care. It is shocking to have a country where children cannot get adequate health care. Guaranteed health care would enable more women to work and would raise their standard of living and quality of life of themselves and their children.

Finally, we should reform, but not abolish or seriously curtail, welfare benefits. Since the low wage labor market does not enable women with children (as well as poor men) to support themselves, we should allow women to be on welfare and work at the same time. If we enact the childcare and health care policies just proposed and reform the low wage labor market, fewer women will need welfare at all. But in the meantime, in order to keep women and children out of poverty, and to enable poor women to leave difficult and violent marriages, we should keep welfare payments. As Spalter-Roth and Hartmann note, women need these payments as part of the "income packaging" they do to survive—the combining of part-time work, welfare payments and other social benefits, and help from families.[14]

Needless to say, making such changes would go against many of our cultural beliefs as well as current political trends. We persist in viewing welfare, increasingly associated with AFDC, as a form of "dependency"—a stigmatizing and derogatory term. Our culture, looking to eradicate "dependency," identifies poverty and hardship as "private" problems rooted in the characteristics of vulnerable groups such as women, particularly minority women. Racism feeds this tendency to view any kind of family help as "dependency." Instead of passing the legislation necessary to reduce poverty, legislators have rushed to restrict benefits for women on welfare. Lost in these discussions of unworthy mothers is a consideration of the fact, noted above, that middle-class families benefit from tax rules which remain hidden from view and from unacknowledged zoning ordinances and insurance and benefit regulations, which cost far more money than we spend on AFDC. We assume that middle-class people are entitled to such subsidies, while lower-income and minority people, mired in "dependence," take money from others.

Such a view is tragically misguided. All families require social supports. We need a new model of social welfare that includes not handouts, but universal benefits for all, such as the right to shelter, health care, income supports for working parents, and family allowances. The goal of such benefits would be to integrate beneficiaries into the social mainstream, unlike current social welfare programs which segregate them.

Despite the arguments of those who oppose Social Welfare programs, we do have the money to fund them. According to Stephanie Coontz:

> Redistributing just 1 percent of the income of America's richest 5 percent would lift one million people above the poverty line. A 1 percent tax on the net wealth of the richest 2 percent of American families would allow us to double federal spending on education and still have almost $20 billion left to spend somewhere else.... One commission has recently suggested that it would be possible to restructure the military to transfer $125 billion a year to other uses over the next ten years.[15]

Perhaps those who oppose strengthening family supports could at least see to providing more benefits for children. We cannot continue to fund children living in single-parent families in such an irresponsible and punitive way. Not only is this unfair, but it is ultimately self-defeating. Investments in children are investments in future citizens and workers, and in the well-being of our society in generations to come.

THE FUTURE OF THE FAMILY

All the recommendations just proposed would strengthen the economic position of the single-parent family. We must make life easier for single-parent families, not blame them for our social ills. It is not enough to wait for the conditions that will improve marriage. There are too many nontraditional families now to deny them resources and support. Further, there is too much violence during marriage and too much conflict, harassment, and poverty after divorce to argue that we can't support alternatives to marriage. In addition, because all groups do not have the same access to marriage, it is unjust to privilege this institution above other family forms. Harsh economic circumstances make stable marriages more difficult for people of low income. Further, for a variety of reasons including personal preference, sexual orientation, or the inability to find a suitable partner, some women do not marry.

Many are opposed, however, to giving any support or legitimacy to the single-parent family, undoubtedly out of fear that doing so could weaken the nuclear family. Policies that provide mothers more social supports for living outside of marriage may in fact encourage some to live outside of marriage. Some social commentators believe this has happened in Scandinavian countries and find the prospect of more single-parent families disturbing. On the other hand, being able to live at an adequate standard of living outside of marriage is obviously a benefit to women who would otherwise remain trapped in difficult or destructive marriages.[16]

We should explore in greater depth why many people are so fearful of the "breakup" of the traditional nuclear family. Some are reluctant to support divorced single-parent families because they believe that they are not good for children. Undeniably divorce is a painful experience for children, and no one wishes children to suffer emotional hardship. There are other factors to consider, however. This study, as well as other research, demonstrates that children's reactions to divorce are variable: some children face destructive or tenuous connections to their fathers within a marriage so that divorce is beneficial for them; others have good relationships with their fathers which continue after divorce, and thus may suffer relatively little for that reason, especially now that many children are aware that there are many other divorced families. Certainly having non-traditional families does not preclude male involvement in the lives of children. If we were really so concerned about children, however, we would direct as much attention to improving the quality of marriage as we do to worrying about the divorce rate. Improving marriage through the reduction of poverty, inequality, and violence would go far to improve the quality of life for children.

People are also afraid of the "breakup" of the traditional nuclear family because they see single-parent families as a threat to the social order. Many believe the nuclear family is necessary to hold society together, to curb people's anti-social impulses, and to properly socialize the next generation, and that without it there would be social disorganization, even anarchy. Perhaps many people also fear that acknowledging the legitimacy of single-parent families may be some kind of admission that men and women don't need each other as much as we think they do. Some may hold on to images of the traditional nuclear family because of an unarticulated fear that if we didn't make the traditional family our standard, the genders would drift apart, or the opposite, that "gender war" might break out.

There are ways to address these concerns and improve family life other than trying to force a uniform conception of the nuclear family on all people. As a society we should make a commitment to helping all families—traditional nuclear families, two-parent, two-earner families, and single-parent families— and to provide adequately for their members, particularly their children. To help families we must reduce female and male poverty, making special efforts to end institutionalized discrimination against minorities. We must also promote equality between men and women in the family. This includes creating new conceptions of what it means to be a father, and what it means to be a partner in a marriage and share family life and household work. It also means taking decisive steps to end violence toward women and children. While the costs of creating humane and just social policies are high, the cost of failing to promote the welfare of family members is far higher.

METHODOLOGICAL
APPENDIX

For most of the important variables in the study, except where noted in the text, fixed-choice questions were asked. In addition, for most of these questions women were asked to elaborate on their answers. Simple closed-ended questions included the following:

- general demographic background about the woman herself, including age, age at marriage, number of children, ages of children, education, income (personal as well as total family income), and employment (occupation and average number of hours worked per week);

- information about the woman's ex-husband, including his education, occupation, income, legal representation, and child support paid.

Women were also asked specific, fixed-choice questions about such topics as their legal representation, custody arrangements, child support agreements, receipt of child support payments, visitation agreements, the violence and the fear they experienced, and the violence they themselves used.

In addition, women were asked to expand on their answers to many of the fixed-choice questions in an open-ended question format. For example, they were asked to elaborate on the circumstances of the violence and their reactions to it, and on what made them fearful during the negotiations for child support, custody, and property. Other subjects on which most divorced women spoke at some length included their reasons for their divorce, how they managed on their reduced incomes, and how they felt about their divorces. Longer, open-ended responses were coded for specific content and themes.

The data set generated by the fixed-choice questions was analyzed using the Stata statistical package. Univariate and bivariate statistics, such as cross-tabulations and group means, were used to develop descriptive profiles of the divorced women in the sample. Chi-square statistics were used to test for significant differences in bivariate distributions of categorical variables (e.g., social class group, race, and whether or not they received child support). Continuous variables were tested using t-tests and comparisons of group means (analysis of variance, with Scheffe test of inter-group differences). The significant results reported below all have p-values of less than .001 unless otherwise noted.

Multivariate statistics were also employed to control for particular background variables in testing for group differences. For example, the analyses of race differences in certain social characteristics employed controls for socioeconomic status in order to separate race-related effects from the effects of the over-representation of minority women among the poor. These analyses employed ordinary least-squares regression methods for continuous dependent variables and logistic regression for dichotomous and categorical variables.

Most data analyses in this study include the 20 women (16% of the sample) who have remarried. However, for analyses focusing on economic resources, the income of women who have remarried is reported separately. The four Hispanic women in the sample are included in all data analyses except those which are explicitly comparisons by race. Comparisons by race are comparisons of black and white women.

The remainder of this appendix describes the specific methods and details regarding the statistical findings included in the volume. The appendix follows the order in which the findings are presented, chapter by chapter.

CHAPTER 2

Figure 2–2. A Portrait of Divorced Mothers

Differences between the social class groups were tested for each variable in the table. Average age was highly significant by class using a one-way analysis of variance test (anova). Scheffe tests of inter-group differences showed that the middle class group was significantly older than each of the two other groups.

The distribution of women by educational level was tested categorically (less than high school, high school diploma, some college, and completed college degree), showing predictable differences consistent with the fact that educational level was used to define each of the social class groups. The average number of years of education was also highly significant (oneway anova), with the main difference again found between the middle-class women and each of the other two groups.

The average age at marriage varied significantly among the three social class groups, with middle class women having married at significantly older ages than those in each of the other two groups.

The average number of children differed significantly by group, with the main inter-group difference found between the poverty-level women and the other groups. Poverty-level women had significantly more children than the other women in the sample.

A chi-square test of the race distribution across social class groups was highly significant, with minority women more likely to be concentrated among the working-class and poverty-level groups (p=.002)

Figure 2–3. The Economic Status of Divorced Mothers

All of the variables showed statistically significant differences by social class group (p<.0001 for all variables), confirming the clear economic distinctions in the way that the groups were defined.

Employment status was analyzed using a chi-square test of significance. Personal income and family income were tested using one-way anova, with Scheffe tests of significant inter-group differences. For each income variable, the Scheffe tests were significant between each pair of groups.

Personal income and family income were further examined for four socioeconomic groups of women: professional middle-class, non-professional middle-class, working-class, and poverty-level. Each of the income variables varied significantly across the four groups, with personal and family incomes of professional women significantly higher than for each of the other groups. Nonprofessional middle-class women had personal incomes that were not significantly different on average from those of the working-class women, but the two groups differed significantly in their total family incomes. The poverty level women were significantly poorer than each of the other groups.

Receipt of child support differed significantly by social class group. Middle-class women were most likely to receive child-support payments; the proportion of those receiving support decreased among the working-class women and was lowest among the poverty-level women.

Figure 2-4. Characteristics of Divorced Women by Race

The average age of the women was not significantly different by race. Multivariate analyses controlling for social class showed a significant class effect (p<.001) but no race difference remained.

The educational levels of the women were not significantly different by race when tested with a chi-square test (p=.11). Logistic regressions were run on each of the four education levels separately in order to assess the effects of race and class. Class is significant for all categories (educational level was an important part of assigning social class designations). Race was not a significant predictor of having a college degree or of not completing high school once social class was controlled.

The average years of education did not differ significantly by race. However, regression analyses showed a significant race effect (p=.039) after controlling for class. Within class groups, black women had more years of education than white women.

The average ages at marriage were not significant by race. Regression analyses including both race and class showed no significant race effect after controlling for class, but class remained significant.

Black women had significantly more children on average than white women (oneway anova, p=.009). Class was highly significant in regression analyses using both race and class, but race was no longer significant after class was controlled.

Figure 2–5. The Economic Status of Divorced Women by Race

These economic variables were examined for race differences. Since all of these variables are part of the social class definitions, it did not make sense to control for class in examining race differences.

Employment status was nearly significant by race using a chi-square test (p=.053). Average personal income was not significantly different by race using a one-way anova, but the difference in average total family income was highly significant (p=.001). Thus, while personal earnings were very similar for both groups, black women had significantly fewer family resources (including child support, as indicated below).

Chi-square tests were used to test each of the following variables for race differences. The proportion of each race group on welfare (AFDC) was highly significant (p=.009), as was the proportion of women with incomes below the official poverty level (p<.0001). Black women were significantly more economically disadvantaged than white women. Black women were significantly more likely to be receiving no child support (p=.001). There was no race difference in women's reports of receiving help from their families.

It should be noted that these analyses of race effects did not include four Hispanic women who were in the sample, in order to restrict the focus to black-white differences. The Hispanic women were similar in characteristics to the black women. Three of the Hispanic women were in the poverty-level group while one was included in the working class.

CHAPTER 3

Figure 3–2. Principal Reasons for Divorce by Social Class

The principal reason for divorce was significantly different by social class groups using a chi-square test (p=.019). Each reason was further examined using logistic regression analyses in order to test significant effects of class and race in predicting a particular reason for divorce.

Social class was a significant predictor of reporting personal dissatisfaction (p=.004) but there was no effect of race. Middle- and working-class women were more likely to identify personal dissatisfaction as their principal reason for divorce.

There were no significant differences by race or class in the cases where women reported that their marriages ended because of their ex-husbands' involvements with other women.

Social class was not a significant predictor of reporting hard living as the reason for divorce, although middle-class women made up a small proportion of hard-living divorces. White women were almost 90 percent more likely than black women to report hard-living as their principal reason for divorce (after controlling for class).

Specifying violence as the principal reason for divorce was significant by social class (p=.041) but not by race. Poverty-level women were more likely than other groups to report violence as their principal reason for divorce.

Figure 3–3 and Figure 3–4.   Violence Experienced within Marriage or after Separation, by Social Class

The frequency of violence experienced by women was divided into five categories: none, once only, sometimes (two or three times), frequent or serious (more than three times, or categorized by a serious level of violence and/or personal injury), and after separation only. The overall distribution of divorced women among these five categories is given in Figure 3–3. Overall chi-square tests indicated significant differences by social class (p=.038) but not by race.

Figure 3–4 shows the distribution of divorced women of each social class by experience of violence for the categories of frequent or serious, sometimes, and after separation only.

The violence categories were then examined more closely using multivariate techniques. First, logistic regressions were run to identify predictors of having ever experienced violence (within marriage or after separation). Neither race nor class were significant—70 percent of the women in the sample had experienced violence at least once during marriage or separation and these women were equally likely to be black or white, middle class, working class, or poverty level.

A logistic regression on whether women experienced frequent or serious violence showed significant effects of race alone (p=.030) and class alone (p=.003), but race was no longer significant after class was controlled. Frequent or serious violence was associated with lower social class status (p=.009).

Logistic regressions on whether violence occurred once or whether violence occurred a few times were not significant by either race or class. Logistic regressions on the experience of violence more than once or after separation was also not significant by race or class. Logistic regression on whether violence occurred only after separation was significant by class (more likely for middle-class women), but was not significant by race.

CHAPTER 4

Figure 4–2. A Profile of the Receipt of Child Support

The amount of annual child support received per child was significantly differently across the social class groups with the main difference found between the middle-class women and each of the other two groups. Regression analyses of race and class showed that each variable was statistically significant alone, but race was no longer significant once class was controlled.

The average amount of annual child support received per year was also significantly related to social class (p=.009), with the main difference again lying between the middle-class women and each of the other two groups.

Regression analyses showed a significant race effect (p=.05) even after controlling for class (p=.003). As noted above, this race difference disappeared once child-support amounts were adjusted for the number of children in each family.

Figure 4–3. Receipt of Child Support by Class

Both race and social class were significantly related to the receipt of child support (p<.001 and p=.002, respectively). A logistic regression of the likelihood of receiving any child support showed that both social class and race were significant when included in a model together. Black women were 64% less likely to be receiving any child support after controlling for social class effects.

Figure 4–4. A Profile of Poverty-level Women

Chi-square tests were used to discern differences between women on AFDC and poverty-level women who were not on AFDC on each of the variables in the table. The significant differences are highlighted on the table. Specifically, the following variables were significant at or below the .05 level: average age, average total family income, percentage of group below the official poverty level, employment status, and health insurance coverage.

CHAPTER 5

Figure 5–3. Women's Fear during Child-support Negotiations as Related to Violence Experienced within Marriage

Reported fear was significantly related to the experience of violence in marriage or after separation. Separate tests of the relationship between fear and ever having experienced violence, more than one experience of violence, and by frequent or serious violence were also significant.

CHAPTER 6

Figure 6–1. Divorced Women with Physical Custody of Their Children but without Legal Custody

Whether or not women had legal custody was highly significant by race and social class. A logistic regression using both race and class to predict legal custody showed that both variables remained highly significant when included in a model together (p=.001). Specifically, black women were 75 percent less likely to have legal custody of their children, and lack of legal custody was associated with being in a lower social class.

Figure 6-3. Frequency of Fathers' Visitation

Chi-square tests on class and race and logistic regressions on both variables together did not show any significant differences.

CHAPTER 7

Women's assessments of their own attitudes toward their divorce and the well-being of their children were examined for significant relationships with other variables. These included race, social class, reasons for divorce, and experience of violence. No significant relationships were found.

NOTES

CHAPTER 1: INTRODUCTION

1. Among politicians, alarm about "family breakdown" was steadily growing during the Republican administrations of Reagan and Bush. One of the most visible symbols of this concern was Murphy Brown, the television show character who had a baby out of wedlock. The show was first attacked by then Vice-President Dan Quayle. While Quayle was lampooned for these attacks, President Clinton and other members of his administration subsequently referred to Quayle's speech as positive, for emphasizing that babies should be born to married couples. A subsequent and widely cited article in the *Atlantic Monthly*, "Dan Quayle Was Right," claimed that recent research "proved" that divorce and out-of-wedlock births harm children. Barbara Dafoe Whitehead, *The Atlantic Monthly*, April 1993, 47–50.

2. The Right throughout the Reagan years claimed that family values had gone wrong. More recently, centrist movements such as the Communitarian movement similarly claim that our commitment to the family has gone astray and and have called for a return to family-centered values. See the work of the founder of the Communitarian movement, Amitai Etzioni, *The Spirit of Community: Rights, Responsibilities, and the Communitarian Agenda* (New York: Crown Publishers, 1993). Signers of the Communitarian platform include Republicans and Democrats—for example, Democratic Senator Daniel Patrick Moynihan. Vice-President Al Gore spoke at a Communitarian teach-in. See *The New York Times*, Sunday, May 24, 1992, "The Weekend Section," 6.

3. For a description and analysis of how politicans and policy makers have increasingly blamed single mothers for a host of social problems, see Martha Fineman, *The Neutered Mother, The Sexual Family and Other Twentieth Century Tragedies.* (New York: Routledge, 1995).

4. For images of black women as "welfare mothers" see Patricia Hill Collins, *Black Feminist Thought* (New York: Routledge, 1991). See also Patricia Hill Collins, "A Comparison of Two Works on Black Family Life," *Signs* 14, 4 (1989): 875–84. My conclusion that we hold images of divorced women as typically rich and white is based on a systematic examination of abstracts for the *Readers Guide to Periodical Literature* over the past four years. The *Readers Guide* abstracts articles from over 250 publications, ranging from *Reader's Digest* and *Good Housekeeping* to *The New York Review of Books* and *The New York Times Book Review*. Overwhelmingly, articles from these publications portray those who are divorcing as well-off and white. They frequently highlight the situation of movie stars and other rich people involved in disputes over large amounts of alimony. Rarely do they address the high rate of poverty among divorced women, and almost never do they feature minority women who are divorced.

5. For the divorce rate being higher among people with less education and less income, see Frank Furstenberg, "History and Current Status of Divorce in the United States," *The Future of Children* 4, no. 1 (Spring 1994): 31; Sharon Price and Patrick McKenry, *Divorce* (Newbury Park, CA: Sage, 1988), 18; H. Carter and P.C. Glick, *Marriage and Divorce: A Social and Economic Study* (Cambridge, MA: Harvard University Press, 1976). Cutright, "Income Family Events. Marital Stability," *Journal of Marriage and the Family* 33: 291–306; Thomas J. Espenshade "The Economic Consequences of Divorce," *Journal of Marriage and the Family*, 1979, 41: 615–25; and Rand D Conger, Glen H. Elder, Frederick O. Lorenz, Katherine J. Conger, Ronald L. Simons, Les B. Whitbeck, Shirley Huck, and Janet N. Melby, "Linking Economic Hardship to Marital Quality and Instability," *Journal of Marriage and the Family* 52 (August 1990): 643–56. For figures on the percentage of women on welfare who are black and white, and the percentage of women on welfare who are separated, divorced, or widowed, see U.S. Bureau of the Census, *Dynamics of Economic Well-Being: Program Participation 1990–1992.* Series P70–41, January 1995.

6. For the divorce rate, see Andrew Cherlin, *Marriage, Divorce, Remarriage* (Cambridge, MA: Harvard University Press, 1992), 24. Forty-four percent of female-headed households composed of women aged 20-64 are headed by divorced women, 18 percent by women who are separated, and 28 percent by women who have never married. See Arlene F. Saluter, "Marital Status and Living Arrangements, March 1993," U.S. Bureau of the Census, Current Population Reports, Series P–20, no. 478 (Washington, DC: U.S. Government Printing Office, 1994). For figures on the number of children affected, see Frank Furstenberg and Andrew Cherlin, *Divided Families* (Cambridge, MA: Harvard University Press, 1991), 96.

7. For remarriage rates, see U.S. Bureau of the Census, Current Population Reports, Series P–23, no. 180, *Marriage, Divorce, and Remarriage in the 1990's* (Washington, DC: U.S. Government Printing Office, 1992). For the percentage of marriages that are second or higher-order, see National Center for Health Statistics, "Supplements to the Vital Statistics Report: Advance Reports, 1987," National Center for Health Statistics, *Vital Health Statistics* 24(4) (1990).

8. For the percentage of divorced women with children under 18 in poverty see U.S. Bureau of the Census, *Poverty in the United States: 1992*, Current Population Reports, Series P-60, no. 185 (Washington, DC: U.S. Government Printing Office, 1993), 79. For figures on women using welfare, see Richard R. Peterson, *Women, Work and Divorce* (New York: State University of New York Press, 1989). For the poverty rate of single-mother families, see Gertrude S. Goldberg, "The United States: Feminization of Poverty Amidst Plenty," in *The Feminization of Poverty: Only in America?* ed. Gertrude S. Goldberg and Eleanor Kremen (New York: Praeger, 1990), 44. For a discussion of how

our family policy continues to be organized around the traditional family with a male wage-earner, see Mimi Abramovitz, *Regulating the Lives of Women: Social Welfare Policy from Colonial Times to the Present* (Boston, Ma: South End Press, 1988); Nancy Fraser and Linda Gordon, "'Dependency' Demystified: Inscriptions of Power in a Keyword of the Welfare State," *Social Politics* 1, no. 1 (Spring 1994): 4–31; L. Gordon, ed., *Women, the State, and Welfare* (Madison, Wis.: University of Wisconsin), 9–35; and Roberta M. Spalter-Roth and Heidi I. Hartmann, "Dependence on Men, the Market, or the State: The Rhetoric and Reality of Welfare Reform," *The Journal of Applied Social Sciences* 18, no. 1 (Fall/Winter 1994): 55–70.

9. Men typically experience a 15 percent rise in their income afer divorce. See Greg J. Duncan and Saul D. Hoffman, "A Reconsideration of the Economic Consequences of Marital Dissolution," *Demography* 22 (November 1985): 485–97. The majority of fathers do not spend much time with their children after divorce. See J. A. Seltzer and S. M. Bianchi, "Children's Contact with Absent Parents," *Journal of Marriage and the Family* 50 (1988): 663–77,

10. For those who believe divorce harms children, see David Blankenhorn, Steven Bayme, and Jean Bethke Elshtain, *Rebuilding the Nest* (Milwaukee, Wis.: Family Service of America, 1990); Barbara Dafoe Whitehead, "Dan Quayle Was Right," *The Atlantic Monthly*, April 1993, 47–50. For those who believe most children adjust and that high conflict marriages are more harmful to children than experiencing divorce, see Frank Furstenberg, "History and Current Status of Divorce in the United States," *Children and Divorce* 4, no. 1 (Spring 1994): 38.

11. Proposals to restrict divorce include things such as Communitarian Amitai Etzioni's support of "braking" mechanisms or waiting periods of up to nine months between when a couple announce their intention to divorce and when they are allowed to divorce. See Etzioni, *The Spirit of Community*, 81. More extreme are proposals by Charles Murray to make marriage "once again the sole legal institution through which parental rights and responsibilities are defined and exercised." A mother having a child out of wedlock would receive no state support at all. If she couldn't support her child, her child would be eligible for an orphanage. While the child's mother could receive no funds, we should be prepared, according to Murray, to "spend lavishly on orphanages." Charles Murray, "The Coming White Underclass," *Wall Street Journal*, October 29, 1993, section A, p. 14, column 4.

12. For a discussion of how divorce rates are higher for younger women, see Sharon Price and Patrick McKenny, *Divorce* (Newbury Park, CA: Sage, 1988), 17.

13. For figures on child support nationally, see U.S. Bureau of the Census, *Child Support and Alimony: 1989*, Current Population Reports, Series P–60, no. 173 (Washington, DC: U.S. Government Printing Office, 1991).

CHAPTER 2: UNDERSTANDING DIVORCE AND DIVORCED WOMEN

1. For a sampling of the work of those who write of divorce as a symptom of family breakdown and decline, see Amitai Etzioni, *The Spirit of Community* (New York: Crown, 1993); David Poponoe, *Disturbing the Nest: Family Change and Decline in Modern Societies* (New York: Aldine De Gruyter, 1988); David Blankenhorn, Steven Bayme, Jean Bethke Elshtain, eds. *Rebuilding the Nest: A New Commitment to the American Family,* (Milwaukee, WI: Family Service of America. 1990); Barbara Defoe Whitehead, "Dan Quayle Was Right," *The Atlantic Monthly*, April 1993: 47–84. For a description of their

organizations, see Peter Steinfels, "A Political Movement Blends Its Ideas From Left and Right," *The New York Times,* May 24, 1992, weekend section, 6; Karen J. Winkler, "Communitarians Move Their Ideas Outside Academic Arena," in *The Chronicle of Higher Education,* April 21, 1993; Judith Stacey, "The New Family Values Crusaders," *The Nation,* July 25/August 1, 1994, 119–22. David Poponoe, *Disturbing the Nest.*

2. Robert Bellah, Richard Madsen, William M. Sullivan, Ann Swidler, and Steven M. Tipton, *Habits of the Heart: Individualism and Commitment in American Life* (New York: Harper & Row, 1985). See also *Poponoe, Disturbing the Nest,* 239. For a critique of *Habits of the Heart,* as well as the work of Poponoe, see Arlene Skolnick, *Embattled Paradise* (New York: Basic Books, 1991): 202–204.

3. All writers in this tradition stress the harmful effects of divorce on children. They particularly cite Judith Wallerstein and Sandra Blakeslee, *Second Chances: Men, Women, and Children a Decade after Divorce* (New York: Ticknor and Fields, 1989); and Judith Wallerstein and & Joan Kelly *Surviving the Breakup: How Children and Parents Cope with Divorce* (New York: Basic Books, 1980), widely publicized longitudinal studies on the effects of divorce on children, as evidence of the long-term negative effects of divorce on children. Whitehead cites this work extensively in her *Atlantic Monthly* article "Dan Quayle Was Right." See also David Blankenhorn, "American Family Dilemmas," in *Rebuilding the Nest,* ed. David Blankenhorn, Steven Bayme, and Jean Bethke Elshtain (Milwaukee, WI: Family Service America, 1990), 3–26; Armand Nicholi, "The Impact of Family Dissolution on the Emotional Health of Children and Adolescents," in *When Families Fail ... The Social Costs,* ed. Bryce Christensen (Lanham, MD: University Press of America, 1990), 27–42; Travis Hirschi, "Family Structure and Crime," in *When Families Fail,* ed. Bryce Christensen, pp. 43–66. For a criticism of these studies and description and analysis of the increasing tendency to blame single mothers not only for their own situation, but for an array of social problems, see Martha Fineman, *The Neutered Mother, The Sexual Family and Other Twentieth Century Tragedies,* (New York: Routledge, 1995).

4. Etzioni, *The Spirit of Community,* 70–72. Poponoe, *Disturbing the Nest* , 238.

5. Myra Marx Ferree, "Beyond Separate Spheres: Feminism and Family Research," *Journal of Marriage and the Family* 52 (1990): 870. For recent excellent work showing the different interests of men and women in marriage and the gendered nature of the family, see also: Evelyn Nakano Glenn, "Gender and the Family," in *Analyzing Gender: A Handbook of Social Science Research,* ed. Beth Hess and Myra Marx Ferree (Newbury Park, CA: Sage Publications, 1987), 348–80; Barrie Thorne, "Feminism and the Family: Two Decades of Thought," in *Rethinking the Family,* ed. Barrie Thorne and Marilyn Yalom (Boston: Northeastern University Press, 1992), 3–30. For the particular position of black women, see Bonnie Thornton Dill, "Our Mother's Grief: Racial Ethnic Women and the Maintenance of Families," *Journal of Family History* 13(1988): 415–31, and Maxine Baca Zinn, "Family, Race, and Poverty in the Eighties," *Signs* 14 (1989): 856–74.

6. For the original formulation of "his" and "her" marriage see Jessie Bernard, *The Future of Marriage* (New York: World Publishers, 1972). For women's experiences at divorce see Terry Arendell, *Mothers and Divorce* (Berkeley, CA: University of California Press, 1986). For the most in-depth comparison of the perspectives of men and women at divorce see Catherine Kohler Riessman, *Divorce Talk* (New Brunswick, N.J.: Rutgers University Press, 1990).

7. For an expanded version of this brief account of the entry of women into the paid labor force and the rise in the divorce rate, see Andrew Cherlin, *Marriage, Divorce, Remarriage* (Cambridge, MA: Harvard University Press, 1992); Frank Furstenberg and Andrew Cherlin, *Divided Families* (Cambridge, MA: Harvard University Press, 1991).

See also Samuel H. Preston and Alan Thomas Richards, "The Influence of Women's Work Opportunities on Marriage Rates," *Demography* 12 (May 1975): 209–22; William Goode, *World Revolution and Family Patterns* (New York: Free Press, 1963); and Carl Degler, *At Odds: Women and the Family in American from the Revolution to the Present* (New York: Oxford University Press, 1980).

8. Barbara Reskin and Irene Padavic, *Women and Men at Work* (Thousand Oaks, CA: Pine Forge Press, 1994), 25.

9. See Furstenberg and Cherlin, *Divided Families,* 6 for a further discussion of emotional gratification as the *sine qua non* of married life. While the public stigma attached to divorce has greatly decreased, Gerstl demonstrates that divorced people still feel a stigma as a result of their status. They believe they are the targets of exclusion, blame, and devaluation by the nondivorced. See Naomi Gerstel, "Divorce and Stigma," *Social Problems* 34, 2 (April 1987): 172–86.

10. Arlie Hochschild, with Anne Machung, *The Second Shift* (New York: Avon Books, 1989), 253

11. Barbara Ehrenreich, *The Hearts of Men* (Garden City, NY: Anchor Press, 1983).

12. Wives could control substantial inherited wealth and, in common law states, they could control their earnings from work outside the home. In community property states, however, the earnings of wives who worked outside the home were subject to control of the husband, because in those states all earnings were considered community property, and control of community property was vested by law in the husband. See "Gender and the Law of Intimate Relationships and Family Life," in Barbara Babcock, Rhonda Copelon, Ann Freedman, Eleanor Holmes Norton, Susan Ross, Nadine Taub, and Wendy Williams, *Sex Discrimination and the Law: Causes and Remedies.* Second Edition (Boston: Little Brown, forthcoming), ch. 3. For the spread of an ideology, equality in marriage, see Judith Stacey, *Brave New Families: Stories of Domestic Upheaval in Late Twentieth-Century America* (New York: Basic Books, 1990); and Lillian Rubin, *Families on the Fault Line: America's Working Class Speaks about the Family, the Economy, Race and Ethnicity* (New York: Harper Collins, 1994)

13. For women's legal control over earnings in the marriage, see Babcock et al., *Sex Discrimination and the Law,* ch. 3; Philip Blumstein and Pepper Schwartz, *American Couples* (New York: Pocket Books, 1983); John Scanzoni, *Sexual Bargaining: Power Politics in the American Marriage* (Chicago: University of Chicago Press, 1982). Lillian Rubin, *Worlds of Pain* (New York: Basic Books, 1976); David Morgan, *The Family, Politics, and Social Theory* (London: Routledge and Kegan Paul, 1985), 253. For polling data, see Linda and Diane Colasanto, "The Gender Gap in America: Unlike 1975, Today Most Americans Think Men Have It Better," *Gallup Poll News Service* 54(37) (1990): 1–7. For further discussion of the role of power and gender in marriage, see Ferree, "Beyond Separate Spheres: Feminism and Family Research," 886–94; and Linda Thompson and Alexis J. Walker, "Gender in Families: Women and Men in Marriage, Work, and Parenthood," *Journal of Marriage and the Family* 51 (November 1989): 845–71.

14. Hochschild, *The Second Shift.* Gallup poll from Janice Steil, "Supermoms and Second Shifts: Marital Inequality in the 1990's," in *Women: A Feminist Perspective,* ed. Jo Freeman, 5th ed., 1995, 149. For further discussion of the dynamics of men's and women's relationship to household labor, see Sarah Fenstermaker Berk, *The Gender Factory: The Apportionment of Work in American Households* (New York: Plenum, 1985); and Judith Lorber, *Paradoxes of Gender* (New Haven: Yale University Press, 1994), ch. 8.

15. On the incidence of domestic violence, see Murray Straus, Richard Gelles, and Suzanne Steinmetz, *Behind Closed Doors* (Garden City, N.Y.: Anchor, 1980); Murray Straus and Richard J. Gelles, "Societal Change and Change in Family Violence from

1975–1985 as Revealed by Two National Surveys," *Journal of Marriage and the Family* 48 (1986): 465–79. For analyses of the causes of domestic violence, see R. Emerson and Russell Dobash *Violence against Wives* (New York: Free Press, 1979); Demie Kurz, "Physical Assaults by Husbands: A Major Social Problem," in *Current Controversies on Family Violence*, ed. Richard J. Gelles and Donileen R. Loseke (Newbury Park, CA: Sage, 1993), 88–103. Kersti A. Yllo, "Through a Feminist Lense: Gender, Power, and Violence," *Current Controversies*, 47–62.

16. Those who believe that black marriages have been relatively egalitarian include D. K. Lewis, "The Black Family: Socialization and Sex Roles," *Phylon* 36, 3 (1975): 221–37; H. Romer & D. Cherry, "Ethnic and Social Class Differences in Children's Sex-Role Concepts," *Sex Roles* 6 (1980): 245–59; Robert Staples, "Masculinity and Race: The Dual Dilemma of Black Men," *Journal of Social Issues* 34, 1 (1978): 169–83. Those who write of inequality in black marriages include Michele Wallace, *Black Macho and the Myth of the Superwoman* (New York: Warner Books, 1980); and Gloria Joseph and Jill Lewis, *Common Differences: Conflicts in Black and White Feminist Perspectives* (New York: Anchor Press, 1981). Pamela M. Wilson writes that both tendencies coexist. See "Black Culture and Sexuality," *Journal of Social Work and Human Sexuality* 4, 3(1986): 29–46.

17. See Daniel Patrick Moynihan, *The Negro Family: The Case for National Action* (Washington, DC: Department of Labor, Office of Policy Planning and Research, 1965).

18. Patricia Hill Collins, "A Comparison of Two Works on Black Family Life," *Signs* 14, 4 (1989): 875–84, for a discussion of the persistence of stereotypes of blacks in the media. See also Joyce Ladner, *Tomorrow's Tomorrow: The Black Woman* (Garden City, N.Y.: Doubleday, 1971).

19. See I. Arafat and B. Yorburg, *The New Woman: Attitudes, Behavior, and Self-Image* (Columbus, Ohio: Charles Merrill, 1976); William T. Bailey, N. Clayton Silver, and Kathleen A. Oliver, "Women's Rights and Roles: Attitudes Among Black and White Students," *Psychological Reports* 66 (1990): 1143–46; see also V. V. P. Rao and V. N. Rao, *Sex Roles* 12, nos. 9/10 (1985): 939–53. H. Edward Ransford and Jon Miller, "Race, Sex and Feminist Outlooks," *American Sociological Review* 48 (February): 46–59. Karen Dugger, "Social Location and Gender-Role Attitudes: A Comparison of Black and White Women," in *The Social Construction of Gender*, ed. Judith Lorber and Susan A. Farrel (Newbury Park, CA: Sage Publications, 1991), 38–59.

20. Terry Arendell, *Fathers & Divorce* (Newbury Park, CA: Sage, forthcoming). For the *New York Times* poll and the American Male Opinion Index, see Susan Falludi, *Backlash* (New York: Doubleday, 1991), 61. For the quote on men, see David Morgan, *The Family, Politics, and Social Theory* (London; Routledge and Kegan Paul, 1985), 61.

21. For the divorce rate as higher among people with less education and less income, see Frank Furstenberg, "History and Current Status of Divorce in the United States," in *The Future of Children* 4, no. 1 (Spring 1994): 31; Sharon Price and Patrick McKenny, *Divorce* (Newbury Park, CA: Sage, 1988), 18; H. Carter and C. Glick, *Marriage and Divorce: A Social and Economic Study* (Cambridge, MA: Harvard University Press, 1976); Phillips Cutright, "Income Family Events: Marital Stability," *Journal of Marriage and the Family* 33: 291–306; Thomas J. Espenshade, "The Economic Consequences of Divorce," *Journal of Marriage and the Family* 41 (1979), 615–65. and Rand D. Conger, Glen H. Elder, Frederick O. Lorenz, Katherine J. Conger, Ronald L. Simons, Les B. Whitbeck, Shirley Huck, and Janet N. Melby, "Linking Economic Hardship to Marital Quality and Instability," *Journal of Marriage and the Family* 52 (August 1990): 643–56. For a discussion of the rise in the divorce rate at all socio-economic levels, see Helen J. Roaschke, "Divorce," in *Handbook of Marriage and the Family*, ed. Marvin B. Sussman

and Suzanne K. Steinmetz (New York: Plenum Press, 1987), 603. For data on how recession and down-sizing continue to disproportionately affect working-class and poorer people, see Lillian Rubin, *Families on the Fault Line: America's Working Class Speaks about the Family, the Economy, Race and Ethnicity* (New York: HarperCollins, 1994).

22. Lillian Rubin, *Worlds of Pain* (New York: Basic Books, 1976) quoting Joseph T. Howell, *Hard Living on Clay Street* (Garden City, N.Y: Anchor Books, 1973); Stacey, "The New Family Value Crusaders," *The Nation* (July 25/August 1): 119–122; Lillian Rubin, *Families on the Fault Line: America's Working Class Speaks about the Family, the Economy, Race and Ethnicity*; Judith Stacey, *Brave New Families: Stories of Domestic Upheaval in Late Twentieth Century America* (New York: Basic Books, 1990); Katherine Newman, *Falling From Grace* (New York: Free Press, 1988), 134–35.

23. William J. Wilson, *The Truly Disadvantaged: The Inner City, the Underclass, and Public Policy* (Chicago: University of Chicago Press, 1987). On divorce rates for blacks, see Andrew Cherlin, *Marriage, Divorce, Remarriage* (Cambridge, MA.: Harvard University Press, 1992), 95. For the 1992 unemployment rate for blacks, see U.S. Bureau of Labor Statistics, "Employment and Earnings," January 1992, as cited in *Statistical Abstract of the United States 1993*, 113th edition, (Washington, DC: U.S. Bureau of the Census, 1993). David Ellwood, *Poor Support* (New York: Basic Books, 1988), 56.

24. Elijah Anderson, *Streetwise: Race, Class and Change in an Urban Community* (Chicago: University of Chicago Press, 1990); Eliot Liebow, *Tally's Corner* (New York: Doubleday, 1967); Robert Staples, "Changes in Black Family Structure: The Conflict between Family Ideology and Structural Conditions," *Journal of Marriage and the Family* 47 (1985): 1005–15. Maxine Baca-Zinn, "Family, Race, and Poverty in the Eighties," *Signs: Journal of Women in Culture and Society* 14, no. 4 (1989); Rose Brewer, "Black Women in Poverty: Some Comments on Female-Headed Families," *Signs* 13 (Winter 1988): 331–39; Patricia Hill Collins, *Black Feminist Thought*.

25. For excellent studies of the economic impact of divorce on women, see Terry Arendell, *Mothers and Divorce*; Leslie A. Morgan, *After Marriage Ends: Economic Consequences for Midlife Women* (Newbury Park, CA: Sage, 1991); Katherine Newman, *Falling from Grace* (New York: Free Press, 1988); Lenore Weitzman, *The Divorce Revolution* (New York: Free Press, 1985). For the percentage of divorced women with children under 18 in poverty, see U.S. Bureau of the Census, *Poverty in the United States: 1992*, Current Population Reports, Series P60–185 (Washington, DC: U.S. Government Printing Office, 1993), 79. For a discussion of the "feminization of poverty," see Diana Pearce, "The Feminization of Poverty: Update," in *Feminist Frameworks*, ed. Alison Jaggar and Paula Rothenberg (New York: McGraw Hill, 1993) 290–96. For figures on the poverty of single-parent families, see Elyce Rotella, "Women and the American Economy," in *Issues in Feminism*, ed. Sheila Ruth (Mountain View, CA: Mayfield Publishing Company, 1995), 331. For a discussion of the racialization of poverty, see Margaret B. Wilkerson and Jewell Handy Gresham, "The Racialization of Poverty," in *Feminist Frameworks*, ed. Alison Jaggar and Paula Rotthenberg (New York: McGraw Hill, 1993), 297–303.

26. For the one-third figure, see Weitzman, *The Divorce Revolution*, 351. On women's decline in standard of living see Saul J. Hoffman and Greg J. Duncan, "What Are the Economic Consequences of Divorce?" *Demography* 25 (1988): 641.

27. For the percentage of their incomes which fathers pay for child support, see Weitzman, *The Divorce Revolution*, 266. For the increase in men's income after divorce, see Greg J. Duncan and Saul D. Hoffman, "A Reconsideration of the Economic Consequences of Marital Dissolution," *Demography* 22 (November 1985).

28, Mary Ann Glendon, *The Transformation of Family Law* (Chicago: University of Chicago Press, 1989), 237.

29. Figures on alimony from E. Mary O'Connell, "Alimony after No-Fault: A Practice in Search of a Theory," *New England Law Review* 23 (1988): 437–513.

30, On how less than half of couples have assets, see Weitzman, *The Divorce Revolution*, 55. For the value of property women receive, see Judith Seltzer and Irwin Garfinkel, "Inequality of Divorce Settlements: An Investigation of Porperty Settlements and Child Support Awards," *Social Science Research* 19 (1990): 82–111. On the family home at divorce, see Weitzman, 79.

31. For new items considered as property, see Sanford Katz, "Historical Perspective and Current Trends in the Legal Process of Divorce," in *The Future of Children: Children and Divorce*, vol. 4, no. 1, (Published by the Center for the Future of Children, The David and Lucile Packard Foundation), 44–62. See also Barbara Babcock, Rhonda Copelan, Ann Freedman, Eleanor Holmes Norton, Deborah Rhode, Sue Deller Ross, Nadine Taub, and Wendy Williams, *Sex Discrimination* (Boston: Little Brown, forthcoming).

32. Weitzman, *The Divorce Revolution,* 504.

33. For figures on custody, see Joan Kelly, "The Determination of Child Custody," in *The Future of Children: Children and Divorce* (The Center for the Future of Children, The David and Lucile Packard Foundation), Spring 1994: 124. For figures on poverty, see Lenore Weitzman, "Child Support: Myths and Reality," in *Child Support: From Debt Collection to Social Policy,* ed. Alfred J. Kahn and Sheila Kamerman (Newbury Park, CA: Sage, 1988), 252.

34. For a discussion of low child-support awards and for how child-support awards don't meet half the costs of childrearing, see Weitzman, *The Divorce Revolution*, 278.

35. Hochschild, *The Second Shift*; Paula England and Barbara Stanek Kilbourne, "Markets, Marriages, and Other Mates: The Problem of Power," in *Beyond the Marketplace: Rethinking Society and Economy,* ed. Roger Friedland and Sandy Robertson (New York: Aldine, 1990), 163–188.

36. Saul J. Hoffman and Greg J. Duncan, "What are the Economic Consequences of Divorce?," p. 641. For divorcees as having the highest labor force participation rate among mothers, see data from the 1992 Current Population Survey, cited by Roberta Spalter-Roth and Heidi Hartmann, "Dependence on Men, the Market, or the State: The Rhetoric and Reality of Welfare Reform" (Washington, DC: Institute for Women's Policy Research, November 1993), 6.

37. For women's earnings as a percentage of men's, see U.S. Bureau of the Census, *Money Income of Households, Families and Persons in the United States 1991,* Current Population Report Series P–60, no. 180, Table 29, 116, 130; Roberta M. Spalter-Roth and Heidi Hartmann, "Dependence on Men." See Goldberg, "The United States: Feminization of Poverty Amidst Plenty," 24 for how women's disadvantage in the workforce persists, whatever their educational level.

38. For data on sex segregation, see Nancy M Thornborrow and Marianne B. Sheldon, "Women in the Labor Force," in *Women: A Feminist Perspective,* ed. Jo Freeman (Mountain View, CA: Mayfield), 210. For the further segregation of black women, see Julianne Malveaux, "The Economic Interests of Black and White Women: Are They Similar?" *Review of Black Political Economy* (Summer 1985): 5–27. For the unemployment rates of black women, see U.S. Department of Labor, Bureau of Labor Statistics (1989): 514–37.

39. For women working at part-time jobs, see U.S. Bureau of the Census, Current Population Reports, "Money Income of Households, Persons, and Families in the United States, 1990," Consumer Income, Series P–60, no. 174, table 19; Teresa L. Amott, "Black Women and AFDC: Making Entitlement out of Necessity," in *Women, the State,*

and Welfare, ed. L. Gordon (Madison, WI: University of Wisconsin Press, 1990), 293; Gertrude Schaffner Goldberg, "The United States: Feminization of Poverty amidst Plenty," in *The Feminization of Poverty: Only in America?* ed. G. S. Coldberg and E. Kremen (New York: Praeger, 1990), 83. For women's earnings as a percentage of men's, see U.S. Bureau of the Census, *Money Income of Households, Families, and Persons in the United States 1991*, Current Population Report, Series P–60, no. 180, Table 29, 116, 130. For AFDC as the poor woman's unemployment compensation, see Diana Pearce, "Welfare Is Not for Women: Why the War on Poverty Cannot Conquer the Feminization of Poverty," in *Women, the State, and Welfare*, ed. Linda Gordon (Madison, WI: The University of Wisconsin Press, 1990), 271.

40. U.S. Merit Systems Protection Board. *Sexual Harassment in the Federal Government: An Update* (Washington, DC: U.S. Government Printing Office, 1988), 16–17. Diana Pearce, "Welfare Is Not for Women", 6.

41. Diana Pearce, ibid. For the poverty level of mothers heading families, see Roberta Spalter-Roth, Heidi Hartmann, and Linda Andrews, in *Sociology and the Public Agenda*, ed. William Julius Wilson (Newbury Park, CA: Sage, 1993); Teresa L. Amott, "Black Women and AFDC," p. 293.

42. For a discussion of the myth of the independent worker and his family, see Gwendolyn Mink, "The Lady and the Tramp: Gender, Race, and the Origins of the American Welfare State," in *Women, the State, and Welfare*, ed. L. Gordon, 10; and Nancy Fraser and Linda Gordon, "'Dependency' Demystified."

43. For percentages of women and children on welfare, see Dorothy Miller, *Women and Social Welfare: A Feminist Analysis* (New York: Praeger, 1990), 30.

44. For data on SSI, see Miller, ibid., p. 35. For data on foster care, see Pearce, 268.

45. The "midnight raids" have been widely documented. For comprehensive histories of welfare and AFDC in this country, see Mimi Abramowitz, *Regulating the Lives of Women: Social Welfare Policiy from Colonial Times to the Present* (Boston, MA: South End Press, 1988), Linda Gordon, *Pitied But Not Entitled: Single Mothers and the History of Welfare, 1890–1935* (New York: Free Press, 1994), and Francis Fox Piven and Richard A. Cloward, *Regulating the Poor: The Functions of Public Welfare* (New York: Vintage Books, 1993). For a discussion of how racism in the United States has shaped the social welfare system, see Jill Quadagno, *The Color of Welfare: How Racism Undermined the War on Poverty* (New York: Oxford University Press, 1994)

46. For decreases in AFDC benefits, see Sara McLanahan and Karen Booth, "Mother-only Families: Problems, Prospects, and Politics," *Journal of Marriage and the Family* 51(3): 557–80. For the relationship between welfare and work, see Abramowitz, *Regulating the Lives of Women*, and Piven and Cloward, *Regulating the Poor*.

47. For problems with the current welfare system, see Roberta M. Spalter-Roth and Heidi Hartmann, "Dependence on Men."

48. For extreme proposals on welfare, see Charles Murray, "The Coming White Underclass," *Wall Street Journal*, October 29, 1993, section A, 14, column 4.

49. For figures on AFDC recipients by race, see U.S. Bureau of the Census, *Dynamics of Economic Well-Being: Program Participation 1990-1992*. Series P70-41, January 1995.

50. William Julius Wilson and Katherine M. Neckerman, "Poverty and Family Structure: The Widening Gap between Evidence and Public Policy Issues," in *Fighting Poverty: What Works and What Doesn't*, ed. Sheldon Danziger and Daniel Weinberg (Cambridge, MA: Harvard University Press, 1986); David Ellwood and Mary Jo Bane, "The Impact of AFDC on Family Structure and Living Arrangements," in Ronald Ehrenberg, ed., *Research in Labor Economics* 7 (1985).

51. For the racial distribution of the city population, see "Philadelphia Health Man-

agement Household Survey" (Philadelphia, PA: The Philadelphia Health Management Corp., 1987).

52. For the response rates of other studies of the divorced, see Weitzman, *The Divorce Revolution*, 408–9.

53. For higher rates of divorce in urban areas, see Sharon J. Price and Patrick C. McKenny, *Divorce* (Newbury Park, CA: Sage, 1988), 16. For higher rates of divorce among African-Americans, see Andrew Cherlin, *Marriage, Divorce, Remarriage*, 95. For higher rates of divorce among people with less education and income, see Frank Furstenberg, "History and Current Status of Divorce in the United States," *The Future of Children* 4, no. 1 (Spring 1994): 31; Sharon Price and Patrick McKenry, *Divorce* (Newbury Park, CA: Sage, 1988), 18.

54. For details of the national sample, see Eleanor Maccoby and Robert Mnookin, *Dividing the Child: Social and Legal Dilemmas of Custody* (Cambridge, MA: Harvard University Press, 1992), 62.

55. Constance Ahrons and R. Rodgers, *Divorced Families: A Multidisciplinary Developmental View* (New York: Norton, 1987).

56. Patricia Ruggles, *Drawing the Line: Alternative Poverty Measures and Their Implications for Public Policy* (Washington, DC: The Urban Institute Press, 1990). The poverty threshold developed by Ruggles provides an updated indicator of minimally adequate living standards based on current normative patterns of need and consumption. While the official poverty level used in government publications has been the widely accepted standard for poverty measurement, Ruggles argues that the official method, originally devised in the mid-1960s, was based on norms and consumption patterns (primarily with regard to family food budgets) which date back to 1955. The threshold has then been adjusted for yearly price changes without any attention to changes in income, relative prices, or consumption patterns that have occurred since the 1950s and 60s. Ruggles argues that the official poverty threshold has, therefore, consistently and vastly underestimated the true minimally adequate living standard of the current U.S. population.

Ruggles proposes two main changes in measurement methods: (1) linking the threshold to changes in income rather than changes in prices over time; and (2) re-estimating the thresholds to account for changes in consumption patterns and in the relative prices of goods consumed. Using an adjustment for income levels and consumption patterns, Ruggles estimates a poverty threshold for a family of three in 1988 at $15,000, compared to the official poverty level of $9,500. For persons in female-headed households in 1987, Ruggles estimates that 52.2 percent lived below a minimally adequate standard of living, while the official poverty level estimates were at 33.6 percent for the same group. For poverty definitions used in the European Community, see Valerie Polakow, *Lives on the Edge: Single Mothers and their Children in the Other America* (Chicago: University of Chicago Press, 1993), 45.

57. For traditional definitions of class, see Melvin Kohn, *Class and Conformity* (Chicago: University of Chicago Press, 1977) and August Hollingshead, *Elmtown's Youth and Elmtown Revisited* (New York: Wiley, 1975). Christine E. Grella, "Irreconcilable Differences: Women Defining Class after Divorce and Downward Mobility," *Gender & Society* 4, 1 (1990): 41–55 and Judith Stacey, *Brave New Families* have pointed out that many definitions of social class are too static and fail to capture how an individual's social class is in a constant process of negotiation and redefinition. For issues in defining the social class of divorced women, see Grella.

58. Most data analyses in this study include the 20 women (16 percent of the sample) who have remarried. However, for analyses focusing on economic resources, the income of women who have remarried is reported separately.

59. The four Hispanic women in the sample are not included in this analysis by race. They are included in all data analyses except those which are explicitly comparisons by race. Comparisons by race are comparisons of black and white women.

60. For the divorce rate being higher among women who marry younger, see Price and McKenry, *Divorce* op. cit. 17. For the particular problems of older divorced women, see Weitzman, *The Divorce Revolution*, 27–28 and Leslie A. Morgan *After Marriage Ends: Economic Consequences for Midlife Women* (Newbury Park, CA: Sage, 1991), and Peter Uhlenberg, Teresa Cooney, Robert Boyd, *Journals of Gerontology* 45, no. 1(1990) S3–11 .

CHAPTER 3: HOW MARRIAGES END

1. For accounts of individualism in American life see Robert Bellah et al., *Habits of the Heart: Individualism and Commitment in American Life* (New York: Harper & Row, 1995); Bruce Hafen, "Individualism in Family Law," in *Rebuilding the Nest,* ed. David Blankenhorn, Steven Bayme, and Jean Bethke Elshtain (Milwaukee, WI: Family Service America, 1990), 161–78, David Poponoe, *Disturbing the Nest: Family Change and Decline in Modern Societies* (New York: Aldine de Gruyter, 1988) For data showing that women initiate the divorce process, see Sharon Price and Patrick C. McKenny, *Divorce* (Newbury Park, CA: Sage, 1988), 40.

2. Sometimes women mentioned that several factors had led to their separation from their ex-husband. However, they almost always stressed one factor as being more important than the others. For more in-depth accounts of the ending of marriages, see Diane Vaughan, *Uncoupling* (New York: Vintage, 1986), who maps the complex processes of couples' disengagement, particularly the dynamics of the leaver and the one left; Catherine K. Riessman, *Divorce Talk* (New Brunswick, NJ: Rutgers, 1990) who has done in-depth analyses of divorce "discourses" and describes how men and women construct different and highly gendered meanings of their divorce. Judith Stacey, in her book *Brave New Families* (New York: Basic Books, 1990), based on extensive participant observation with a selected group of working-class, "postmodern" families, shows the social pressures on a family type at a particular point in time. For "his" accounts of divorce, see Terry Arendell, *Fathers & Divorce* (Newbury Park, CA: Sage, forthcoming) For a discussion of how people's accounts of their divorce can change over the course of the divorce process, see Gay Kitson and William M. Holmes, *Portrait of Divorce* (New York: Guilford Press, 1992), 143–46.

3. I refer to the body of research on self-reported causes of divorce, often described as "sources of marital dissatisfaction." See the following: William J. Goode, *After Divorce* (New York: Free Press, 1956); George Levinger, "Sources of Marital Dissatisfaction among Applicants for Divorce," *American Journal of Orthopsychiatry* 36 (1966): 803–7. Gay Kitson and Marvin Sussman, "Marital Complaints, Demographic characteristics and Symptoms of Mental Distress in Divorce," *Journal of Marriage and the Family* 44 (1982): 87–101; B.L. Bloom et al., "Sources of Marital Dissatisfaction among Newly Separated Persons," *Journal of Family Issues* 6 (1985): 359–73; Gay Kitson and Willima Holmes, *Portrait of Divorce,* chapter 5.

4. Joseph T. Howell, *Hard Living on Clay Street* (Garden City, NY: Anchor Books, 1973).

5. Class remained a highly significant predictor for personal dissatisfaction and violence-related divorces after controlling for race. For hard-living divorces, class was not

significant, but black women were 90 percent less likely to cite hard living as the principal reason for divorce (after controlling for class).

6. Scott, "Gender: A Useful Category of Historical Analysis," *American Historical Review* 91 (1986): 1067.

7. Lillian Rubin, *Worlds of Pain* (New York: Basic Books, 1976), and *Intimate Strangers: Men and Women Together* (New York: Harper & Row, 1983).

8. Myra Marx Ferree, "Beyond Separate Spheres," *Journal of Marriage and the Family* 52 (November 1990): 874.

9. Barbara Finlay, Charles E. Starnes, and Fausto B. Alvarez, "Recent Changes in Sex-Role Ideology among Divorced Men and Women: Some Possible Causes and Implications," *Sex Roles* 12 (1985): 637–53.

10. For statistics on the incidence of domestic violence, see Murray Straus and Richard J. Gelles, "Societal Change and Change in Family Violence from 1975–1985 as Revealed by Two National Surveys," *Journal of Marriage and the Family* 48 (1986): 465–79; Murray Straus, Richard Gelles, and Suzanne Steinmetz, *Behind Closed Doors* (New York: Doubleday, 1980). For statistics on deaths, see Ann Jones, *Next Time She'll Be Dead* (Boston, MA: Beacon Press, 1994), 87. For statistics on injuries, see Surgeon General Antonia C. Novello, quoted in "Physicians Begin a Program to Combat Family Violence," *New York Times*, Oct. 17, 1991, 15; Kathleen Waits, "The Criminal Justice System's Response to Battering: Understanding the Problem, Forging the Solutions," *Washington Law Review* 60 (1985): 267, 273. For estimates that half of all incidents of domestic violence go unreported, see Waits, 275–313 and Straus, Gelles, and Steinmetz, *Behind Closed Doors*, 35. For the effect of domestic violence on children, see "Silent Victims: Children Who Witness Violence," *Journal of the American Medical Association* 269, no. 2 (January 13, 1993): 262–64. For the criminal justice response to battered women, see Eve S. Buzawa and Carl G. Buzawa, eds., *Domestic Violence: The Changing Criminal Justice Response* (Westport, CT: Auburn House, 1992). For the healthcare response, see Centers for Disease Control, *Surgeon General's Workshop on Violence and Public Health: Sourcebook* (Atlanta, GA: U.S. Public Health Service. 1985); Demie Kurz, "Interventions with Battered Women in Health Care Settings," *Violence and Victims* 5, no. 4 (1990). For the prevalence and limitations of gender-neutral perspectives on domestic violence, see Demie Kurz, "Social Science Perspectives on Wife Abuse: Current Debates and Future Directions," *Gender and Society* 3, 4 (December 1989): 489–505. For analyses of the causes of domestic violence, see R.E. Dobash and R. Dobash, *Violence against Wives* (New York: Free Press, 1979); Demie Kurz, "Physical Assaults by Husbands: A Major Social Problem," In *Current Controversies on Family Violence*, ed. R. J. Gelles and D. R. Loseke (Newbury Park, CA: Sage, 1993), 88–103. See also Kersti A. Yllo, "Through a Feminist Lens: Gender, Power, and Violence," in *Current Controversies*, 47–62.

11. To measure acts of physical violence, a modified version of the Conflict Tactics Scales was used. See Murray Straus, "Measuring Intrafamily Conflict and Violence: The Conflict Tactics (CT) Scales," *Journal of Marriagae and the Family* 41(1979): 75–88.

12. Joseph Howell, *Hard Living on Clay Street*; Lillian Rubin, *Families on the the Fault Line* (New York: Harper, 1994); Katherine Newman, *Falling From Grace* (New York: The Free Press, 1988); Rubin, *Worlds of Pain* (New York: Basic Books, 1976). While it is not clear how many people abuse alcohol or drugs, many use both. According to a survey conducted in 1988, 21.1 million Americans reported having used marijuana in the past year, and 65.7 had used it at least once. National Institute on Drug Abuse, "National Household Survey on Drug Abuse: Population Estimates 1988," DHHS Publication No. (ADM) 89–1636 (Washington, DC: U.S. Department of Health and Human Services, 1989).

13. Judith Stacey, *Brave New Families*, 257.

14. See David Halle, *America's Working Man: Work, Home, and Politics Among Blue-Collar Property Owners* (Chicago: University of Chicago Press, 1984).

15. Elijah Anderson, *Streetwise: Race, Class and Change in an Urban Community* (Chicago: University of Chicago Press, 1990).

16. Data on marital fidelity come from a 1992 survey conducted by the National Opinion Research Center, University of Chicago, cited in *The New York Times*, October 7, 1994, A1.

17. For higher divorce rates among women who marry younger, see Frank Furstenberg, "History and Current Status of Divorce in the United States," in *The Future of Children*, The Center for the Future of Children 4, no. 1 (1994): 31; Lillian Rubin, *Worlds of Pain*.

18. For statistics on violence during marriage, see note 11. For figures on violence reported by divorcing couples, see M. D. Fields, "Wife-beating: Facts and Figures," *Victimology* 2, nos. 3–4 (1978): 643–47. Barbara Parker and Dale N. Schumacher, "The Battered Wife Syndrome and Violence in the Nuclear Family of Origin: A Controlled Pilot Study," *American Journal of Public Health* 67(8) (1977): 760–61. Mark A. Schulman, *A Survey of Spousal Violence against Women in Kentucky*, study no. 792701 for the Kentucky Commission on Women (Washington, DC: U.S. Department of Justice, 1979); Murray Straus et al., *Behind Closed Doors*.

19. For data from Canada, see Desmond Ellis and Walter Dekeseredy, "Marital Status and Woman Abuse: Dad Model," *International Journal of the Sociology of the Family* 19 (1989): 67–87 and Desmond Ellis and Walter Dekeseredy, *The Wrong Stuff: An Introduction to the Sociological Study of Deviance*, 2nd edition (Toronto: Allyn and Bacon, 1995), Martha Mahoney, "Legal Images of Battered Women: Redefining the Issue of Separation," *Michigan Law Review* 90, no. 1 (October 1991): 1–94.

20. For no class differences, see Mildred Pagelow, *Family Violence* (New York: Praeger, 1984) and Lenore Walker, *The Battered Woman* (New York: Harper, 1979). Straus et al., *Behind Closed Doors*.

21. Robert Staples, *Black Masculinity* (San Francisco: The Black Scholar Press, 1982).

22. For figures on marital rape, see Diana Russell, *Rape in Marriage* (New York: Macmillan, 1990).

23. Dobash and Dobash, *Violence Against Wives*; Mildred Pagelow, *Family Violence*; Elizabeth Stanko, *Intimate Intrusions* (London: Routledge and Kegan Paul, 1985); Evan Stark, Ann Flitcraft, and William Frazier, "Medicine and Patriarchal Violence: The Social Construction of a 'Private' Event," *International Journal of Health Services* 98 (1979): 461–93.

24. See Dobash and Dobash, *Violence Against Wives*.

25. Martha Mahoney, "Legal Images of Battered Women: Redefining the Issue of Separation," 71–72. For others who believe that violence escalates during separation, see Desmond Ellis, "Post-Separation Woman Abuse: The Contribution of Lawyers as 'Barracudas,' 'Advocates,' and 'Counsellors,'" *International Journal of Law and Psychiatry* (1987): 403, 408; Cynthia Gillespie, *Justifiable Homicide* (Columbus: Ohio State University Press, 1989); Terry Arendell, *Fathers & Divorce*.

26. See Murray Straus and Richard Gelles, "Societal Change and Change in Family Violence."

27. The most commonly used way of measuring violence is the Conflict Tactics Scales. See Straus et al., *Behind Closed Doors*, and Straus and Gelles, "Societal Change and Change in Family Violence." Straus argues that the scales demonstrate that women are as violent as men. See Murray Straus, "Physical Assaults by Wives: A Major Social

Problem," in *Current Controversies on Family Violence,* ed. Richard Gelles and Donileen Loseke (Newbury Park, CA: Sage, 1993), 67–87. For a critique of these scales and their interpretation, see Demie Kurz, "Physical Assaults by Husbands: A Major Social Problem," in *Current Controversies on Family Violence,* ed. Gelles and Loseke, 88–103; R. P. Dobash et al., "The Myth of Sexual Symmetry in Marital Violence," *Social Problems* 39 (1992): 71–91; Daniel Saunders, "Wife Abuse, Husband Abuse, or Mutual Combat?" in *Feminist Perspectives on Wife Abuse,* ed. Kersti Yllo and Michelle Bograd (Newbury Park, CA: Sage, 1988), 90–113. Richard Berk et al., "Mutual Combat and Other Family Violence Myths," in *The Dark Side of Families,* ed. David Finkelhor et al (Beverly Hills, CA: Sage, 1983), 197–212.

CHAPTER 4: COPING WITH DIVORCE

1. Saul D. Hoffman and Greg J. Duncan report a 30 percent reduction in women's income at divorce. S. Hoffman and G.J. Duncan, "What Are the Consequences of Divorce?" *Demography* 25(1988): 641–45. Women must support themselves and their children on this reduced income. For the 39 percent of divorced women with children under 18 in poverty, see U.S. Bureau of the Census, *Poverty in the United States: 1992.* Current Population Reports, Series P60–185 (Washington, DC: US Government Printing Office, 1993), 79, and U.S. Bureau of the Census, *Child Support and Alimony: 1989,* Current Population Reports, Series P–60, no. 173, (Washington, DC: U.S. Government Printing Office, 1991).

2. Data on employment figures come from unpublished data in the 1992 Current Population Survey, as cited in Roberta M. Spalter-Roth and Heidi Hartmann, "Dependence on Men, the Market or the State: The Rhetoric and Reality of Welfare Reform" (Washington, DC: Institute for Women's Policy Research, November 1993).

3. For middle-class women's drop in income, see Thomas Espenshade, "The Economic Consequences of Divorce," *Journal of Marriage and the Family* 41 (1979): 615–25; Robert S. Weiss, "The Impact of Marital Dissolution on Income and Consumption in Single-Parent Households," *Journal of Marriage and the Family* 46 (1984): 115–27.

4. For federal expenditures see Stephanie Coontz, *The Way We Never Were: American Families and the Nostalgia Trap* (New York: Basic Books, 1992), 86. According to Sara McLanahan and Irwin Garfinkel, *New York Times,* July 29, 1994, A-27, "We cut poverty rates among the elderly by two-thirds from 1967 to 1993."

5. For remarriage as the best way for women to reduce hardship and improve their economic circumstances at divorce, see Jay D. Teachman and Kathleen M. Paasch, "Financial Impact of Divorce on Children and Their Families," in *The Future of Children* 1, no. 4 (Center for the Future of Children, The David and Lucile Packard, Spring 1994), 69.

6. For figures on women using welfare, see Richard R. Peterson, *Women, Work and Divorce* (New York: State University of New York Press, 1989), 49–51. For the percentage of divorced women in poverty, see U.S. Bureau of the Census *Poverty in the United States: 1991.*

7. Diane Dodson, "The Relationship between Child Support and Alimony," *Journal of the American Academy of Matrimonial Lawyers* 25, 4 (1988): 35–36.

8. Roberta Spalter-Roth, et al., "Dependence on Men, the Market, or the State: The Rhetoric and Reality of Welfare Reform."

9. Lenore Weitzman, *The Divorce Revolution* (New York: Free Press, 1985), 504.

10. Women received alimony in this sample as follows: 19 percent of the middle-class women (5) received alimony from their ex-husbands. The median amount was $400 per month, although two women received three to four times that amount. In most cases the alimony will end after six years. Only three working-class mothers were awarded alimony. One never received any of the alimony that was ordered, one received alimony for a year, and the third woman said that the alimony she received was actually child support money which her ex-husband re-classified as alimony to claim a tax deduction. No poverty-level women received alimony. For how less than half of all women receive any significant amounts of property, see Deborah Rhode, *Justice and Gender* (Cambridge, MA: Harvard University Press, 1989), 150; Weitzman, *The Divorce Revolution*, 55. For the study of property, see Judith Seltzer and Irwin Garfinkel, "Inequality of Divorce Settlements: An Investigation of Property Settlements and Child Support Awards," *Social Science Research* 19 (1990): 82–111.

11. Child support accounts for 18.5 percent of the income of divorced women nationwide. See U.S. Bureau of the Census. *Child Support and Alimony: 1989*, Current Population Reports, Series P–60, no. 173 (U.S. Government Printing Office, 1991). For estimates that child-support typically covers less than half the costs of childrearing, see Weitzman, *The Divorce Revolution*, 278. For estimates that child support awards do not even cover the costs of childcare, see Carol Bruch, "Developing Standards for Child Support Payments: A Critique of Current Practice," *University of California at Davis Law Review* 16, 1(1982): 49–64.

12. Amy Hirsch, "Income Deeming in the AFDC Program: Using Dual Track Family Law to Make Poor Women Poorer," *New York University Review of Law and Social Change* 16, no. 4 (October 1988): 713–40.

13. For figures showing that less than half of all divorced mothers receive child support, see Jay D. Teachman and Kathleen M. Paasch, "Financial Impact of Divorce on Children and Their Families," *The Future Children* 1 no. 4 (Center for the Future of Children, The David and Lucile Packard Foundation, Spring 1994): 73. As in the sample, national figures show black mothers receiving less child support than white mothers. See Frank F. Furstenberg, Jr., "History and Current Status of Divorce in the United States," *The Future of Children* 1, no. 4 (Center for the Future of Children, The David and Lucile Packard Foundation, Spring 1994): 32.

14. Roberta Spalter-Roth and Heidi Hartmann, "AFDC Recipients as Care-givers and Workers: A Feminist Approach to Income Security Policy for American Women," *Social Politics* 1 (Spring 1994): 193.

15. Sara S. McLanahan, "Family Structure and Stress: A Longitudinal Comparison of Two-Parent and Female-Headed Families," *Journal of Marriage and the Family* (May 1984): 347–57.

16. For the role of gender in seeking help from kin, see See Naomi Gerstl, "Divorce and Kin Ties: The Importance of Gender," *Journal of Marriage and the Family* 50 (February 1988): 209–19. For the number of divorced women living with their parents, see James A. Sweet and Larry L. Bumpass, *American Families and Households* (New York: Russell Sage Foundation, 1988). For help from grandparents, see Andrew J. Cherlin and Frank F. Furstenberg, Jr., *The New American Grandparent: A Place in the Family, A Life Apart* (New York: Basic Books, 1986).

17. For how working-class families are oriented toward kin, see Claude S. Fischer, *To Dwell among Friends: Social Networks in Town and City* (Chicago: University of Chicago Press, 1982). For help-seeking among black families, see Carol B. Stack *All Our Kin: Strategies for Survival in a Black Community* (New York: Harper, 1974).

18. For conflicts over receiving help from parents, see Robert S. Weiss, *Going It Alone* (New York: Basic Books, 1979); and Leigh A. Leslie and Katherine Grady, "Changes in Mothers' Social Networks and Social Support Following Divorce," *Journal of Marriage and the Family* 47 (August 1985): 663–73.

19. Kimberle W. Crenshaw, "Mapping the Margins: Intersectionality, Identity Politics, and Violence Against Women of Color," in *The Public Nature of Private Violence,* ed. Martha A. Fineman and Roxanne Mykitiuk (New York: Routledge, 1994), 93–118. See also Jody Raphael, "Domestic Violence and Welfare Reform," *Poverty & Race* 4, no. 1 (January/February 1995): 19–29, for a discussion of how job training and other programs for poor women should include services for women who have been abused.

20. For a discussion of the reactions to divorce of men and fathers, and for a comprehensive review of the literature on this subject, see Terry Arendell, *Fathers & Divorce*; Catherine K. Riessman, *Divorce Talk: Women and Men Make Sense of Personal Relationships* (New Brunswick, NJ: Rutgers University Press, 1990); Robert Weiss, *Going It Alone* (New York: Basic Books, 1979); and Deborah Luepnitz, *Child Custody: A Study of Families after Divorce* (Lexington, MA: D.C. Heath, 1982)

CHAPTER 5: DIVIDING RESOURCES

1. For discussion of how child support would keep women out of poverty, see Ann Nichols-Caseboldt, "The Economic Impact of Child Support Reform on the Poverty Status of Custodial and Noncustodial Families," in *Child Support Assurance*, ed. Irwin Garfinkel, Sara McLanahan and Philip Robins, (Washington, DC: Urban Institute Press, 1992), 196. For figures on those who don't receive child support, see U.S. Bureau of the Census, *Child Support and Alimony: 1989*, Current Population Reports, Series P–60, No. 173 (Washington, DC: Government Printing Office, 1991), Table C, 5. For low child-support awards, see Lenore Weitzman, *The Divorce Revolution* (New York: The Free Press, 1985), 278. For difficulty of getting increases in child-support awards, see: Irwin Garfinkel, *Assuring Child Support* (New York: Russell Sage Foundation, 1992), 98.

2. "Child Support Enforcement: Credit Bureau Reporting Shows Promise," HEHS–94–175, June 3, 1994, letter report. Washington, DC: U.S. General Accounting Office.

3. For a description of the public and private system, see Paula G. Roberts, "Child Support Orders: Problems with Enforcement," in *The Future of Children: Children and Divorce* 4, no. 1 (The David and Lucile Packard Foundation, Spring 1994): 101–20.

4. For a description of the child support system for women on welfare, see Deborah Harris, "Child Support for Welfare Families: Family Policy Trapped in Its Own Rhetoric," *New York University Review of Law and Social Change* 16 (October 1988): 19–57.

5. For problems of the IV–D system, see Roberts, ibid. For figures on case workers, see U.S. Department of Health and Human Services, Administration of Children and Families, Office of Child Support Enforcement, *Sixteenth Annual Report to Congress* (Washington, D.C: DHHS, 1993). AFDC regulations apply to all of a woman's children, even if a mother has a child not covered by AFDC who is receiving child support from the father independent of AFDC, that child must be considered part of the AFDC grant. This practice, called "income deeming," was introduced in the Deficit Reduction

Act of 1984. See Amy Hirsch, "Income Deeming in the AFDC Program: Using Dual Track Family Law to Make Poor Women Poorer," *New York University Review of Law and Social Change* 16, no. 4 (October 1988): 713–40.

6. For a description of the Family Support Act, see Irwin Garfinkel, Marygold S. Melli, and John G. Robertson, "Child Support Orders: A Perspective on Reform," in *The Future of Children: Children and Divorce* 4, no. 1 (Spring 1994): 86. For initial evaluation of income withholding, see Irwin Garfinkel, *Assuring Child Support*, 46. For information on wage withholding as the most effective form of child-support enforcement, see Department of Health and Human Services, Office of Child Support Enforcement, "Seventeenth Annual Report to Congress" (Washington, DC: DHHS, 1994) 20.

7. Paula Roberts, *Ending Poverty as We Know It: The Case for Child Support Enforcement and Assurance* (Washington, DC: The Center for Law and Social Policy, 1994).

8. For a discussion of health insurance coverage, see Roberts, "Child Support Orders: Problems with Enforcement," 110.

9. For this 30% figure, see Garfinkel, *Assuring Child Support*, 76.

10. For a study on the effectiveness of guidelines, see Nancy Thoennes, Patricia Tjaden, and Jessica Pearson, "The Impact of Child Support Guidelines on Award Adequacy, Award Variability, and Case Processing Efficiency," *Family Law Quarterly* 25 (Fall 1991): 325–45. For a report of the Massachusetts study, see Department of Health and Human Services, Office of Child Support Enforcement, *Seventeenth Annual Report to Congress*. For the expectation that guidelines could increase awards by 50 percent, see Irwin Garfinkel, Donald Oellerich, and Philip Robins, "Child Support Guidelines: Will They Make a Difference?" *Journal of Family Issues* 12 (1991): 404–29.

11. For loopholes in the law, see Garfinkel, *Assuring Child Support*, 72–73; for problems arising when there is joint custody, see Thoennes, Tjaden, and Pearson, "The Impact of Child Support Guidelines on Award Adequacy."

12. For a general critique of guidelines, see Sally Goldfarb, "What Every Lawyer Should Know about Child Support Guidelines," *Family Law Reporter* 13, 30/31 (1987): 3036-37.

13. Isabel V. Sawhill, "Developing Normative Standards for Child Support and Alimony Payments," Working Paper 992–04, Washington, DC, The Urban Institute, September 1977. For judicial attitudes towards child support, see Lenore Weitzman, *The Divorce Revolution*, 193; On the survey of Maryland residents, see Barbara Bergmann and Sherry Wetchler, "Child Support Awards: State Guidelines versus Public Opinion," unpublished paper; Garfinkel, *Assuring Child Support*, 76, believes that raising child-support awards too high will lead more men to evade paying child support.

14. On the value of adopting the percentage of income standard, see Irwin Garfinkel, Marygold Melli, and John Robertson, "Child Support Orders: A Perspective on Reform," in *The Future of Children*, 92. On the problems of raising child-support awards, see Garfinkel, *Assuring Child Support*, 73.

15. Nancy Duff Campbell et al., "A Vision of Child Support Reform," Washington, DC: Center for Law and Social Policy, 1994 (prepared by Nancy Duff Campbell and Sarah Craven, National Women's Law Center; Diane Dodson, Women's Legal Defense Fund; Nancy Ebb, Children's Defense Fund; Paula Roberts Center for Law and Social Policy). More specifically, Campbell et al. suggest that there be a $3,000 minimum assured benefit for one child, and more for larger families. They feel this is very reasonable given that it is estimated that, for single parents with incomes of less than $30,000, the expenses for raising one child for one year are $5,030 (1990 figures). For higher income families they estimate the expense at $9,330.

16. For figures on divorced women's receipt of child support, see Jay D. Teachman and Kathleen M. Paasch, "Financial Impact of Divorce on Children and Their Families," in *The Future of Children*, 64.

17. Terry Arendell, *Fathers & Divorce* (Newbury Park, CA: Sage, forthcoming).

18. Fifty to 66 percent of child support cases are handled outside the IV–D system according to Margaret C. Haynes, "Supporting Our Children: A Blueprint for Reform," *Family Law Quarterly* 27, no. 1 (Spring 1993). For a description of the child support enforcement system, see P. Roberts, "Child Support Orders: Problems with Enforcement," 105.

19. See Frank Furstenberg and Andrew Cherlin, *Divided Families* (Cambridge, MA: Harvard University Press, 1991); Eleanor Maccoby and Robert Mnookin, *Dividing the Child: Social and Legal Dilemmas of Custody* (Cambridge, MA: Harvard University Press, 1992); and Judith Seltzer, "Legal Custody Arrangements and Children's Economic Welfare," *American Journal of* Sociology 96 (1991): 895-929 on how those with lawyers secure more favorable custody outcomes. For data showing that women with lawyers gained more child support even after the institution of guidelines, see Thoennes, Tjaden, and Pearson, "The Impact of Child Support Guidelines on Award Adequacy."

20. For costs of lawyers, see Sanford N. Katz, "Historical Perspectives and Current Trends in the Legal Process of Divorce," in *The Future of Children*, 55. For abuses of women clients by divorce lawyers, see James Dao, "Divorce Lawyers Assailed in Study by Albany Panel," *The New York Times*, Wednesday, May 5, 1993, 1A. For example, some lawyers have been able to take their clients' homes when women were unable to pay their legal fees. A ruling by Chief Judge Judith Kaye of the New York Court of Appeals established new rules which divorce lawyers must use with their clients, such as providing a written fee schedule and itemized bills. These rules also forbid a lawyer to take a woman's home as payment for fees. See also the article by Jan Hoffman, entitled "New York's Chief Judge Imposes Strict Rules for Divorce Lawyers," *The New York Times*, August 17, 1993, A1, col. 5.

21. For difficulties which lawyers and clients can have in their negotiations with each other, see William L.F. Felstiner and Austin Sarat, "Enactments of Power: Negotiating Reality and Responsibility in Lawyer-Client Interactions," *Cornell Law Review* 77 (1992): 1447.

22. For the advantages of a *pro se* system for women, see Emily Joselson and Judy Kaye, "Pro Se Divorce: A Strategy for Empowering Women," in *Family Matters*, ed. Martha Minow (New York: The New Press, 1993), 377–80. For the problems with the *pro se* system, see Paula Roberts, "Child Support Orders: Problems with Enforcement," 106.

23. Arendell, *Fathers & Divorce*.

24. For reporting systems, see Paula Roberts, *Ending Poverty as We Know It*, 22–23.

25. See Garfinkel, *Assuring Child Support*, 76, for the percentage of child-support cases which are out of state. For out-of-state problems, see U.S. General Accounting Office, *Mothers Report Receiving Less Support from Out-Of-State Fathers* (Washington, DC: Government Printing Office, 1992), 3.

26. Garfinkel, ibid., 75, claims that most states have computerized systems. For the flaws in the computerization process, see U.S. General Accounting Office, *Timely Action Needed to Correct Systems Development Problems* (GAO IMTEC–92–46) (1992).

27. Arendell, *Fathers & Divorce*.

28. For those who argue that custody blackmail exists, see Weitzman, *The Divorce Revolution* and Nancy Polikoff, "Why Are Mothers Losing? A Brief Analysis of Criteria Used in Child Custody Determinations," *Women's Rights Law Reporter* 7, 3 (1982):

235–43. See also Richard Neely, "The Primary Caretaker Parent Rule: Child Custody and the Dynamics of Greed," *Yale Law and Public Policy Review* 3 (1984): 168–86. For those who find no evidence of custody blackmail, see Eleanor Maccoby and Robert Mnookin, *Dividing the Child: Social and Legal Dilemmas of Custody* (Cambridge, MA: Harvard University Press, 1992), 273.

29. For a discussion of separation assault, see Martha R. Mahoney, "Legal Images of Battered Women: Redefining the Issue of Separation,." *Michigan Law Review* 90, 1 (1991): 1-89. Note also that the number of women in this sample experiencing violence or threats of violence during the separation could have been higher. As noted earlier, women who reported violence during the marriage unfortunately were not questioned further about the violence they experienced during the separation. However eleven women who experienced violence during the marriage also described incidents of violence during the separation, and an additional six women described immediate threats of violence during the separation. See also Terry Arendell, *Fathers & Divorce*, forthcoming.

30. Weitzman, *The Divorce Revolution*, 313–16.

31. Personal communication, Melinda Dutton, Staff Attorney, Brooklyn Legal Services, Brooklyn, NY, 8 June 1995.

. 32. For the proportionately higher rates of payment and incarceration of poor men, see Garfinkel, *Assuring Child Support*, 76–77. For the income of men on AFDC, see Roberts, *Ending Poverty as We Know It*, 37.

33. Jay D. Teachman and Kathleen M. Paasch, "Financial Impact of Divorce on Children and Their Families," 74.

34. Paula Roberts on the 25 percent proposal in *Ending Poverty as We Know It*, 37. On the advantages of the percentage of income approach see Garfinkel, Melli, and Robertson, "Child Support Orders: A Perspective on Reform," 92.

35. For a description of these projects, see Paula Roberts, *Ending Poverty as We Know It*, 37–38.

36. For the 28 percent figure, see Jay D. Teachman and Kathleen M Paasch, "Financial Impact of Divorce on Children and Their Families," in *The Future of Children*, 75.

37. "A Vision of Child Support Reform," by Ayuda, Clinica Legal Latina, Center for Law and Social Policy, Children's Defense Fund, National Women's Law Center, Office of Domestic Social Development, United States Catholic Conference, Women's Legal Defense Fund (Washington, DC: Jan. 1994).

38. For the Pennsylvania law, see Karen Czapanskiy "Child Support and Visitation: Rethinking the Connections," *Rutgers Law Journal* 20 (1989): 619–65.

39. On the need for federalization, see Roberts, "Child Support Orders: Problems with Enforcement," 101–20.

40. See Garfinkel, *Assuring Child Support*, chapter 6.

41. Harry D. Krause, "Child Support Reassessed: Limits of Private Responsibility and the Public Interest," in *Divorce Reform at the Crossroads*, ed. Stephen Sugarman and Harma Hill Kay (New Haven: Yale University Press, 1990), 166–90.

CHAPTER 6: MOTHERS NEGOTIATE FOR CUSTODY AND VISITATIONS

1. For visitation figures, see Judith A. Seltzer, "Relationships Between Fathers and Children Who Live Apart: The Father's Role after Separation," *Journal of Marriage and the Family* 53, 1 (1991): 79–101. For the decrease in visitation rates over time, see Frank Furstenberg and Andrew Cherlin, *Divided Families* (Cambridge, MA: Harvard

University Press, 1991), 35–36: "Almost half of the children of recently separated couples saw their fathers at least once a week, and a third had not seen them at all in the past year. Among the children of marriages disrupted for ten or more years—that is, since early childhood—only one in ten had weekly contact with their fathers and almost two-thirds had no contact in the past year."

2. Furstenberg and Cherlin, ibid., 107, report that there is no clear relationship between frequency of fathers' visits and the well-being of children. Emery summarizes studies claiming it is better for children to have an ongoing relationship with both parents after a divorce. See Robert E. Emery, *Marriage, Divorce, and Children's Adjustment* (Newbury Park, CA: Sage, 1988).

3. Eleanor E. Maccoby and Robert H. Mnookin, *Dividing the Child: Social and Legal Issues of Custody* (Cambridge, MA: Harvard University Press, 1992). For an analysis of the activities and policies of the fathers' rights movement see Scott Coltrane and Neal Hickman, "The Rhetoric of Rights and Needs: Moral Discourse in the Reform of Child Custody and Child Support Laws," *Social Problems* 39, 4 (1992): 400–420. Mary Becker, in "Maternal Feelings: Myth, Taboo, and Child Custody," *Review of Law and Women's Studies* 1 (1992): 133–224, notes that there are also other procedures and policies which serve to encourage shared custody. For example, many states urge or require mediation of custody disputes, and mediators typically favor joint custody as the optimal legal arrangement. Also, in many states, even if mediation fails, mediators are influential because they make recommendations to the court. Naomi R. Cahn, "Civil Images of Battered Women: The Impact of Domestic Violence on Child Custody Decisions," *Vanderbilt Law Review* 44 (1991): 1060, on states which interpret the best interest of the child as a "presumption for awarding joint custody."

4. For a discussion of the fathers' rights movement, see Coltrane and Hickman, "The Rhetoric of Rights and Needs." Maccoby and Mnookin discuss how the introduction of joint custody statutes has not resulted in greater payment of child support by fathers.

5. For an argument favoring joint custody see Katherine T. Bartlett and Carol B. Stack, "Joint Custody, Feminism, and the Dependency Dilemma," *Berkeley Women's Law Journal* 2 (1986): 9–41. For those who fear increased father influence, see Mary Becker, "Maternal Feelings: Myth, Taboo, and Child Custody," and Martha Fineman, *The Illusion of Equity* (Chicago: University of Chicago Press, 1991).

6. The following argue that custody blackmail does take place: Nancy Polikoff, "Gender and Child-Custody Determinations: Exploding the Myths," in *Families, Politics and Public Policies: A Feminist Dialogue on Women and the State*, ed. Irene Diamond (New York: Longman, 1983), 195; Lenore Weitzman, *The Divorce Revolution* (New York: The Free Press, 1985), 310–18; Richard Neely, "The Primary Caretaker Parent Rule: Child Custody and the Dynamics of Greed," *Yale Law and Policy Review* 3 (1984). Weitzman argues that fathers are more often awarded custody in contested cases, 233. Martha Fineman, *The Illusion of Equality*, part 2.

7. "Legal Responses to Domestic Violence," *Harvard Law Review* 106 (1993): 1498–1620; Martha R. Mahoney, "Legal Images of Battered Women: Redefining the Issue of Separation," *Michigan Law Review* 90 (1991): 2–3. For harm done to children by domestic violence, see the review by Peter Jaffe, David Wolfe, and Susan Kaye Wilson, "Children of Battered Women," *Developmental Clinical Psychology and Psychiatry* 21 (Newbury Park, CA: Sage, 1990). This review concludes that children who are exposed to physical violence between their parents have more behavioral problems, emotional difficulties, and reduced social competence than children who are not exposed to violence. However, Johnston notes that there are variations in children's responses to violence. While some children are very negatively affected, others are not. According to

Johnston, children's reactions are mediated by the child-parent relationship. A good relationship with the primary parent can buffer a child against the negative effects of witnessing domestic violence. See Janet R. Johnston, "High-Conflict Divorce," in *The Future of Children: Children and Divorce*. The David and Lucile Packard Foundation 4, no. 1 (Spring 1994): 165–82.

8. Karen Czapanskiy, "Volunteers and Draftees: The Struggle for Parental Equality," *UCLA Law Review* 38 (1991): 1415–81.

9. Other reseachers who have found that parents report similar patterns of custody and visitation include: Terry Arendell, *Fathers & Divorce*; Anne-Marie Ambert, "Relationship Between Ex-Spouses: Individual and Dyadic Perspectives," *Journal of Social and Personal Relationships* 5 (1988): 327–46; and Robert Mnookin, Eleanor E. Maccoby, Catherine R. Albiston, and Charlene E. Depner, "Private Ordering Revisited: What Custodial Arrangements Are Parents Negotiating?" in *Divorce Reform at the Crossroads*, ed. Stephen D. Sugarman and Herman Hill Kay, (New Haven, CT: Yale University Press), 37–74.

10. Christy M. Buchanan, Eleanor E. Maccoby, and Sanford M. Dornbusch, "Caught Between Parents: Adolescents' Experience in Divorced Homes," *Child Development* 62, 5 (1991): 10008–1029; Janet R. Johnston, L. E. G. Campbell, and S. Mayes, "Latency Children in Post-Separation and Divorce Disputes," *Journal of the American Academy of Child Psychiatry* 24 (1985): 563–74; Eleanor Maccoby and Robert Mnookin, *Dividing the Child;* Janet Johnston, "High Conflict Divorce," in *The Future of Children: Children and Divorce*.

11. Recent studies indicate that in as many as 15 percent of cases, fathers may have physical custody of the children. See Joan Kelly, "The Determination of Child Custody," in *The Future of Children*, 124. In three of the six father-custody cases in this study, fathers had joint physical custody with the mother. In the other three cases, one father had custody of most of the children, the second father had custody of one child while the mother had one child, and the third had kidnapped the children. Only one of the fathers with some form of physical custody also had joint legal custody of his children. In seven other cases, fathers had joint legal custody with the mothers. In these cases, the mothers still had physical custody and the fathers tended to visit with their children at the same rate as fathers without joint legal custody.

12. Maccoby and Mnookin, in their California study of 1,124 families with 1,875 children, reported that 10 percent of families reported "substantial" legal conflict over custody and access to the children, and 15 percent reported "intense" legal conflict.

13. Terry Arendell, *Fathers & Divorce* (Newbury Park, CA: Sage, forthcoming). For figures on abduction, see David Finkelhor, Gerald Hotaling, and Andrea Sedlak, *Missing, Abducted, Runaway, and Thrownaway Children in America* (Washington, DC: U.S. Dept. of Justice, 1990). Finkelhor et al. state: "There were an estimated 354,100 *Broad Scope Family Abductions* in 1988," defined as "situations where a family member (1) took a child in violation of a custody agreement or decree, (2) in violation of a custody agreement or decree failed to return a child at the end of a legal or agreed-upon visit, with the child being away at least overnight" (ix). "Most of the ... abductions were perpetrated by men, noncustodial fathers and father figures" (xi). In contrast, there were an estimated 3,200 to 4,000 *"Legal Definition Non-Family Abductions"* known to law enforcement in 1988 (xii). Quoted in Terry Arendell, "After Divorce: Investigations into Father Absence," *Gender & Society* 6, no. 4 (December 1992): 562–86. Mahoney, "Legal Issues of Battered Women: Redefining the Issue of Separation."

14. See note 9

15. Maccoby and Mnookin, *Dividing the Child,* report that 29 percent of their sam-

ple engaged in "cooperative coparenting," with high communication and low discord; 41 percent in "disengaged coparenting," with low communication and low discord; and 24 percent engaged in "conflicted coparenting," with low communication and high discord.

16. Furstenberg and Cherlin, *Divided Families*, ch. 2; Terry Arendell, *Fathers & Divorce*.

17. Terry Arendell, *Fathers & Divorce*.

18. Arlene Daniels, "Invisible Work," *Social Problems* 34 (1987): 403–15.

19. Jay Teachman, "Contributions to Children by Divorced Fathers," *Social Problems* 38 (1991): 358–71; Furstenberg and Cherlin, *Divided Families*, 36.

20. Furstenberg and Cherlin, ibid.

21. For those who believe that fathers fail to see their children because of conflicts with mothers, see Denise Donnelly and David Finkelhor, "Does Equality in Custody Arrangement Improve the Parent-Child Relationship?" *Journal of Marriage and the Family* 54, 4 (1992): 837–45; and Janet Johnston, "High-Conflict Divorce." For ongoing conflict over visitation, see Judith W. Wallerstein and Joan B. Kelly, *Surviving the Breakup: How Children and Parents Cope with Divorce* (New York: Basic Books, 1980) and Constance R. Ahrons, "The Continuing Coparental Relationship Between Divorced Spouses," *American Journal of Orthopsychiatry* (1981) 51: 415–428.

22. Terry Arendell, in *Fathers & Divorce*, reports that many fathers fear that they can be unjustly charged with sexual abuse of their children as a way for mothers to prevent visitation. However, according to Arendell and others, false allegations of child abuse by mothers are rare. See also Jan E. Paradise, Anthony L. Rostain, and Madeleine Nathanson, "Substantiation of Sexual Abuse Charges when Parents Dispute Custody or Visitation," *Pediatrics* 81 (1988): 835–39; Katherine Coulborn Faller, "Possible Explanations for Child Sexual Abuse Allegations in Divorce," *American Journal of Orthopsychiatry* 61, 1 (1991): 86–91.

23. Arendell, *Fathers & Divorce*.

24. William Goode, *Women in Divorce* (New York: Free Press, 1965), 313.

25. Karen Czapanskiy, "Child Support and Visitation: Rethinking the Connections," *Rutgers Law Journal* 20 (1989): 619–65.

26. Maccoby and Mnookin, *Dividing the Child*, 159.

27. For a discussion of women's loss of custody because of "failure" to protect the children, see Martha Mahoney, "Legal Issues of Battered Women: Redefining the Issue of Separation."

28. Arendell, *Fathers & Divorce*.

29. Czapanskiy, "Child Support and Visitation: Rethinking the Connections."

30. Czapanskiy, ibid., 1474.

CHAPTER 7: WOMEN AND CHILDREN AT DIVORCE

1. Many researchers have focused on the psychological problems of the divorced. See Gay Kitson, *Portrait of Divorce: Adjustment to Marital Breakdown* (New York: The Guilford Press, 1992); Bernard L. Bloom, Stephen W. White, and Shirley J. Asher, "Marital Disruption as a Stressful Life Event," in *Divorce and Separation: Context, Causes, and Consequences*, ed. George Levinger and Oliver C. Moles (New York: Basic

Books, 1979); Judith Wallerstein, "Women After Divorce: Preliminary Report from a Ten-Year Follow-Up," *American Journal of Orthopsychiatry* 56: 65–77; Robert S. Weiss, *Marital Separation* (New York: Basic Books, 1975); E. Mavis Hetherington, Martha Cox, and Roger Cox, "Stress and Coping in Divorce: A Focus on Women," in *Psychology and Women in Transition,* ed. Jeanne Gullahorn (New York: B. J. Winston, 1979). Some researchers have also noted greater illness and mortality on the part of the divorced. See Lois M. Verbrugge, "Marital Status and Health," *Journal of Marriage and the Family* 41 (1979): 267–85. On the other hand, other researchers report that separated and divorced men and women have a greater sense of well-being after divorce and believe that life has improved for them. See Graham B. Spanier and Linda Thompson, *Parting: The Aftermath of Separation and Divorce* (Newbury Park, CA: Sage, 1987); John P. Robinson and Philip R. Shaver, "Measures of Social Psychological Attitudes" (Ann Arbor, MI: Survey Research Center, Institute for Social Research, 1973); Angus Campbell, Philip E. Converse, and Willard L. Rodgers, *The Quality of American Life* (New York: Russell Sage Foundation, 1976). A few researchers believe that women in particular, despite their greater symptoms of depression and stress, gain an increased sense of competency and control through successfully negotiating the difficult tasks of divorce. See Carol Brown, "Mothers, Fathers, and Children: From Private to Public Patriarchy," in *Women and Revolution,* ed. Lydia Sargent (Boston, MA:South End Press, 1981), 239–268. . Still others report that men's and women's adjustment to divorce is mixed. Sharon Price and Patrick McKenry, *Divorce* (Newbury Park, CA: Sage, 1988), 55–72, in their review of the literature on adjustment to divorce, cite data showing divorce as a "very positive life event." However, they point out that there is also extensive data showing that most people who divorce experience some pain and distress.

2. Catherine K. Riessman, *Divorce Talk* (New Brunswick, NJ: Rutgers University Press, 1990); Terry Arendell, *Mothers and Divorce* (Berkeley: University of California Press, 1986). For polling data, see Susan Faludi, *Backlash* (New York: Doubleday, 1991), 61.

3. Many more of the middle-class husbands are remarried (42 percent), compared to working-class (28 percent) and poverty-level ex-husbands (9 percent). At the same time, far fewer middle-class ex-husbands (12 percent) are living with someone than working-class (26 percent) and poverty-level ones (39 percent).

4. Many researchers report negative consequences of divorce for children. For a summary of these negative consequences, see Paul Amato, "Life-Span Adjustment of Children to Their Parents' Divorce," *The Future of Children: Children and Divorce* 1, no. 4 (Spring 1994): 149–52; Robert Emery, *Marriage, Divorce, and Children's Adjustment* (Newbury Park, CA: Sage, 1988); Sara McLanahan and Karen Booth, "Mother-Only Families: Problems, Prospects, and Politics," *Journal of Marriage and the Family* 51, 3 (1989): 557–80. Those who write in the "decline of the family" tradition cite studies showing many harmful effects of divorce on children. As noted in chapter 2, many of these researchers believe that the problems that children of divorce suffer are a major reason to try and curb the divorce rate. See Barbara Defoe Whitehead, "Dan Quayle Was Right," *The Atlantic Monthly,* April 1993, 47–84. See Armand Nicholi, "The Impact of Family Dissolution on the Emotional Health of Children and Adolescents," in *When Families Fail,* ed. Bryce Christensen (Lanham, MD: University Press of America, 1991), 27–42. Nicholi cites a number of other studies that he believes conclusively demonstrate that, apart from poverty, divorce itself has a very negative effect on the mental health of children. He claims that the absence of one parent due to death, divorce, or a time-demanding job "contributes to the many forms of emotional disorder, especially the anger, rebelliousness, low self-esteem, depression, and antisocial behavior that

characterizes those adolescents who take drugs, become pregnant out of wedlock, or commit suicide" (31). He claims that several recent studies have found that children with a father absent for long periods tend to have low motivation for achievement, inability to defer immediate gratification for later rewards, low self-esteem, and susceptibility to group influence and to juvenile delinquency.

5. See Frank Furstenberg and Andrew Cherlin, *Divided Families* (Cambridge, MA: Harvard University Press, 1991); Paul Amato, "Life-Span Adjustment of Children to Their Parents' Divorce"; and Susan E. Krantz, "The Impact of Divorce on Children," in *Feminism, Children, and the New Families,* ed. Sanford M. Dornbusch and Myra H. Strober (New York: Guilford, 1988), 249–73. Terry Arendell argues that studies fail to take into account the impact on children of their downward mobility at divorce. See Arendell, *Mothers and Divorce,* 88; and Robert Emery, *Marriage, Divorce, and Children's Adjustment,* 102. For studies based on clinical samples, see Judith Wallerstein and Sandra Blakeslee, *Second Chances: Men, Women, and Children a Decade After Divorce* (New York: Ticknor and Fields, 1989). Wallerstein and Blakeslee conducted a widely publicized study reporting that divorce had strong negative effects on half of all children in their clinical sample of sixty middle-class divorced families, including anger, anxiety, and underachievement. Wallerstein and Blakeslee claim that their families are "representative of the way normal people from a white, middle-class background cope with divorce." However, others argue that we should not generalize from Wallerstein's sample because it was drawn from a clinic population, which would have a history of greater psychological problems than a truly representative sample.

6. Frank Furstenberg and Andrew Cherlin, *Divided Families* (Cambridge, MA: Harvard University Press, 1991), 69. See also, Amato, "Life-Span Adjustment of Children to Their Parents' Divorce," 146.

7. See Amato, ibid., 151. See also Andrew Cherlin, Frank Furstenberg, and P.L. Chase-Lansdale, "Longitudinal Studies of Effects of Divorce on Children in Great Britain and the United States," *Science* 252 (1991): 1386–89; Jeanne H. Block, Jack Block, and Per R. Gjerde, "The Personality of Children Prior to Divorce," *Child Development* 57 (1986): 827–40; Frank Furstenberg and Julien Teitler, "Reconsidering the Effects of Marital Disruption," *Journal of Family Issues* 15, no. 2 (June 1994): 173–90.

8. Susan Krantz, "The Impact of Divorce on Children," in *Feminism, Children, and the New Families,* ed. S. M. Dornbusch and M. H. Strober (New York: Guilford, 1988), 255.

9. See also Paul Amato, "Life-Span Adjustment of Children to Their Parents' Divorce," 149.

10. Furstenberg and Cherlin report that child well-being is not related to contact with the father, while Judith S. Wallerstein and Joan B. Kelly, in *Surviving the Breakup: How Children Actually Cope with Divorce* (New York: Basic Books, 1980); and E. Mavis Hetherington, Martha Cox, and Roger Cox, in "The Aftermath of Divorce," in *Mother-Child, Father-Child Relations,* ed. Joseph H. Stevens and Marilyn Matthews, (Washington, DC: National Association for the Education of Young Children, 1978), report that it is.

11. See Peter Jaffe, David Wolfe, and Susan K. Wilson, "Children of Battered Women," *Developmental Clinical Psychology and Psychiatry* 21 (Newbury Park, CA: Sage, 1990); Janet R. Johnston, "High Conflict Divorce," *The Future of Children: Children and Divorce.* The David and Lucile Packard Foundation 4, no. 1 (Spring 1994): 165–82.

12. Terry Arendell, *Mothers and Divorce.*

13. Arlie Hochschild, *The Second Shift* (New York: Avon Books, 1989),

CHAPTER 8: CONCLUSION

1. For the number of children affected by divorce, see Frank F. Furstenberg, Jr. "History and Current Status of Divorce in the United States," in *The Future of Children: Children and Divorce* 4, no. 1 (Spring 1994), The David and Lucile Packard Foundation, 35. For the poverty rate of single-mother families, see Jay D. Teachman and Kathleen M. Paasc, "Financial Impact of Divorce on Children and Their Families," in *The Future of Children*, Center for the Future of Children, The David and Lucile Packard Foundation 1, no. 4 (Spring 1994), 69.

2. Fortunately there is increased attention to how masculinity is constructed in our culture. Harry Brod, Michael Kimmelman, and Robert Connell, among others, have done excellent work in this field. For a brief sampling of their work, see Harry Brod and Michael Kimmelman, ed., *Theorizing Masculinities* (Newbury Park, CA: Sage, 1994) For two recent interview studies of men, see Kathleen Gerson, *No Man's Land: Men's Changing Commitments to Family and Work* (New York: Basic Books, 1993) and Terry Arendell, *Fathers & Divorce* (Newbury Park, CA: Sage, forthcoming).

3. Naomi Cahn, "Civil Images of Battered Women: The Impact of Domestic Violence on Child Custody Decisions," *Vanderbilt Law Review* 44 (1991): 1040–1097.

4. For discussion of a range of program possibilities for families in conflict, see "High-Conflict Divorce," in *The Future of Children: Children and Divorce*, The David and Lucile Packard Foundation 4, no. 1 (Spring 1994).

5. David Finkelhor, Gerald Hotaling, and Andrea Sedlak, *Missing, Abducted, Runaway, and Thrownaway Children in America* (Washington, DC: U.S. Department of Justice, 1990).

6. Among those favoring a primary caretaker presumption are: Terry Arendell, *Fathers & Divorce*, Frank Furstenberg and Andrew Cherlin, *Divided Families* (Cambridge, MA: Harvard University Press, 1991), 116; Martha Fineman, *The Illusion of Equality* (Chicago: University of Chicago Press, 1991), 183; David Chambers, "Rethinking the Substantive Rules for Custody Disputes in Divorce," *Michigan Law Review* 80 (1984): 1614–34. See also Barbara Bennett Woodhouse, "Hatching the Egg: A Child-Centered Perspective on Parents' Rights," *Cardozo Law Review* 14, 6 (1993): 1747–1865, especially 1851 on how the primary caretaker standard can be beneficial to the interests of children.

7. Terry Arendell, *Fathers & Divorce*.

8. Karen Czapanskiy, "Volunteers and Draftees: The Struggle for Parental Equality," *UCLA Law Review* 38 (1991): 1415–81.

9. According to Sara McLanahan and Irwin Garfinkel, *New York Times*, July 29, 1994, 27, "We cut poverty rates among the elderly by two-thirds from 1967 to 1993." Pearce says, "Older Americans, whose poverty frequently occurred because of a health crisis or the lack of housing, and inadequate social security, have benefitted from programs targeted to their needs: Medicare, elderly housing, and broadened and indexed social security benefits. As a result, the overall poverty rate for the elderly is actually less than that of the population as a whole." Diana Pearce, "The Feminization of Poverty: Update," in *Feminist Frameworks*, ed. Alison Jaggar and Paula Rothenberg, third edition (New York: McGraw Hill, 1993), 292. Middle-class tax subsidies are disguised as "earned benefits," for example, in social security. As economist Sawhill says, "A dollar spent on housing, health care, or capital investment through the tax code has the same effects on the allocation of resources and the distribution of income as a dollar in direct spending for the same purposes. Yet, because tax expenditures are hidden and do not

affect calculations of the "size of government" as measured by the ratio of outlays to GNP, they receive far less scrutiny than regular budget accounts." Isabel Sawhill, "Escaping the Fiscal Trap," *The American Prospect* (Spring 1990): 21. For the United States as at an extreme point, see Mary Ann Glendon, *The Transformation of Family Law* (Chicago: University of Chicago Press, 1989), 237. Also Glendon, *Abortion and Divorce in Western Law* (Cambridge, MA: Harvard University Press, 1987).

10. Martha Fineman, *The Illusion of Equality: The Rhetoric and Reality of Divorce Reform* (Chicago: University of Chicago Press, 1991). Mary O'Connell, "Alimony After No-Fault: A Practice in Search of a Theory," *New England Law Review* 23(1988): 437–513. Jana Singer, "Divorce Reform and Gender Justice," *North Carolina Law Review* 67 (1989): 1118. Stephen Sugarman, "Dividing Financial Interests on Divorce," in *Divorce Reform at the Crossroads*, ed. Stephen Sugarman and Herma Hill Kay (New Haven: Yale University Press, 1991), 130–65; June Carbone and Margaret Brinig, "Rethinking Marriage: Feminist Ideology, Economic Change, and Divorce Reform," 65 *Tulane Law Review* 953 (1991): 953-1010.

11. Singer, ibid., 1110–21; O'Connell, ibid.

12. Roberta Spalter-Roth and Heidi Hartmann, "AFDC Recipients as Caregivers and Workers," *Social Politics* 1, no. 2 (Summer 1994): 190–210. For policies to pay people for work of "comparable worth," see Ronnie Steinberg, "Evaluating Jobs," *Society* 22 (July/August 1985): 44–54; and Jerry Jacobs and Ronnie Steinberg, "Compensating Differentials and the Male-Female Wage Gap: Evidence from the New York State Comparable Worth Study," *Social Forces* 69 (December 1990): 439–68.

13. Barbara Bergmann, "Child Care: The Key to Ending Child Poverty," Paper presented at the Conference on Social Policies for Children, Woodrow Wilson School of Public and International Affairs, Princeton University, May 25–27, 1994.

14. Roberta M. Spalter-Roth and Heidi Hartmann, "AFDC Recipients as Care-givers and Workers."

15. Stephanie Coontz, *The Way We Never Were* (New York: Basic Books, 1992), 286.

16. David Poponoe, in *Disturbing the Nest: Family Change and Decline in Modern Societies* (New York: Aldine De Gruyter, 1988), states that social welfare policies in Scandinavia have caused an increase in single parent families and finds this a disturbing trend.

REFERENCES

Abramovitz, Mimi. 1988. *Regulating the Lives of Women: Social Welfare Policy from Colonial Times to the Present.* Boston, MA: South End Press.

Ahrons, Constance. 1981. "The Continuing Coparental Relationship Between Divorced Spouses." *American Journal of Orthopsychiatry* 51 (1981): 415–428.

Ahrons, Constance and R. Rodgers. 1987. *Divorced Families: A Multidisciplinary Developmental View* (New York: W.W. Norton).

Amato, Paul. 1994. "Life-Span Adjustment of Children to Their Parents' Divorce." *The Future of Children: Children and Divorce* 1, No. 4 (Spring): 149–152

Ambert, Anne-Marie. 1988. "Relationship Between Ex-Spouses: Individual and Dyadic Perspectives." *Journal of Social and Personal Relationships* 5: 327–46.

Amott, Teresa L. 1990. "Black Women and AFDC: Making Entitlement Out of Necessity." In *Women, the State, and Welfare*, ed. Linda Gordon, 208–298. Madison, Wisconsin: University of Wisconsin Press.

Anderson, Elijah. 1990. *Streetwise: Race, Class and Change in an Urban Community.* Chicago: University of Chicago Press.

Angel, Ronald & Jacqueline L. Worobey. 1988. "Single Motherhood and Children's Health." *Journal Of Health and Social Behavior* 29 (March): 38–52.

Arafat, I. and B.Yorburg. 1976. *The New Woman: Attitudes, Behavior, and Self-Image.* Columbus, Ohio: Charles Merrill.

Arendell, Terry. 1986. *Mothers and Divorce: Legal, Economic, and Social Dilemmas.* Berkeley: University of California Press.

_____.1987. "Women and the Economics of Divorce in the Contemporary United States." *Sign*, 13: 121–135.

_____.1992. "After Divorce: Investigations into Father Absence." *Gender & Society* Vol. 6, No. 4 (December): 562–586

_____.(forthcoming) *Fathers & Divorce.* Newbury Park, CA: Sage.

Ayuda, Clinica Legal Latina. 1994. Center for Law and Social Policy, Children's Defense Fund, National Women's Law Center, Office of Domestic Social Development United States Catholic Conference, Women's Legal Defense Fund. "A Vision of Child Support Reform" (January) Washington, DC.

Babcock, Barbara, Rhonda Copelon, Ann Freedman, Eleanor Holmes Norton, Susan Ross, Nadine Taub, and Wendy Williams. Forthcoming. *Sex Discrimination and the Law: Causes and Remedies.* Second Edition. Boston: Little Brown.

Baca Zinn, Maxine. 1990. "Family, Feminism, and Race in America." *Gender & Society* 4, No. 1 (March): 68–82.

Bailey, William T., N. Clayton Silver, and Kathleen A. Oliver. 1990. "Women's Rights and Roles: Attitudes Among Black and White Students." *Psychological Reports* 66, 1143–1146.

Bartlett, Katherine T. and Carol B. Stack. 1986. "Joint Custody, Feminism, and the Dependency Dilemma," *Berkeley Women's Law Journal* 2: 9–41.

Becker, Mary. 1992. "Maternal Feelings: Myth, Taboo, and Child Custody." *Review of Law and Women's Studies* Vol. 1: 133–224.

Bellah, Robert, Richard Madsen, William M Sullivan, Ann Swidler, and Steven M. Tipton. 1985. *Habits of the Heart: Individualism and Commitment in American Life.* New York: Harper & Row.

Bergmann, Barbara. 1994. "Child Care: The Key to Ending Child Poverty." Paper presented at the Conference on Social Policies for Children, Woodrow Wilson School of Public and International Affairs, Princeton University, Princeton, NJ, May 25–27, 1994.

Bergmann, Barbara and Sherry Wetchler, "Child Support Awards: State Guidelines Versus Public Opinion." Department of Economics, University of Maryland.

Berk, Sarah Fenstermaker. 1985. *The Gender Factory: The Apportionment of Work in American Households.* New York: Plenum Press.

Berk, Richard, Sarah Fenstermaker Berk, Donileen R. Loseke, and David Rauma. 1983. "Mutual Combat and Other Family Violence Myths." In *The Dark Side of Families,* ed. David Finkelhor, Richard J. Gelles, Gerald T. Hotaling, and Murray A. Straus, 197–212. Beverly Hills, CA: Sage.

Bernard, Jessie. 1972. *The Future of Marriage.* New York: World Publishers.

Blankenhorn, David. 1990. "American Family Dilemmas." In *Rebuilding the Nest,* ed. David Blankenhorn, S. Bayme, and Jean B. Elshtain, 3–26. Milwaukee, WI: Family Service America.

Block, Jeanne H., Jack Block, and Per F. Gjerde. 1986. "The Personality of Children Prior to Divorce." *Child Development* 57: 827–840.

Bloom, B.L., Niles, R.L. and Tatcher, A.M. "Sources of Marital Dissatisfaction Among Newly Separated Persons." *Journal of Family Issues* 6: 359–373.

Bloom, Bernard L., Shirley J. Asher, and Stephen W. White. 1979. "Marital Disruption as a Stressful Life Event." In *Divorce and Separation: Context, Causes, and Consequences,* ed. George Levinger and Oliver C. Moles. New York: Basic Books.

Blumstein, Philip and Pepper Schwartz. 1983. *American Couples*. New York: Pocket Books.

Brewer, Rose 1988. "Black Women in Poverty: Some Comments on Female-Headed Families." *Signs* 13 (Winter): 331–9.

Brod, Harry and Michael Kimmelman, ed., 1994. *Theorizing Masculinities*. Newbury Park, CA: Sage.

Brown, Carol. 1981. "Mothers, Fathers, and Children: From Private to Public Patriarchy." In *Women and Revolution*, ed. Lydia Sargent, 239–268. Boston, MA: South End Press.

Bruch, Carol. 1982. "Developing Standards for Child Support Payments: A Critique of Current Practice." *University of California at Davis Law Review* 16 (1): 49–64.

Buchanan, Christy M., Eleanor E. Maccoby, and Sanford M. Dornbusch. 1991. "Caught Between Parents: Adolescents' Experience in Divorced Homes." *Child Development* 62(5): 1008–1029.

Bumpass, Larry. 1984. "Children and Marital Disruption: A Replication and Update." *Demography* 21(1): 71–82.

Buzawa, Eve S. and Carl G. Buzawa, eds. 1992. *Domestic Violence: The Changing Criminal Justice Response*. Westport, CT: Auburn House.

Cahn, Naomi R. 1991. "Civil Images of Battered Women: The Impact of Domestic Violence on Child Custody Decisions." *Vanderbilt Law Review* 44: 1041–1097.

Campbell, Angus, Philip Converse, and Willard Rodgers. 1976. *The Quality of American Life*. New York: Russell Sage Foundation.

Campbell, Nancy D., Sarah Craven, Diane Dodson, Nancy Ebb, and Paul Roberts. 1994. "A Vision of Child Support Reform." Washington, D.C.: Center for Law and Social Policy.

Carbone, June and Margaret Brinig. 1991. "Rethinking Marriage: Feminist Ideology, Economic Change, and Divorce Reform." *Tulane Law Review* 65: 953–1010.

Carter, H. and P.C. Glick. 1976. *Marriage and Divorce: A Social and Economic Study*. Cambridge, MA: Harvard University Press.

Cazenave, Noel and Murray A. Straus. 1979. "Race, Class, Network Embeddedness and Family Violence: A Search for Potent Support Systems." *Journal of Comparative Family Studies* 10: 281–300.

Centers for Disease Control (ed.) 1985. *Surgeon General's Workshop on Violence and Public Health: Sourcebook*. Atlanta, GA: U.S. Public Health Service.

Chambers, David. "Rethinking the Substantive Rules for Custody Disputes in Divorce." *Michigan Law Review* 88: 477–569.

Cherlin, Andrew. 1990. "Recent Changes in American Fertility, Marriage and Divorce." *Annals, AAPSS*, 510 (July): 145–154.

_____.1992. *Marriage, Divorce, Remarriage*. Cambridge, MA: Harvard University Press.

Cherlin, Andrew, Frank Furstenberg, and P. Lindsay Chase-Lansdale. 1991. "Longitudinal Studies of Effects of Divorce on Children in Great Britain and the United States." *Science* 252: 1386–1389.

Clatterbaugh, Kenneth. 1990. *Contemporary Perspectives on Masculinity*. Boulder, CO: Westview Press.

Colasanto, Linda and Diane Colasanto. 1990. "The Gender Gap in America: Unlike 1975, Today Most Americans Think Men Have It Better." *Gallup Poll News Service* 54(37): 1–7.

Collins, Patricia Hill. 1989. "A Comparison of Two Works on Black Family Life," *Signs* 14, 4: 875–884.

_____. 1991. *Black Feminist Thought.* New York: Routledge.

Collins, Randall. 1988. *Sociology of Marriage and the Family.* Chicago: Nelson-Hall.

Coltrane, Scott and Neal Hickman. 1992. "The Rhetoric of Rights and Needs: Moral Discourse in the Reform of Child Custody and Child Support Laws." *Social Problems* 39, 4: 400–420.

Conger, Rand D., Glen H. Elder, Frederick O. Lorenz, Katherine J. Conger, Ronald L. Simons, Les B. Whitbeck, Shirley Huck, and Janet N. Melby. 1990. "Linking Economic Hardship to Marital Quality and Instability." *Journal of Marriage and the Family* 52(August): 643–656.

Coontz, Stephanie. 1992. *The Way We Never Were.* New York: Basic Books.

Crenshaw, Kimberle. 1994. "Mapping the Margins: Intersectionality, Identity Politics, and Violence Against Women of Color." In *The Public Nature of Private Violence,* eds. Martha A. Fineman and Roxanne Mykitiu, 93–118. New York: Routledge.

Cutright, Phillips. 1971. "Income Family Events: Marital Stability." *Journal of Marriage and the Family* 33: 291–306.

Czapanskiy, Karen. 1989. "Child Support and Visitation: Rethinking the Connections." *Rutgers Law Journal* 20: 619–665.

_____. 1991. "Volunteers and Draftees: The Struggle for Parental Equality." *UCLA Law Review* 38: 1415–1481.

Daniels, Arlene K. 1987. "Invisible Work." *Social Problems* 34, 5: 403–415.

Dao, James. 1993. "Divorce Lawyers Assailed in Study By Albany Panel." *The New York Times,* Wednesday. May 5, A1.

Degler, Carl. 1980. *At Odds: Women and the Family in American from the Revolution to the Present.* New York: Oxford University Press.

DeStefano, Linda & Colasanto, Diane. 1990. "The Gender Gap in America: Unlike 1975, Today Most Americans Think Men Have It Better.," *Gallup Poll News Service* 54(37): 1–7.

Dill, Bonnie Thornton. 1988. "Our Mother's Grief: Racial Ethnic Women and the Maintenance of Families." *Journal of Family History* 13: 415–431.

Dobash, R. Emerson and Russell Dobash. 1979. *Violence Against Wives.* New York: Free Press.

_____. 1992. "The Myth of Sexual Symmetry in Marital Violence." *Social Problems* 39: 71–91.

Dodson, Diane. 1988. "The Relationship Between Child Support and Alimony." In *Journal of the American Academy of Matrimonial Lawyers* 4: 25–56.

Donnelly, Denise and David Finkelhor. 1992. "Does Equality in Custody Arrangement Improve the Parent-Child Relationship?" *Journal of Marriage and the Family* 54, 4: 837–845.

Dugger, Karen. 1991. "Social Location and Gender-Role Attitudes: A Comparison of Black and White Women." In *The Social Construction of Gender,* ed. Judith Lorber and Susan A. Farrell, 38–59. Newbury Park, CA: Sage Publications.

Duncan, Greg J. and Saul Hoffman. 1985. "A Reconsideration of the Economic Consequences of Marital Dissolution." *Demography* 22: 485–97.

Ehrenreich, Barbara. 1983. *The Hearts of Men: American Dreams and the Flight From Commitment.* Garden City, NY: Anchor Press.

Ellis, Desmond. 1987. "Post-Separation Woman Abuse: The Contribution of Lawyers as 'Barracudas,' 'Advocates,' and 'Counsellors,'" *International Journal of Law and Psychiatry* 10: 403–411.

Ellis, Desmond and Walter Dekeseredy. 1989. "Marital Status and Woman Abuse: Dad Model." *International Journal of the Sociology of the Family* 19: 67–87.

_____. 1995. *The Wrong Stuff: An Introduction to the Sociological Study of Deviance,* 2nd edition. Toronto: Allyn and Baco, 1995.

Ellwood, David T. 1988. *Poor Support.* New York: Basic Books.

Ellwood, David and Bane, Mary Jo. 1985. "The Impact of AFDC on family structure and living arrangements." In Ronald Ehrenberg, ed. *Research in Labor Economics 7.*

Elshtain, Jean Bethke. 1981. *Public Man, Private Woman: Women in Social and Political Thought.* Princeton: Princeton University Press.

_____. 1990. "The Family and Civic Life." In *Rebuilding the Nest,* ed. David Blankenhorn, Steven Bayme, and Jean B. Elshtain, 161–178. Milwaukee, WI: Family Service America.

Emery, Robert. 1988. *Marriage, Divorce, and Children's Adjustment.* Newbury Park, CA: Sage.

England, Paula and Barbara Stanek Kilbourne. 1990. "Markets, Marriages, and Other Mates: The Problem of Power." In *Beyond the Marketplace: Rethinking Society and Economy,* ed. Roger Friedland and Sandy Robertson, 163–188. New York: Aldine.

Espenshade, Thomas. 1979. "The Economic Consequences of Divorce." *Journal of Marriage and the Family* 41: 615–625.

Etzioni, Amitai. 1993. *The Spirit of Community.* New York: Crown.

Fagen, Jeffrey A., Douglas K. Steward, and Karen V. Hansen. 1983. "Violent Men or Violent Husbands? Background Factors and Situational Correlates." In *The Dark Side of Families: Current Family Violence Research,* eds. David Finkelhor, Richard J. Gelles, Gerald Hotaling, and Murray A.Straus, 49–68. Beverly Hills: Sage.

Faller, Katherine Couler. 1991. "Possible Explanations for Child Sexual Abuse Allegations in Divorce." *American Journal of Orthopsychiatry* 61, 1: 86–91.

Faludi, Susan. 1991. *Backlash.* New York: Doubleday.

Felstiner, William L. and Austin Sarat. 1992. "Enactments of Power: Negotiating Reality and Responsibility in Lawyer-Client Interactions." *Cornell Law Review,* 77: 1447–1498.

Ferree, Myra Marx. 1990. "Beyond Separate Spheres: Feminism and Family Research," *Journal of Marriage and the Family* 52: 886–94.

Fields, Marjory D. 1978. "Wife-beating: Facts and Figures." *Victimology* 2(3–4): 643–647.

Fineman, Martha A. 1991. *The Illusion of Equality: The Rhetoric and Reality of Divorce Reform.* Chicago: University of Chicago Press.

_____. 1995. *The Neutered Mother, The Sexual Family and Other Twentieth Century Tragedies.* New York: Routledge.

Finkelhor, David Gerald Hotaling, and Andrea Sedlak. 1990. *Missing, Abducted, Runaway, and Thrownaway Children in America.* Washington, DC: U.S. Dept. of Justice.

Finlay, Barbara, Charles E. Starnes, and Fausto B. Alvarez. 1985. "Recent Changes in Sex-Role Ideology Among Divorced Men and Women: Some Possible Causes and Implications." *Sex Roles* 12: 637–653.

Fischer, Claude S. 1982. *To Dwell Among Friends: Social Networks in Town and City.* Chicago: University of Chicago Press.

Fraser, Nancy and Linda Gordon. 1994. "'Dependency' Demystified: Inscriptions of Power in a Keyword of the Welfare State." *Social Politics* 1, No. 1 (Spring): 4–31.

Furstenberg, Jr., Frank F. 1988. "Marital Disruptions, Child Custody, and Visitation." In *Child Support: From Debt Collection to Social Policy,* ed. A. Kahn and Sheila Kamerman. Newbury Park, CA: Sage. 277–305.

_____. 1994. "History and Current Status of Divorce in the United States" *The Future of Children: Children and Divorce* 1, No. 4 (Sprint): 29–43.

Furstenberg, Jr., Frank F., Christine W. Nord, James L. Peterson, and Nicholas Zill. 1983. "The Life Course of Children of Divorce: Marital Disruption and Parental Contact." *American Sociological Review* 48, no.10: 656–68.

Furstenberg, Jr., Frank F. and Graham G. Spanier. 1984. *Recycling the Family: Remarriage After Divorce.* Beverly Hills: Sage.

Furstenberg, Jr., Frank F., S. Phillip Morgan, and Paul D. Allison. 1987. "Paternal Participation and Children's Well-Being after Marital Dissolution." *American Sociological Review* 52: 695–701.

Furstenberg, Jr., Frank F. and Andrew Cherlin. 1991. *Divided Families.* Cambridge MA: Harvard University Press.

Furstenberg, Jr., Frank F. and Julien Teitler. 1994. "Reconsidering the Effects of Marital Disruption." *Journal of Family Issues* 15, 2 (June): 173–190.

Garfinkel, Irwin. 1992a. *Assuring Child Support: An Extension of Social Security.* New York: Russell Sage.

_____. 1992b. "Bringing Fathers Back In, The Child Support Assurance Strategy." *The American Prospect* 9 (Spring): 74–83.

Garfinkel, Irwin and Sara McLanahan. 1986. *Single Mothers and Their Children.* Washington, D.C.: Urban Institute Press.

Garfinkel, Irwin, Marygold S. Melli, and John G. Robertson. 1994. "Child Support Orders: A Perspective on Reform." In *The Future of the Family: Children and Divorce.* 4, No. 1 (Spring): 86.

Garfinkel, Irwin, Donald Oellerich, and Philip Robins. 1991. "Child Support Guidelines: Will they make a Difference?" *Journal of Family Issues* 12: 404–429.

Gerson, Kathleen. 1993. *No Man's Land: Men's Changing Commitments to Family and Work.* New York: Basic Books.

Gerstel, Naomi. 1987. "Divorce and Stigma," *Social Problems* 34, 2 (April): 172–186.

_____. 1988. "Divorce and Kin Ties: The Importance of Gender." *Journal of Marriage and the Family* 50 (February): 209–219.

Gillespie, Cynthia. 1989. *Justifiable Homicide.* Columbus: Ohio State University Press.

Glendon, Mary Ann. 1987. *Abortion and Divorce in Western Law.* Cambridge, MA: Harvard University Press, 1987.

_____. 1989. *The Transformation of Family Law.* Chicago: University of Chicago Press.

Glenn, Evelyn Nakano. 1987. "Gender and the Family." In *Analyzing Gender: A Handbook of Social Science Research*, ed. Beth Hess and Myra Marx Ferree, 348–369. Newbury Park, CA: Sage Publications

Goldberg, Gertrude S. 1990. "The United States: Feminization of Poverty Amidst Plenty." In *The Feminization of Poverty: Only in America?*, ed. Gertrude S. Goldberg and Eleanor Kremen, 17–58. New York: Praeger.

Goldfarb, Sally. 1987. "What Every Lawyer Should Know About Child Support Guidelines." *Family Law Reporter* 13: 3036–37.

Goldstein, Judith, Anna Freud, and A.J. Solnit. 1973. *Beyond the Best Interests of the Child*. New York: The Free Press.

Goode, William J. 1956. *After Divorce*. New York: Free Press.

_____. 1965. *Women in Divorce*. New York: The Free Press.

_____. 1963. *World Revolution and Family Patterns*. New York: Free Press.

Gordon, Linda. 1990. "The New Feminist Scholarship on the Welfare State." In *Women, the State, and Welfare*, ed. Linda Gordon, 9–35. Madison, Wisconsin: University of Wisconsin.

_____. 1994. *Pitied But Not Entitled: Single Mothers and the History of Welfare, 1890–1935*. New York: Free Press.

Grella, Christine E. 1990. "Irreconcilable Differences: Women Defining Class After Divorce and Downward Mobility." *Gender & Society* 4, 1: 41–55.

Groves, Betsy M., B. Zuckerman, S. Marans, D. Cohen. 1993. "Silent Victims: Children Who Witness Violence." *Journal of the American Medical Association* 269, No. 2 (January 13): 262–264.

Hafen, Bruce 1990. "Individualism in Family Law." In *Rebuilding the Nest*, ed. David Blankenhorn, Steven Bayme, and Jean B. Elshtain, 161–178. Milwaukee, WI: Family Service America.

Halle, David. 1984. *America's Working Man: Work, Home, and Politics Among Blue-Collar Property Owners*. Chicago: University of Chicago Press.

Hampton, Robert, Richard J. Gelles, and J. Harrop. 1989. "Is Violence in Black Families Increasing? A Comparison of 1975 and 1985 National Survey Rates." *Journal of Marriage and the Family* 51 (Nov.): 969–980.

Harris, Deborah, 1988. "Child Support for Welfare Families: Family Policy Trapped in Its Own Rhetoric." *New York University Review of Law and Social Change* 16 (October) 19–57.

Hartmann, Heidi I. 1987. "Changes in Women's Economic and Family Roles in Post-World War II United States." In *Women, Households and the Economy*, ed. L. R. Benaria and C.R. Stimpson, 33–64. New Brunswick, NJ: Rutgers.

Harvard Law Review. 1993. "Developments in the Law: Legal Responses to Domestic Violence." *Harvard Law Review* 106: 1498–1620.

Haynes, Margaret C. 1993. "Supporting Our Children: A Blueprint for Reform." *Family Law Quarterly* 27, No. 1 (Spring): 7–29.

Hetherington, E. Mavis, Martha Cox, and Roger Cox. 1979. "Stress and Coping in Divorce: A Focus on Women." In *Psychology and Women in Transition*, ed. Jeanne Gullahorn, 95–128. New York: B.J. Winston.

Hetherington, E. Mavis, and Roger Cox. 1978. "The Aftermath of Divorce." In *Mother-*

Child, Father-Child Relations, ed. Joseph H. Stevens & Marilyn Matthews, 149–176. Washington, DC: National Association for the Education of Young Children.

Hirsch, Amy, 1988. "Income Deeming in the AFDC Program: Using Dual Track Family Law to Make Poor Women Poorer." *New York Review of Law and Social Change* 16 (October): 713–740.

Hochschild, Arlie. 1989. *The Second Shift.* New York: Viking.

Hoffman, Jan. 1992. "New York's Chief Judge Imposes Strict Rules for Divorce Lawyers." *New York Times*, A1.

Hoffman, Saul D. and Greg D. Duncan. 1988. "What are the Consequences of Divorce?" *Demography* 25: 641–645.

Hollingshead, August. 1975. *Elmtown's Youth and Elmtown Revisited.* New York: Wiley.

Howell, Joseph T. 1973. *Hard Living on Clay Street.* Garden City, NY: Anchor Books.

Jacobs, Jerry and Ronnie Steinberg. 1990. "Compensating Differentials and the Male-Female Wage Gap: Evidence from the New York State Comparable Worth Study." *Social Forces* 69 (December): 439–468.

Jaffe, Peter, David Wolfe, and Susan K. Wilson. 1990. "Children of Battered Women." *Developmental Clinical Psychology and Psychiatry.* Newbury Park, CA: Sage.

Johnston, Janet. 1994. "High Conflict Divorce." *The Future of Children: Children and Divorce* 4, No. 1 (Spring): 165–182.

Johnston, Janet R., Linda E. Campbell, and Sharon Mayes. 1985. "Latency Children in Post-Separation and Divorce Disputes." *Journal of the American Academy of Child Psychiatry* 24: 563–574.

Jones, Ann. 1994. *Next Time She'll Be Dead.* Boston: Beacon Press.

Joselson, Emily and Judy Kaye. 1993. "Pro Se Divorce: A Strategy for Empowering Women." In *Family Matters*, ed. Martha Minow, 377–380. New York: The New Press.

Joseph, Gloria and Jill Lewis. 1981. *Common Differences: Conflicts in Black and White Feminist Perspectives.* New York: Anchor Press.

Journal of the American Medical Association. n.a. 1993. "Silent Victims: Children Who Witness Violence." *Journal of the American Medical Association* 269, No. 2 (January 13): 262–264.

Kamerman, Sheila B. and Alfred J. Kahn. 1988. *Mothers Alone.* New York.

Katz, Sanford. 1994. "Historical Perspective and Current Trends in the Legal Process of Divorce." In *The Future of Children: Children and Divorce.* The David and Lucile Packard Foundation 4, No. 1 (Spring): 44–62.

Kelly, Joan. 1993. "The Determination of Child Custody." *The Future of Children: Children and Divorce.* The David and Lucile Packard Foundation 4, No. 1, (Spring): 121–142.

Kitson, Gay C. 1985. "Marital Discord and Marital Separation: A County Survey." *Journal of Marriage and the Family* 47: 693–700.

_____. 1992. *Portrait of Divorce: Adjustment to Marital Breakdown.* New York: The Guilford Press.

Kitson, Gay C. and Marvin Sussman. 1982. "Marital Complaints, Demographic Characteristics and Symptoms of Mental Distress in Divorce." *Journal of Marriage and the Family* 44: 87–101.

Kohn, Melvin. 1977. *Class and Conformity.* Chicago: University of Chicago Press.

Komarovsky, Mirra. 1962. *Blue-Collar Marriage.* New York: Vintage.

Krantz, Susan. 1988. "The Impact of Divorce on Children." In *Feminism, Children and the New Families,* ed. Sanford M. Dornbusch and Myra H. Strober, 249–273. New York: Guilford Press.

Krause, Harry D. 1990. "Child Support Reassessed. Limits of Private Responsibility and the Public Interest." In *Divorce Reform at the Crossroads,* ed. Stephen Sugarman and Herma Hill Kay, 166–275. New Haven: Yale University Press.

Kurz, Demie. 1989. "Social Science Perspectives on Wife Abuse." *Gender & Society* 3, no. 4 (December): 489–505.

_____. 1990. "Interventions with Battered Women in Health Care Settings." *Violence and Victims* 5, no. 4: 243–256.

_____. 1993. "Physical Assaults by Husbands: A Major Social Problem." In *Current Controversies on Family Violence,* ed. Richard J. Gelles and Donileen R. Loseke. Newbury Park, CA: Sage. 88–103.

Ladner, Joyce. 1971. *Tomorrow's Tomorrow: The Black Woman.* Garden City, NY: Doubleday.

Leslie, Leigh A. and Katherine Grady. 1985. "Changes in Mothers' Social Networks and Social Support Following Divorce." *Journal of Marriage and the Family* 47 (August): 663–673.

Levinger, George. 1966. "Sources of Marital Dissatisfaction Among Applicants for Divorce." *American Journal of Orthopsychiatry* 36: 803–807.

Lewis, D.K. 1975. "The Black Family: Socialization and Sex Roles." *Phylon* 36(3): 221–37.

Liebow, Eliot. 1967. *Tally's Corner.* New York: Doubleday.

Lockhart, Lottie. 1991. "Spousal Violence: A Cross-Racial Perspective." In *Black Family Violence,* ed. Robert L. Hampton, 85–101. Lexington, MA: Lexington Books.

Lorber, Judith. 1994. *Paradoxes of Gender.* New Haven: Yale University Press.

Luepnitz, Deborah A. 1982. *Child Custody: A Study of Families After Divorce.* Lexington, MA: D.C. Heath.

Maccoby, Eleanor. E. and Robert H. Mnookin. 1992. *Dividing the Child: Social and Legal Dilemmas of Custody.* Cambridge, MA: Harvard University Press.

Mahoney, Martha. 1991. "Legal Images of Battered Women: Redefining the Issue of Separation." *Michigan Law Review* 90, 1: 1–94.

Malveaux, Julianne. 1985. "The Economic Interests of Black and White Women: Are They Similar?" *Review of Black Political Economy* (Summer): 5–27.

McLanahan, Sara S. 1984. "Family Structure and Stress: A Longitudinal Comparison of Two-Parent and Female-Headed Families." *Journal of Marriage and the Family* (May): 347–357.

McLanahan, Sara S. and Larry Bumpass. 1988a. "Intergenerational Consequences of Family Disruption." *American Journal of Sociology* 94 (July): 30–52.

_____. 1988b. "A Note on the Effect of Family Structure on School Enrollment." In *Divided Opportunities: Minorities, Poverty, and Social Policy,* ed. G. Sandefur and M. Tienda, 195–203. New York: Plenum Press.

McLanahan, Sara and Karen Booth. 1989. "Mother-Only Families: Problems, Prospects, and Politics." *Journal of Marriage and the Family* 51, 3 (1989): 557–580.

McLanahan, Sara and Irwin Garfinkel. 1994. "We Cut Poverty Rates Among the Elderly by Two-Thirds from 1967 to 1993." *New York Times*. July 29, A–27,

Miller, Dorothy C. 1990. *Women and Social Welfare: A Feminist Analysis*. New York: Praeger.

Mink, Gwendolyn. 1990. "The Lady and the Tramp: Gender, Race, and the Origins of the American Welfare State." In *Women, the State, and Welfare*, ed. Linda Gordon, 92–122. Madison, Wisconsin: The University of Wisconsin Press.

Mnookin, Robert and L. Kornhauser. 1979. "Bargaining in the Shadow of the Law." *Yale Law Journal* 88(950): 952–958.

Mnookin, Robert, Eleanor E. Maccoby, Catherine R. Albiston, and Charlene E. Depner. 1990. "Private Ordering Revisited: What Custodial Arrangements Are Parents Negotiating?" In *Divorce Reform at the Crossroads*, ed. Stephen D. Sugarman and Herman Hill Kay, 37–74. New Haven, CT: Yale University Press.

Morgan, David. 1985. *The Family, Politics, and Social Theory*. London: Routledge and Kegan Paul, 1985.

Morgan, Leslie A. 1991. *After Marriage Ends: Economic Consequences for Midlife Women* Newbury Park, CA: Sage.

Moynihan, Daniel P. 1965. *The Negro Family: The Case for National Action*. Washington, D.C.: U.S. Dept. of Labor, Office of Planning and Research.

_____. 1986. *Family and Nation*. New York: Harcourt Brace Jovanovich.

Murray, Charles. 1993. "The Coming White Underclass." *Wall Street Journal*. Oct. 29, Section A., 14, col. 4.

National Center for Health Statistics. 1990. "Supplements to the Vital Statistics Report: Advance Reports, 1987." National Center for Health Statistics. *Vital Health Statistics* 24(4) (1990).

National Institute on Drug Abuse. 1989. "National Household Drug Survey on Drug Abuse: Population Estimates 1988," DHHS Publication No. (ADM) 89-1636. Washington, DC: U.S. Department of Health and Human Services.

Neely, Richard. 1984. "The Primary Caretaker Parent Rule: Child Custody and the Dynamics of Greed." *Yale Law and Public Policy Review* 3: 168–186.

Newman, Katherine S. 1988. *Falling From Grace*. New York: Free Press.

Nicholi, Armand M. 1991. "The Impact of Family Dissolution on the Emotional Health of Children and Adolescents." In *When Families Fail. . .The Social Costs*, ed. Bryce J. Christensen, 27–41. New York: University Press of America.

Nichols-Caseboldt, Ann. 1992. "The Economic Impact of Child Support Reform on the Poverty Status of Custodial and Noncustodial Families." In *Child Support Assurance*, ed. Irwin Garfinkel, Sara McLanahan and Philip Robins,189–202. Washington, DC: Urban Institute Press.

O'Connell, Mary E. 1988. "Alimony After No-Fault: A Practice in Search of a Theory." *New England Law Review* 23: 437–513.

Office of Child Support Enforcement. 1992. *Child Support Enforcement: Seventeenth Annual Report to Congress*. Washington, DC: Department of Health and Human Services.

Pagelow, Mildred. 1984. *Family Violence*. New York Praeger.

Paradise, Jan A., Anthony Rostain, and Madeleine Nathanson. 1988. "Substantiation of

Sexual Abuse Charges When Parents Dispute Custody or Visitation" *Pediatrics* 81: 835–839.

Parker, Barbara and Dale N. Schumacher. 1977. "The Battered Wife Syndrome and Violence in the Nuclear Family of Origin: A Controlled Pilot Study." *American Journal of Public Health* 67(8): 760–761.

Pearce, Diana. 1989. "Welfare Is Not for Women: Toward a Model of Advocacy to Meet the Needs of Women in Poverty." Washington, DC: Institute for Women's Policy Research."

_____. 1993. "The Feminization of Poverty: Update." In *Feminist Frameworks*, ed. Alison Jaggar and Paula S. Rothenberg, 290–296. Third Edition. New York: McGraw Hill.

Peterson, Richard R. 1989. *Women, Work and Divorce*. New York: State University of New York Press, 1989.

Philadelphia Health Management Corporation. 1988. "Philadelphia Health Management Household Survey 1987." Philadelphia, PA: The Philadelphia Health Management Corp.

Piven, Francis Fox and Richard Cloward. 1993. *Regulating the Poor: The Function of Public Welfare*. New York: Vintage Books.

Polakow, Valerie. 1993. *Lives On the Edge: Single Mothers and their Children in the Other America*. Chicago: University of Chicago Press.

Polikoff, Nancy D. 1982. "Why Are Mothers Losing? A Brief Analysis of Criteria Used in Child Custody Determinations." *Women's Rights Law Reporter* 7(3): 235–243.

_____. 1983. "Gender and Child-Custody Determinations: Exploding the Myths." In *Families, Politics and Public Policies: A Feminist Dialogue on Women and the State*, ed. Irene Diamond, 183–202. New York: Longman.

Popenoe, David. 1988. *Disturbing the Nest: Family Change and Decline in Modern Societies*. New York: Aldine de Gruyter.

Preston, Samuel H. and Alan T. Richards. 1975. "The Influence of Women's Work Opportunities on Marriage Rates." *Demography* 12 (May): 209–222

Price, Sharon J. and Patrick McKenny, 1988. *Divorce*. Newbury Park: Sage.

Quadagno, Jill. 1994. *The Color of Welfare : How Racism Undermined the War on Poverty*. New York: Oxford University Press.

Ransford, H. Edward and Jon Miller. 1983. "Race, Sex and Feminist Outlooks." *American Sociological Review* 48 (February): 46–59

Rao, V. V. P. and V. N. Rao. 1985. *Sex Roles* 12, nos. 9/10: 939–53.

Raschke, Helen J. 1987. "Divorce." In *Handbook of Marriage and the Family*, ed. Marvin B. Sussman and Suzanne Steinmetz, 597–624. New York: Plenum Press.

Rhode, Deborah. 1989. *Justice and Gender*. Cambridge, MA: Harvard University Press.

_____. 1990. "Reforming the Questions, Questioning the Reforms: Feminist Perspectives on Divorce Law." In *Divorce Reform at the Crossroads*, ed. Stephen Sugarman and Herma Hill Kay, 191–210. New Haven: Yale University Press.

Riessman, Catherine K. 1990. *Divorce Talk: Women and Men Make Sense of Personal Relationships*. New Brunswick: Rutgers University Press.

Riessman, Catherine K. and N. Gerstel. 1985. "Marital Dissolution and Health: Do Males or Females Have Greater Risk?" *Social Science and Medicine* 20(6): 627–635.

Roberts, Paula G. 1994. "Ending Poverty As We Know It: The Case for Child Support Enforcement and Assurance." Washington, DC: The Center for Law and Social Policy.

————. 1994. "Child Support Orders: Problems with Enforcement." *The Future of Children: Children and Divorce.* The David and Lucile Packard Foundation 4, No. 1 (Spring): 101–120.

Robinson, John P. and Philip Shaver. 1973. "Measures of Social Psychological Attitudes." Ann Arbor, MI: Survey Research Center, Institute for Social Research.

Romer, H. and D. Cherry. 1980. "Ethnic and Social Class Differences in Children's Sex-Role Concepts. *Sex Roles* 6: 245–259.

Rotella, Elyce. 1995. "Women and the American Economy." In *Issues in Feminism,* ed. Sheila Ruth, 320–333. Mountain View, California: Mayfield Publishing Company, 1995.

Rubin, Lillian B. 1976. *Worlds of Pain.* New York: Basic Books. 1976.

————. 1983. *Intimate Strangers: Men and Women Together. New York* : Harper & Row.

————. 1994. *Families on the Fault Line.* New York: Harper 1994.

Ruggles, Patricia. 1990. *Drawing the Line: Alternative Poverty Measures and Their Implications for Public Policy.* Washington, DC: The Urban Institute Press.

Saluter, Arlene F. 1994. "Marital Status and Living Arrangements, March 1993." U.S. Bureau of the Census, Current Population Reports, Series P-20, no. 478. Washington, DC: U.S. Government Printing Office.

Saunders, Daniel. 1988. "Wife Abuse, Husband Abuse, or Mutual Combat?" In *Feminist Perspectives on Wife Abuse,* ed. Kersti Yllo & Michelle Bograd, 90–113. Newbury Park, CA: Sage.

Sawhill, Isabel V. 1977. "Developing Normative Standards for Child Support and Alimony Payments." Working Paper (September): 992–1004. Washington, DC: The Urban Institute.

————. 1990. "Escaping the Fiscal Trap." *The American Prospect* 1 (Spring): 19–25.

Scanzoni, John. 1982. *Sexual Bargaining: Power Politics in the American Marriage.* Chicago: Univeristy of Chicago Press. Second Edition.

Schulman. 1979. *A Survey of Spousal Violence Against Women in Kentucky.* Study #792701 for the Kentucky Commission on Women. Washington, DC: U.S. Department of Justice.

Scott, Joan. 1986. "Gender: A Useful Category of Historical Analysis." *American Historical Review* 91: 1067.

Seltzer, Judith. 1991a. "Legal Custody Arrangements and Children's Economic Welfare." *American Journal of Sociology* 96: 895–929.

————. 1991b. "Relationships Between Fathers and Children Who Live Apart: The Father's Role After Separation." *Journal of Marriage and the Family* 53(1): 79–101.

Seltzer, Judith A. and Suzanne M. Bianchi. 1988. "Children's Contact With Absent Parents." *Journal of Marriage and the Family* 50: 663–677.

Seltzer, Judith and Irwin Garfinkel. 1991. "Inequality of Divorce Settlements: An Investigation of Property Settlements and Child Support Awards." *Social Science Research* 19: 82–11.

Singer, Jana. 1989. "Divorce Reform and Gender Justice." *North Carolina Law Review* 67: 1110–1121.

Skolnick, Arlene. 1991. *Embattled Paradise: The American Family in an Age of Uncertainty.* New York: Basic Books.

Spalter-Roth, Roberta M. and Heidi Hartmann. 1994a. "AFDC Recipients as Care-Givers and workers: A Feminist Approach to Income Security Policy for American Women." *Social Politics* 1, No. 2 (Summer): 190–210.

_____. 1994b. "Dependence on Men, the Market, or the State: The Rhetoric and Reality of Welfare Reform." *The Journal of Applied Social Sciences* 18, No. 1 (Fall/Winter): 55–70.

Spanier, Graham and Linda Thompson. 1984. *Parting: The Aftermath of Separation and Divorce.* Beverly Hills: Sage.

Stacey, Judith. 1994. "The New Family Values Crusaders." *The Nation* (July 25/August 1): 119–122.

_____. 1990. *Brave New Families: Stories of Domestic Upheaval in Late Twentieth Century America.* New York: Basic Books.

Stack, Carol B. 1974. *All Our Kin: Strategies for Survival in a Black Community.* New York: Harper.

Stanko, Elizabeth. 1985. *Intimate Intrusions.* London: Routledge and Kegan Paul.

Staples, Robert. 1978. "Masculinity and Race: The Dual Dilemma of Black Men." *Journal of Social Issues* 34, 1: 169–183.

_____. 1982. *Black Masculinity.* San Francisco: The Black Scholar Press.

_____. 1985. "Changes in Black Family Structure: The Conflict between Family Ideology and Structural Conditions." *Journal of Marriage and the Family* 47: 1005–1015.

Stark, Evan, Ann Flitcraft, and William Frazier. 1979. "Medicine and Patriarchal Violence: The Social Construction of a 'Private' Event." *International Journal of Health Services* 98: 461–93.

Steil, Janice. 1995. "Supermoms and Second Shifts: Marital Inequality in the 1990s." In *Women: A Feminist Perspective,* ed. Jo Freeman, 149–161.

Steinberg, Ronnie. 1985. "Evaluating Jobs." *Society* 22(Jul/Aug): 44–54

Steinfels, Peter. 1992. "A Political Movement Blends Its Ideas From Left and Right." *The New York Times.* May 24, Weekend section, 6.

Straus, Murray. 1979. "Measuring Intrafamily Conflict and Violence: The Conflict Tactics (CT) Scales." *Journal of Marriage and the Family* 41:75–88.

Straus, Murray A. 1993. "Physical Assaults by Wives: A Major Social Problem." In *Current Controversies on Family Violence,* ed. Richard J. Gelles and Donileen R. Loseke. Newbury Park: Sage, 1993, 67–87.

Straus, Murray A. and Richard J. Gelles. 1986. "Societal Change and Change in Family Violence from 1975–1985 as Revealed by Two National Surveys." *Journal of Marriage and the Family* 48 : 465–479.

Straus, Murray A, Richard J. Gelles, and Suzanne Steinmetz. 1980. *Behind Closed Doors.* New York: Doubleday.

Sugarman, Stephen. 1991. "Dividing Financial Interests on Divorce." In *Divorce Reform at the Crossroads,* ed. Stephen Sugarman and Herma Hill Kay, 130–165. New Haven: Yale University Press, 1991.

Sweet, James A. and Larry L. Bumpass. 1988. *American Families and Households.* New York: Russell Sage Foundation.

Teachman, Jay D. 1991. "Contributions to Children by Divorced Fathers." *Social Problems* 38: 358–371.

Teachman, Jay D. and Kathleen M. Paasch. 1994. "Financial Impact of Divorce on Children and Their Families." In *The Future of Children*. Center for the Future of Children, The David and Lucile Packard Foundation 1, No. 4, Spring.

Thoennes, Nancy, Patricia Tjaden, and Jessica Pearson. 1991. "The Impact of Child Support Guidelines on Award Adequacy, Award Variability, and Case Processing Efficiency." *Family Law Quarterly* 25 (Fall): 325–345.

Thompson, Linda and Alexis J. Walker. 1989. "Gender in Families: Women and Men in Marriage, Work, and Parenthood." *Journal of Marriage and the Family* 51 (November): 845–871.

Thornborrow, Nancy M. and Marianne B. Sheldon. 1995. "Women in the Labor Force." In *Women: A Feminist Perspective*, ed. Jo Freeman, 197–219. Mountain View, CA: Mayfield.

Thorne, Barrie. 1992. "Feminism and the Family: Two Decades of Thought." In *Rethinking the Family*, ed. Barrie Thorne and Marilyn Yalom, 3–30. Boston: Northeastern University Press.

Thurner, M. C.B. Fenn, J. Melichar, and D.A. Chiriboga. 1983. "Sociodemographics: Perspectives on Reasons for Divorce." *Journal of Divorce* 6: 25–35.

Uhlenberg, Peter, Teresa Cooney, and Robert Boyd. 1990. "Divorce for Women After Midlife." *Journals of Gerontology* 45, No. 1: S3–11.

U.S. Bureau of the Census. 1986. *Statistical Abstract of the United States, 1985: National Data Book and Guide to Sources.* Washington, DC: Government Printing Office, 1986.

U.S. Bureau of the Census. 1989a. *Changes in American Family Life.* Current Population Reports, Series P–23, No. 163. Washington, DC: U.S. Government Printing Office.

U.S. Bureau of the Census. 1989b. *Marital Status and Living Arrangements: March 1988.* Current Population Reports. Series P–20, No. 433. Washington, DC: U.S. Government Printing Office.

U.S. Bureau of the Census. 1989c. *Money Income and Poverty Status in the United States: 1988.* Current Population Reports. Series P–60, No. 166 (Advance Data from the March 1989 Current Population Survey) Washington, DC: U.S. Government Printing Office.

U.S. Bureau of the Census. 1991. *Child Support and Alimony: 1989.* Current Population Reports, Series P–60, No. 173. Washington, DC: U.S. Government Printing Office.

U.S. Bureau of the Census. 1992a. *Marriage, Divorce, and Remarriage in the 1990's.* Current Population Reports, p23–180. Washington, DC: U.S. Government Printing Office.

U.S. Bureau of the Census. 1992b. *Money Income of Households, Families and Persons in the United States 1991*, Current Population Report Series P–60, no. 180, Table 29, pp. 116 and 130. Washington, DC: U.S. Government Printing Office.

U.S. Bureau of the Census. 1992c. *Poverty in the United States: 1991.* Current Population Reports, Series P–60, No. 181. Washington, DC: U.S. Government Printing Office.

U.S. Bureau of the Census. 1995. *Dynamics of Economic Well-Being: Program Participation 1990–1992.* Series P70–41 (January).

U.S. Department of Health and Human Services Administration of Children and Families, Office of Child Support Enforcement. 1993. *Sixteenth Annual Report to Congress*. Washington, DC: Department of Health and Human Services.

U.S. Department of Labor, Bureau of Labor Statistics. 1989. *Labor Force Statistics Derived From the Current Population Survey, 1948–1987*. Bulletin 2307. Washington, DC: U.S. Government Printing Office.

U.S. General Accounting Office. 1992a. *Mothers Report Receiving Less Support From Out-Of-State Fathers*. Washington, DC.: Government Printing Office.

U.S.General Accounting Office. 1992b. *Timely Action Needed to Correct Systems Development Problems* (GAO IMTEC–92–46). Washington, DC: U.S. Government Printing Office.

U.S. General Accounting Office. 1994. "Child Support Enforcement: Credit Bureau Reporting Shows Promise." Letter Report HEHS–94–175 (June 3) Washington, DC: U.S. General Accounting Office.

U.S. Merit Systems Protection Board. 1988. *Sexual Harassment in the Federal Government: An Update*. Washington, D.C.: U.S. Government Printing Office.

Vaughan, Diane. 1986. *Uncoupling*. New York: Vintage.

Verbrugge, Lois M. 1979. "Marital Status and Health." *Journal of Marriage and the Family* 41: 267–285

Waits, Kathleen. 1985. "The Criminal Justice System's Response of Battering: Understanding the Problem, Forging the Solutions." *Washington Law Review* 60: 267, 273.

Walker, Lenore. 1979. *The Battered Woman*. New York: Harper.

Wallace, Michele. 1980. *Black Macho and the Myth of the Superwoman*. New York: Warner Books.

Wallerstein, Judith S. 1986. "Women After Divorce: Preliminary Report From a Ten-Year Follow-Up." *American Journal of Orthopsychiatry* 56: 65–77.

Wallerstein, Judith S. and Sandra Blakeslee. 1989. *Second Chances: Men, Women, and Children a Decade After Divorce*. New York: Ticknor and Fields.

Wallerstein, Judith and D. Huntington. 1983. "Bread and Roses: Nonfinancial Issues Related to Fathers' Economic Support of Their Children Following Divorce." In *The Parental Child Support Obligation*, ed. Judith Cassetty, 135–156. Lexington, MA: D.C. Heath.

Wallerstein, Judith and Joan Kelly. 1980. *Surviving the Breakup: How Children and Parents Cope with Divorce*. New York: Basic Books.

Weiss, Robert S. 1975. *Marital Separation*. New York: Basic Books.

_____. 1979. *Going It Alone*. New York: Basic Books.

_____. 1984. "The Impact of Marital Dissolution on Income and Consumption in Single-Parent Households." *Journal of Marriage and the Family* 46: 115–127.

Weitzman, Lenore J. 1985. *The Divorce Revolution*. New York: The Free Press.

_____. 1988. "Child Support: Myths and Reality." In *Child Support: From Debt Collection to Social Policy*, ed. Alfred J. Kahn and Sheila Kamerman, 251–276. Newbury Park, CA: Sage.

Whitehead, Barbara Defoe. 1993. "Dan Quayle Was Right." *The Atlantic* (April): 47–84.

Wilkerson, Margaret B. and Jewell Handy Gresham. 1993. "The Racialization of

Poverty." In *Feminist Frameworks*, ed. Alison Jaggar and Paula Rothenberg, 297–303. New York: McGraw Hill.

Wilson, Pamela. 1986. "Black Culture and Sexuality." *Journal of Social Work and Human Sexuality* 4(3): 29–46.

Wilson, William J. 1987. *The Truly Disadvantaged: The Inner City, the Underclass, and Public Policy*. Chicago: University of Chicago Press, 1987.

Wilson, William J. and Katherine M. Neckerman. 1986. "Poverty and Family Structure: The Widening Gap Between Evidence and Public Policy Issues." In *Fighting Poverty: What Works and What Doesn't*, ed. Sheldon Danziger and Daniel Weinberg. Cambridge, MA: Harvard University Press.

Winkler, Karen J. 1993. "Communitarians Move Their Ideas Outside Academic Arena." *The Chronicle of Higher Education*, April 21.

Woodhouse, Barbara Bennett. 1993. "Hatching the Egg: A Child-Centered Perspective on Parents' Rights." *Cardozo Law Review* 14 (6): 1747–1865.

Yllo, Kersti A. 1993. "Through a Feminist Lens: Gender, Power, and Violence." In *Current Controversies on Family Violence*, ed. Richard J. Gelles and Donileen R. Loseke, 47–62. Newbury Park, CA: Sage.

Zinn, Maxine Baca. 1989. "Family, Race, and Poverty in the Eighties." *Signs* 14: 856–74.

INDEX